QuarkXPress for Windows
Inside & Out

To all the PC-based desktop publishers who instinctively knew there had to be a better way

Contents at a Glance

Contents

Part I • Getting Comfortable with QuarkXPress

Part II • *Building an Intelligently Structured Document*

Part IV • Graphics, Color, and Layout Power

Part V · *Output*

Part VI · *Additional Resources*

Acknowledgments

It takes quite a crew to turn an idea into a finished book, and this book is no exception. Many individuals contributed to the final product. Thanks go first to Frances Stack, who recruited us for the project; her diplomacy and talent for keeping cool under pressure were greatly appreciated. Linda Briggs proved an insightful tech editor. Barry Bergin kept the channels of communication to the Production department open, helping us surmount the inevitable output obstacles and surprises that accompany software under development. Also deserving of commendation is Yvonne Johnson, who jumped in to speed the preparation of two chapters and patiently rewrote early drafts until we were able to take over.

At Quark, we're grateful to Pete Richardson for meeting us more than halfway with technical information. Peter Warren and Greg Morton also did their best to respond to the queries of pesky authors under tight deadlines.

Finally, Wendy Rinaldi deserves special mention for an unbelievable job of coordinating, communicating, and keeping track of absolutely every detail. Thanks for pulling it all together, Wendy!

Introduction

QuarkXPress for Windows is the page layout package of choice for anyone running Microsoft Windows. No other package offers such a blend of typographical sophistication and design-oriented features for enhancing documents creatively with graphics and color. Now that Quark is here, page layout professionals who use DOS-based machines need no longer envy their Macintosh cousins.

This book is designed for Quark users at all levels: beginning, intermediate, and advanced. We know that while you may be new to Quark, you might already know about desktop publishing through your experience with other page layout or word processing packages. *QuarkXPress for Windows Inside & Out* will not disappoint you, no matter what your depth of previous experience. Desktop publishing novices will find explanations of all industry terms as well as in-depth coverage of Quark features. Intermediate and advanced users who are more familiar with other page layout packages will find a wealth of graphic examples and applications-oriented tips that they can use in the real-world documents they create every day.

To help get your feet wet, the following gives a brief summary of the topics covered in this book on a chapter-by-chapter basis.

Part I: Getting Comfortable with QuarkXPress

This book begins with an overview of the "look and feel" of Quark—the palettes, menus, dialog boxes, and document-structuring conventions that make it possible to work so intuitively. Whether you are new to desktop publishing or a seasoned veteran of other page layout packages, Chapter 1 quickly acquaints you with the features that make Quark unique and powerful.

Hands-on experimentation is the most effective learning tool that exists, so Chapter 2 contains a structured tutorial. With it you practice basic word processing, style sheet development, and layout skills while creating a one-page newsletter that includes graphics, rules, and text.

Part II: Building an Intelligently Structured Document

Depending on how you set up a new Quark document, you can standardize document features automatically and save yourself a great deal of layout time. Chapters 3 and 4 show you the secrets of building intelligence into a new document. Chapter 3 explores templates, master pages, and the Document Layout palette, while Chapter 4 delves into the many Preferences settings that determine both the structure of a document and how you work with it.

Part III: Editing and Formatting Text

Text is an important component of most types of documents, and Quark boasts some of the most sophisticated yet flexible typographic controls of any page layout package. Chapter 5 introduces you to Quark's word processing features, including text entry and editing, spell checking, custom dictionaries, search and replace, and formatting text on the character level. Chapter 6 takes you one step further and explores techniques for formatting text on the paragraph level. Here, you will learn about developing and using style sheets, which allow you to format text automatically. You also will encounter Quark's user-definable hyphenation and justification options and advanced kerning and tracking controls. Chapter 7 discusses the ins and outs of importing and exporting text and using XPress Tags to preformat text in your favorite word processor.

Part IV: Graphics, Color, and Layout Power

When it comes to layout, the use of pictures, and the power of color, QuarkXPress has no rivals. The six chapters in this section of the book explore the many ways you can use Quark to design effective, attention-getting layouts. Chapter 8 shows you how to import and manipulate graphics and how to use OLE (object linking and embedding) to incorporate pictures and tables from other programs into a Quark document. Chapter 9 takes an in-depth look at using and enhancing photographs and bitmaps in a document. Chapter 10 covers all you need to know about defining and applying colors, when and how to use trapping, and preparing color-intensive documents for printing.

Chapter 11 reviews the basics of page layout in Quark. You'll learn about grouping, arranging, aligning, and spacing items, numbering pages automatically according to any scheme you desire, and using libraries to organize frequently used elements of a publication. Chapter 12 offers real-world tips and tricks for using runaround, anchored text, and picture boxes to manage interaction between text and graphics. Finally, Chapter 13 discusses the best techniques for designing and laying out specific types of documents such as newsletters, books, and promotional material.

Part V: Output

What good is a document if you can't print it correctly? Chapter 14 goes beyond the basics of using Quark's print-related commands and controls to discuss when and *why* you might want to apply each one. You will also find useful tips for managing fonts, picture files, and non-standard Quark settings; working with a service bureau and selecting an imagesetter; creating PostScript output files; choosing halftone screen settings; outputting documents that contain high-quality digital photographs; and printing documents that contain spot or process color elements.

Part VI: Additional Resources

Keep in mind that QuarkXPress is not an island. New third-party utilities that enhance Quark's printing and publishing capabilities under Windows appear daily, and in Appendix A, you will find out how to learn more about them.

Typographical Conventions

We have adopted a few conventions in this book for making information easy to find when you need it quickly.

☐   The first time an unfamiliar term is used in context, it appears in *italics* to signal that its definition is about to follow. For example: *Trapping* is a set of techniques for creating overlaps between adjacent colors so that misregistration won't cause a problem during commercial printing.

☐   If you are asked to enter information in a field or type it in a Quark document, the information appears in boldface. For example: Enter the abbreviation **pt** to specify measurements in terms of points.

☐   Icons for Quark tools appear in the margin to the left of a paragraph the first time the tool is mentioned in a chapter.

☐   Special icons accompany four types of paragraphs in this book that provide additional information about Quark features.

Tip   provides useful real-world hints that may be of interest to intermediate and advanced Quark users.

Remember   reminds you of information that you should always keep in mind in order to make a particular feature work properly.

 Caution   warns you of actions to avoid and their possible negative consequences.

 Note   provides miscellaneous technical information about Quark features.

PART I

Getting Comfortable
with QuarkXPress

CHAPTER

The Quark Environment

uarkXPress for Windows is far more than just another page layout package; it is an all-encompassing desktop communications tool. Its publication design capabilities are outstanding, but "Quark," as users often call it, is also a sophisticated word processor, a powerhouse graphics enhancement package, and a complete color separation studio all in one. Put simply, Quark does it all.

QuarkXPress is designed to be intuitive and to boost your creativity. Using Quark creatively, though, requires that you first acquaint yourself with the user interface. This chapter guides you through the Quark interface or *environment*, which contains the visual aids that help you exploit QuarkXPress to its fullest.

Starting QuarkXPress

QuarkXPress for Windows

When you installed QuarkXPress, the program created its own group window within the Windows Program Manager and placed the program icon inside it. If you have organized your group windows differently, your QuarkXPress for Windows icon may be located somewhere else.

To start QuarkXPress, follow these steps:

1. Run Microsoft Windows.

2. Locate the QuarkXPress for Windows icon and double-click it.

The QuarkXPress logo appears in the center of your screen as Quark loads. Then, the blank Quark application window appears as shown in Figure 1-1.

Application Windows and Document Windows

During a QuarkXPress session, you are actually working in at least two different windows: the main Quark *application window* and one or more *document windows*. In Figure 1-1, the Tool palette, Measurements

The QuarkXPress application window

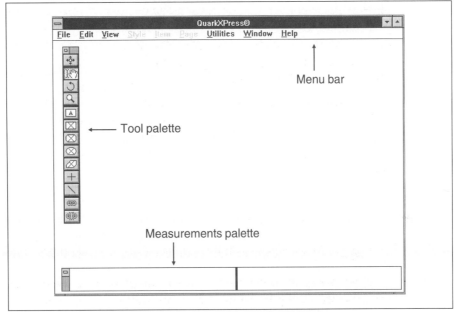

palette, and menu bar appear in the application window because they are available to all documents that are open during a work session. To use these and other Quark interface aids meaningfully, though, you need to open or create at least one document. Each document appears in its own document window within the Quark application window, and you can have up to seven documents open at one time.

Note   Other palettes may appear in your Quark application window if you or another QuarkXPress user has displayed them during previous sessions. QuarkXPress "remembers" your preferred interface elements from one session to the next.

Opening an Existing Document

QuarkXPress for Windows contains several example documents. If you are new to QuarkXPress and have not yet created documents of your own, you can open one of the sample documents to learn how Quark's intuitive user interface works.

To open an existing document in QuarkXPress (including one of the sample documents), follow these steps:

1. Choose the Open command in the File menu or use the keyboard shortcut, CTRL-O. The Open dialog box shown in Figure 1-2 appears. If this is your first QuarkXPress session, the xpress folder representing the xpress directory is open and the List Files of Type list box is set to "All QuarkXPress files." With this setting, any files that Quark can open appear in the Files list box at the left side of the dialog box.

2. If the Open dialog box displays the contents of some other drive or directory, use the Drives and Directories list boxes pointed out in Figure 1-2 to change to the xpress directory. Consult your *Microsoft Windows User's Guide* for assistance on moving between directories; the conventions are slightly different for Microsoft Windows versions 3.0 and 3.1.

3. If you would like to open one of the sample documents provided with QuarkXPress, double-click the samples directory icon and its desired subdirectory in the Directories list box. The list of available sample documents appears in the files list box with the file extension .qxd. If you would rather open a document of your own creation—preferably one that contains graphics—find the desired directory name in the Directories list box and double-click it.

4. To select and open the desired document file, double-click its name in the Files list box.

FIGURE 1-2   The Open dialog box

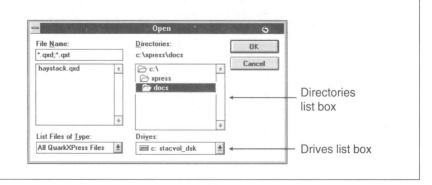

After a moment, the document opens in its own document window
as shown in Figure 1-3. How much of the document you see at one
time depends on the page size of your document, the resolution of
your monitor, and whether you have changed the default (100% or
Actual Size) viewing magnification of the document during a previous Quark session. (If you have opened the same document previously, Quark saves any adjustment you made to the viewing
magnification.)

Tip   If you have a 14-inch monitor or a display adapter that supports
less than a 1024 x 768 pixel resolution, you can significantly increase
the viewable area of a page by calibrating your monitor in Quark. See the
"Calibrating a Monitor" section later in this chapter for more details.

Now that your Quark application window contains at least one open
document window, you are ready to take a tour through the intuitive user
interface.

FIGURE 1-3   Elements of a Quark document window

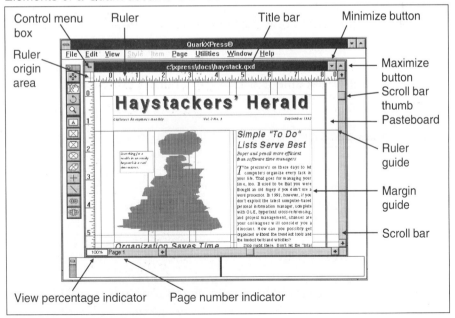

Document Window Elements

A document window contains several standard elements that make your editing and file management tasks easier. The following sections cover the elements pointed out in Figure 1-3.

Title Bar   The title bar displays the filename of the document. When more than one document is open, the title bar of the active document window is highlighted so you can recognize it.

Minimize and Maximize Buttons   Minimize and maximize buttons let you alter the amount of space a document window takes up. When you minimize a document window, it becomes a small icon at the lower-left edge of the Quark application window, like this:

c:\xpresdoc\haystack.qxd

Minimizing document windows reduces clutter on your screen when you have multiple documents open. Maximizing a document window lets you see more of the page. If you have a 14-inch monitor, you should probably maximize the document window you just opened.

Control Menu   The control menu contains commands that let you move, size, minimize, maximize, and close a document window, or move from one document window to another. To close a document window quickly, double-click its control menu box.

Rulers   Rulers help you precisely lay out your document and position guidelines. Rulers appear with all documents by default, but you can turn off the display of rulers by choosing Hide Rulers from the View menu (the keyboard shortcut is CTRL-R). You can adjust the *zero point* of the rulers—the point at which the marker reads zero—by dragging the mouse pointer from the ruler origin downward and to the right, as shown in Figure 1-4. To restore the zero point to its original position, double-click in the ruler origin area.

Ruler Guides   Ruler guides like the one shown in Figure 1-3 assist you in precisely positioning text boxes, picture boxes, and lines on a page.

Changing the ruler zero point

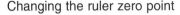

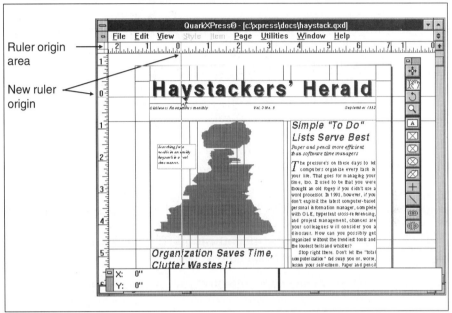

By default, ruler guides appear in green on a color monitor. To place a ruler guide in a document, move the mouse pointer into the horizontal or vertical ruler and drag inward or downward onto the page. To delete all existing horizontal or vertical ruler guides, place the pointer on the horizontal or vertical ruler, press ALT, and click.

Margin Guides   Margin guides show the margins you have defined for a document. By default margin guides appear in blue. You can position guides in front of or behind other objects in your document. You can simultaneously display ruler guides, master guides, and margin guides in your document if you wish. See Chapters 2, 3, and 4 for more about specifying and positioning all types of guides.

Pasteboard   The pasteboard may or may not be visible in your document, depending on the size of your page and your current viewing magnification. The pasteboard lets you move items on and off the current page and can be quite handy during a layout or design process. See the "Setting General Preferences" section of Chapter 4 for more information about defining the pasteboard.

Scroll Bars   Scroll bars enable you to see different areas of a page and to move manually to different pages within a document. Scroll bars are just one tool to carry out these tasks; keyboard shortcuts and the Document Layout palette offer even faster, more intuitive ways to move through a document.

Page Number Indicator   The page number indicator displays the number of the page currently in view.

View Percentage Indicator   The view percentage indicator lets you change the viewing magnification of a page quickly and intuitively. To change your view of a document, double-click the percentage value and type a new value over it. Figure 1-5 shows that as the viewing percentage *decreases* below 100%, a larger area of your page becomes visible, but at a smaller viewing magnification. The reverse is true when you *increase* the viewing percentage above 100%.

These basic elements are part of every document window. Your document may contain additional elements if you have already customized the Quark interface or your document preferences. Chapters 2, 3,

FIGURE 1-5   As the view percentage decreases, more of the document becomes visible

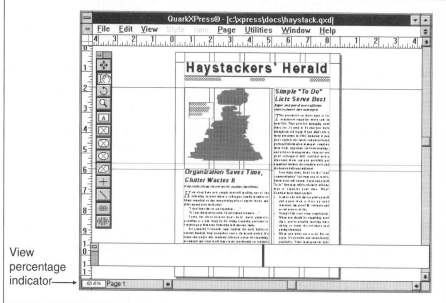

View percentage indicator⟶

and 4 provide more opportunities to try out these and other interface aids.

Shortcuts: Document Windows

QuarkXPress makes available a large number of keyboard shortcuts for every kind of desktop publishing task. There are so many different keyboard shortcuts in Quark that listing all of them would simply result in a hard-to-use table. Instead, throughout this book, keyboard shortcuts are given at the end of appropriate sections. You may find it easier to remember shortcuts if you can associate them with the Quark functions you have just learned.

Table 1-1 features a summary of keyboard shortcuts that should help you get around in a QuarkXPress document window.

Calibrating a Monitor

The *display resolution* of a monitor is a function of monitor size, *dot pitch* (the distance between dots on a screen), and display adapter

TABLE 1-1 Shortcuts: Working with Document Windows

Function	Shortcut
Open a document	CTRL-O
Close a document	Double-click control menu box
Minimize a document	Click minimize button
Maximize a document	Click maximize button
Resize a document window	Drag from document window edge or corner
Show/Hide rulers	CTRL-R
Adjust ruler zero point	Drag from upper-left corner of document window
Place a new ruler guide	Drag from ruler into document
Delete horizontal/vertical ruler guides	ALT + click any ruler guide
Change view percentage	Double-click in View Percentage window, overtype current value

capabilities. Desktop publishing experts maintain that a display resolution of 72 dots per inch (dpi) is desirable for an accurate view of documents. At this resolution, desktop publishing is *WYSIWYG* (what you see is what you get), because one inch on the monitor represents exactly one inch on a ruler. If all monitors featured a 72 dpi display resolution, fonts and graphics in a given document would look exactly the same on every computer.

On the DOS platform, however, monitors come in a multitude of sizes and vary in their dot pitch. Display adapters also support many different pixel resolutions: 640 x 480, 800 x 600, 1024 x 768, or even 1280 x 1024. This lack of standards works against WYSIWYG desktop publishing, because specific fonts and graphics in a document look different on different computers. If you are part of a desktop publishing workgroup, such display variations can be annoying.

QuarkXPress for Windows has a solution to this problem: *monitor calibration,* or adjusting the monitor display. Using the Preferences/Application command in the Edit menu, you can manipulate the monitor display so that one inch on any standard ruler equals one inch on your screen. If you always work at the same pixel resolution (1024 x 768, for example), you need to calibrate your monitor only once, when you first begin using QuarkXPress. If you have a 14-inch monitor, or if your display adapter supports a resolution lower than 1024 x 768, calibrating your monitor lets you see a larger area of a page.

To calibrate a monitor for true WYSIWYG desktop publishing under QuarkXPress, follow these steps:

1. With a document window open, choose Actual View in the View menu. This sets the display to a baseline 100 percent viewing magnification.

2. Choose the Preferences command in the Edit menu and then the Application command in the submenu. The dialog box shown in Figure 1-6 appears.

3. Look at the Display DPI Value field in the lower-right area of the dialog box. The value for this in Figure 1-6 is 96, which is the standard value for a display adapter that supports a 640 x 480 pixel resolution. If your display adapter supports a higher resolution, the value you see will be higher.

FIGURE 1-6 Calibrating the monitor to the rulers

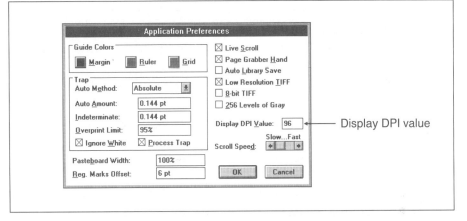

Display DPI value

4. Take a ruler and hold it up to the horizontal ruler in the active document window. If an inch on the ruler on the screen takes up more space than an inch on the ruler in your hand, you need to *reduce* the Display DPI Value. If a screen inch takes up less space than an inch on the ruler, you need to *increase* the Display DPI value.

5. To change the value, double-click the Display DPI Value field and then type a new value. Click the OK button to save this new setting.

6. Hold the ruler in your hand up to the horizontal ruler of the document ruler once more. If they still do not match perfectly, choose the Preferences/Application command in the Edit menu again and readjust the value until the rulers match inch per inch.

Document Elements: QuarkXPress Items

In QuarkXPress, an *item* is a specific term that means the type of graphic element you are dealing with on the screen. QuarkXPress documents contain only three basic types of items: *text boxes*, *picture boxes*, and free-standing *lines*. All text in a document is contained within text boxes, while all line drawings, photographs, and other images are contained within picture boxes. Figure 1-7 shows the items used in a simple publication in QuarkXPress. Keep in mind that Quark

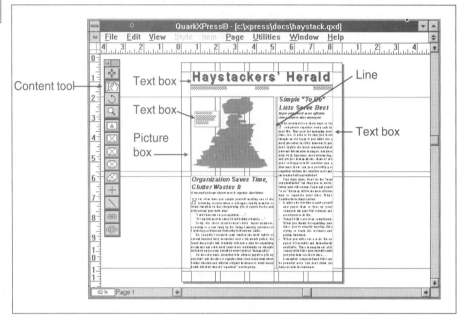

FIGURE 1-7   Items in a QuarkXPress document

distinguishes between items (for example, text boxes) and their contents (the text inside the text boxes).

In order to work effectively with the Tool palette, the Measurements palette, or other palettes, and even some menu commands, you often have to select a document item or its contents. Understanding a document in terms of the three items that comprise it is therefore one of the most important concepts you can master in QuarkXPress.

QuarkXPress Menus

The nine drop-down menus in the QuarkXPress menu bar—File, Edit, View, Style, Item, Page, Utilities, Window, and Help—provide commands and options that help you edit your documents. To choose a menu command, click the menu name and click the name of the command you want to highlight.

Not all menus are available at all times; when you first open a document, for example, the Style and Item menus are grayed, indicating that you cannot access them. To make these menus available, click anything in the document when the Content tool in the Tool palette is active (see Figure 1-7). This tool is automatically active when you first open a document.

Menu Conventions

As Figure 1-8 shows, menus contain or give you access to several kinds of information. If there is a keyboard shortcut for a certain menu command, for example, that shortcut appears next to the command name. Remembering the shortcut the next time you need to use the command can save time, making you more productive.

In some cases, triangular arrows appear to the right of a menu command (note the arrow at the end of Color, the first menu command in Figure 1-8). An arrow indicates that the command gives you access to a *submenu* containing a fixed set of options. To access a submenu like the one shown in Figure 1-8, click the main menu command. The submenu pops out; move the mouse pointer across the arrow into the submenu and click the desired command.

An ellipsis (. . .) next to a menu command (note the Open command in Figure 1-9) signals that you access a dialog box when you choose the command. *Dialog boxes* contain several types of controls that you can use to enter information when you select a command that requires additional information before Quark can execute it. Dialog boxes appear

FIGURE
1-8

Menus offer a variety of ways to choose options

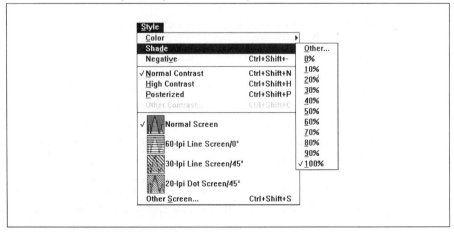

The File menu

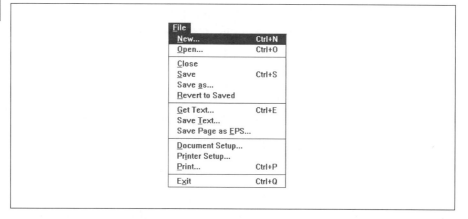

whenever Quark needs more information in order to carry out the command. The next sections familiarize you with the layout and functions of QuarkXPress menus.

The File Menu

The File menu, shown in Figure 1-9, controls operations that affect entire documents or files. Use this menu to open, save, and close documents; set up new document parameters; import text and pictures; print documents to disk or to a printer; and exit QuarkXPress.

The Edit Menu

Use the commands in the Edit menu (Figure 1-10) to undo your most recent actions, copy, cut, and paste data between documents or applications, or import data or graphics from Windows applications that support OLE (Object Linking and Embedding). The Find/Change command in this menu is useful for word processing search-and-replace functions. The Edit menu also lets you customize interface elements throughout QuarkXPress as well as typographic settings, tools, interface elements, colors, style sheets, and hyphenation and justification settings for particular documents. Chapter 4 gives more information about setting a variety of preferences through the Edit menu.

The Edit menu

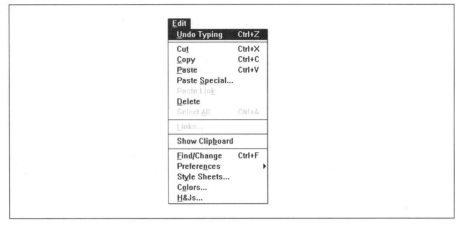

The View Menu

The View menu, shown in Figure 1-11, is "Grand Central Station" for customizing the QuarkXPress interface. From the View menu, you can adjust the viewing size of your documents, hide or display grids, rulers, and other interface aids, and hide or display the floating palettes that help you make intuitive editing choices. (You will learn about floating palettes shortly.)

The View menu

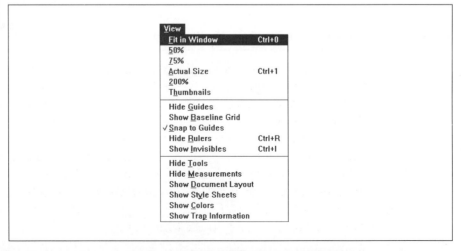

The Style Menu

The Style menu is available only when the Content tool in the Tool palette is active and you have selected some item—text box, picture box, or line—within a document. (You might want to select an item in the document you have just opened to see how this works.) The content of this menu changes according to the currently selected item. When a text box is active, as shown in Figure 1-12, you can use the Style menu to change every imaginable typographic attribute and to apply style sheets to paragraphs. (A *style sheet* is a set of text attributes that you can define and then apply automatically to an entire paragraph—you will learn more about these in "The Style Sheets Palette" section later in this chapter.) When a picture box is active, as shown in Figure 1-13, the Style menu contains controls for applying color, adjusting contrast levels, and setting halftone screen parameters for output. When a line is active, you can use the Style menu to change line style, entraps, width, color, and shade, with this menu:

You can effect these changes through the intuitive Measurements palette, too.

Chapters 6, 9, and 10 devote more attention to the varied functions of the Style menu.

FIGURE 1-12   The Style menu when a text box is selected

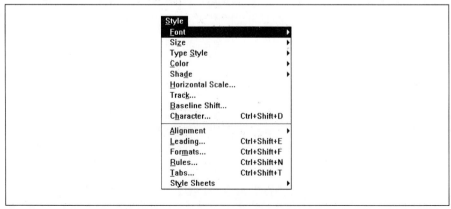

FIGURE
1-13

The Style menu when an image is selected

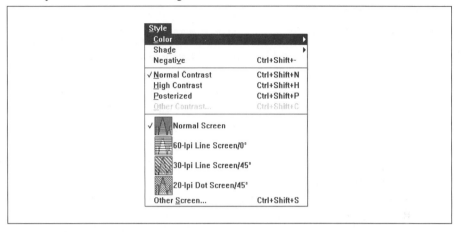

The Item Menu

The Item menu, shown in Figure 1-14, is available only when you have made a selection in a document using either the Item or the Content tool. It contains commands for formatting text and picture boxes, determining runarounds for all items, grouping and arranging items, and creating special graphic effects. Chapters 5, 8, 11, and 12 explore the Item menu functions in greater detail.

FIGURE
1-14

The Item menu

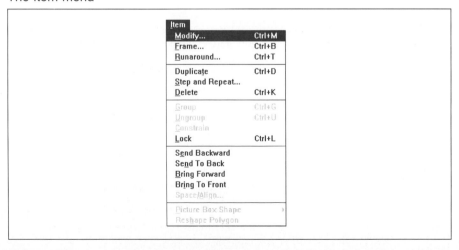

The Page Menu

The Page menu, shown in Figure 1-15, helps you move between pages in a document, add, delete, and move pages, number pages in a complex document, and manipulate elements of master pages. The Document Layout palette duplicates some of these functions, as you will see in the "Quark's Floating Palettes" section later in this chapter.

The Utilities Menu

The Utilities menu, shown in Figure 1-16, covers a wide range of functions. Word processing functions include a spell checker and educable dictionary. You can customize typography with hyphenation exceptions, kerning, and tracking controls. The Utilities menu also features powerful file and document management controls: Font Usage, Picture Usage, and Library. Chapters 5, 6, 8, and 13 cover these functions in greater detail.

The Window Menu

The Window menu, shown in Figure 1-17, lets you manage document windows when you have more than one document open at a time. You can tile or cascade document windows, arrange the icons for documents

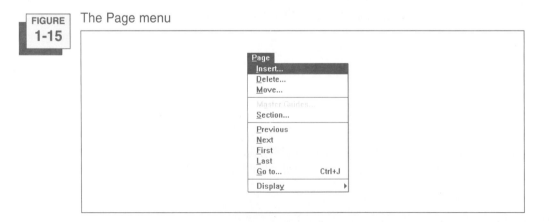

FIGURE 1-15   The Page menu

FIGURE
1-16
The Utilities menu

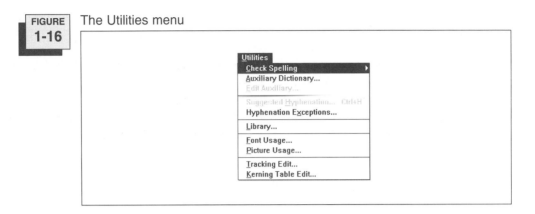

that have been minimized, close all open windows, and move easily between open documents.

The Help Menu

Stuck? Turn to the Help menu, shown in Figure 1-18, to obtain help for menus, keyboard shortcuts, commands, and QuarkXPress procedures. The Help menu also lets you access a comprehensive index of help topics. Quark's help file follows common Microsoft Windows conventions; if you are not familiar with using Help under Windows, refer to your *Microsoft Windows User's Guide.*

Quark XTensions in Menus

A number of third-party software developers have created *XTensions* for the Macintosh version of QuarkXPress. These XTensions cover a broad

FIGURE
1-17
The Window menu

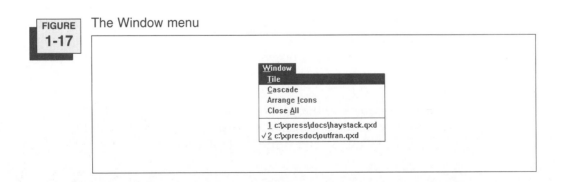

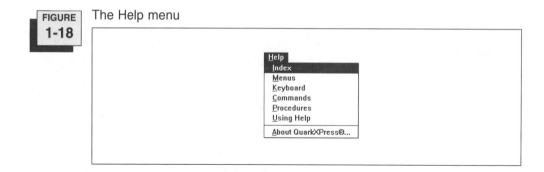

FIGURE 1-18

The Help menu

range of add-on functions, ranging from high-end advertising layouts, to color image enhancement programs, to indexing or print imposition utilities, and more. Some of these vendors have released or are planning to develop these utilities for use with the Windows version of QuarkXPress. If you purchase and install XTensions, they appear in various Quark menus depending on their functions. See the Appendix to find out which utilities are available under Windows and what they do.

Shortcuts: QuarkXPress Menus

Table 1-2 contains a handy summary of keyboard shortcuts for accessing menu commands in QuarkXPress.

Dialog Boxes

Whenever you click a menu command that appears with an ellipsis (. . .), a dialog box pops up asking you to specify more information. The dialog boxes in Figures 1-19 and 1-20 show most of the controls you are likely to encounter in dialog boxes. To move from one control in a dialog box to the next, either press TAB or click the desired field or control.

Text Entry Field   You use text entry fields (see Figure 1-19) when you need to specify detailed information rather than just clicking a preset option. Sometimes you enter numerical information; in other cases, you

Keyboard Shortcuts: Menu Commands

Menu Command	Function	Keyboard Shortcut
File menu		
New	Create new document	CTRL-N
Open	Open existing document	CTRL-O
Save	Save document	CTRL-S
Print	Print document	CTRL-P
Exit	Quit QuarkXPress	CTRL-Q
Edit menu		
Undo	Undo last edit	CTRL-Z
Cut	Cut data to clipboard	CTRL-X
Copy	Copy data to clipboard	CTRL-C
Paste	Paste data from clipboard	CTRL-V
Delete	Delete active item/content	DEL
Select All	Select all items or text	CTRL-A
Find/Change	Search and replace text	CTRL-F
View menu		
Fit in Window	View entire page	CTRL-0
Actual Size	100% viewing magnification	CTRL-1
Show/Hide Rulers	Display or hide rulers	CTRL-R
Show/Hide Invisibles	Show/hide tabs, paragraph marks, etc.	CTRL-I
Style menu, Text selected (Content tool)		
Character	Format selected characters	CTRL-SHIFT-D
Leading	Define interline spacing	CTRL-SHIFT-E
Formats	Format current paragraph	CTRL-SHIFT-F
Rules	Format paragraph rules	CTRL-SHIFT-N
Tabs	Set tabs for a paragraph	CTRL-SHIFT-T
Style menu, Picture selected (Content tool)		
Negative	Invert color values	CTRL-SHIFT- -

TABLE 1-2   Keyboard Shortcuts: Menu Commands (*continued*)

Menu Command	Function	Keyboard Shortcut
Normal Contrast	Undo contrast modifications	CTRL-SHIFT-N
High Contrast	Convert grayscale image to black and white	CTRL-SHIFT-H
Posterized	Convert grayscale image to 6 levels of gray	CTRL-SHIFT-P
Other Contrast	Customize contrast values	CTRL-SHIFT-C
Other Screen	Customize halftone screen	CTRL-SHIFT-S
Item menu		
Modify	Format text/picture box	CTRL-M
Frame	Define frame attributes	CTRL-B
Runaround	Define relationship to other objects	CTRL-T
Duplicate	Create copy of item	CTRL-D
Delete	Clear selected item	CTRL-K
Lock	Freeze item in place	CTRL-L
Page menu		
Go to	Go to selected page	CTRL-J
Utilities menu		
Suggested Hyphenation	Customize hyphenation	CTRL-H

need to enter a filename. Often you can make information appear in a text entry field by highlighting a predefined choice with your mouse; this is shown in Figure 1-19.

Drives and Directories List Boxes   Dialog boxes that deal with opening, printing, and saving files provide Drives and Directories list boxes to help you choose a source or destination for the file. As with the list box in the Save Page as EPS dialog box (Figure 1-19), open folder icons indicate directories that are above the current directory level, while closed

FIGURE
1-19
Some typical dialog box controls

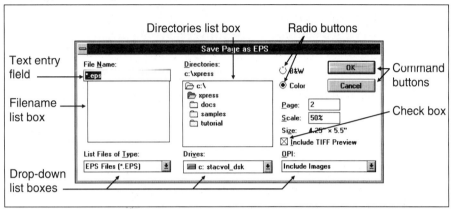

folder icons indicate subdirectories below the current directory level. A shaded open folder icon indicates the current directory. Double-click a drive or directory icon to change drives or directories.

Filename List Box   The Filename list box displays any files in the current directory that are available. The easiest way to select a file is to double-click its filename.

Radio Buttons   Radio buttons indicate choices that are mutually exclusive—that is, only one radio button can be selected at a time.

FIGURE
1-20
More typical dialog box controls

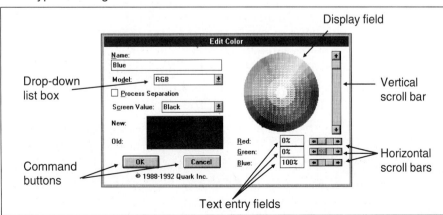

Command Buttons   Command buttons (or simply buttons), the broad rectangular buttons that appear in both Figure 1-19 and Figure 1-20, carry out a command instantly. Most dialog boxes contain OK and Cancel command buttons; another way to exit out of a dialog box without making changes is to press ESC. Some command buttons open another dialog box when you click them.

Drop-Down List Boxes   When multiple preset choices exist for a dialog box setting, a drop-down list box like the one shown in Figure 1-20 is available. Think of drop-down list boxes as submenus within a dialog box. Click the arrow, and a list of choices appears, like this:

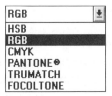

To select one of the options, click it and then release the mouse button.

Check Boxes   Check boxes, unlike radio buttons, represent options that you can mix and match by turning on as many or as few as you like. Click an empty check box to select it. Clicking a check box that already contains an "x" deselects that option.

Display Field   A few dialog boxes in QuarkXPress contain graphics like the example shown in Figure 1-20. A display field lets you preview the changes you make in the dialog box.

Scroll Bars   In dialog boxes that require numeric values, you can often use a scroll bar to select a value instead of typing it into a text entry field. Clicking the scroll arrow at the right side of the scroll bar increases the numeric value; pressing and holding the mouse button over the scroll arrow increases this value continuously. In the same way, clicking or pressing the scroll arrow at the left side of the scroll bar decreases the numeric value. The Edit Color dialog box in Figure 1-20 shows two different types of scroll bars: a horizontal scroll bar for specifying numeric values and a vertical scroll bar for selecting colors visually.

Shortcuts: Dialog Boxes

Table 1-3 summarizes the keyboard shortcuts you can use to get around in QuarkXPress dialog boxes.

There Are Easier Ways...Alternatives to Using Menus

Using menus and dialog boxes can be a time-consuming way to carry out a task. Fortunately, QuarkXPress provides you with several different ways to arrive at most goals. Often, you can achieve the same end by choosing a menu command, changing settings interactively through a floating palette, or invoking a keyboard shortcut. Many users prefer to use floating palettes and keyboard shortcuts for most tasks because they save time and are more intuitive than menu commands.

Quark's Floating Palettes

Constantly walking a mouse back and forth between menus and your document can seem like unnecessary effort. Traveling through a series of dialog boxes every time you want to make a tiny change can be counterproductive.

TABLE 1-3	Keyboard Shortcuts: Dialog Boxes

Task	Keyboard Shortcut
Go to next field	TAB
Go to previous field	SHIFT-TAB
Move down list or drop-down list	DOWN ARROW
Move up list or drop-down list	UP ARROW
Exit, saving changes	ENTER
Exit, cancel changes	ESC

There is a better, faster, more intuitive way to do desktop publishing in QuarkXPress—you use movable elements on your screen called *floating palettes*. Floating palettes help you make instant design and editing choices without wasting time. Figure 1-21 shows the full range of floating palettes available to you in QuarkXPress. Two of these palettes, the Tool palette and the Measurements palette, always appear within the application window when you first start Quark, unless you hid them during a previous session. The other five palettes you encounter in Quark—the Document Layout palette, Style Sheets palette, Colors palette, Trap Information palette, and Library palette—are linked to the specific documents in which you use them.

Palette Conventions

Techniques for moving, sizing, displaying, and hiding floating palettes in Quark are similar for all palettes. The next section reviews common palette conventions before delving into how specific palettes function.

FIGURE 1-21

The QuarkXPress floating palettes

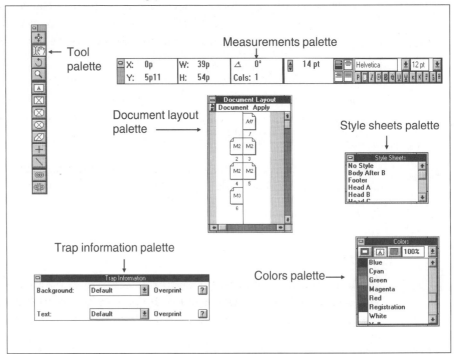

Hiding a Palette

To hide a floating palette when you do not need to use it in a document, double-click the control menu box at the upper-left corner of the palette, as shown here:

Control menu box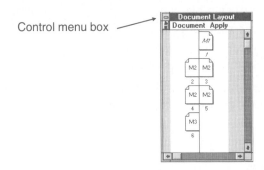

Try removing the Tool palette from your screen now by double-clicking its control menu icon.

Displaying a Palette

To display a specific floating palette, choose the appropriate command from the View menu. The Show Tools, Show Measurements, Show Document Layout, Show Style Sheets, Show Colors, and Show Trap Information commands toggle between Show and Hide depending on whether a palette is currently visible on your monitor.

You can display the Tool and Measurements palettes using special keyboard shortcuts. To display the Tool palette, press CTRL-TAB. To display the Measurements palette, press CTRL-ALT-M.

 Note   If no item or content of a document is selected when you display a floating palette, that palette remains empty. The only exception is the Tool palette.

Moving a Palette

The highlighted area to the right of a floating palette's control menu box is known as a title bar, even if the palette bears no title. To move a floating palette, simply drag it by its title bar to the desired position on your screen.

Sizing a Palette

The Style Sheets, Document Layout, and Colors palettes are flexible in size because the needs of your documents determine how much information they contain. If one of these palettes contains more information than is currently visible, you can increase its size by positioning the mouse at the lower-right corner of the palette and then dragging vertically, horizontally, or diagonally. You can decrease the size of these palettes in the same way; just drag in the opposite direction.

The Tool, Measurements, and Trap Information palettes are fixed in size. The amount of information they contain remains constant.

The Tool Palette

The Tool palette shown in Figure 1-22 displays the 13 tools you use when creating and editing documents. To select a tool, click it; the tool's icon becomes highlighted.

Tool functions in the Tool palette

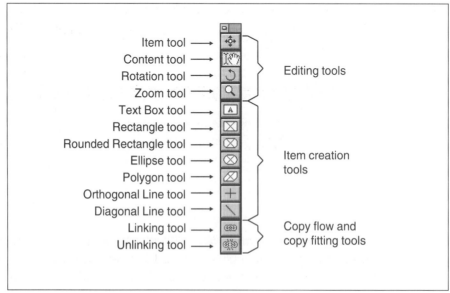

The tools in Figure 1-22 encompass three broad types of functions:

☐   *Editing tools* The top four tools are the Item tool, the Content tool, the Rotation tool, and the Zoom tool. They help you edit existing elements in a document.

☐   *Item creation tools* Use the Text Box tool, the four Picture Box tools, the Orthogonal line tools, and the Diagonal Line tools to create text boxes, picture boxes of several different shapes, and lines.

☐   *Copy flow and copyfitting tools* The Linking and Unlinking tools help you determine the relative placement of text and multiple stories in a document.

An overview of the major functions of each tool in the Tool palette follows.

The Item Tool

QuarkXPress makes a clear distinction between *items* in a publication—picture boxes, text boxes, and lines—and the *content* of those items. The Tool palette reflects this distinction. The Item tool acts upon items only, while the Content tool affects the graphics or text the item contains.

When you click a text box, picture box, or line with the Item tool selected, you activate that item. Eight handles appear around the item to indicate that it is active, as shown here:

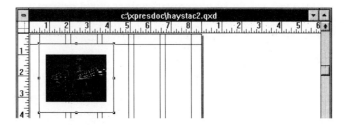

Once you activate an item, you can use the Item tool to move, resize, group, arrange, copy, cut, or paste it. Moving the item is as simple as dragging it with the mouse. To resize an item, position the mouse pointer over one of the selection handles and drag in the desired direction. The mouse pointer takes on the appearance of a hand, like this:

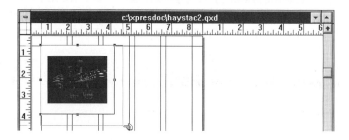

Chapters 8, 11, and 12 provide more detailed information on using the Item tool.

 Tip   The Measurements palette and Item menu commands also provide controls for moving and resizing items in a publication.

The Content Tool

    The Content tool is always active when you first start QuarkXPress (refer back to Figure 1-1). It lets you select an item for the purpose of editing its content. When you click a text box with the Content tool active, you can apply style sheets, select and format text, copy, cut and paste text, type new text, or adjust text trapping. When you click a picture box with the Content tool active, you can import and edit images, manipulate pictures, apply background colors, and adjust image trapping.

The Rotation Tool

    The Rotation tool allows you to select and rotate any item (text box, picture box, or line) by sight. To rotate an item, first select the Rotation tool and then click the item you want to rotate. Then drag the item in the desired direction.

 Tip   Normally, you see only a blank outline of an item as you rotate it. If you press and hold the mouse button for one-half second before you begin rotating, you can see a WYSIWYG copy of the original item as you rotate it.

To rotate an item by precise degrees rather than manually, use the Measurements palette described later in this chapter.

The Zoom Tool

The Zoom tool provides one technique for changing the viewing magnification of your document. (Another is the view percentage bar, described in Chapter 2.) There are two ways to use the Zoom tool:

☐ Click (activate) the Zoom tool to make the pointer turn into an image of a magnifying glass with a + in it. Then, click the item you want to magnify. (If you want to *reduce* viewing magnification, press and hold the CTRL key while clicking the item. The + in the pointer symbol changes to a –.) The viewing magnification changes by a preset increment, depending on your settings in the Tool Preferences dialog box. See Chapter 4 and the "Customizing the Tools" section later in this chapter.

☐ Activate the Zoom tool and then drag the mouse pointer across the area you want to magnify. A dotted rectangular area or *marquee* follows the path of the pointer, as shown here:

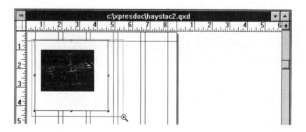

When you release the mouse button, the area indicated by the marquee enlarges as much as 400 percent, depending on your monitor and display adapter combination.

The Text Box Tool

 The Text Box tool has a single purpose: to create a new text box into which you can then import or type text. To begin creating a text box, activate the Text Box tool by clicking it. Then position the pointer (now appearing as a crosshair) where you want the upper-left corner of the text box to be and drag downward and to the right. An empty box grows as you move the pointer. When you release the mouse button, eight handles appear around the new text box to show that it is the currently selected item, and the Content tool becomes active.

The Four Picture Box Tools

With the four picture box tools—the Rectangle tool, the Rounded Rectangle tool, the Ellipse tool, and the Polygon tool—you can create picture boxes of various shapes to contain your line art or photographic artwork. Of course, you can also use picture boxes as independent graphics.

To draw a picture box, activate the desired picture box tool and then position the pointer where you want to locate the upper-left corner of the picture box. If you are using one of the first three picture box tools, drag downward and to the right until the picture box is the size you want. The Polygon picture box tool works differently, letting you shape an irregular picture box by pointing and clicking. You can always refine the sizing and location of a picture box using the Measurements palette described later in this chapter.

 Note   An "x" always appears in picture boxes that contain no imported artwork.

 Rectangle Tool   Use the Rectangle tool to create a rectangular picture box or graphic. Pressing the SHIFT key as you draw the box creates a perfect square.

 Rounded Rectangle Tool   The Rounded Rectangle tool creates a rectangular picture box or graphic with rounded corners. You can use the Measurements palette or the Preferences/Tools command to change the curvature of the corners. Press the SHIFT key to create a rounded rectangle with sides of equal length.

 Ellipse Tool Use the Ellipse tool to create an oval-shaped picture box or graphic. Pressing the SHIFT key as you draw the picture box results in a perfect circle.

 Polygon Tool The Polygon Picture Box tool lets you draw odd-shaped graphics or picture boxes that are ideal for unusual picture cropping effects. To draw such a picture box, activate the Polygon Picture Box tool and then click where you want the first corner to appear. Continue clicking to place each desired corner. After achieving the shape you want, close the polygon by clicking at the point of origin.

The Line Tools

These two tools let you draw lines of different types. To draw a line, activate the desired Line tool and click where you want the first endpoint to appear. Click again at the desired second endpoint to complete the line. After drawing a line, you can change its length, width, position, and other attributes using the Measurements palette or the commands in the Item menu.

 Orthogonal Line Tool *Orthogonal* means intersecting or lying at right angles; the lines you draw with this tool are straight vertical or horizontal lines.

 Diagonal Line Tool Use the Diagonal Line tool to draw lines at any angle. To avoid jagged lines, you can use the SHIFT key to constrain your lines to 45-degree angles.

The Linking Tools

These two tools help you automate copy flow in a document that contains multiple text boxes, such as a newsletter. Chapters 3 and 11 describe the uses of these tools in greater detail.

 The Linking Tool The Linking tool helps you link two or more text boxes so that copy flows between them automatically. The effect of the

Linking tool varies, depending on whether you use it on master pages or on document pages; this will be covered fully in Chapter 3.

 The Unlinking Tool   The Unlinking tool icon looks like a broken chain. Use this tool to disrupt automatic copy flow between two or more text boxes that are currently linked. As with the Linking tool, the effect of the Unlinking tool depends on whether you use it on master pages or on document pages.

Selecting Tools

When you first start QuarkXPress for Windows, the Content tool is automatically active. Clicking a tool icon is just one way to select a different tool. If you want to activate the tool just below the currently active one, press CTRL-TAB. To select the tool just above the currently active one, press CTRL-SHIFT-TAB.

Customizing the Tools

Eight of the tools in the Tool palette—the Zoom, Text Box, the four Picture Box tools, and two Line tools—have *user-customizable settings*, which means you can change the way these tools behave using the Preferences/Tools command in the Edit menu. Choosing this command or double-clicking the tool you want to customize brings up the Tool Preferences dialog box shown in Figure 1-23.

QuarkXPress saves tool preferences with a document, so that you can set different line end styles, zoom increments, and so forth for every publication. Chapter 4 gives more information about customizing tool behavior.

The Measurements Palette

Imagine having most of the settings for a given text box, picture box, or line right at your fingertips. Imagine being able to change those settings with just a couple of clicks or keystrokes. Thanks to the Measurements palette, you can edit attributes for any element in your document precisely and intuitively.

The Tool Preferences dialog box

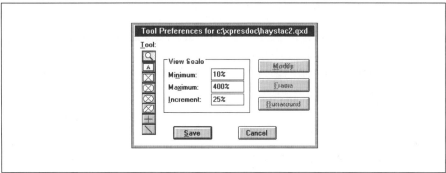

The contents of the Measurements palette varies according to two factors:

☐ Whether the Item tool or the Content tool is active

☐ Which item in the document is currently selected

Changing values in the Measurements palette is as easy as clicking an icon, double-clicking a value and typing over it, highlighting an option in a pop-up list, or adjusting a number using a scroll arrow. If you prefer to use keyboard commands, you can move between fields in the Measurements palette by pressing TAB (to move forward one field) or SHIFT-TAB (to move backward one field).

Measurements Palette: Text Box Selected

Figure 1-24 shows the kinds of information the Measurements palette contains when you select a text box in a document. The upper portion of the figure shows how the Measurements palette looks when you select a text box with the Item tool. The lower portion of the figure shows the Measurements palette when you select the same text box with the Content tool.

X and Y Coordinates   The X and Y coordinates specify the location of the upper-left corner of the text box. Changing the X and Y coordinate

FIGURE
1-24

The Measurements palette when a text box is active

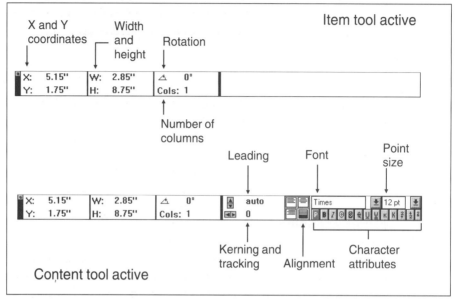

values moves the text box to a different location. Since you can specify values in extremely precise increments—in thousandths of an inch, for example—the Measurements palette offers the most exact method for positioning elements.

To change an X or Y coordinate value, simply double-click the existing value and type a new value to replace it. If you specify a different unit of measurement for the new value, QuarkXPress translates your values to the current unit of measurement (picas into inches, for example).

Tip You can specify a different unit of measurement for the new values by typing the appropriate abbreviation (**pt** for points, **p** for picas, " for inches, **cm** for centimeters). To change the default unit of measurement that appears in the Measurements palette, choose the Preferences/General command in the Edit menu and change the Horizontal Measure and Vertical Measure settings.

Width and Height The width and height values let you adjust the size of the text box precisely. To change the current value, double-click it and type the new value.

Degree of Rotation   This control lets you rotate the text box more precisely than if you used the Rotation tool in the Tool palette. To change the degree of rotation, double-click the current value and type a new one over it.

Columns   The Cols control lets you change the number of columns in a text box, up to a maximum of 30 columns. The number of columns you can implement in a specific document depends on the font and point size of your text.

Leading   You can change the *leading* (the amount of space between each line of a paragraph) of text using this control. If you do not want to type a new value over the existing one, use the up or down scroll arrow to specify a value.

Tracking and Kerning   *Kerning* is the process of adjusting the amount of space between two consecutive characters. *Tracking* involves adjusting the spacing between larger numbers of consecutive characters. You can adjust kerning and tracking by either typing in a new value or using the scroll arrow. See Chapter 6 for more information about kerning and tracking units.

Alignment   To change the alignment of the paragraph where the Content tool pointer is located, simply click the desired icon. The icons represent left, center, right, and justified alignment, respectively.

Font   Use the drop-down Font list box to change the current font of selected text to one of the other fonts available on your system. Chapter 6 gives more details on specifying fonts.

Point Size   To change the current point size of text, use the drop-down list box or enter the desired numeric value.

Character Attributes   The set of icons below the font and point size indicators control the attributes of selected text. Click the desired icon(s) to apply bold, italic, outline, shadow, strike-through, underline, small caps, all caps, superscript, subscript, or superior attributes.

Measurements Palette: Picture Box Selected

When a picture box is the active item, the Measurements palette looks like those shown in Figure 1-25. If you selected the picture box with the Item tool, only the information on the left side of the Measurements palette is available. If you selected the picture box with the Content tool, the information on the right side of the Measurements palette is available as well.

X and Y Coordinates   These coordinates indicate the position of the upper-left corner of the picture box. You can change the position of the picture box by typing new values just as you would for a text box.

Width and Height   These controls indicate the current size of the picture box. You can change them in the same way as the width and height controls for text boxes.

Degree of Rotation   Double-click and type over the value here to change the degree of rotation of the picture box.

FIGURE 1-25

The Measurements palette when a picture box is active

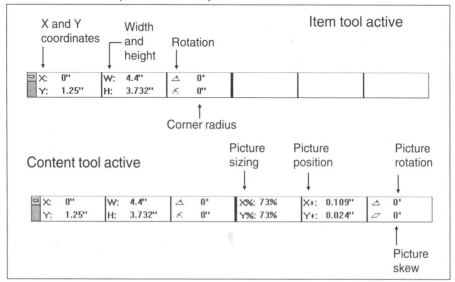

Corner Radius (Rounded Rectangle Picture Boxes)   If the selected item is a rounded rectangle picture box, you can use the corner radius control to adjust the curve of the rounded corners of the picture box.

Picture Sizing   If you use the Content tool to select a picture box, the picture sizing controls are available. To change the *width* of the picture, double-click the current X value and enter a new one. Changing the Y value alters the *height* of the picture. Changing the picture sizing values adjusts the size of the imported picture, not the picture box itself.

Picture Position   These X and Y values change the position of the image within its picture box and are therefore a valuable aid in cropping. Changing the numeric value specifies the increment by which the picture moves; changing the + or – causes the picture to move to the right or left, respectively. See Chapters 8 and 11 for more information about changing picture position.

Rotation and Skew   Edit these values to adjust the degree of rotation or skew (slant) of an image within its picture box. Remember, these adjustments affect only the picture, not the box that contains it.

Line Selected

When a free-standing rule or line is the active item, the Measurements palette resembles one of those shown in Figure 1-26. Your choice of a measurement start point determines which types of information appear in the palette.

Measurement Start Point   The drop-down list box for the measurement start point lets you determine the point relative to which Quark measures the line. To select an option, highlight and click the choice from the list box as shown:

The Measurements palette when a line is active

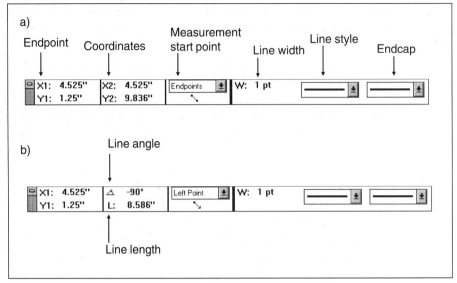

If Endpoints is the setting (Endpoints is the default), the Measurements palette displays the location of both endpoints, as shown in Figure 1-26a. If you select Left point, Right point, or Midpoint, the Measurements palette displays the location of the chosen point, plus the angle and length of the line as shown in Figure 1-26b. By adjusting the angle and length values, you can change the direction and length of a line precisely.

X and Y Coordinates   If you measure the active line relative to the Left point, Right point, or Midpoint, one set of X and Y coordinates appears on the Measurements palette. If you measure the line relative to Endpoints, two sets appear. The first set shows the position of the endpoint furthest to the left, while the second set shows the position of the remaining endpoint. Altering these values adjusts the length and/or direction of the line.

Angle and Length Indicators   These indicators, available when you measure a selected line relative to the Left, Right, or Midpoint, let you adjust the direction and length of a line precisely. To change the values, double-click the existing number and type over it. The angle and length indicators do not appear when you measure a line relative to Endpoints.

Width The value next to "W" on the Measurements palette indicates the width of the active line in points. You can enter any width value in any unit of measurement, and Quark converts your value to points.

Line Styles and Endcaps Quark provides 11 preset solid, dotted, and dashed line styles that you can apply through the Measurements palette. Six preset types of endcaps are also available. To apply a style or endcap, click the appropriate list box arrow and then highlight your choice from the pop-up menu that appears.

Grouped Items and the Measurements Palette

The Measurements palette displays yet another screen of information when you activate grouped items. Chapter 12 gives further details.

The Style Sheets Palette

As you learned earlier, a style sheet is a set of text attributes—for example, font, leading, and point size—that you can define and then apply automatically to an entire paragraph. There are two ways to apply style sheets that you have created within a document. The standard method is to use the Style Sheets command submenu in the Edit menu. A faster, more intuitive way is to click one of the style sheet names in the Style Sheets palette shown here:

To display all the style sheets available for the active document window (along with any keyboard shortcuts you have assigned to them), choose the Show Style Sheets command in the View menu. To apply one of the style sheets, activate the Content tool, click anywhere in the desired paragraph, and then click a style sheet name in the Style Sheets palette. Chapter 6 covers many more tips and tricks on using the Style Sheets palette efficiently.

The Document Layout Palette

The Document Layout palette shown here is a powerful tool for designing, arranging, and managing pages and spreads throughout a publication.

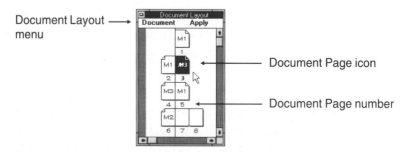

Document Layout menu

Document Page icon

Document Page number

QuarkXPress for Windows lets you design multiple *master pages*, which you set up as patterns that you want subsequent pages to follow. You then apply master page designs to specific actual pages. Using the Document Layout palette, you can do all these things:

☐ Specify multiple page designs within a single document

☐ Add pages to a document in any order or throw pages away

☐ Apply a page design to the pages that you choose

☐ Rearrange and renumber pages automatically

☐ Go to specific page numbers or view master pages

☐ Design spreads for odd layouts such as brochures and advertisements

Chapter 3 introduces you to the basic techniques for working with the Document Layout palette.

The Colors Palette

QuarkXPress lets you apply color to document elements in many different ways. You can apply a colored outline to a text or picture box; apply a single color to the background of a picture box, text box, or line;

highlight selected text in color; or blend two colors at any angle within a text or picture box. The tool that allows you to do all these things easily is the Colors palette, which is shown here:

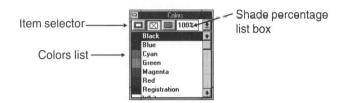

To display the Colors palette, choose the Show Colors command in the View menu. The appearance of this palette varies according to which tool you are using, how many colors you have defined for the current document, and whether you are interested in applying a solid color or a blend. In general, though, there are three basic steps involved in applying color with this palette:

1. Click the icon in the top row that specifies whether you want to use color for an outline, a background, or selected content or item (type or a line).

2. Click the item to which you want to apply the color in your document.

3. In the lower area of the Colors palette click the color that you want to apply. You also can specify a tint of that color using the Shade percentage list box in the upper row of the Colors palette.

To apply a color blend to an object, follow the additional steps given in Chapter 10, which thoroughly explains color tips and tricks in QuarkXPress for Windows.

The Trap Information Palette

Color printing is an art, not a science. Commercial printers must deal with the problem of achieving "clean" side-by-side color when two or more colors overlap or are adjacent to one another. *Trapping* is a set of procedures developed in response to this problem. You can control trapping (and make your print vendor happy!) by learning how to use the Trap Information palette shown here:

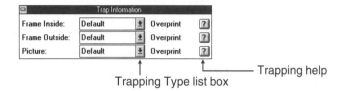

Trapping help

Trapping Type list box

Quark sets up default trapping techniques for different colored objects and their backgrounds, but you can change these techniques for specific objects using the Trap Information palette. This palette includes help information explaining each trapping technique and the circumstances in which it is appropriate. When you are ready to delve into the mysteries of color publishing and trapping, refer to Chapter 10 for a full exploration of the Trap Information palette and other Quark trapping aids.

Shortcuts: Working with Palettes

Table 1-4 provides a summary of keyboard and mouse shortcuts you can use when editing documents with a floating palette.

Exiting QuarkXPress

To exit QuarkXPress at the end of a session, you have several options:

☐   Choose the Exit command from the File menu

☐   Use the keyboard shortcut CTRL-Q

☐   Double-click the control menu box in the application window

If any open documents remain unsaved when you try to exit, a message box appears asking you if you want to save the document(s). Click Yes to save the documents or No if you do not want to save changes.

TABLE 1-4

Shortcuts: Working with Floating Palettes

Palette Function	Shortcut
Hide palette	Double-click control menu
Move palette	Drag palette title bar
Size palette (Style Sheets, Colors, Layout)	Drag from side or corner
Tool palette	
Display Tool palette	CTRL-TAB
Activate next tool	CTRL-TAB
Activate previous tool	CTRL-SHIFT-TAB
Keep tool selected	ALT + click tool while selecting
Set tool preferences	Double-click tool
Measurements palette	
Display Measurements palette	CTRL-ALT-M
Highlight next field	TAB
Highlight previous field	SHIFT-TAB
Apply change	ENTER
Style Sheets palette	
Edit style sheet	Double-click style sheet name
Colors palette	
Edit colors	Double-click color name

Chapter 1 has provided you with a whirlwind tour of the QuarkXPress interface and the QuarkXPress tools that make publishing more creative and efficient. Chapter 2 gives you hands-on experience creating your own QuarkXPress document. You will find Chapter 2 particularly helpful if you have beginning or intermediate desktop publishing skills or if most of your desktop publishing experience has been with other software. If you are a professional designer or want more detailed information about setting up new documents, move ahead to Chapter 3.

CHAPTER

Creating a Document

*T*here is no substitute for hands-on experimentation, especially with a layout package as rich in features as QuarkXPress. This chapter leads you through a simple project—a one-page newsletter—in which you can explore the basics of word processing, layout, typography, and graphics manipulation. You will learn how to carry out these tasks:

☐ Adjust the user interface to suit your working style

☐ Set up new document parameters

☐ Adjust the viewing area in a variety of ways

☐ Define a layout grid

☐ Create, size, and format text and picture boxes

☐ Enter text and format text locally

☐ Create style sheets for automatic paragraph formatting

☐ Set tabs and define ruling lines

☐ Import, size, and position pictures

☐ Use the Measurements and Style Sheets palettes

Your final document should resemble the one shown in Figure 2-1.

Note The document you create in this chapter uses several standard PostScript Type 1 fonts. If you do not have Adobe Type Manager (ATM) installed, you may substitute the equivalent TrueType fonts supplied with Windows 3.1.

Setting Up the Interface

Before creating or editing any document, it is good practice to customize the QuarkXPress user interface in a way that promotes a comfortable working environment. You customize some interface elements using the commands in the View menu and others using the Preferences/Application command in the Edit menu.

FIGURE 2-1

A simple one-page newsletter created in QuarkXPress

Haystackers' Herald

Clutterers Anonymous monthly   *Vol. 3 No. 9*   *September 1992*

Searching for a needle in an untidy haystack is a real time-waster.

Organization Saves Time, Clutter Wastes It

New study shows clutter works against timeliness

*H*ow often have you caught yourself making one of the following excuses when a colleague, family member, or friend remarked on that ever-growing pile of papers, books, and disks around your work area?

"I don't have time to get organized. . . ."

"If I put this mess in order, I'd fall behind schedule. . ."

Sorry, but those excuses won't hold water anymore, according to a new study by Dr. Irving Lundeby, professor of Psychology at Newtown University in Newtown, Idaho.

Dr. Lundeby's research team studied the work habits of several hundred busy executives over a six-month period. He found that people who routinely followed a plan for organizing documents and other work items were consistently on schedule with their projects and described stress levels as "manageable."

On the other hand, executives who allowed papers to pile up and didn't take the time to organize them often found themselves behind schedule and suffered a higher incidence of stress-related health disorders than the "organized" control group.

Simple "To Do" Lists Serve Best

Paper and pencil more efficient than software time managers

*T*he pressure's on these days to let computers organize every task in your life. That goes for managing your time, too. It used to be that you were thought an old fogey if you didn't use a word processor. In 1992, however, if you don't exploit the latest computer-based personal information manager, complete with OLE, hypertext cross-referencing, and project management, chances are your colleagues will consider you a dinosaur. How can you possibly get organized without the trendiest tools and the loudest bells and whistles?

Stop right there. Don't let the "total computerization" fad sway you or, worse, lessen your self-esteem. Paper and pencil "to do" lists may still be the most efficient way to organize your time. Why? Consider these simple points.

- It takes a lot less time to grab a pencil and paper than to boot up your computer, run your PIM software, and access your to-do list.
- Today's PIMs are often complicated. When you should be organizing your time, you're usually wasting time trying to learn the software and getting frustrated.
- When you write out a to-do list on paper, it's portable and immediately available. Time management aids created with PIMs aren't portable until you print them out. More time. . . .

Remember: computer-based PIMs *can* be powerful tools. Just don't throw the baby out with the bathwater.

Note Application-wide preferences apply to all Quark documents, not just the one on which you are currently working. Chapter 4 gives more details on preferences that Quark allows you to save with a particular document.

To customize the user interface for the one-page newsletter, follow these steps:

1. Start QuarkXPress.

2. If the Tool palette and the Measurements palette are not both visible, choose the Show Tools and Show Measurements commands in the View menu (shortcuts are CTRL-TAB and CTRL-ALT-M, respectively). Hide any other palettes using the appropriate commands in the View menu.

3. Save preferences that Quark applies to all documents. To do this, choose the Preferences command in the Edit menu and the Application submenu command. The Application Preferences dialog box, shown in Figure 2-2, appears.

4. If you have a color monitor, make sure the Margin, Ruler, and Grid guide colors are different so you can distinguish between them during the layout process. If the colors of any two guide types seem too similar, click the color you want to change. The Guide Color dialog box for the selected guide type pops up as shown in Figure 2-3.

 FIGURE 2-2   The Application Preferences dialog box

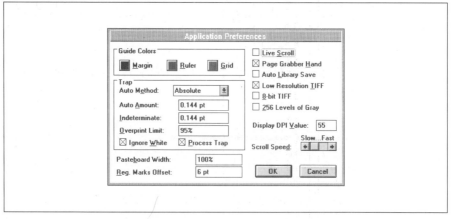

The Margin Guide Color dialog box

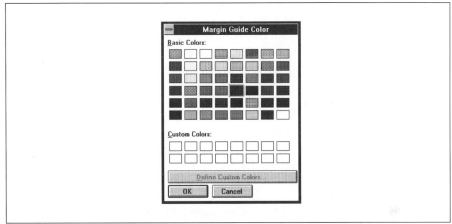

Simply click the color you want to switch to in the dialog box and select OK.

5. Make certain that an "x" appears in the check box next to the Page Grabber Hand option. Setting this allows you to scroll the view of a page by pressing ALT and dragging the mouse. If this check box is blank, click it to activate it.

6. Check to see that an "x" appears in the Low Resolution TIFF check box. If you decide to import a TIFF image into the newsletter, this setting speeds up screen redraw without affecting the quality of the image file.

7. Click OK to exit the dialog box and save these settings. QuarkXPress saves your preferences in the xpress.prf file located in the same directory as the program.

You have customized the interface, and are now ready to open a new document.

Creating and Saving a New Document

To open and save a new document, follow these steps:

1. Choose New from the File menu or use the keyboard shortcut CTRL-N. The New dialog box appears.

2. Enter settings in the New dialog box to match the ones given here:

   Page Size: 8.5" x 11"
   Margin Guides: 0.5" (or 3p) for Top, Bottom, Left, and Right
   Columns: 5
   Gutter: 1p6 (1 pica, 6 points, equal to 0.167 inches)

3. If the Automatic Text Box check box contains an "x," click once to deselect it. You need to add text boxes manually for this exercise. Make sure the Facing Pages check box remains unselected, too; your newsletter will be single-sided.

4. Click OK. A blank document appears on the screen at 100 percent viewing magnification (actual size). Depending on your monitor and display adapter combination, you may be able to see only a portion of the page.

5. Make sure that a check mark appears in front of the Snap to Guides command in the View menu; click the command if no check mark is visible. This command makes precision layouts possible by forcing items that you create to snap automatically to guidelines.

6. Save the new document by choosing the Save (CTRL-S) or Save As command in the File menu. The Save As dialog box shown in Figure 2-4 appears.

7. Set the Save File as Type list box to Documents (.QXD) as in Figure 2-4. If you do not want to save the document in the default xpress directory, use the Directories list box to save it to the directory you prefer.

8. By default, doc1 appears in the File Name entry box and is high-lighted. Type over this name with the filename **haystack** and then click OK. Quark saves the document with the extension .qxd.

9. Click the maximize button of the document window to make the document fill the application window.

Before going on, take a moment to adjust a number of preferences that QuarkXPress saves with the document.

FIGURE
2-4

The Save As dialog box

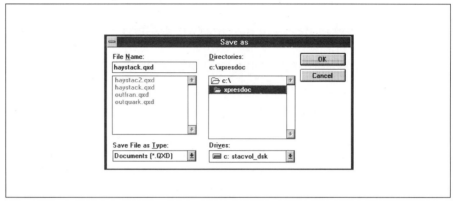

Adjusting Document Preferences

You can adjust general preferences that Quark saves with the document file. This means that every time you open the haystack.qxd file, the current preferences settings will change to match the requirements for that document.

The preferences that Quark saves with a document fall into three categories: General, Typographic, and Tools. General Preferences have to do with interface-related and miscellaneous defaults; Typographic Preferences control special character formatting attributes; and Tool Preferences determine the behavior of Quark tools in a specific document. You do not need to know about all of them here; refer to Chapter 4 for further information.

General Preferences

To adjust interface-related preferences for the new document, choose the Preferences/General command in the Edit menu. Change settings if necessary to match those in the General Preferences dialog box shown in Figure 2-5. A few of these settings deserve comment here:

☐ The *Horizontal Measure* and *Vertical Measure* settings determine the unit of measure that appears on the rulers accompanying a document window. You can set the two rulers to different units of measure, but in this case use inches for both.

☐ Set *Guides* to Behind. This setting prevents you from accidentally moving the margin or ruler guides when you are working with a text box, picture box, or line.

☐ Set *Auto Picture Import* to On. With this setting, Quark updates imported graphics automatically. If you edit a graphics file contained in the document between sessions, Quark displays a screen representation of the updated file next time you open the document.

☐ The *Snap Distance* setting aids in positioning text boxes, picture boxes, and lines precisely. With a setting of 6, objects within 6 points of margin and ruler guides snap to those guidelines automatically.

☐ Activate the *Greek Pictures* check box to maintain a reasonably speedy screen redraw. Quark still displays a picture whenever you are editing it, but the rest of the time you see a gray box.

When your settings match the ones in Figure 2-5, click OK.

FIGURE 2-5

The General Preferences dialog box for haystack.qxd

General Preferences for c:\xpresdoc\haystack.qxd	
Horizontal Measure: Inches	Points/Inch: 72
Vertical Measure: Inches	Ciceros/cm: 2.1967
Auto Page Insertion: End of Section	Snap Distance: 6
Framing: Inside	☐ Vector Above: 72 pt
Guides: Behind	☒ Greek Below: 7 pt
Item Coordinates: Page	☒ Greek Pictures
Auto Picture Import: On	☐ Accurate Blends
Master Page Items: Keep Changes	☐ Auto Constrain
	OK Cancel

Tool Preferences

You will use the Zoom tools, Text Box, and Picture Box to develop the new document. To customize the use of these three tools, choose the Preferences/Tools command from the Edit menu. The Tool Preferences dialog box shown in Figure 2-6 appears.

Zoom Tool Preferences

Match the Zoom tool settings on your screen to the ones in Figure 2-6. These settings allow a minimum zoom of 10 percent actual size and a maximum zoom of 400 percent actual size. The incremental zoom setting indicates that you magnify in 25 percent increments each time you click an area with the Zoom tool selected.

Text Box Tool Preferences

To check the settings for the Text Box tool, follow these steps:

1. Click the Text Box tool icon in the dialog box and then on the Modify button in the dialog box. Match the Text Box Specifications dialog box settings to the ones shown in Figure 2-7, then click OK. (Settings that are grayed are not available for tool preferences.)

FIGURE 2-6   The Tool Preferences dialog box for haystack.qxd

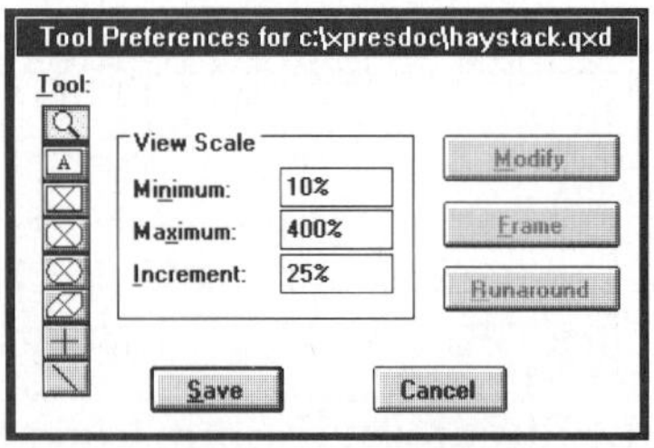

FIGURE
2-7

Setting text box specifications for haystack.qxd

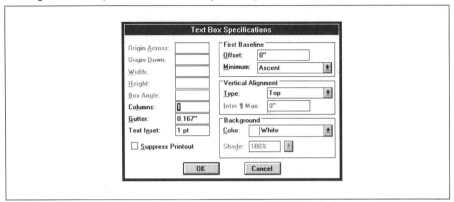

2. Click the Frame button and match your settings to the ones shown in Figure 2-8. No frame should be visible around any text box you create, so be sure to set Width to 0 pt. Click the OK button when finished.

3. Click the Runaround button and match your settings to the ones shown in Figure 2-9. The Mode should be Item and all margin values should be 1 pt. Click OK to save these settings.

Picture Box Tool Preferences

To check preferences for the Rectangular Picture Box tool, follow these steps:

1. Click the Rectangular Picture Box tool icon in the Tool preferences dialog box.

2. Click the Modify button and match the settings in the Picture Box Specifications dialog box to the ones in Figure 2-10. Click OK to return to the Tool preferences dialog box.

3. Click the Frame button and use the same Frame Specification settings you chose for the Text Box tool (refer back to Figure 2-8). Then click OK.

4. Click the Runaround button to access the Runaround Specifications dialog box. Your settings here should be the same as for the Text Box tool (refer back to Figure 2-9).

FIGURE 2-8

Setting frame specifications for the haystack.qxd

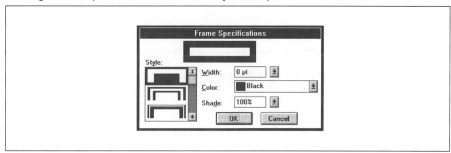

FIGURE 2-9

Setting runaround specifications for haystack.qxd

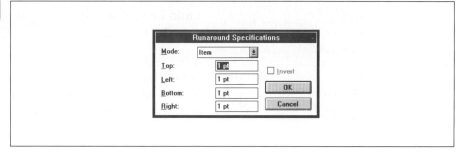

FIGURE 2-10

Setting picture box preferences for haystack.qxd

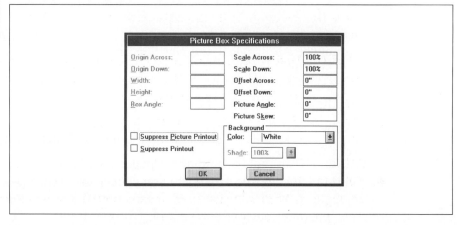

5. Click OK here and then click Save in the Tool Preferences dialog box to return to the document.

Adjusting the View

Different desktop publishing tasks require that you view a document at different magnification levels. To check a layout, for example, you may want to see an entire page (or two facing pages) at once. To edit text, an actual size view may be desirable. And to position or edit graphics, you may want to zoom in to an even higher magnification level.

QuarkXPress offers a number of convenient ways to adjust your view of a document. No matter what the size of your monitor or the pixel resolution of your display adapter, you can view any area of a page you specify. To customize the view, you can use any or all of the following:

☐ View menu commands and the Page Grabber hand

☐ Scroll bars

☐ The Zoom tool

☐ The view percentage indicator

☐ Keyboard and mouse shortcuts

View Menu Commands and the Page Grabber

Unless you have a high-resolution 19- or 20-inch monitor, you probably cannot see a full page of the new document. To view the entire page centered on your screen, choose the Fit in Window command in the View menu or use the keyboard shortcut, CTRL-0. The document should now look like the one in Figure 2-11.

The View menu also offers commands for viewing a document at preset magnifications of 50 percent, 75 percent, Actual Size (100 percent), 200 percent, and Thumbnails (miniature pages). When you choose one of these options, the area in which you last clicked the mouse becomes the center of the new viewing area. To reposition the viewing area more precisely, you need the help of the Page Grabber hand.

A Fit in Window view of the new document

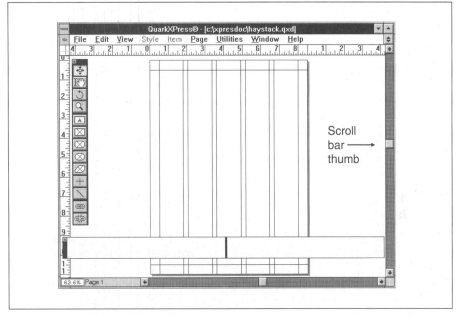

Change the view of your new document using View menu commands and the Page Grabber hand. Follow these steps:

1. Starting from a Fit in Window view, choose the 200% command from the View menu.

2. Activate the Content tool in the Tool palette and move the mouse pointer onto the page area.

3. While pressing the ALT key, drag the pointer in the direction in which you want to scroll the page view. The pointer takes on the shape of a hand as you drag.

4. Release the mouse button when you can see the desired area of the page.

Scrolling the Page

A more familiar way to adjust the page view is to use the horizontal and vertical scroll bars that are part of every document window. To view an area of the page that lies to the right of the visible area, you can press and hold the scroll bar arrow at the right edge of the document window, or drag the scroll bar *thumb* (the square button on the scroll bar) toward the right.

Dragging the scroll bar thumb toward the left brings into view an area of the page that lies to the left of the currently visible area. The same principle applies to using the vertical scroll bar.

Using the Zoom Tool

 The Zoom tool offers another technique for increasing or reducing the viewing area in preset increments. There are several ways to use the Zoom tool:

☐ To zoom in preset increments, activate the Zoom tool in the Tool palette and then click in the area you want to magnify. You can change the default zoom increment for a particular document using the Preferences/Tools command in the Edit menu.

☐ To *reduce* viewing magnification in preset increments, activate the Zoom tool, press and hold the CTRL key, and then click in the area you want to zoom out on.

☐ To magnify a precise area as much as the monitor allows (up to a maximum of 400 percent), activate the Zoom tool and drag the pointer across the area you want to zoom in on. A marquee follows the pointer, as shown in this example:

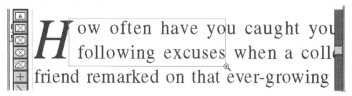

The View Percentage Indicator

An especially intuitive way to adjust magnification is to change the value in the view percentage indicator. This handy interface aid appears at the lower-left corner of every document window, as shown in the following example:

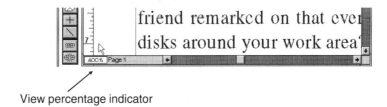

View percentage indicator

The view percentage of a new document is always 100 percent (actual size). To change the current view percentage, simply double-click in the view percentage indicator and type the desired value.

Tip You may find it convenient to control your viewing area using Quark's view percentage indicator in conjunction with the Page Grabber. After adjusting the view percentage, press and hold ALT and use the Page Grabber to drag the desired area into view.

Shortcuts: Keyboard/Mouse Combination

QuarkXPress offers a number of keyboard and mouse shortcuts for controlling both the level of viewing magnification *and* the area that you magnify. When you use one of these combinations, you define the area of the page that appears in the document window by clicking. Table 2-1 lists these combinations. Table 2-2 lists other handy shortcuts you can use to adjust the view.

Defining a Grid

If you are familiar with newsletter publishing, you know that it is important to define a *grid*, or a pattern of horizontal and/or vertical lines across your screen. Grids let you position elements precisely on the page, permitting flexible design choices within a fixed matrix. When you specify

**TABLE
2-1** Zooming In and Out: Keyboard/Mouse Combination Shortcuts

Zoom Function	Shortcut
Switch from any view to Actual Size (100%)	Right mouse button click
Switch from Actual Size to Fit in Window	Right mouse button click
Switch from any view to 200%	CTRL + right mouse button click
Switch from 200% to Actual Size (100%)	CTRL + right mouse button click
Zoom in once in preset increment	SHIFT + right mouse button click
Zoom out once in preset increment	CTRL-SHIFT + right mouse button click

five columns for the newsletter page you are defining, you are setting up just such a flexible grid.

To get a better look at the grid for your new document, choose the Fit in Window command in the View menu. If you have a color monitor, you can see ten blue vertical guidelines and two horizontal ones, as shown in Figure 2-11. These are *margin guides*. The horizontal guides and the

**TABLE
2-2** Adjusting the View: Additional Keyboard/Mouse Combination Shortcuts

View Adjustment Function	Shortcut
Fit in Window, page centered	CTRL-0
Actual Size (100%)	CTRL-1
Zoom in in preset increments	Click (Zoom tool active)
Zoom out in preset increments	CTRL + click (Zoom tool active)
Zoom in to maximum (up to 400%)	Drag (Zoom tool active)
Scroll page view with Page Grabber	ALT + drag (Content tool active) (see Preferences)
Scroll page view with scroll bars	ALT + drag scroll box (see General Preferences dialog box)

two vertical guides closest to the edge of the document define the page margins, while the other vertical guides demarcate the boundaries and the gutters of the five columns you specified.

The newsletter you are creating has just two columns. However, the five-column grid you set up lets you place the broader column on the left or right side of the page as your needs dictate. If the lengths of your stories and the sizes of available images vary from one issue to the next, you need the kind of flexibility a five- or seven-column grid offers. Grids of this type also help you avoid static, too-symmetrical page designs.

 Tip In QuarkXPress, margin guides are suggested boundaries only; QuarkXPress does not force you to confine design elements within the guide lines.

Now that you have had practice manipulating page view, you can begin the real work of designing a layout.

Creating a Masthead

The *masthead* of a newsletter usually contains the newsletter's title, the date of publication, and other information about the publication's sponsors. To create the masthead for *Haystacker's Herald*, you'll add ruler guides, create a text box, add text, and format it using Quark's Style Sheets palette.

Positioning Ruler Guides

Like margin guides, ruler guides help you precisely position the elements of a publication. You will use both margin and ruler guides in creating a text box to hold the masthead. Follow these steps:

1. Adjust the document view if necessary, so that just the top half of the page is visible.

2. If the Measurements palette is not visible, press CTRL-ALT-M to display it.

3. Place the mouse pointer in the horizontal ruler, then press the mouse button and drag the pointer downward within the document. A ruler guide follows the pointer.

4. Continue dragging the ruler guide downward until it reaches the 1.75 inch mark on the vertical ruler. Let the Measurements palette tell you when you have reached this point, as shown here:

This new ruler guide will form the lower boundary of the masthead text box.

QuarkXPress is so precise (to the nearest thousandth of an inch) that you may not be able to position the ruler guide exactly at the 1.75 inch mark. Don't worry about this; you can fine-tune the sizing of the text box after you create it.

Adding and Positioning a Text Box

To create a text box for the masthead, follow these steps:

1. Activate the Text box in the Tool palette by clicking it once.

2. Position the mouse pointer at the intersection of the topmost and leftmost margin guides on the page (0.5 inches on both the horizontal and vertical rulers). Press and hold the mouse button and drag downward and to the right; the outline of a text box follows the pointer.

3. When you reach the intersection of the ruler guide and the rightmost margin guide, release the mouse button. The text box snaps to the guides and eight handles appear around it to show that it is the active item, as shown in Figure 2-12.

4. Note the text box information in the Measurements palette. If the H, or height, value is not precisely 1.25 inches due to the placement of the ruler guide, double-click this value and adjust it.

Adding a text box for the masthead

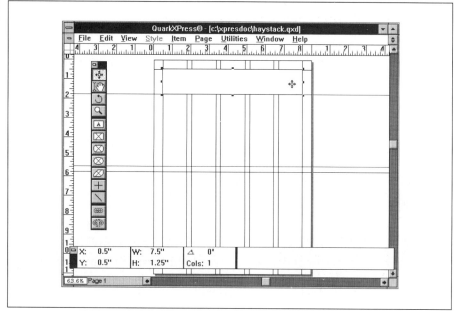

Look at the text box information in the Measurements palette. The X and Y fields indicate the position of the upper-left corner of the text box. If you wanted to move the text box without using the mouse, you could do so by changing these numerical values. If you wanted to change the *size* of the text box numerically, you would alter the W (width) and H (height) values.

Adjusting the Text Box Margins

To ensure that the text you add in this text box formats properly, you need to fine-tune the margins. To adjust the margins, follow these steps:

1. With the new text box selected and the Item tool in the Tool palette active, choose the Modify command in the Item menu. The Text Box Specifications dialog box appears, as shown in Figure 2-13. Note that the left side of this dialog box contains much the same information as the Measurements palette.

2. Change the Text Inset value to 0 pt, and then click OK. This permits text to flow all the way to the edges of the text box.

Adding Text

Next, type the nameplate information (information about the publication's sponsors, date, and volume) inside the text box, with the following steps. For a more thorough introduction to Quark's word processing capabilities, see Chapters 5, 6, and 7.

1. Click the Content tool. Since the new text box is already active, a blinking text cursor appears inside it. Note also that the right side of the Measurements palette fills with information about the default text attributes such as auto leading, left alignment, and Helvetica 12 pt plain, as shown here:

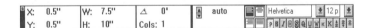

Your Measurements palette may show default attributes that are different from these.

FIGURE 2-13 Modifying text box parameters for the masthead

Text Box Specifications

		First Baseline	
Origin Across:	0.5"	Offset:	0"
Origin Down:	0.5"	Minimum:	Ascent
Width:	7.5"		
Height:	1.25"	Vertical Alignment	
Box Angle:	0°	Type:	Top
Columns:	1	Inter ¶ Max:	0"
Gutter:	0.167"	Background	
Text Inset:	0pt	Color:	White
☐ Suppress Printout		Shade:	100%

OK   Cancel

2. Choose the Show Invisibles command from the View menu so you can see paragraph returns and tabs in text.

3. Type the following text:

   Haystacker's Herald
   Clutterers Anonymous monthly TAB Vol. 3 No. 9 TAB September 1992

   Press ENTER after "Herald" and insert two tabs: one after "monthly" and one after "No. 9."

   To achieve a finished look, format the text as described in the next section.

Creating Style Sheets

There are two ways to format text in QuarkXPress. You can select characters, words, or lines and edit their attributes one at a time (called *local formatting*), or you can define style sheets that apply formatting automatically to an entire paragraph or an entire document (called *global formatting*).

In Chapter 1 you saw that style sheets are an efficient way to format text, saving you time and energy. You will create two different style sheets for the masthead: one for the newsletter title and another for the nameplate information.

Defining the Masthead Style Sheet

To define a style sheet, you need to place the text cursor somewhere in the paragraph you want to format, display the Style Sheets palette, and edit attributes using the Style Sheets dialog box.

1. Display the Style Sheets palette by choosing the Show Style Sheets command from the View menu. Since this document is new, only two default style sheet names, No Style and Normal, appear in the palette.

2. Make sure the Content tool is still active, and then click anywhere in the paragraph that contains the newsletter title. The Normal stylesheet becomes highlighted, like this:

3. Press CTRL and click the Normal style sheet option. The Style Sheets dialog box, shown in Figure 2-14, appears.

4. Click the New button to access the Edit Style Sheet dialog box shown in Figure 2-15. The pointer appears in the Name field automatically. The default attributes for the No Style style sheet on which this paragraph is based appear at the bottom of the dialog box.

5. To name the new style sheet, type **Masthead** in the Name field.

Tip   If you like, you can assign a keyboard shortcut to this style sheet. To do so, press TAB to access the Keyboard Equivalent field and then press the keyboard sequence (two or three keys) that you want to use as a shortcut. Be sure to press the actual keys; don't try to type the key names.

Assigning Style Sheet Attributes   As the Edit Style Sheet dialog box shows, a style sheet consists of several types of attributes. Examples of

FIGURE 2-14   Accessing the Style Sheets dialog box

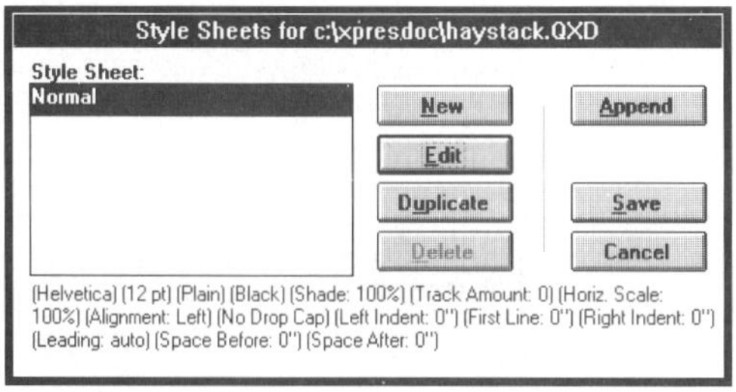

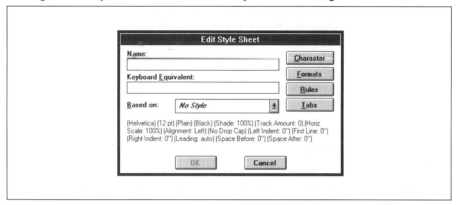

FIGURE 2-15 Adding a new style sheet with the Edit Style Sheet dialog box

character attributes are fonts, type styles (bold or italic, for example), type size, and color. *Formats attributes* pertain to alignment, spacing, and the relationships between paragraphs. *Rule attributes* let you define ruling lines that accompany a paragraph automatically. *Tab attributes*, finally, have to do with the spacing and alignment of tabs.

Assign Character, Formats, and Rules attributes to the Masthead style sheet with these steps:

1. Click the Character button in the Edit Style Sheet dialog box. The Character Attributes dialog box shown in Figure 2-16 appears.

FIGURE 2-16 Setting character attributes for the Masthead style sheet

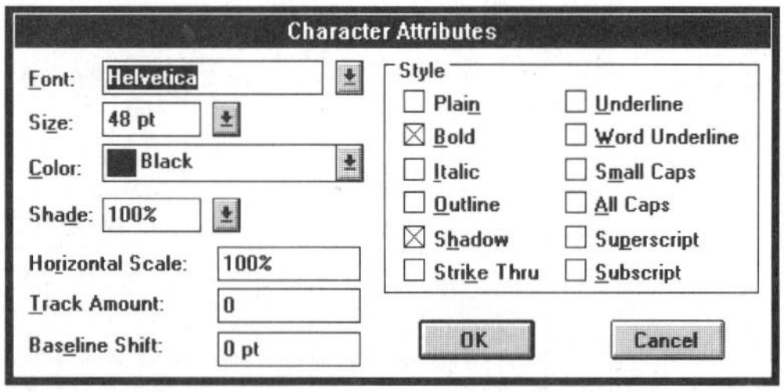

2. Match the attributes of the style sheet to the ones shown in Figure 2-16: Helvetica, 48 pt, Bold and Shadow, Black, 100%. Leave Horizontal Scale, Track Amount, and Baseline Shift at their default values of 100%, 0, and 0 pt, respectively. (If you do not have Adobe Type Manager, use the Arial font.)

3. When finished with character attributes, click OK to return to the Edit Style Sheet dialog box.

4. To access the Paragraph Formats dialog box, shown in Figure 2-17, click the Formats button.

5. Match your paragraph format settings to the ones in Figure 2-17. Change the Leading value to 60 pt and Alignment to Centered; leave other attributes at their default values.

6. Click OK to return to the Edit Style Sheet dialog box.

7. A ruling line between the Masthead paragraph and the one that follows it will add visual interest. To define a rule, click the Rules button. The Paragraph Rules dialog box appears, containing only two check box options, as shown here:

FIGURE
2-17

Setting paragraph format attributes for the Masthead style sheet

8. Click the Rule Below check box. The dialog box expands to contain several attribute options as shown in Figure 2-18.

9. Match the Length, Offset, Style, Width, and Shade options to the ones shown in Figure 2-18 and then click OK to return to the Edit Style Sheet dialog box.

10. Click the OK button in the Edit Style Sheets dialog box.

11. To save the new style sheet and return to the document, click the Save button in the Style Sheets dialog box. The new style sheet name appears in the Style Sheets palette, but the masthead paragraph continues to retain the Normal style sheet until you apply the new one (in step 13).

12. Adjust the view so that you can see just the upper half of the page.

13. Make sure that the text cursor is still somewhere in the masthead paragraph (Haystacker's Herald). Then, click Masthead in the Style Sheets palette to apply the new style sheet. The newsletter title reformats to look like the one shown here:

FIGURE 2-18 Setting paragraph rule attributes for the Masthead style sheet

14. The newsletter title should really span the entire width of the text box. One way to achieve this effect is to stretch the text horizontally. First, select the entire paragraph by clicking four times anywhere in the paragraph. The paragraph becomes highlighted, like this:

15. Choose the Horizontal Scale command from the Style menu to access the Horizontal Scale dialog box shown here:

Change the value to 106% and then click OK. The text redisplays with a slightly stretched appearance, extending all the way to the text box margins.

The format of the Masthead paragraph is now complete. You still need to format the nameplate information below it, though.

Defining the Nameplate Style Sheet

The information about your newsletter's sponsor, volume number, and date contains tabs. In defining a style sheet for this paragraph, you need to assign two different kinds of tabs and become acquainted with the Paragraph Tabs dialog box.

To define a style sheet for the nameplate information, follow these steps:

1. With the Content tool still selected, click anywhere in the paragraph that contains the nameplate information. The Normal style sheet in the Style Sheets palette becomes highlighted.

Setting character attributes for the Nameplate style sheet

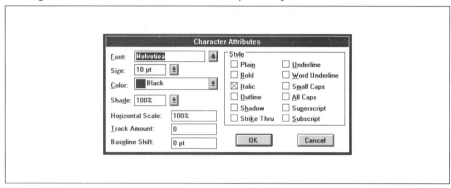

2. Double-click the Normal style sheet name to access the Style Sheets dialog box.

3. Click the New button. When the Edit Style Sheet dialog box appears, type **Nameplate** in the Name field.

4. Click the Character button and change the settings in the Character Attributes dialog box to match the ones shown in Figure 2-19: Helvetica 10 pt. Italic, Black, 100%. (Use the Arial font if you do not have Adobe Type manager.) Click OK to return to the Edit Style Sheets dialog box.

5. Click the Formats button and change the settings in the Paragraph Formats dialog box to match the ones in Figure 2-20: Left alignment, Space before 0.167" (or 12 pt). Click OK to return to the Edit Style Sheets dialog box once more.

6. Click the Tabs button to access the Paragraph Tabs dialog box shown here:

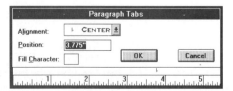

The pixel resolution of your monitor determines how far the ruler in the dialog box extends.

The first tab you define determines the placement of the volume number information, which should fall exactly in the center of the text box. The second tab determines the placement of the date information, which must right-align to the edge of the text box.

7. To set the first tab, choose Center from the Alignment drop-down list box and type **3.75"** in the Position field. If you prefer a graphical approach, you can click just above the 3.75 inch mark on the ruler to determine the tab position. The equivalent value appears in the Position field as you click.

Tip   If the value in the Position field is not exact, you can backspace over it and enter the exact value.

8. To define the second tab, choose Right from the Alignment drop-down list box and type **7.5"** in the Position field. Then click OK to return to the Edit Style Sheet dialog box.

9. Click OK in the Edit Style Sheet dialog box and Save in the Style Sheets dialog box.

FIGURE 2-20

Setting paragraph attributes for the Nameplate style sheet

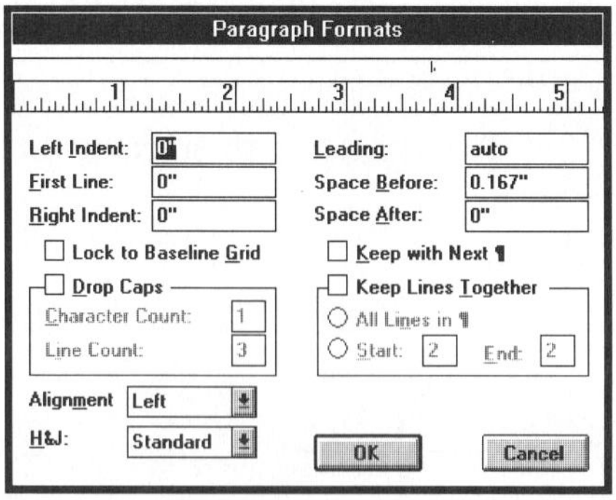

10. Click in the paragraph to which you want to assign the Nameplate style sheet and then click the style sheet name in the palette. The Nameplate paragraph reformats as shown in Figure 2-21, with the volume and number information centered exactly in the text box and the date aligned perfectly against the right margin.

11. Save the work you have done so far by pressing CTRL-S.

Adding Copy

The remaining elements of this one-page newsletter are two additional text boxes for stories, a picture box to contain an illustration, and a ruling line. In general, it is wise to add graphics to a document last, since the presence of image data can slow screen redraw. Create the additional text boxes and add copy as the next step.

FIGURE 2-21   Applying the Nameplate style sheet to a paragraph

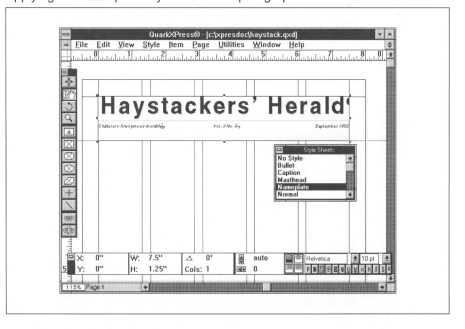

Adding and Positioning Text Boxes

The two text boxes that contain newsletter stories will define the actual columns of the newsletter. This issue of the newsletter contains two columns: a wide one that spans three of the five columns you set up for the page, and a narrower one that spans the remaining two columns.

To add, position, and format the two text boxes, follow these steps:

1. Zoom out to a Fit in Window view of the document.

2. Pull down a horizontal ruler guide and align it with the 5.25 inch mark on the vertical ruler. Use the Measurements palette to help you position the guide.

3. Press and hold ALT and click the Text Box Tool icon; then, release the ALT key *before* you begin drawing a text box. Pressing ALT before you activate the Text tool tells Quark to keep the tool selected so that you can create multiple items without pausing. You can use this keyboard shortcut with the Picture Box tools as well.

4. Position the pointer at the intersection of the new ruler guide and the leftmost margin guide. To create the first text box, drag from this point downward and outward until you reach the intersection of the sixth vertical margin guide and the bottommost horizontal margin guide. Then release the mouse button to make the new text box snap to the guides.

5. To add the second text box, position the pointer at the intersection of the top horizontal margin guide and the seventh vertical margin guide. Drag downward and to the right until you reach the intersection of the bottom horizontal margin guide and the rightmost (tenth) vertical margin guide. When you release the mouse button, the second text box snaps to the guides, and the page should now resemble Figure 2-22.

6. Click the Item tool to activate it and view the information in the Measurements palette (the second text box should still be selected). If the dimension and coordinate information differs from what you see in Figure 2-22, change the values in the Measurements palette to match those.

A Fit in Window view after adding two text boxes

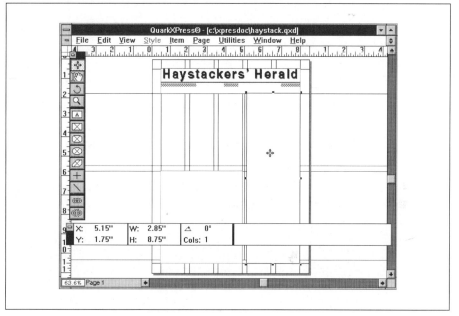

7. With the Item tool still active, click the first text box and check the values for it in the Measurements palette. Adjust the values as necessary to match the ones shown here:

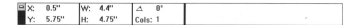

These new text boxes adhere to the defaults you set up for the Text Box tool preferences earlier, so they do not require any special formatting.

Adding Text

Next, you will add stories to the text boxes and format them with style sheets. You can either type text directly into the text boxes or import text from your word processor (importing text will be explained fully in

Chapter 7). If you choose to import the stories into Quark, do not use any special formatting in your word processor.

To enter the text for the newsletter stories directly into QuarkXPress, follow these steps:

1. Zoom in until just the leftmost text box is visible in its entirety.

2. Click the Content tool to activate it. If the text box on the left side of the page is still the active element, a blinking pointer immediately appears in it. If that text box is no longer the active element, click it once.

3. Type the text shown in Figure 2-1 into this text box. Where paragraph breaks occur in the figure, press ENTER.

 Tip   To obtain typographically correct double quotation marks instead of the inch marks the computer keyboard substitutes, type ALT-SHIFT-[for an open double quote and ALT-SHIFT-] for a closed double quote.

4. When text entry for the first text box is complete, adjust the document view so that the second text box is visible in its entirety. Then click in the second text box and type the text that appears there in Figure 2-1.

Creating More Style Sheets

The stories in the finished newsletter (see Figure 2-1) are to contain five different style sheets: Story Head for the primary headings, Story Subhead for the subheadings, Story for the body copy, Story Para 1 for the first paragraph in a story, and Bullet for the three bulleted items in the second of the two stories. Begin by creating style sheets for the primary and secondary heads.

Story Head

To create and apply the Story Head style sheet, follow these steps:

1. Adjust the document view so you can see the top half of the page clearly.

2. With the Content tool still selected, click anywhere within the first paragraph in the text box to the left. The Normal style sheet in the Style Sheets palette becomes highlighted.

3. Double-click the Normal style sheet to access the Style Sheets dialog box.

4. Click the New button. When the Edit Style Sheet dialog box appears, type **Story Head** in the Name field.

5. Click the Character button to access the Character Attributes dialog box. Set the attributes as follows:

   Font: Helvetica (or Arial if you are not using ATM)
   Size: 24 pt
   Style: Bold and Italic

   Leave the other options at their default values and click OK to return to the Edit Style Sheet dialog box.

6. Click the Formats button. When the Paragraph Formats dialog box displays, set Leading to 28 pt and activate the Keep with Next check box. Leave the other values unchanged and return to the Edit Style Sheet dialog box by clicking OK.

7. Click OK in the Edit Style Sheet dialog box and Save in the Style Sheets dialog box. The new style sheet name should now appear in the Style Sheets palette.

8. With the pointer still in the first paragraph of the text box, click Story Head in the Style Sheets palette to apply the new style sheet.

9. Click somewhere in the first paragraph of the second text box. Apply the Story Head style sheet to this paragraph, too.

Story Subhead

The paragraph immediately under the primary head in both text boxes is a subhead with different formatting characteristics. To create and apply a style sheet to these paragraphs, follow these steps:

1. Double-click Normal in the Style Sheets palette to access the Style Sheets dialog box.

2. Click the New button and type **Story Subhead** in the Name field.

3. Click the Character button to access the Character Attributes dialog box. Set the attributes as follows:

Font:	Times (or Times New Roman if you are not using ATM)
Size:	14 pt
Style:	Italic

   Leave the other attributes unchanged and click OK to return to the Edit Style Sheet dialog box.

4. Click the Formats button. When the Paragraph Formats dialog box displays, change settings to match these:

Leading:	14 pt
Space Before:	0.056" or 4 pt
Space After:	0.139" or 10 pt
Keep with Next:	Active

5. Click OK twice to exit the Paragraph Formats and Edit Style Sheet dialog boxes. Click Save to exit the Style Sheets dialog box.

6. Position the text cursor anywhere in the second paragraph of either text box. Apply the Story Subhead style sheet by clicking it in the Style Sheets palette.

7. Apply this style sheet to the second paragraph of the other text box in the same way.

Story, Story Para 1, Bullet

The last three style sheets you create for this newsletter have several typographic elements in common. After creating the first one (Story), you can save yourself time and effort by basing the remaining style sheets on it. Follow these steps:

1. Click anywhere in the paragraph following one of the Subhead paragraphs.

2. Double-click Normal in the Style Sheets palette. When the Style Sheets dialog box appears, click the New button, type **Story** in the Name field of the Edit Style Sheet dialog box, and then click the Character button.

3. In the Character Attributes dialog box, define the text attributes as follows:

Font:	Times (or Times New Roman)
Size:	12 pt
Style:	Plain

   Return to the Edit Style Sheet dialog box by clicking OK.

4. Click the Formats button. In the Paragraph Formats dialog box, change the following default settings to these:

First Line:	0.25"
Alignment:	Justified

   The First Line setting creates an indent for the first line of each paragraph.

5. Click OK twice to exit the Paragraph Formats and Edit Style Sheet dialog boxes and return to the Style Sheets dialog box.

6. Without exiting the Style Sheets dialog box, click the New button. When the Edit Style Sheet dialog box appears, type **Story Para 1** in the New field.

7. Select Story from the Based on drop-down list box. This tells Quark that you want to use the existing attributes for the Story style sheet as a basis for Story Para 1.

8. You need to change only a few Formats attributes to finish defining this style sheet. Click the Formats button and, using the controls in the Paragraph Formats dialog box, define these settings:

First Line:	0"
Drop Caps:	Character Count 1, Line Count 2

The First Line setting removes the first line indent that is characteristic of Story. The Drop Caps setting formats the first letter of a Story Para 1 paragraph in a large point size exactly two lines high.

9. Click OK twice to exit the Paragraph Formats and Edit Style Sheet dialog boxes and return to the Style Sheets dialog box.

10. To begin defining the third style sheet, click the New button and type **Bullet** in the Name field of the Edit Style Sheet dialog box. Choose Based on: Story for this paragraph, too.

11. Click the Formats button and set the following attributes for the Bullet style sheet:

Left Indent: 0.25"
First Line: –0.25"

These settings create a hanging indent when you insert a bullet and a tab at the beginning of the paragraph.

12. When you are finished, click OK twice to exit the Paragraph Formats and Edit Style Sheet dialog boxes. Click the Save button in the Style Sheets dialog box to save the document along with all three of the new style sheets.

Formatting the Newsletter Copy

All that remains is to format text with the style sheets you have created and to fine-tune a few characters with local formatting. To apply style sheets to the copy in the two text boxes:

1. With the Content tool selected, place the pointer somewhere in the first paragraph below the subhead in either text box.

2. Click in Story Para 1 in the Style Sheets palette to apply this style sheet.

3. In the other text box, click in the first paragraph after the subhead and apply the Story Para 1 style sheet in the same way.

4. Click anywhere in the paragraph beginning "I don't have time . . ." in the leftmost text box. Press and hold the mouse button and drag downward until at least some text in all the remaining paragraphs is selected, as shown in Figure 2-23.

5. Click Story in the Style Sheets palette to apply this style sheet to all the selected paragraphs. Notice that Quark applies the formatting to every paragraph in which you had highlighted at least some text.

6. In the second text box, click somewhere in the paragraph that begins "Stop right there. . ." Highlight text in all the remaining paragraphs of the text box just as you did in step 4.

7. Apply the Story style sheet to these paragraphs as you did in step 5.

8. Highlight text in the three paragraphs beginning "It takes a lot less time. . ." and ending "until you print them out. More time. . ."

9. Apply the Bullet style sheet to these paragraphs by clicking Bullet in the Style Sheets palette. These paragraphs reformat with the first line outdented.

FIGURE 2-23   Selecting text in multiple paragraphs in order to apply a style sheet

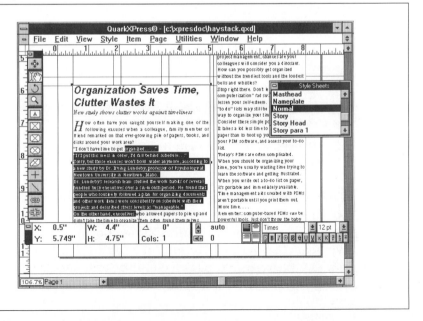

So far, there are no bullets in the Bullet style sheet. The next section shows you how to add them.

Applying Local Formatting: Bullets and Tracking

To finalize the text in this newsletter, you need to add bullets to the Bullet paragraphs, fine-tune letter spacing in the Story Para 1 paragraphs, and convert inch marks to typographically correct quotation marks. These operations involve *local formatting*—applying formatting selectively to letters, words or characters on a case-by-case basis. Style sheets, on the other hand, format entire paragraphs automatically every time you apply them.

To add bullets to the paragraphs formatted with the Bullet style sheet:

1. With the Content tool active, position the text cursor just in front of the first character in the first Bullet paragraph. Adjust the page view if necessary so that these paragraphs are visible.

2. Choose the Font command in the Style menu and select Symbol from the font list that appears. The next character that you type will be in this font.

3. With the Num Lock key turned on, press and hold ALT and type the sequence **0183** on the numeric keypad of your keyboard. This produces a thick bullet.

4. Press TAB to insert a default tab with a .25-inch indent. The rest of the first line aligns with the remaining lines of the paragraph, as shown in Figure 2-24.

5. Repeat steps 1 through 5 with the remaining two Bullet paragraphs in the text box.

Tip   Under Windows 3.1, you can use the Character Map program (located in the Accessories group window) to copy and paste a Symbol bullet character into the QuarkXPress document. Consult your *Microsoft Windows User's Guide* for instructions on how to use Character Map.

FIGURE
2-24

After tabbing, the first line aligns with the other lines in the paragraph

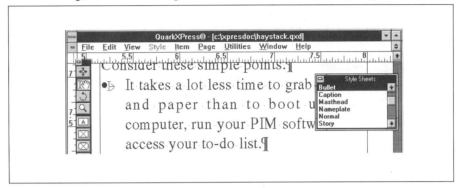

You may have noticed that in the final document pictured in Figure 2-1, the first character of the Story Para 1 paragraphs are Bold Italic rather than simply Bold, and that a little extra space has been added between that drop cap and the text that follows it. You can obtain the same results by following these steps:

1. Highlight the drop cap "H" in the first text box.

2. Choose the Typestyle command from the Style menu and highlight Italic. If you prefer keyboard shortcuts to menu commands, press CTRL-SHIFT-I to italicize the selected drop cap.

3. Repeat steps 1 and 2 with the "T" drop cap in the second text box.

4. Introduce a little extra kerning (letter spacing) between the drop cap and the letters that follow it. With the drop cap "T" still highlighted, adjust the kerning value in the Measurements palette from 0 (the default value) to 20, as shown here:

Kerning value

You can adjust the value in one of two ways: either press the right scroll arrow until the value reaches 20, or double-click the existing value and type **20** in its place. Note how the text in the first two lines of the paragraph moves over to make room for the bold italic drop cap.

5. Highlight the "H" drop cap in the other text box and increase the kerning value in the same way.

At this point, your document should resemble the one in Figure 2-25. You are done formatting the copy in this newsletter. Now comes the fun part: importing and manipulating an illustration.

Adding a Graphic

QuarkXPress for Windows gives you more control—and more intuitive control—over graphics than other popular page layout packages do. You can size and position pictures and picture boxes interactively and

FIGURE 2-25   Haystack.qxd with all text entered and formatted

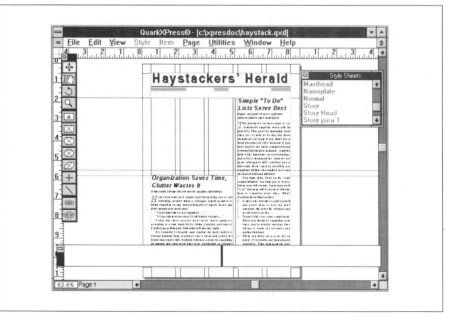

precisely, rotate picture boxes or their contents, add a variety of frames, and even perform image enhancement. In this chapter, you practice a few basic picture management techniques: creating a picture box, importing a picture, sizing it, and changing its position. When you are ready to take advantage of all of Quark's graphics-related bells and whistles, delve into Chapters 8, 9, and 10.

Adding and Formatting a Picture Box

The first step in importing a picture into Quark is creating a picture box to contain it. Ruler guides and the Measurements palette help you precisely define the size and placement of a picture box. Several types of picture boxes are available, too. For this newsletter, add a basic rectangular picture box by following these steps:

1. Adjust the document view so that the top half of the page is clearly visible.

2. Drag a horizontal ruler guide down to the 5.0 inch mark on the vertical ruler.

3. Activate the Rectangular Picture Box tool by clicking it.

4. Position the pointer at the intersection of the leftmost margin guide and the ruler guide at the 1.25 inch mark. This is the ruler guide that you used to help define the narrower of the two text boxes.

5. Press and hold the mouse button and drag. The outline of a rectangular picture box follows the pointer. When you reach the intersection of the sixth vertical margin guide and the ruler guide at the 5.0 inch mark, release the mouse button. The picture box snaps to these guides, as shown in Figure 2-26, and the Item tool becomes active.

6. Check the Measurements palette at this point. If the X, Y, W, and H values do not match the ones in Figure 2-26, change them.

7. To add a frame around the picture box, choose the Frame command in the Item menu. Change the settings in the Frame Specifications dialog box to match the ones in Figure 2-27: Width 0.5 pt, Color Black, Shade 100%, default Style (top option).

FIGURE
2-26 Adding a rectangular picture box

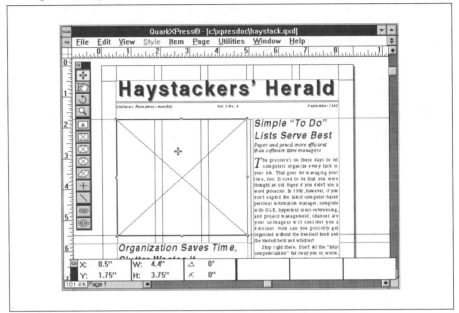

Importing a Picture

You are ready to import a picture into the picture box. QuarkXPress accepts a broad variety of graphics and image formats. Chances are that you can easily export images from your current drawing software, photo editing package, or clipart collection to QuarkXPress.

 Creating a .5 pt frame around the picture box

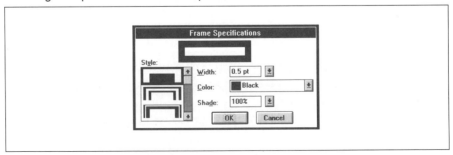

Tip The most commonly accepted graphics file formats in desktop publishing are Encapsulated PostScript (.eps) for line drawings and TIFF (.tif) for bitmaps. Files in these formats usually print easily and contain the most information about the graphic. If you have clipart in one of these formats, or if your drawing or image editing software can save in one or both of them, they are probably your best choices.

The graphic in the finished sample document (see Figure 2-1) is a clipart file exported to an .eps (PostScript) format from CorelDRAW!. You may substitute any fitting line art or image files at your disposal. The subject matter isn't really important; what is important is that you gain hands-on experience in importing and manipulating a graphic.

To import a graphic into the picture box, follow these steps:

1. With the picture box still selected, activate the Content tool. The Content tool makes it possible to import a graphic into a picture box.

2. Choose the Get Picture command from the File menu, or press the keyboard shortcut CTRL-E. The Get Picture dialog box, shown in Figure 2-28, appears.

3. Set List Files of Type to All Picture Files if necessary. This causes picture files in any compatible file format to become available in the Files list box.

FIGURE 2-28

The Get Picture dialog box

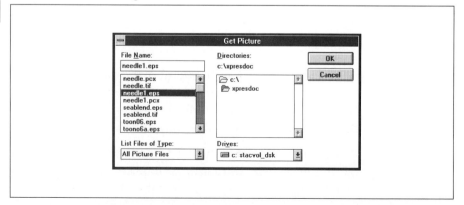

4. Using the Directories list box, find the directory that contains the file you want to import. Available filenames appear in the files list box.

5. Double-click the selected filename to exit the dialog box and import the picture.

After a moment, a screen representation of the chosen graphic appears in the picture box. Depending on the file format chosen, this representation may or may not be WYSIWYG; .eps files, for example, carry only a rough image header to help you position the image.

By default, the picture fills the picture box at actual size (100 percent), with the upper-left corner of the picture at the upper-left corner of the picture box. The X% and Y% values in the Measurements palette are both 100 percent, indicating that the graphic is at actual size. If the original picture is smaller than the picture box, you can see some empty space. If the picture is larger than the picture box, not all of it is visible. Quark makes it easy to crop, position, and resize a picture, regardless of its size.

Centering, Sizing, and Repositioning the Picture

Perhaps the graphic you have chosen isn't any larger than the picture box. But if it is, Quark offers some handy shortcuts for automatically resizing a picture. You can also center and reposition the picture automatically using keyboard shortcuts.

To resize, center, and/or reposition the picture within its picture box, follow these steps:

1. With the Content tool active and the picture box selected, press CTRL-SHIFT-M to center the illustration within the picture box. The X+ and Y+ values in the Measurements palette show you how far the graphic is offset horizontally and vertically when centered.

2. If you still cannot see the entire picture, it may be larger than the picture box itself. To resize the illustration automatically so that it

FIGURE
2-29

Importing, centering, and automatically resizing a graphic to fit in its picture box

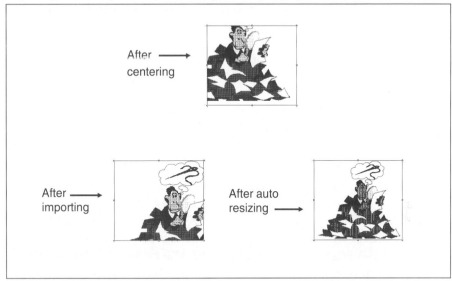

fits wholly within the picture box without becoming distorted, press CTRL-ALT-SHIFT-F. The X% and Y% values in the Measurements palette reflect the change in picture size.

Figure 2-29 shows how the picture in the sample document looked when first imported, after centering, and after auto-resizing.

Caution Be careful about arbitrarily resizing a bitmapped (paint or photographic) image. If you make it much larger or smaller than its original size, image quality may suffer. Pictures from drawing programs have no such limitations; you can resize them proportionally without loss of quality. Chapters 8 and 9 tell more about the differences between bitmapped and line art image data.

3. It may be that you would like to resize or reposition the picture further to achieve just the right look. To change picture size, double-click in the X% field of the Measurements palette and enter a new value. Then press TAB to access the Y% field, and type the same value there. The X% and Y% values must be the same to avoid distorting the picture.

4. If you would like to reposition the image further, you can drag it around using the Grabber hand that appears in the picture box when the Content tool is active.

Tip   You can also use keyboard shortcuts to nudge a picture in very small increments within its picture box. See Table 2-3.

5. When the picture is in position and at the size you want it to be, save the document.

Shortcuts: Adjusting Graphics with the Keyboard

Table 2-3 lists the keyboard shortcuts that you can use to move a graphic up, down, to the left, or to the right in 1-point or .1-point increments within its picture box.

Greeking the Picture

Generally speaking, screen redraw is slower for documents that contain pictures than for documents that contain only text. The speed of

TABLE 2-3   Keyboard Shortcuts: Nudging a Picture within Its Picture Box

Move Picture . . .	Keyboard Shortcut
Left 1 point	LEFT ARROW
Right 1 point	RIGHT ARROW
Up 1 point	UP ARROW
Down 1 point	DOWN ARROW
Left 1/10 point	ALT-LEFT ARROW
Right 1/10 point	ALT-RIGHT ARROW
Up 1/10 point	ALT-UP ARROW
Down 1/10 point	ALT-DOWN ARROW

your computer, the amount of memory on your display adapter, the file format of the picture, and the drawing or painting program from which it comes can all affect just how much slower screen redraw might be.

If you find the time you spend waiting for screen redraw annoying, you can *greek* the pictures in a document. When a picture is greeked and the picture box is not active, you see a gray area in the shape of the picture box, as shown in Figure 2-30.

At the beginning of the chapter, you turned greeking on for this document using the General Preferences dialog box (Preferences/General command, Edit menu). To see how your picture looks when greeked, click one of the newsletter text boxes to deactivate the picture box.

 Note A picture that is greeked becomes visible again whenever you activate its picture box with the Item, Content, or Rotation tool selected. Thus, you can edit a greeked picture when you need to, without sacrificing speed of operation.

 A greeked graphic

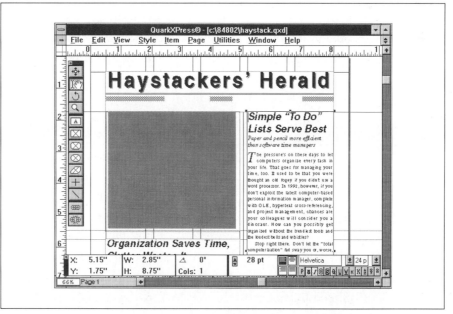

Adding a Caption

A typical newsletter photo or clipart image might contain a caption. The graphic used in the sample document does not completely fill the picture box, so we chose to position the caption text box in an empty area on top of the picture box. If the illustration you are using fills the picture box completely, you can forego adding a caption. But if you have room for one, follow along. You will add a text box, enter text, create a new style sheet, and position the text box according to the needs of the picture you are using for this document. Follow these steps:

1. Add a text box. Activate the Text Box tool and position the pointer at the desired location on top of the picture box, then drag to create a text box of the appropriate size.

2. Activate the Content tool to position the pointer at the upper-left corner of the text box.

3. Type the following caption text:

   Searching for a needle in an untidy haystack is a real time-waster.

   If you prefer, you can use some other caption.

4. Double-click Nameplate in the Style Sheets palette. When the Style Sheets dialog box appears, click the New button.

5. In the Edit Style Sheet dialog box, type **Caption** in the Name field. Using the Based On drop-down list box, choose Nameplate as the style sheet on which Caption is based.

6. You still need to change a few character and paragraph format attributes on the new style sheet. Click the Character button and set Font in the Character Attributes dialog box to Times, then click OK.

7. To change paragraph format attributes, click the Formats button in the Edit Style Sheet dialog box. Change Leading to 12 pt and change the Space Before value to 0". Click OK to return to the Edit Style Sheet dialog box.

8. To save the new style sheet, click the OK button in the Edit Style Sheet dialog box and the Save button in the Style Sheets dialog box.

9. Apply the Caption style sheet by clicking Caption in the Style Sheets palette.

10. If you need to resize the text box that contains the caption, either drag from any corner with the Item tool active, or change the W and H values in the Measurements palette.

11. To reposition the caption text box, activate the Item tool and drag the text box to the desired location. If you prefer, you can change the X and Y values in the Measurements palette to achieve the same end.

There are other methods of integrating pictures and text beyond the simple one you used here. Chapter 12 discusses the ins and outs of customizing text runaround to achieve special stylistic effects.

Adding an Intercolumn Rule

Ruling lines enhance the design of any publication and draw the eye in certain directions. As a finishing touch to this one-page newsletter, add an *intercolumn rule* that aligns with the baseline of the last line of text on the page.

To add, size, and position an intercolumn rule, follow these steps:

1. Adjust the view of your document so you can see the bottom half of the page and the last few lines of text clearly.

2. Drag a horizontal ruler guide down until it aligns to the baseline of the last line of text in both text boxes, as shown in Figure 2-31.

 Note You have designed this newsletter so that text in the adjoining text boxes should align. If it does not, check the position of the text boxes and the various style sheet attributes against the instructions in this chapter.

3. Zoom out to a full view of the page using your choice of techniques: the Fit in Window command in the View menu, the keyboard shortcut CTRL-0, or a click of the right mouse button.

FIGURE 2-31   Aligning a ruler guide to the baseline of story text

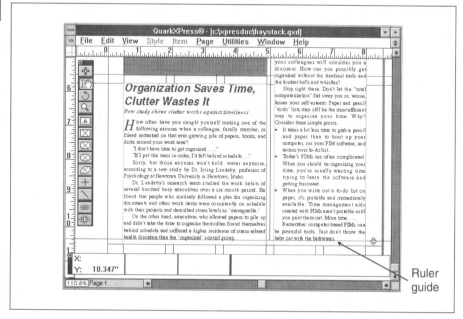

Ruler guide

4. Activate the Orthogonal Line tool and position the pointer where the gutter between the two story text boxes meets the ruler guide you have just placed.

5. Drag until the pointer reaches the ruler guide that marks the upper edge of the picture box and text box. When you release the mouse button, a straight line extends between the two ruler guides.

6. With the ruling line still selected, check the Measurements palette and adjust the ruling line specifications to match these:

Adjusting these settings has the effect of centering the ruling line in the gutter and establishing a line width of 1 point.

7. Zoom out to a Fit in Window view of the page and save the document.

The one-page newsletter is now complete. Except for the graphic, your page should resemble the one shown in Figure 2-1. You will have an opportunity to print this document in Chapter 13.

This chapter has introduced you to the basics of creating a new document. Now that you have scratched the surface, you may be interested in the next step. Chapter 3 offers a more high-level discussion of the rich design possibilities—templates, multiple master pages, spreads, libraries, and more—available to you when designing a new document with QuarkXPress for Windows.

Building an Intelligently Structured Document

CHAPTER

Designing a New Publication

*Q*uarkXPress lets you create fully automated, visually sophisticated designs for every type of document imaginable. The key to achieving this goal is to intelligently structure a document during the initial setup process. Using templates and master pages, you can plan for automatic headers, footers, repeating graphic elements, page numbering, copy flow, multiple-page spreads, and more. Strategically planning a new document before creating it means much less work to do during the layout process.

Intelligent document design with Quark means mastery of templates and master pages.

☐   *Templates* are preformatted "model" documents that you can reuse many times as a pattern when creating new documents. Newsletters and magazines, which are produced on a regular basis and must have continuity of design from one issue to the next, are excellent candidates for templates. Not every document requires the use of a template.

☐   *Master pages* are the basic building blocks of every Quark document. They contain repeating formatting elements, such as headers, footers, or page numbers, that are common to all the pages in a document or to a group of document pages. A document can contain up to 127 master pages, each with a different design.

This chapter teaches the skills you need to use templates and master pages effectively. You will learn to develop sound templates that can serve as models for a series of related documents, understand and exploit the differences between master pages and document pages, use the Document Layout palette, and develop master pages that include the basic repeating design elements for an entire document. The first and most important step in developing an intelligent design, however, is to know what kind of document you want to produce.

Know Your Application

Different types of documents require differing amounts of automation. To determine how much intelligence you need to build into a document during the initial setup, ask yourself these questions:

☐ *Am I going to use the design for this document more than once?* Flyers, posters, and other brief documents intended for a single use rarely require templates. A single master page is often sufficient for such documents. On the other hand, newsletters, magazines, business reports, and books in a series often follow formats that you use over and over again. Rather than design documents like these from scratch every time you produce them, develop a template and multiple master pages to ensure consistency and make setup easier.

☐ *Will the document have a uniform layout on every page, or will there be variable layouts?* Common business documents such as reports and proposals often repeat the same design on every page. Relatively simple templates based on a single master page are sufficient for these. However, books, magazines, newsletters, and brochures often contain pages with many different design schemes. The use of multiple master page designs for these variable layouts can save you time during production.

☐ *Is the document based on single-sided pages, facing pages, or unique spreads?* Single-sided documents such as reports usually require only one master page and a minimum of design automation. On the other hand, most published books, newsletters, and magazines are based on facing pages and thus have at least two potential master page designs (right and left). If a document contains specially formatted pages or pull-out sections, additional master pages may be necessary.

Refer to Table 3-1 for suggestions on using templates and master pages with typical types of documents. Chapter 13 provides further tips and tricks for designing specific types of documents.

Defining New Document Parameters

Once you know what type of document you want to create and its likely design requirements, open a new document by invoking the New command in the File menu (keyboard shortcut: CTRL-N). The New dialog box shown next appears, with settings to define page size, the number and

TABLE 3-1 Suggested Use of Template and Master Pages by Document Type

Document Type	Template	Single Master Page	Multiple Master Pages
Brochure			✓
Advertising & collateral		✓	
Business cards		✓	
Posters, flyers		✓	
Resumes	✓	✓	
Newsletters	✓		✓
Magazines, journals	✓		✓
Reports, memos	✓	✓	
Books, manuals	✓		✓

placement of margin and column guides, and a single- or double-sided page layout. You can also use this dialog box to insert an automatic text box that controls copy flow.

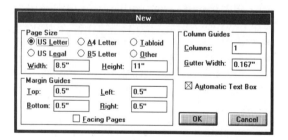

This section describes how to define these parameters when you first create a document. The "Modifying a Master Page" section later in this chapter teaches how to modify page size, guide placement, or other document parameters later in the layout process.

Page Size

Some desktop publishing packages define page size as the size of the paper that your printer or an imagesetter can output. In QuarkXPress, however, page size is the size of a page in the document. You control output paper size through the Printer Setup command in the File menu.

QuarkXPress offers five preset page sizes. US Letter, US Legal, and Tabloid are the most common American page sizes, while A4 and B4 are common European sizes. Table 3-2 provides the measurements for each of these in inches, picas, points, and centimeters. Current settings in the General Preferences dialog box (Preferences/General command, Edit menu) determine the unit of measurement used for page dimensions in the New dialog box.

To define a custom page size for a new document, simply click the Other button and enter the desired measurements in the Width and Height fields. If you enter custom measurements while any other button is selected, the Other button will become highlighted automatically.

Margin Guides

The Margin Guides area of the New dialog box has two main functions:

☐   It lets you determine the *live area* of all standard document pages—the area within which text and graphics normally appear.

☐   The Facing Pages check box lets you specify whether a new document will have single-sided pages as in a flyer or report, or facing (double-sided) pages like those seen in books, magazines, and newsletters.

QuarkXPress places visible *margin guides* on each page of a document to show the margins you have set. As Figure 3-1 shows, you can set

TABLE 3-2   Preset Page Sizes in Inches, Picas, Points, and Centimeters

Page Size	Inches	Picas/Points	Centimeters
US Letter	8.5 x 11	51p x 66p	21.6 x 27.94
US Legal	8.5 x 14	51p x 84p	21.6 x 35.56
Tabloid	11 x 17	66p x 102p	27.94 x 43.18
A4	8.27 x 11.69	49p7.3 x 70p1.9	21.0 x 29.7
B4	6.93 x 9.84	41p6.9 x 59p.7	17.6 x 25.0

different margins for all four sides of the page. Quark never forces you to place all text boxes, picture boxes, and ruling lines within these guides. You can position or extend items beyond any margin guide as your page design requires.

Margin Guides for Facing-Pages Documents

When the Facing Pages check box is blank, you create a document with single-sided pages. Single-sided pages are appropriate for documents such as business reports, memos, letters, flyers, and posters. If you are creating a newsletter, book, magazine, or other document that eventually will be printed on double-sided pages, click the Facing Pages check box to make an "x" appear in it.

FIGURE
3-1

Margins, columns, and gutters define the live area of a page

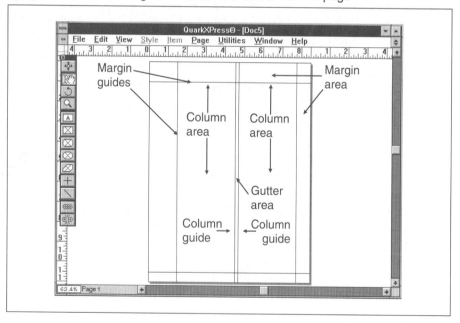

When the Facing Pages check box is active, the Margin Guides section of the New dialog box refers to Inside and Outside margins (rather than Left and Right), as shown here:

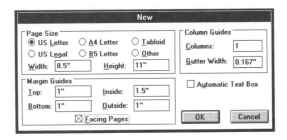

Inside and Outside margins differ because books, magazines, and other facing-pages documents need to have slightly wider margins on the page sides closest to the center or binding of the publication. These wider Inside margins or *binding margins*, shown in Figure 3-2, let text and graphics near the inside edge of a page remain readable even after the print vendor or book binder has fastened all the pages together. Documents with facing pages should always have an Inside margin that is at least 3/16 of an inch (0.188 inches) wider than the Outside margin.

 Note The Inside margin is the right margin of left pages and the left margin of right pages. The Outside margin is the left margin of left pages and the right margin of right pages.

QuarkXPress displays single-sided and facing-pages documents differently. Pages in a single-sided document appear alone, and are arranged vertically; you can scroll from one page to the next simply by using the vertical scroll bar. On the other hand, left and right pages in a facing-pages document (except for page one) always appear together on the screen, as shown in Figure 3-2. To move from a left page to its opposite right page, scroll across using the horizontal scroll bar or the Page Grabber hand described in Chapter 2.

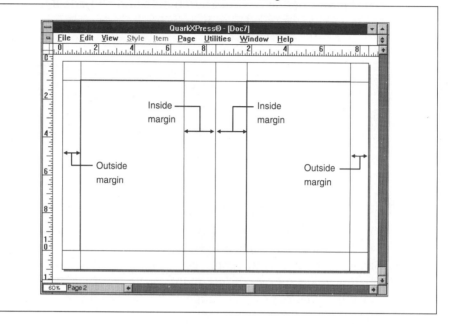

FIGURE 3-2   Inside margins should be wider than Outside margins

Column Guides

The Column Guides area of the New dialog box lets you define both the number of column guides per page and the width of the *gutter*, or blank space, between each column. The maximum number of column guides you can display on a page is 30. If Quark does not let you create as many column guides as you would like, reduce the width of the gutters. Columns always fall within the margin guides you set up for a document.

Column guides are just that—guides. The text boxes, picture boxes, and rules you create can span any number of whole or partial columns. Many newsletter and magazine publishers like to use Quark's column guides as a flexible grid that helps them develop asymmetrical column layouts such as the one shown in Figure 3-3. If the Snap to Guides command in the View menu is active, newly created or resized items will snap to column guides whenever the pointer is within a few points of the guides. You used column guides as a grid when you created the one-page newsletter in Chapter 2.

Using column guides as a flexible layout grid: two text boxes span three columns

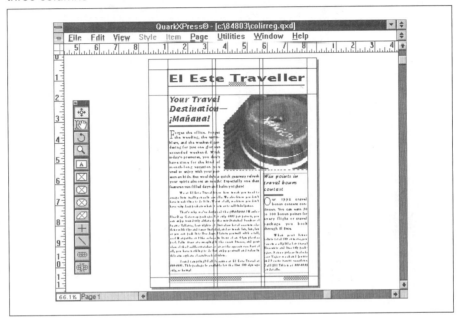

Tip To change the default distance at which items snap to margin, column, and ruler guides in a document, choose the Preferences/General command in the Edit menu and alter the Snap Distance value in the General Preferences dialog box. Quark saves this setting with the active document.

Automatic Text Box

When an "x" appears in this check box, Quark places a single text box on every page of the document. Copy that you type or import into the document then flows automatically from one page to the next. As Figure 3-4 shows, an automatic text box extends all the way to the margins and includes the number of columns you specify in the Column Guides section of the New dialog box.

FIGURE
3-4 A document page containing a single-column automatic text box

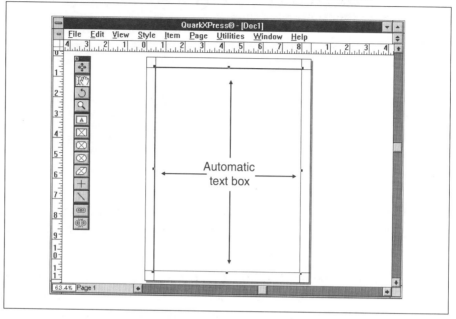

In general, use Automatic Text Box only for books, memos, reports, and other documents that contain a single text box per page. Newsletters, magazines, and documents that contain graphics and multiple text boxes on every page usually require more complex layouts and a different method of managing copy flow. See Chapter 11 and the section "Modifying a Master Page" later in this chapter for more tips on automating copy flow.

Modifying New Document Parameters

Once you exit the New dialog box and create a new document, you must use other techniques to change the basic document parameters just discussed.

☐ To change the page size or to switch from a single-sided to a facing-pages layout, choose the Document Setup command in the

File menu. The Document Setup dialog box shown here lets you alter these parameters:

 Note   If a document already has a facing-pages layout, you cannot use the Document Setup dialog box to switch back to single-sided pages.

To change page margins, the number of columns, or gutter widths between columns, you must first display a master page and then choose the Master Guides command in the Page menu. See the "Document Layout Palette" section later in this chapter.

Retaining New Dialog Box Settings

QuarkXPress "remembers" the settings you used most recently in the New dialog box. The next time you open a new document, this dialog box retains the page size, margin, and column settings you used the last time.

Saving a New Document: Documents and Templates

Always save a new document soon after you open it. The question is, should you save it as a document (extension .qxd) or as a template (extension .qxt)? If you plan to base other, similar documents on the one just created, save it as a template. If the new document is to be a short, one-time publication, save it as a document.

To save a new document, follow these steps:

1. Choose the Save (CTRL-S) or Save As command in the File menu. In either case, the Save As dialog box shown here appears, because you have not saved this document previously:

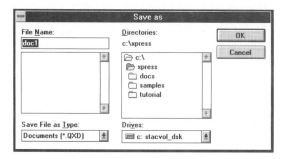

2. If necessary, use the Drives and Directories list boxes to change to the drive and/or directory where you want to save the new document.

3. If you prefer to save the new document as a template on which to base other documents, set the Save File as Type option to Templates (.QXT).

4. Double-click the File Name entry box and type the desired filename for the new document or template. You do not need to add an extension.

5. Press ENTER or click Save to save the new document. Quark adds the correct extension (.qxd or .qxt) based on your selection in the Save File as Type list box.

As you continue to develop the document, save it frequently. If you initially saved it as a Quark document, you can save over the existing filename by choosing the Save command in the File menu or pressing CTRL-S. If you initially saved the document as a template, the rules are a bit trickier.

Resaving a Template

QuarkXPress is smart. When you press CTRL-S to save an existing template, Quark assumes you want to derive a separate new document from the template. Consequently, the Save As dialog box appears, with the Save File as Type option set to Documents (.QXD) to prevent you from accidentally overwriting the template. If you are developing the existing template and really do want to overwrite it, follow these steps:

1. Press CTRL-S to save the existing template. The Save As dialog box appears.

2. In the File Name entry box, enter the existing template filename, including the extension .qxt. Or, if you prefer, change the Save File as Type setting to Templates (.qxt) and then type the existing template filename in the File Name entry box without an extension.

3. Press ENTER or click the Save button. When the Save As warning box appears, as shown next, type **Y** to overwrite the existing template file:

Creating a New Document from a Template

Think of Quark templates as electronic cookie cutters that let you stamp clones of a document design again and again. A template file should include all the repeating design elements that you expect to find in each issue of a periodical, each section of a book, or each printout of a memo or other business document. Such elements may include headers, footers, page numbers, style sheets, and one or more master pages.

The beauty of templates is that once you create a new document from one, you can customize that document without altering the master design. Take a typical newsletter, for example. Every issue of the newsletter contains the same number of columns per page, but the placement of photos and the length of stories tend to vary from one issue to the next. If your template file contains headers, footers, page numbers, a masthead logo, text boxes for standard columns, and a few empty picture boxes, you can save the template as a new document, change the dates in the masthead, resize picture boxes and text boxes, and *voilà!* You are ready to import the stories and graphics for the new issue—while the original design remains safeguarded in the template for the next use.

To create a new document from a fully designed template, follow these steps:

1. With the template file open, choose Save from the File menu or press CTRL-S. The Save As dialog box appears, with the File Name entry box highlighted and the Save File as Type list box automatically set to Documents (.QXD).

2. Type the desired filename for the new document, omitting the file extension, and then press ENTER. QuarkXPress automatically saves the file as a separate document.

The master pages that store repeating design elements form the foundation for any good template file. The Document Layout palette and the magic of master pages make the task of designing a new document or template enjoyable and creatively challenging.

Master Pages and Document Pages

Most documents contain repeating design elements such as headers, footers, page numbers, bleeds, or repeating icons. Through master pages, QuarkXPress puts at your disposal a powerful yet intuitive feature for storing, changing, and applying these repeating elements to pages in your documents.

Just as a template in Quark can serve as a pattern for many documents, so does a master page serve as a pattern for many document pages. QuarkXPress always creates one master page automatically when you open a new document, and every page in a newly created document has that master page as its model. However, you can create up to 127 master pages per document to accommodate pages with different designs.

The relationship between master pages and document pages in QuarkXPress is a designer's dream, just as flexible as it is powerful. For example:

☐ Any document or template can contain multiple master pages, each with different design elements.

☐ You can apply the design of any master page to any document page.

☐ You can turn master pages off for some document pages by basing them on a *blank* master page. A blank master page makes it possible to create custom formatting for those document pages.

☐ You also can choose to edit a document page *locally*—changing its formatting directly, without affecting the master page on which it is based. Local modifications take precedence over master page design in Quark.

☐ You can view and edit master pages just as you would a document page. Changes to the design of a master page immediately take effect on the document pages to which that master page applies. The only exceptions are document pages that you have modified locally.

Your ally in the design of master and document pages is Quark's Document Layout palette. The next section explores the components of this palette.

The Document Layout Palette

The Document Layout palette is a powerful aid in designing, arranging, and moving between pages. With the help of this palette, you can perform all of the following tasks:

☐   Create and name new master pages for single-sided or facing-pages documents

☐   Insert new document pages based on a master page or a blank (unformatted) page

☐   Delete master and/or document pages

☐   Create spreads with unusual page configurations

☐   Reformat specific document pages by applying a master page to them

☐   Move between pages in a document

☐   Display master or document pages

☐   Rearrange pages in a document

To display the Document Layout palette, choose the Show Document Layout command in the View menu. Two factors determine the components of the palette at this point: the current mode of the palette and the layout of the active document.

Document Page Mode and Master Page Mode

The Document Layout palette features two modes: *document page mode* and *master page mode*. Both the menus and the layout area of the palette vary according to the current mode. When you choose the Show Document Layout command, Quark remembers the mode you were using most recently and displays the palette in that mode.

Switching Between Modes

To switch the Document Layout palette quickly from document page mode to master page mode, click the mode toggle button shown in Figure

3-5, or choose the Show Master Pages command in the Document menu of the palette. To switch from master page mode to document page mode, click the mode toggle button again or choose the Show Document Pages command in the Masters menu of the palette.

Document Page Mode

In document page mode, the Document Layout palette contains icons that represent all the pages in the active document. Figure 3-5 shows how the document page mode might look for two different documents: a typical six-page facing-pages newsletter based on three different master page designs, and a four-page single-sided business memo based on a single master page.

The Document Menu   The Document menu, available only when the Document Layout palette is in document page mode, contains commands

FIGURE 3-5

The appearance of the Document Layout palette in document page mode varies with document structure

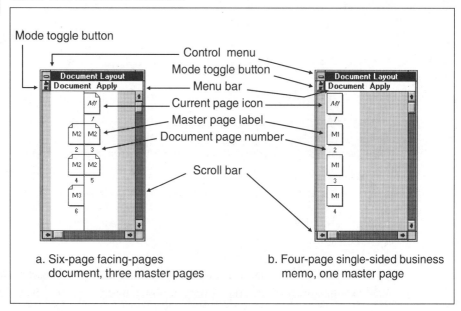

a. Six-page facing-pages
   document, three master pages

b. Four-page single-sided business
   memo, one master page

that let you insert new pages, delete existing pages, or show the master page(s) for the current document, as shown here:

The Insert command contains a submenu that lets you choose which type of document page to insert. The type of page available depends on whether the current document has single-sided or double-sided (facing) pages and on the number of master pages it contains. The Insert submenu for a six-page facing-pages newsletter based on three different master pages looks like this:

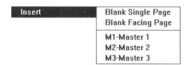

The Insert submenu for a simple single-sided business memo based on one master page looks like this:

The "Inserting Document Pages" section later in this chapter leads you through the process of adding one or more new document pages.

The Apply Menu   When the Document Layout palette is in document page mode, use the commands in the Apply menu to apply master page formatting to the currently selected document page. The number of commands available depends on the number of master pages in the current document and on whether it is based on single-sided or double-sided pages. The Apply menu for the six-page newsletter just mentioned looks like this:

The Apply menu for the single-sided business memo looks like this:

For specific details on how to reformat a document page, see "Applying a Master Page to a Document Page" later in this chapter.

Document Page Icons   In document page mode, each icon in the Document Layout palette represents a single page in the document. The appearance of each icon gives you clues about the master page on which it is based, the current page number, and whether it is a single-sided or facing page. Figure 3-6 points out the kinds of information you can glean from a document page icon in the Document Layout palette.

FIGURE 3-6   Icons in the document page mode of the Document Layout palette

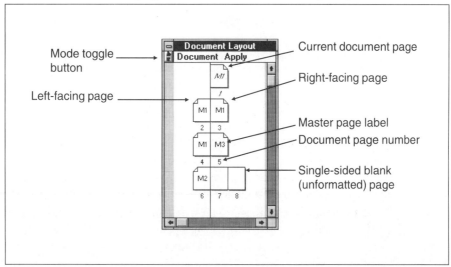

Notice also that the label of one document page icon is always highlighted. The highlighted icon represents the page that is currently displayed in the document window.

Note   If a page icon is blank, displaying no master page label, master page formatting has been turned off for that page. See "Inserting Document Pages" later in this chapter.

Master Page Mode

In master page mode, the Document Layout palette displays icons representing all the master pages in the document. Figure 3-7 shows how the palette looks in master page mode for the two documents previously discussed: the six-page facing-pages newsletter based on three different master page designs and the four-page single-sided business memo based on a single master page.

The Masters Menu   The Masters menu, available only when the Document Layout palette is in master page mode, contains commands

FIGURE 3-7   The appearance of the Document Layout palette in master page mode varies with the number and type of master pages

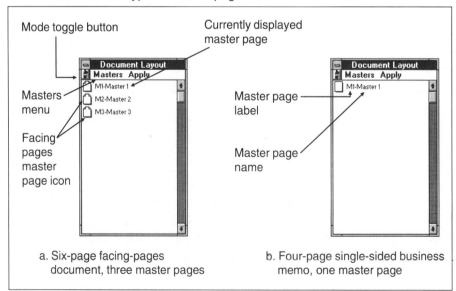

Mode toggle button

Currently displayed master page

Masters menu

Facing pages master page icon

Master page label

Master page name

a. Six-page facing-pages document, three master pages

b. Four-page single-sided business memo, one master page

that let you add new master page designs, delete existing master pages, or switch to document page mode for the current document, as shown here:

The Insert command contains a submenu that lets you choose which type of master page to add. You can format a new master page from scratch or base a new master page on the design of an existing one. The type of page available depends on whether the current document has single-sided or double-sided (facing) pages and on the number of master pages it contains.

The Apply Menu When the Document Layout palette is in master page mode, you use the commands in the Apply menu to reformat the currently selected master page instantly. The number of commands available depends on the number of master pages in the current document and on whether it is based on single-sided or double-sided pages. The Apply Menu for the six-page facing-pages newsletter already discussed looks like this:

Master Page Icons In master page mode, the layout area of the Document Layout palette contains icons representing each of the master pages used in the active document. As Figure 3-8 shows, the shape of a master page icon indicates whether the page is single-sided or double-sided. Both the label and the full name of the master page appear to the right of the icon. You can edit the full name of any master page and even the label if you need to; see the "Naming and Renaming a Master Page" section later in this chapter.

FIGURE
3-8

Icons in the master page mode of the Document Layout palette

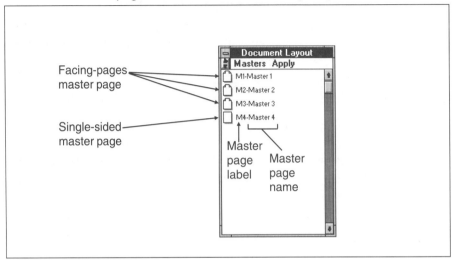

Note All documents may contain single-sided master pages, but only facing-pages documents may contain double-sided master pages.

Now that you are familiar with the modes and components of the Document Layout palette, learn how to use it to manipulate master and document pages. Let's begin with master pages, since they are the foundation of any document.

Master Page Basics

Master pages are, as you have seen, the models for actual pages in a document. Browse through this section for specific help on using the Document Layout palette to insert, delete, display, name, and apply master pages. For help on formatting or modifying a master page, see the "Essential Master Page Elements" and "Modifying a Master Page" sections later in this chapter.

Displaying a Master Page

A new document always contains one master page: M1-Master 1. In a single-sided document, M1 is one page, and its icon in the master page mode of the Document Layout palette resembles a single-sided blank page, as shown here:

M1-Master 1

In a facing-pages document, M1-Master 1 consists of both a left and a right page. Its icon in the Document Layout palette appears "dog-eared" to indicate this:

M1-Master 1

There are two ways to display a master page: from the Document Layout palette or from the Page menu.

Displaying a Master Page: Document Layout Palette Method

To display a master page for the current document with the help of the Document Layout palette, follow these steps:

1. Display the Document Layout palette by choosing the Show Document Layout command from the View menu.

2. If the palette is not already in master page mode, click the mode toggle button. The icons representing the master pages for the current document appear in the layout area of the Document Layout palette.

3. Double-click the icon that represents the master page you want to display. The master page appears as shown in Figure 3-9. Note that the title of the selected master page icon in the Document Layout palette becomes highlighted.

Displaying a master page using the Document Layout palette

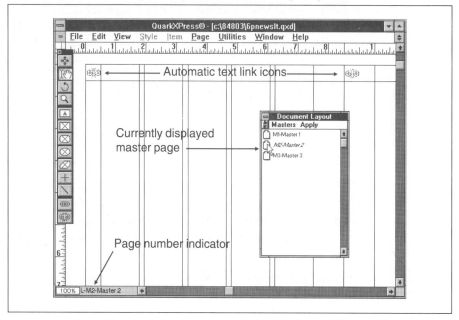

Displaying a Master Page: Page Menu Method

To display a master page using a command from the Page menu, choose the Display command from the Page menu. The submenu that pops out contains the names of all the master pages currently in the document, as shown here:

Click the name of the master page you want to display. After a moment, it appears in the active document window.

Figure 3-9 points out two visual clues that help you tell master pages and document pages apart:

☐   The upper-left corner of a master page always contains an automatic text link icon to help manage copy flow. (See "Modifying Text Links" later in this chapter.)

☐   The page number indicator in the lower-left corner of the document window displays the master page name.

Adding Master Pages

A Quark document can store up to 127 different master page designs. To generate master pages beyond the original one created with every new document, use the Insert command in the Masters menu of the Document Layout palette. Quark gives you flexible choices: You can generate a blank master page and then format it from scratch, or you can base a new master page on the design of an existing one.

Inserting a New Unformatted Master Page

To generate a new unformatted master page, follow these steps:

1. Decide whether to add a single-sided or a facing-pages master page.

 Note   Single-sided documents can contain only single-sided master pages, but facing-pages documents can contain both double-sided and single-sided master pages.

2. Display the Document Layout palette using the Show Document Layout command in the View menu.

3. Switch to master page mode if necessary by clicking the mode toggle button.

4. Choose the Insert command in the Masters menu. If the current document contains only single-sided pages, choose the Blank Single Master command from the Insert submenu, as shown here:

The pointer takes on the appearance of a double-sided page icon. If the current document is a facing-pages document, choose the Blank Facing Master command from the Insert submenu, as shown here:

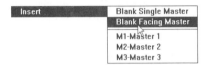

The pointer takes on the appearance of a double-sided page icon.

   Tip   To create a special spread within a facing-pages document, insert a Blank Single Master.

5. Determine where you want to place the new master page within the existing master page list. Then, move the pointer into the layout area of the palette and position it either *before* or *after* the desired existing master page icon. At any of these points, the pointer takes on the appearance of a stylized arrow, as shown here:

Master page
insertion pointer

6. Click to fix the new master page icon in the list. No matter where you position the new icon, its label and name include the next available number, as shown here:

You can rename and reposition the icon later; see the "Naming and Renaming a Master Page" and "Rearranging Master Pages" sections for more information.

7. Display the new master page by double-clicking its icon in the Document Layout palette. Modify its layout as described in the "Modifying a Master Page" section of this chapter.

Basing a New Master Page on an Existing One

You do not always need to design a new master page from scratch. One time-saving approach is to use the Document Layout palette to base a new master page on the design of an existing master page. This approach works especially well when you want a new master page to look somewhat similar to one that you have set up previously.

To generate a master page based partially on the design of an existing one, follow these steps:

1. Display the Document Layout palette using the Show Document Layout command in the View menu.

2. If the palette is in document page mode, switch to master page mode by clicking the mode toggle button. The layout area of the palette now contains one or more master page icons.

3. Choose the Insert command in the Masters menu and click the submenu command that represents the existing master page you want to use as a model. For instance, if the document currently contains three master pages and you want to base a new master on M3-Master 3, click the M3-Master 3 command in the Insert submenu, as shown in this example:

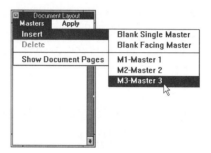

4. Determine where you want to place the new master page within the existing master page list. Then, move the pointer into the layout area of the palette and position it either *before* or *after* the desired existing master page icon.

5. Click to fix the new master page icon in place.

You can now display the new master page and refine its design. Since you have modeled it on an existing master page, you need to make fewer modifications than if you were to design the master page from scratch.

Reformatting a Master Page Automatically

When a document contains multiple master pages, you may choose to reformat one master page according to the design of another. You can do this automatically using the commands in the Apply menu of the Document Layout palette.

To reformat a master page automatically, follow these steps:

1. With a document open, display the Document Layout palette.

2. Switch to master page mode if necessary.

3. Click the icon that represents the master page you want to reformat. It becomes highlighted.

4. From the Apply menu, click the name of the master page with which you want to reformat the selected master page. Quark displays a dialog box asking if you are sure you want to replace the formatting of the existing master page:

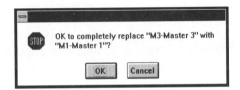

The selected master page icon does not change its appearance when you reformat it this way. However, if you display the master page by double-clicking its icon, the layout will change.

Naming and Renaming a Master Page

A master page name consists of two parts: a two-character label and a full name. Quark automatically assigns both the full name and the abbreviated label when you create a new master page. However, in some situations you might prefer to set up your own master page naming system for documents that contain multiple master pages.

For example, imagine you are developing a newsletter that features separate layouts for the front page, internal feature stories pages, and the company calendar page. Your document would feature three master pages, initially called M1-Master 1, M2-Master 2, and M3-Master 3. To help distinguish the purpose of each master page, you might rename them M1-Masthead, M2-Features, and M3-Calendar. These names would appear in the layout area of the Document Layout palette in master page mode.

To rename a master page, follow these steps:

1. With a document open, display the Document Layout palette.

2. If necessary, switch the palette to master page mode by clicking the mode toggle button.

3. Click the desired master page icon or its name once. Both the icon and its name become highlighted, and a box surrounds the name, as shown here:

4. Type the desired name in the box and then press ENTER. The master page still retains its original two-character label, but the new name follows it after a hyphen, as shown here:

Tip   Document page icons always carry the two-character label of the master pages on which they are modeled. In some cases, using a different set of labels—B1, B2, B3, and so on for master pages in a book, for instance—might help you remember the functions of a document's master pages better. There is only one way to change the default M1-sequence label when you rename a master page, however: follow the first two characters of the new page name with a hyphen. For example, when renaming a book's master pages in the case just cited, you could call them B1-Title, B2-Contents, B3-Acknowledgments, and so on.

Rearranging Master Pages

To change the sequence of master pages as they appear in the Document Layout palette, follow these steps:

1. Display the Document Layout palette.

2. If necessary, click the mode toggle button to switch to master page mode.

3. To select the first master page you want to move, click it once. It becomes highlighted.

4. Press and hold the mouse button and drag the icon slowly toward the place in the layout area of the palette where you want to reposition it. A shadow icon and arrow follow the pointer.

5. When the pointer reaches the desired position (and takes on the shape of a stylized arrow), release the mouse button. The master page icon reappears in the new position.

Deleting a Master Page

To delete a master page when the Document Layout palette is in master page mode, simply click it to highlight it and then choose the Delete command from the Masters menu. If the document contains at least one page based on the selected master page, Quark presents this dialog box:

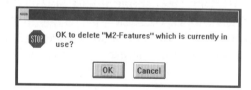

If you choose OK, document pages that you have already formatted with this master page remain in the document and retain their current formatting. However, you can no longer update their formatting automatically, because they no longer retain links to any master page or to each other. As shown in Figure 3-10, these document pages lose their labels and become like individually formatted "blank" pages.

Essential Master Page Elements

You can put any repeating item on a master page. When first created, however, a master page always contains at least three elements: margin

FIGURE 3-10   After a master page is deleted, Quark no longer updates the formatting of associated document pages automatically

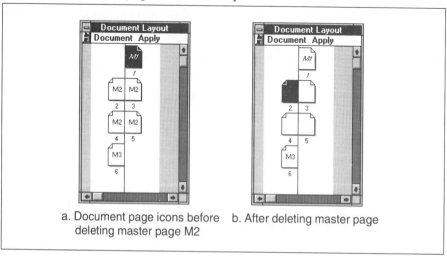

a. Document page icons before deleting master page M2

b. After deleting master page

guides, column guides, and an automatic text link icon. If you specified an Automatic Text Box when you first set up the document, the master page contains one of these also. Figure 3-11 shows a typical master page with all four basic elements.

Margin and Column Guides

Margin and column guides on a master page apply to every page in the document that has this master page as its model. You cannot move or add guides using the mouse; instead, you must use the Master Guides command in the Page menu, as described in the "Modifying a Master Page" section later in this chapter.

FIGURE 3-11   Typical elements of a master page

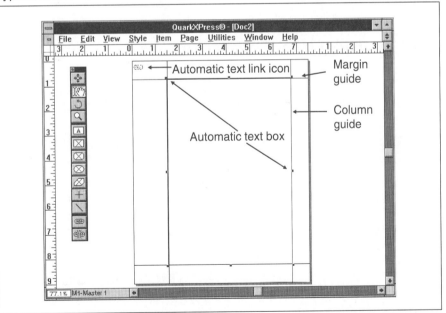

The Automatic Text Link Icon

The automatic text link icon in the upper-left corner of every master page (refer to Figure 3-14) helps you control the flow of text in a document. This icon can have one of two different appearances:

 ☐ In a master page that contains an automatic text box (see "Modifying Text Links" later in this chapter), the automatic text link icon looks like an unbroken chain and is called an *intact text link icon.* Every document page associated with this master page contains a text box, and copy flows from one document page to the next when a text box overflows.

 ☐ A master page that contains no automatic text box displays a *broken text link icon* in its upper-left corner. This means that the associated document pages contain no text boxes except the ones you add directly to each document page. Copy on associated document pages does not flow automatically from one page to another unless you create manual text links as described in the "Modifying Text Links" section later in this chapter.

The Automatic Text Box

The customary place to add an automatic text box is in the New dialog box, when you first open a new document. Quark is so flexible, though, that with the help of the automatic text link icon, you can create one or more automatic text boxes in a master page at any time. The "Modifying Text Links" section of this chapter explains how.

Quark does not allow you to type in the automatic text box of a master page. You must enter or import text directly into document pages. However, you can use the Modify, Frame, and Runaround commands in the Item menu to format an automatic text box and prepare its layout for text.

Modifying a Master Page

You can edit essential master page elements and add new repeating items (both text and graphics) at any time during the document layout process. When you update a master page, Quark also updates all document pages that are based on it, except for any document pages you may have edited locally. This section briefly reviews techniques for modifying common elements of a master page: margin and column guides, automatic text boxes, headers, footers, page numbers, and repeating graphics and text.

Modifying Margin and Column Guides

QuarkXPress lets you edit most page formatting elements from either a master page or a document page. Margin and column guides are different. Once you exit the New dialog box, the only way you can change page margins or the number or position of columns in a document is by choosing the Master Guides command in the Page menu when a master page is displayed.

To modify margin and/or column guides in a document:

1. Display the master page for which you want to edit margin and/or column guide values. You can either double-click the desired master page icon in the Document Layout palette or choose the appropriate master page through the Display submenu in the Page menu.

2. Choose the Master Guides command in the Page menu. The Master Guides dialog box appears, as shown next. Depending on your original document setup, the values you see may be different from the ones in the illustration.

3. To change page margins, edit the values in the Margin Guides section of the dialog box.

4. To change the number of columns or the width of all column gutters, edit the values in the Column Guides section of the dialog box.

5. Click OK to save the new settings and return to the master page.

Modifying Text Links

An efficient way to control copy flow in document pages is to add, link, and modify automatic text boxes in a master page. Even if you did not specify an automatic text box when you first opened a document, you can create one (or more) at any time during the page layout process. You also can unlink text boxes that you have linked previously.

Creating and Linking Automatic Text Boxes

There are many cases in which you might want a master page to contain more than one automatic text box. Imagine, for example, that you publish a two-column professional journal in which feature articles flow across both columns from one page to the next. A useful document design strategy might be to create a master page for each feature article, add two text boxes to each master page, and link the two text boxes with the help of the automatic text link icon and the Linking tool in the Tool palette.

Here is how you might proceed:

1. Open a new facing-pages document, specifying two columns (but no automatic text box) in the New dialog box.

2. Display the Document Layout palette and click the mode toggle button to switch the palette to master page mode.

3. To create a new master page based on M1, choose the Insert/M1-Master 1 command from the Masters menu and click below the M1 icon in the palette.

4. Display the new master page (M2) by double-clicking its icon.

5. Zoom out to a Fit in Window view of the master page (keyboard shortcut: CTRL-0) and ensure that the Snap to Guides command in the View menu is active.

6. Press ALT momentarily as you click the Text box tool in the Tools palette, and then release ALT immediately.

Note Briefly pressing ALT as you select a tool lets you apply the tool more than once without having to reselect it.

7. Move the pointer until it becomes a + and then draw a text box that fills all of column 1 on the left master page. If you begin and end the text box where the margin and column guides intersect, the text box snaps precisely to the guides.

8. With the Text Box tool still selected, draw a second text box that fills the whole of column 2.

9. Draw text boxes for the two columns on the right master page in the same way. The left and right master pages of M2 should now look like Figure 3-12.

    Since they are components of a master page, the two text boxes will appear on any left or right document page you generate from this master page. At this point, however, they are not *automatic* text boxes because you have established no automatic copy flow. In order to generate such a flow, you need to link these text boxes to each other in sequence.

10. Zoom in on the top half of the left master page by activating the Zoom tool and drawing a marquee around that area.

11. Activate the Linking tool in the Tool palette and click the automatic text link icon in the upper-left corner of the master page. An animated marquee appears around the icon to show you are in

FIGURE
3-12

Completed text boxes on left and right facing master pages

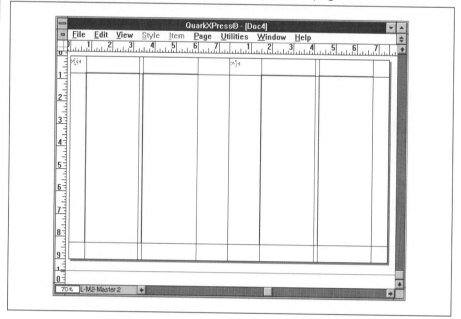

text link mode, and the pointer takes on the appearance of the Linking tool.

12. Click the outline of the first text box on the left master page. A small arrow points from the automatic text link icon to the text box to show that this is now an automatic text box, as shown here:

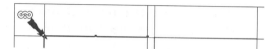

The outline of the text box also becomes an animated marquee.

13. Zoom out to a full view of the left master page and then click the second text box to link it to the first. As shown in Figure 3-13, a much longer arrow appears between the two text boxes indicating the direction of the link.

FIGURE 3-13 A series of continuously linked text boxes on left and right master pages

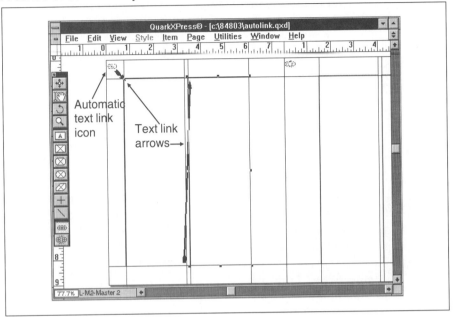

At this point, the Linking tool in the Tools palette is no longer active, because you have linked all the text boxes on the current page.

 Note When creating automatic text boxes on a facing-pages master page, link the text boxes on the left page to the ones on the right. That way, copy will flow automatically between left and right document pages based on this master.

14. Activate the Linking tool once more. The link arrows should reappear automatically, because the second text box on the left master page is still selected. If it is not, click this text box to make the link arrows visible again.

15. Click the automatic text link icon on the right master page to display the animated marquee. This tells Quark that you want to continue the link from one page to the next.

16. Click the outline of the first text box on the right master page. A linking arrow appears from the automatic text link icon to this text box.

17. Click the outline of the second text box on the right master page. A second linking arrow appears. You have linked all the text boxes on these two pages successfully.

Note Linking arrows are never visible on more than one page at a time. You can always continue the link from one master page to another, though, by first clicking the automatic text link icon in the corner of the next page you wish to link.

Text link arrows on a master page always indicate the direction of the link and thus the flow of copy. These arrows are visible only when the Linking tool or the Unlinking tool is active and you have selected either the automatic text link icon or a text box on the master page. If you ever need to review the relationship between automatic text boxes on a master page, simply display the master page, temporarily activate the Linking tool, and click the automatic text link icon.

Remember Link text boxes *in the order* in which you want text to flow in document pages.

Unlinking Linked Text Boxes

To break the link between linked text boxes on a master page, follow these steps:

1. Display the master page that contains the automatic text boxes you want to unlink.

2. To determine which text boxes are currently linked, activate the Linking tool in the Tools palette and click the automatic text link icon in the upper-left corner of the master page.

3. Activate the Unlinking tool in the Tools palette. If you plan to unlink more than one text box, press ALT briefly as you select the tool.

4. Click the *head* of the linking arrow that touches the text box you want to unlink. The linking arrow that extended to that text box disappears.

5. If you pressed ALT when you first selected the Linking tool, the tool remains active. You can continue unlinking additional text boxes by first selecting the next text box you want to unlink and then clicking the head of the linking arrow.

Setting up an Automatic Text Chain in Master Pages

When a master page contains one or more automatic text boxes, text flows automatically between existing pages in a document. But if you want QuarkXPress to add *new* pages automatically when you type more text or import large text files, you must tell the program how and where to do so. You can choose to add new pages at the end of a story, at the end of a section, at the end of a document, or not at all. Quark calls this process setting up an *automatic text chain*, and you control it through the General Preferences dialog box.

To set up an automatic text chain, have the desired document open and then choose the Preferences/General command in the Edit menu (keyboard shortcut: CTRL-Y). Click the Auto Page Insertion option to view the choices in the drop-down list box. You have four options:

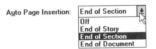

☐ *Off* means that Quark does not insert any new pages automatically when existing pages fill with text. This setting is useful when setting up a document that must have a fixed number of pages, such as an issue of a newsletter or a magazine. You can still add new pages manually after selecting Off.

☐ *End of Story* tells Quark to insert new pages at the end of the active text chain. Depending on whether you have linked text boxes on master pages or in document pages, the end of the active text chain could fall at the end of the story controlled by the current master page, or somewhere else.

☐ *End of Section* (the default) means Quark adds new pages at the end of what you designate as a section in a document. Inserted pages take on the master page format of the last page in the section. See Chapter 11 for more about assigning sections to control page numbering.

☐ *End of Document* tells QuarkXPress to add new pages automatically at the very end of a document. Inserted pages take on the master page format of the last page in the document. This setting is most appropriate for documents based on a single master page, where text flow is continuous from the beginning to the end of a document.

Every document has different layout requirements, and not every document can benefit from setting up automatic text chains at the master page level. For example, layouts for some newsletters and magazines are so unpredictable from issue to issue that you need more flexibility than the foregoing method provides. In cases like these, you might prefer to create normal (repeating) text boxes at the master page level and then link them manually in document pages. See "Controlling Copy Flow Locally (Linking/Unlinking)" at the end of this chapter.

Adding Headers and Footers

Repeating information about a document's title, section or chapter number, subject, and page number usually appears in a *header* at the top of each page or in a *footer* at the bottom. Headers and footers in QuarkXPress can consist of almost anything: text, ruling lines, shaded bars, graphic icons, or any combination of these. This shows an example of a graphically interesting header that combines text, pictures, and color:

To make headers and footers appear on every page of a document, you simply create them on a master page. You can use ruler guides and the Measurements palette to help you position headers and footers precisely in the margin area. Thanks to the flexible relationship between master and document pages in Quark, you can then delete headers and footers from specific pages in a document without affecting them on other document pages.

Adding Bleeds

A *bleed* is a repeating design element that appears at the extreme top, bottom, or outside edge of pages. A thumb tab that marks each right page in chapters of a book, such as the one shown in Figure 3-14, is a good example of a bleed.

In a finished print job, bleeds extend exactly to the edge of a page. Within QuarkXPress, bleeds extend a little *beyond* the edge of a page. The reason for this is that commercial printing equipment can sometimes trim page edges imprecisely. Conscientious desktop publishers overextend bleed elements by a fixed amount to avoid having unwanted white space appear at the edge of pages.

A bleed that includes both text and graphics

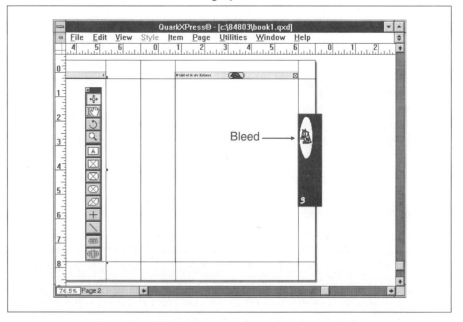

Adding Page Numbers

In QuarkXPress, you control automatic page numbering through master pages. To make page numbers appear automatically on all document pages associated with a master page, follow these steps:

1. Display a master page using either the Display command in the Page menu or the Document Layout palette.

2. Create a normal (unlinked) text box on the master page. If the page numbering is to be part of a header or footer, you may already have created a text box for it.

3. With the Content tool active, click in the text box and type the page number code CTRL-3. The text sequence <#> appears on the master page, as shown here:

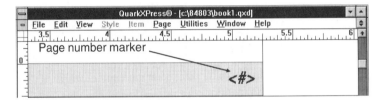

4. If the current master page is a facing-pages master, repeat steps 2 and 3 for the other facing page.

Adding Other Repeating Text Elements

You can enter text in any master page text box except for automatic text boxes. The contents of such text boxes repeat on all associated document pages. Quark's graphics capabilities make it easy to create repeating text elements with special effects, such as automatic drop shadows (Chapter 6), rotation, and gradient fills (Chapter 10).

An empty text box on a master page is a repeating text element, too. If a document contains multiple columns, you can control copy flow by creating repeating text boxes in the master page and then resizing them as needed on specific document pages.

 Tip Although you cannot type in automatic text boxes, you can assign a style sheet to them. Text that you type directly into the automatic text boxes document pages will appear in the assigned style sheet. See Chapter 6 for more details.

Using Step and Repeat to Create Multiple Columns

The Step and Repeat command in the Item menu can save you time when you need to create multiple same-size columns on a master page. If you know the exact horizontal distance by which you want to space each column's text box, you might proceed with steps like these:

1. Display the master page to which you want to add the repeating text columns.

2. Create the first text box with the help of ruler guides and/or the Measurements palette. The text box remains selected after you create it.

3. Choose the Step and Repeat command in the Item menu to display the dialog box shown here:

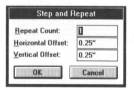

4. In the Repeat Count field, enter the number of *additional* text boxes you want to create per page.

5. In the Horizontal Offset field, enter the desired distance from the left edge of the first text box to the left edge of the next text box.

6. Enter 0 (zero) in the Vertical Offset field. This setting causes any duplicate text boxes to align vertically with one another.

7. Click OK to create the desired number of additional text boxes instantly.

Adding Repeating Graphic Elements

Many desktop publishers like to use ruling lines, repeating icons, or small illustrations as part of a header or footer. You have seen examples of this earlier in the chapter.

A large illustration can even serve as a repeating background graphic (Figure 3-15 shows this) provided you place it on the bottom layer, give it a runaround setting of None, and give it a shade that does not overwhelm any overlying text. Chapters 8 through 12 provide more information on setting up runarounds, layers, and shades for effects like these.

Moving Items Between Master Pages

Multiple master pages in a document sometimes retain a few design elements in common. With the help of the Copy, Cut, and Paste com-

FIGURE 3-15

Using a large image as a repeating background graphic

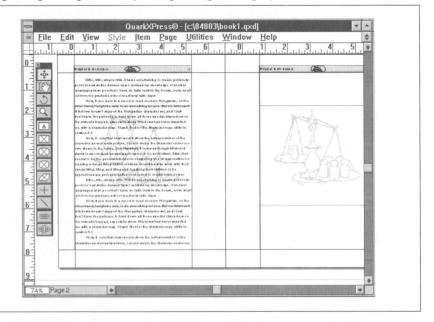

mands in the Edit menu, you can easily copy or move design elements between different master pages.

To copy or move design elements from one master page to another, follow these steps:

1. Display the master page that contains the design element you want to copy or move.

2. With the Item tool active, click the item you want to copy or move.

3. To copy the item to the clipboard while leaving the original in the current master page, choose Copy from the Edit menu. To remove the item from the current master page entirely, choose the Cut command from the Edit menu.

4. Display the master page to which you want to copy or move the item.

5. Choose Paste. If the item falls in a spot other than where you want it, you may either move it manually with the Item tool or change its position using the Measurements palette.

Master Page Tips for Facing-Pages Documents

A master page for a facing-pages document consists of both a left and a right page. While the principles of developing master pages are the same for both single-sided and facing-pages documents, facing-page documents present special opportunities and challenges. This section describes several tips for streamlining your work when setting up facing-pages documents.

Setting Rulers to Span Facing Pages

By default, both the Measurements palette and rulers in a document window reflect the width of a single page at a time. In a facing-pages document, however, it may be more convenient to draw picture boxes, text boxes, and lines if measurements correspond to the combined width of two pages.

To set rulers to span facing pages, choose the Preferences/General command in the Edit menu. Change Item Coordinates from Page to Spread as shown here:

When Item Coordinates is set to Spread, the horizontal ruler measures continuously from the upper-left corner of the left page to the upper-right corner of the right page as shown in Figure 3-16.

Duplicating Elements with the Step and Repeat Command

Many master page items in a facing-pages document—text columns, headers, footers, and page numbers, for example—appear on both facing

Ruler spanning facing pages for easier layout

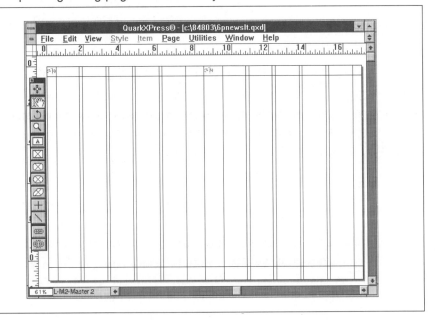

pages, although often in different positions. One way to quickly duplicate such repeating items is to use the Step and Repeat command described in the "Using Step and Repeat to Create Multiple Columns" section earlier in this chapter.

You should specify a Vertical Offset value of zero and a Horizontal Offset value that represents the point where you want to place the upper-left corner of the duplicate item. (To ease your task, set Item Coordinates to Spread in the General Preferences dialog box.)

Using the Measurements Palette to Copy and Paste Attributes

If you want to copy item *attributes* (not the items themselves) between facing master pages, the Measurements palette and the Copy and Paste commands in the Edit menu can assist you. For example, suppose you have set up text columns of different sizes on facing master pages and only later decide you want facing-page columns to be the same size. You could resize text boxes manually, of course, but copying and pasting text box dimensions using the Measurements palette might save you time. In cases like these, try the following steps:

1. Display the facing-pages master page that contains the items whose attributes you want to edit.

2. With the Item or Content tool active, click the item that has the attribute you want to copy.

3. Double-click the desired attribute field (width, height, font, and so forth) in the Measurements palette.

4. Choose the Copy command in the Edit menu to copy the attribute to the clipboard.

5. Click the item on the facing page to which you want to copy the attribute.

6. Choose Paste from the Edit menu. The item reformats to reflect the change in values.

Document Page Basics

Once you have set up repeating design elements in master pages, you are ready to begin manipulating actual document pages. The document page mode of the Document Layout palette and commands in the Page menu let you add, delete, and rearrange pages; display the page of your choice; and reformat pages in a variety of ways.

Inserting Document Pages

You can use either the Insert command in the Page menu or the Document Layout palette to insert one or more new pages into a document. Generally, the Insert command is more convenient for adding multiple pages. The Document Layout palette technique can be quicker if you are adding one page at a time.

Inserting Pages with the Insert Command

To insert one or more pages into a document using a menu command, follow these steps:

1. Open the document into which you want to insert pages.

 Note If the current document contains an active text chain and you want to link the inserted page(s) to it, you must first go to the document page to which you want to link the inserted pages, activate the Item or Content tool, and click the text box at the end of the chain.

2. Choose the Insert command in the Page menu. The Insert Pages dialog box appears, as shown here:

3. In the Insert field, specify the number of pages you want to insert.

4. Click the radio button that best describes where you want to insert pages. If you choose Before Page or After Page, you must also specify the target page number. You do not need to specify a page number if you choose At End of Document.

5. If the Link to Current Text Chain check box is available, you may choose to link the inserted page(s) to a specific linked text box. (This option is available only if you selected such a text box before choosing the Insert command.)

6. Click the Master Page drop-down list box and highlight the master page on which to base the inserted page(s).

7. Click OK to insert the page(s) with the specified formatting at the location you have chosen.

Inserting Pages with the Document Layout Palette

Using the Document Layout palette in document page mode, you can add new pages to a document one at a time. Quark renumbers the existing pages in a document automatically as you add new ones.

To insert a page with the help of the Document Layout palette, follow these steps:

1. Open the document to which you want to add a page.

2. Display the Document Layout palette if it is not currently visible (Show Document Layout command, View menu). If the palette currently displays master page icons, switch to document page mode by clicking the mode toggle button.

3. Choose the Insert submenu command in the Document menu and click the type of master page you want to use to format the new document page. The choices available to you depend on the layout (single-sided or double-sided) of the current document and on the number of master pages you have already created.

4. Release the mouse button. A shadow page icon and miniature page icon appear at the pointer position, as shown here:

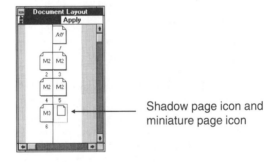

Shadow page icon and miniature page icon

5. Drag this page icon to the desired position before a page, after a page, or at the end of the current page list in the layout area of the palette. A stylized arrow appears when you drag the pointer past the locations where a click would result in fixing the new page in position.

6. Release the mouse button. A new document page icon appears in the position you have chosen, and Quark renumbers all other pages. The shape of the new document page icon shows whether it is a single-sided, left-facing, or right-facing page. The icon also includes the new page number and the label of the master page (if any) used to format it.

Developing Multiple-Page Spreads

The intuitive Document Layout palette makes it possible to design *spreads*: series of two, three or more pages that form a continuous but separate unit within a document. A reader request card, a fold-out advertisement in a magazine, and a multi-panel brochure are examples of common spreads.

A spread can consist of any number of pages with a total width of 48 inches or less. In a single-sided document, you can use single-sided blank and master pages to build a spread. Within a facing-pages document, you can build a spread from any combination of single-sided and facing-pages blank and master pages. The icons in the Document Layout palette let you see the arrangement of the spread and its position relative to the rest of a document.

To build a spread using the Document Layout palette, follow these steps:

1. Open the document into which you want to insert a spread.

2. Display the Document Layout palette by choosing the Show Document Layout command from the View menu. If necessary, switch to document page mode by clicking the mode toggle button.

3. Choose Insert from the Document menu. From the Insert submenu, click the name of the blank or master page on which you want to base the first added page of a spread.

4. Drag a copy of the chosen master page icon into the layout area of the palette.

5. Position the new page at one of the following locations and then release the mouse button:

   ☐ To the right of an existing single-sided page (single-sided documents)

   ☐ To the right of an existing right-facing page (facing-pages documents)

   ☐ To the left of an existing left-facing page (facing-pages documents)

Caution   Do not position the new page icon to the left of a right-facing page or to the right of a left-facing page. If you do, Quark simply adds a new page to the standard document layout and renumbers pages accordingly.

The new document page icon appears in the spot where you have placed it, complete with a page number and the label of the master page on which it is based. Quark renumbers the pages that follow the new page, as the previous illustration shows.

6. If you wish, continue adding pages in the same way. Here is a completed four-page spread as the Document Layout palette represents it:

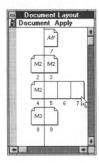

Both spreads and facing-pages documents can contain text or graphic elements that extend across more than one page. Let this fact stoke the fire of your imagination when you need to develop creative document designs.

Deleting Document Pages

You can delete one or more document pages using either the Delete command in the Page menu or the Delete command in the Document menu of the Document Layout palette.

Deleting Document Pages Using the Document Layout Palette

To delete document pages with the help of the Document Layout palette, follow these steps:

1. Display the Document Layout palette and, if necessary, switch to document page mode by choosing the Show Document Pages command from the Document menu.

2. Click the icon of the document page you want to delete. If you want to delete more than one, press and hold CTRL and click to select each document page icon. The selected icons become highlighted.

3. Choose the Delete command from the Document menu of the Document Layout palette. Quark displays a warning message asking you to confirm deletion of the selected pages, as shown here:

Are you sure you want to remove these pages?

OK   Cancel

4. Choose Yes to delete the selected page(s). Quark renumbers the remaining page icons in the Document Layout palette automatically.

Note   There is no way to Undo a page deletion unless you choose the Revert to Saved command in the File menu. This returns the document to the version that you saved most recently; you lose any changes made since the last save.

Deleting a Series of Pages Using the Delete Command

To delete a continuous series of document pages, choose the Delete command from the Page menu. The Delete Pages dialog box appears, as shown here:

Enter the page numbers of the first and last pages in the series of pages you want to delete and then click OK.

Labeling Document Pages

Whenever you insert a new document page, Quark automatically assigns to it the label of the master page on which it is based. If you base a document page on a blank single-sided or facing page, the document icon contains no label at all.

The label of a document page changes automatically if you apply a different master page to the document page, or if you change the label of the associated master page.

Moving Between Document Pages

To view and move between document pages, you can use menu commands, keyboard shortcuts, or the Document Layout palette. Table 3-3 summarizes the commands in the Page menu that let you move between document pages. Table 3-4 lists the keyboard shortcuts that you

TABLE 3-3 Moving Between Document Pages: Page Menu Commands

To Move	Use This Command
Forward one page	Next
Backward one page	Previous
To page 1 in a document	First
To the last page in a document	Last
To a specific page	Go To

Moving Between Document Pages: Keyboard Shortcuts

To Move	Use This Shortcut
Forward one page	CTRL-PGDN
Backward one page	CTRL-PGUP
To page 1 in a document	CTRL-HOME
To the last page in a document	CTRL-END
To a specific page	CTRL-J

can use to jump from one page to another. To view a specific page when the Document Layout palette is in document page mode, simply double-click the desired document page icon.

Rearranging Document Pages

When laying out a newsletter, magazine, or other document that contains many components, you sometimes need to change the order of pages. Quark lets you rearrange pages either by dragging icons in the Document Layout palette or by using the Move command in the Page menu.

Note   When you rearrange pages that contain linked text boxes, Quark reflows the text automatically.

Using the Move Command

To rearrange document pages using a menu command:

1. With a document open, choose the Move command in the Page menu. The Move Pages dialog box appears, as shown here:

2. Use the Move Page(s) . . . Thru entry boxes to designate a page or span of pages that you want to move. If you wish to move a single page, enter its number in the first entry box. To move a span of pages, enter the first page number in the first entry box and the last page number in the second.

3. Click one of the three radio buttons (Before Page, After Page, To End of Document) to select the target location for the pages you have specified. If you choose Before Page or After Page, you must also specify a page number in the adjoining entry box.

4. Click OK to exit the dialog box and move the specified page(s) to the target location. Quark renumbers all of the document pages automatically.

Using the Document Layout Palette

The Document Layout palette is convenient to use when you need to move a single page or several nonadjacent pages to one location in the document.

To move one or more pages using the Document Layout palette, follow these steps:

1. Open the document and display the Document Layout palette using the Show Document Layout command in the View menu. Switch to document page mode if necessary.

2. Highlight the first page you want to move by clicking its icon once. If you want to move several pages to the same location, press CTRL as you highlight each icon.

3. Drag the page icon(s) to the desired location and release the mouse button. Quark renumbers pages automatically.

Caution   Exercise care when rearranging pages in a facing-pages document. If you move a left page to the right of a right page or a right page to the left of a left one, you may leave one page without a partner and create a lopsided layout.

4. To move additional pages to other locations, repeat steps 2 and 3.

Modifying a Document Page

You usually make many changes to each document page during the layout process. For example, you might add and manipulate new text boxes, picture boxes, and ruling lines to accommodate the needs of specific document pages. This chapter focuses on changes to *master items*: the repeating document structures that you set up on master pages. For help with normal layout, refer to Chapters 11 and 12.

Quark offers several ways to edit the master items that appear on a document page. You can modify the master page on which a document page is based, apply a new or different master page to a document page, or modify master items and text links directly on a document page. The following sections explore each of these options.

Editing Items on a Master Page

When you edit repeating items directly on a master page (see the section on "Modifying a Master Page" earlier in this chapter), Quark normally updates these items on all document pages that use the master page as a model. There is one exception: If you previously edited these items on a specific document page (local formatting), Quark leaves that page unaltered because local formatting always takes precedence over master page formatting. You can override local formatting only by reapplying a master page to a document page.

For example, imagine that you have used a master page to set up automatic text box columns for a newsletter. On one document page, however, you change the height of one text column for copyfitting purposes. If you later change the dimensions of the automatic text boxes on the master page, the document page you already edited does not reflect those changes automatically. You can update the document page your-self by applying the master page to it as described in the next section.

Applying a Master Page to a Document Page

There are two common reasons for applying a master page to a document page:

☐ To reformat a document page that you have modified locally

☐ To model a document page on a master page *other* than the one to which you originally assigned it

To apply a master page to a document page with the help of the Document Layout palette, follow these steps:

1. Open a document and display the Document Layout palette. If the palette is in master page mode, switch to document page mode by clicking the mode toggle button.

2. Click the document page icon to which you want to apply a specific master page. If you plan to apply the same master page to several document pages at once, press CTRL and click those document page icons one at a time.

3. From the Apply menu of the palette, choose the type of master page with which you want to reformat the selected document pages. When you release the mouse button, the labels of the selected document pages change to reflect the master page you have just applied.

 Note If you are simply reapplying the current master page to a docu-ment page, no visual change takes place; the updating occurs in the formatting of the actual document page(s).

 Tip To turn automatic master page formatting off for a particular page, apply one of the blank (unformatted) master page icons to it. Depending

on the current Master Page Items setting in the General Preferences dialog box, the document page either loses all master page formatting or retains it, but without any further links to master pages.

What happens to a document page when you apply a master page to it depends on the current setting for the Master Page Items option in the General Preferences dialog box.

Retaining or Overriding Local Formatting

As soon as you create a new document, set the Master Page Items option in the General Preferences dialog box (General/Preferences command, Edit menu). This option controls how Quark transfers formatting from a master page to a document page that you have modified locally. Two settings are possible:

☐   *Keep Changes*   This is the default setting. A document page *retains* any previous local modifications to master items when you apply or reapply a master page.

☐   *Delete Changes*   When you apply a master page with this setting active, Quark *overrides* previous local changes to a document page and reformats all its master items. If you apply a master page other than the one you originally assigned, Quark removes all the original master page margins, columns, and items and replaces them with the ones from the new master page.

Modifying Master Items Locally

Master page items in Quark are not just overlays: they are actually present on each document page. Thanks to this feature, you can edit headers and footers, change page numbers, modify or delete repeating graphics, and delete or alter automatic text boxes and text links directly on document pages. Changes to master items on a document page have no effect on the original master page.

Later in the layout process, you may decide to undo local changes to master page items and revert to original master page formatting. You can do this by reapplying the master page, as long as Master Page Items in the General Preferences dialog box is set to Delete Changes.

Controlling Copy Flow Locally (Linking/Unlinking)

Quark's Linking and Unlinking tools let you create, modify, and delete text links on any document page. If you have set up automatic text links on master pages, any local modifications you make to them in document pages take precedence.

Creating Text Chains in Document Pages

To create a text chain among two or more text boxes on document pages, follow these steps:

1. Open the document and display the first page to which you want to add text links.

2. If the text boxes you want to link do not yet exist, create them now using the Text Box tool in the Tools palette. To draw multiple text boxes in a row, press ALT briefly while activating this Text Box tool; this keeps the tool active.

3. Click the Linking tool to activate it. The pointer turns into an unbroken chain icon. If you plan to link more than two text boxes in a chain, press ALT briefly while selecting the Linking tool to keep it active.

4. Click the text box that you want as the first in the chain. The pointer "blinks" to indicate that you have begun the process.

5. Click the text box that you want as the second in the chain. The arrow that appears shows the direction of the link, as shown in Figure 3-17.

6. To link additional text boxes on this and other document pages (and if you pressed ALT to keep the Linking tool active), continue clicking each text box in sequence. As long as the Linking tool is active, arrows remain visible on all of the text boxes that contain links on a given page.

Deleting Text Links in Document Pages

To delete links in an existing automatic or local text chain, follow these steps:

1. Open the document and display a page that contains linked text boxes.

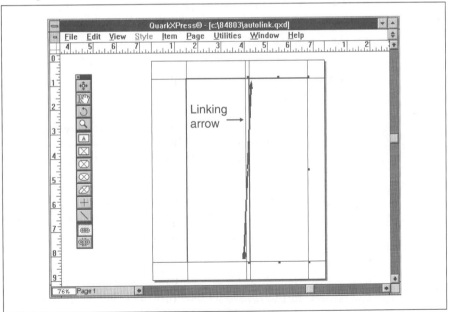

FIGURE 3-17

Linking two text boxes manually on a document page

2. Activate the Unlinking tool in the Tools palette. If you plan to remove the links from more than one text box, press ALT briefly as you activate the tool.

3. Click one of the text boxes from which you want to remove existing links. Selection handles appear around the text box, and the pointer takes on the appearance of a broken chain link. An arrow appears indicating both the direction of the link and the text box to which the active text box is linked.

4. To remove the link, click either the head or the tail of the linking arrow. The linking arrow between the two text boxes disappears.

5. If you pressed ALT before activating the Unlinking tool, continue removing links from additional text boxes in the same way. Click each linked text box to make the linking arrows visible and then click the head or tail of the linking arrow.

In some documents, you may want to *rearrange* existing text links on specific document pages. That is, you may choose to reroute copy flow from one text box to another. In these cases, first use the Unlinking tool to remove existing links and then the Linking tool to reestablish them.

This chapter has provided a fairly thorough introduction to the process of setting up new documents of all types. In the initial setup phase, your main concerns are with templates and master pages. To learn more about the process of page-by-page layout (including the use of document libraries), see Chapters 11, 12, and 13.

CHAPTER

Working Smart: Setting Preferences and Defaults

*Q*uarkXPress is like a tailor-made wardrobe: you can customize its functions to fit your working style and the needs of typical documents. Many Quark functions have predefined settings or defaults (also known as preferences), which are in effect when you first install the program. You can change a wide variety of default settings using the Preferences, Style Sheets, Colors, and H&Js commands in the Edit menu.

Preferences and defaults can be either application-wide or document-specific. *Application-wide preferences* apply to all documents, both new and existing, and usually (though not always) affect the user interface. The color of margin and ruler guides is one example of an application-wide default. Quark stores application-wide preferences from one session to the next. *Document-specific preferences* apply only to the particular document in which you set them, or as defaults for new documents. Tool behavior, color sets, and ruler measurement units are examples of default settings that can vary from one document to another.

This chapter describes each of the user-definable functions (application-wide and document-specific) found in Quark's Edit menu. You will learn how to change preset defaults and the effects your changes have on general Quark functions, specific documents, or both. The wise use of preferences and defaults can streamline the document production process.

Setting Application-Wide Preferences

The Preferences command in the Edit menu contains a submenu with four commands: Application, General, Typographic, and Tools, as shown here:

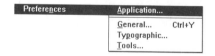

The Application command in this submenu accesses a dialog box that controls application-wide Quark functions. Quark stores these defaults in a file called xpress.prf. Only one xpress.prf file can be active at a time. If you change any of the current application-wide defaults, the previous settings no longer apply to any documents, either new or existing.

Accessing the Application Preferences Dialog Box

To begin editing application-wide preferences in Quark, choose the Preferences/Application command in the Edit menu. The Application Preferences dialog box appears, as shown in Figure 4-1. The following sections explain each default, its function, and how to edit it.

Guide Colors

The Guide Colors section of the Application Preferences dialog box lets you edit the colors Quark uses to represent margin guides, ruler guides, and baseline grid guides in all documents. The default colors are blue for margin guides, green for ruler guides, and magenta for baseline grid guides. If you have a grayscale rather than a color monitor, you can use these controls to change the shades of gray that represent different types of guides.

To change the current color (or shade of gray) of a particular type of guide, follow these steps:

1. In the Application Preferences dialog box, click either the name of the guide or its associated color block. The appropriate Guide Color dialog box appears, as Figure 4-2 shows.

The Application Preferences dialog box

FIGURE
4-2 The Margin Guide Color dialog box

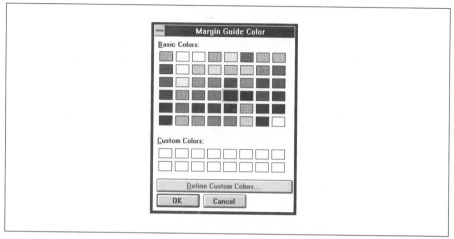

2. You now have three options. You can choose a predefined color, select a custom color that you have defined previously, or define a new custom color.

❑ To choose a predefined color, click one of the color blocks in the Basic Colors area of the dialog box.

❑ To select a custom color that you have defined previously, click its color block in the Custom Colors area. If you have not defined any custom colors, only blank white blocks appear here.

❑ To define a new custom color, click the Define Custom Colors button to access the Edit Color dialog box. Here, you define a new color by clicking in the color wheel or specifying the new color in terms of mathematical values, and then clicking OK. See Chapter 10 for more information on using the Edit Colors dialog box.

3. Click OK to return to the Application Preferences dialog box. The guide color you chose replaces the previous one.

Trapping Preferences

Trapping is the process of allowing adjacent colors in a document to overlap slightly to correct for potential shifts of the printing press.

Commercially printed documents that use color in ruling lines, text, line art, or photographs require trapping to avoid unsightly gaps between adjacent colors. The Trap options in the Application Preferences dialog box control the default trapping methods and amounts that Quark applies when you output any document to a PostScript printer or imagesetter.

The Trap options in this dialog box are the lowest level of trapping controls in Quark. Trapping parameters that you define in either the Trap Specifications dialog box (Colors command, Edit menu) or the Trap Information palette (Show Trap Information, View menu) take precedence over the current Application Preferences Trap options and override them. See Chapter 10 for more advanced information on trapping and working with color.

Auto Method

Quark can employ its own sophisticated algorithms to trap adjacent colors automatically. This automatic trapping method applies by default to all colors in a document and is useful for most color work. The Auto Method option in the Application Preferences dialog box lets you decide how *much* trapping Quark applies to colors that trap automatically.

Absolute   If you set Auto Method to Absolute, Quark applies the exact amount of trapping that you specify in the Auto Amount field of the Application Preferences dialog box. Just how the foreground and background colors overlap depends on which of the two colors is darker. Figure 4-3 shows an exaggerated example of what happens during trapping when the background color is lighter than the foreground color. The lighter background color is *choked*, which means that the darker background color encroaches on its "territory." Figure 4-4 illustrates trapping principles when the background color is darker than the object on top of it. The lighter foreground color *spreads* into the darker background color.

Proportional   Choose the Proportional setting to let Quark trap colors automatically according to a calculated fraction of the amount you specify in the Auto Amount field. (The next section explains this further.) Quark determines this fraction by comparing the differences in the degree of darkness, or *luminance*, between foreground and background colors.

FIGURE
4-3
An exaggerated example of trapping when the background color is lighter than the foreground color

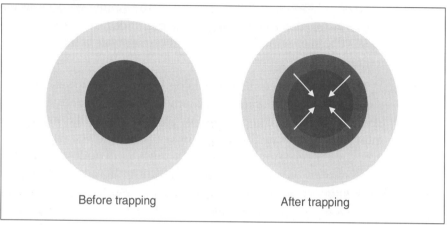

Before trapping   After trapping

Auto Amount

The value in the Auto Amount field tells Quark how much trapping to apply to all automatically trapped colors during the printing process. You

FIGURE
4-4

An exaggerated example of trapping when the background color is darker than the foreground color

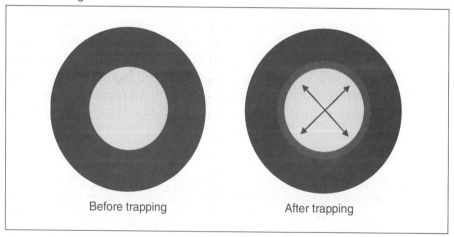

Before trapping   After trapping

can enter any value from 0 points to 36 points in .001-point increments. Consult with your print vendor to determine the appropriate amount; the default value (.0144 points) may be too low for all but the most sophisticated types of printing presses.

Indeterminate

An *indeterminate* background is one that contains multiple colors. Color photographs, full-color line art graphics, and any item containing a color blend are examples of indeterminate color elements in a document. Any object that overlays multiple elements of different colors has an indeterminate background. By specifying a value in the Indeterminate field of the Application Preferences dialog box, you tell Quark how much trapping to apply in such cases. You can enter any value from 0 points to 36 points in .001-point increments. Again, check with your print vendor for this number.

Overprint Limit

Overprinting occurs when you elect to print one color directly on top of another color. As you will see in Chapter 10, overprinting multiple colors is usually not a good idea unless you do so to create special effects. The Overprint Limit option in the Application Preferences dialog box is important for trapping black. It also affects trapping for colors for which you have specified a trapping method of Overprint instead of Automatic in the Trap Specifications dialog box. The Overprint Limit percentage (the default value is 95 percent) tells Quark the shade at which a foreground (object) color directly overprints its background color. If the overprint color is lighter than the Overprint Limit shade, no overprinting occurs; instead, Quark traps the foreground and background colors according to the current Auto Amount in the Applications Preferences dialog box.

For example, if you specify overprint trapping for Green and set Overprint Limit to 90 percent, an object that is 91 percent Green will print directly on top of whatever color is underneath it. If the green object is only 89 percent Green, however, trapping occurs according to the current Auto Amount value.

Ignore White

When you first install QuarkXPress, the Ignore White option is checked. This option tells Quark *not* to take white into account when trapping an object against a background that includes white along with other colors. Instead, Quark bases trapping solely on the other color or colors in the background. If you deselect the Ignore White check box, Quark traps multicolored backgrounds that contain some white according to the Indeterminate value in the Application Preferences dialog box.

Process Trap

The Process Trap option provides added flexibility to color-savvy designers who produce documents containing process color elements. When a check mark appears here (the default setting), Quark applies separate trapping values for each of the four process color plates (cyan, magenta, yellow, and black) during printing. When this option is turned off, Quark automatically traps all four color plates using the same values. See Chapter 10 to learn more about process color and Chapter 14 for information about printing documents that use process color.

Pasteboard Width

The *pasteboard* is the blank area that appears on all sides of a page. You can use the pasteboard as a place to store items temporarily while you experiment with page design.

QuarkXPress measures the size of the pasteboard in terms of a percentage of page width. You can specify a pasteboard width between 0 percent and 100 percent (100 percent is the default). Do be aware of two limitations:

❑   The pasteboard is always at least 1/2 inch wide, no matter how low a percentage you specify.

❑   The total width of a document plus its pasteboard cannot exceed 48 inches. This is a concern only if a document contains multiple-page spreads or exceptionally large pages.

Note In Quark, the pasteboard is always linked with the specific page with which it appears. If you place an item in the pasteboard and then move to a different page in the document, you will no longer be able to view that item.

Reg. Marks Offset

The purpose of printing *registration marks* and *crop marks* with each page of a document is to help commercial print vendors align plates for accurate printing (see Figure 4-5). The Reg. Marks Offset option in the Application Preferences dialog box lets you specify how far from the corners of the page to place these marks. The default value is 6 points, but you can enter any value from 0 to 30 points in .0001-point increments.

FIGURE 4-5 Registration marks and crop marks help commercial print vendors align plates accurately

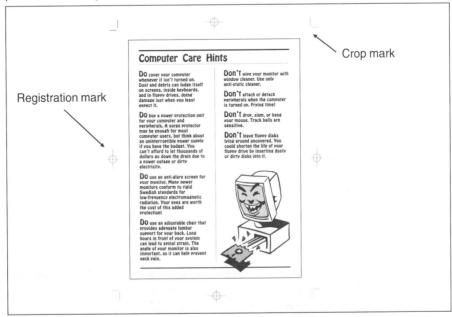

Live Scroll

Dragging the scroll box in the horizontal or vertical scroll bar of a document window is a fast way to move across facing pages or through a document. However, Quark does not normally update the screen until you release the scroll box. You can force Quark to update the document view in real time if you activate the Live Scroll check box in the Application Preferences dialog box. Be prepared: real-time screen redraw slows program operation in a document that contains lots of graphics. You may find the Page Grabber hand a more convenient way to move around in a document.

Page Grabber Hand

When the Page Grabber Hand check box is active (the default setting), you can scroll the view of a document in any direction, including diagonally. Just press and hold ALT and drag the hand-shaped pointer across the screen in the desired direction.

Auto Library Save

Documents that contain many different graphics or other design elements are easier to manage if you store those elements in a library file (extension .qxl). If you want Quark to save the contents of a library automatically every time you add something to it, activate the Auto Library Save check box. See Chapter 11 for more about using libraries.

Low Resolution TIFF

This option controls how images imported in the TIFF file format (extension .tif) appear on your monitor. When this option is active (the default setting), Quark displays TIFF images at only half the monitor's display resolution—for instance, at 48 dpi (dots-per-inch) if your monitor and display adapter support a standard VGA display resolution of 96 dpi. The low-resolution display of images speeds screen redraw and in no way affects the quality of the digital image. To display all TIFF images at full screen resolution, deselect the Low Resolution TIFF check box. Be aware, however, that full-resolution display tends to slow the speed of screen redraw.

8-Bit TIFF

Today's scanners and image editing packages make it possible to edit 24-bit True Color images containing 16 million colors. You can import these images into QuarkXPress, but screen redraw will be slow if Quark displays all 16 million colors. To speed screen redraw for 24-bit color image files, make sure the 8-Bit TIFF option in the Application Preferences dialog box is checked. At this setting, Quark displays 24-bit color images as though they were 8-bit images containing only 256 colors. This type of color reduction is for display purposes only and in no way affects the print quality of True Color images.

256 Levels of Gray

The 256 Levels of Gray option affects the display of imported grayscale images. Activate this option if your monitor can display 256 different shades of gray and if you want all 256 shades to appear on the screen. By default, this option is unchecked, and Quark displays only 16 levels of gray in grayscale images to speed screen redraw.

Display DPI Value

On the DOS platform, monitors and display adapters support many different display resolutions. When you first install QuarkXPress, the Display DPI Value option shows you the default display resolution of your video card in dots per inch (dpi). The Display DPI Value for a standard VGA screen is 96, as shown in the example in Figure 4-1. You can assign any Display DPI Value from 36 to 300 in increments of .01 dot. You can also use this option to calibrate a monitor so that one inch on a document window ruler equals exactly one inch on the screen. See the "Calibrating a Monitor" section of Chapter 2 to review how to use the Display DPI Value option for this purpose.

Scroll Speed

The Scroll Speed option lets you set the speed at which you scroll through a document using the vertical and horizontal scroll bars in a document window.

Setting General Preferences

The options you access through the General, Typographic, and Tools commands in the Preferences submenu apply to specific documents. In this respect they differ from the application-wide preferences available through the Preferences/Application command.

When you choose the General command in the Preferences submenu (keyboard shortcut: CTRL-Y), the General Preferences dialog box shown in Figure 4-6 appears. Most of the options in this dialog box control interface-related functions.

Quark saves general preferences in one of two ways: with the active document and as defaults for new documents.

Saving Preferences with the Active Document If you choose the Preferences/General command when a document window is open, Quark saves your settings with that document. When multiple documents are open, the active document window is the one to which the new preferences apply. The name of the active document always appears in the title bar of the dialog box, as shown here:

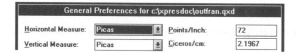

FIGURE
4-6

The default General Preferences dialog box when no document window is open

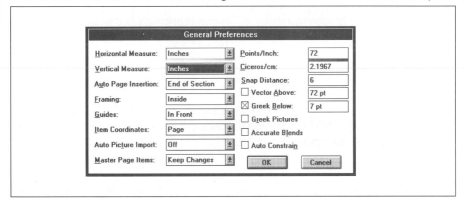

Saving Preferences as Defaults for New Documents   If you choose the Preferences/General command when no document windows are open, the title bar of the General Preferences dialog box resembles the one displayed in Figure 4-6 in that it contains no reference to a document file. This tells you that Quark will save any new settings as defaults for future new documents.

Horizontal Measure, Vertical Measure

The Horizontal Measure and Vertical Measure options determine the units of measurement Quark uses to display rulers in a document window. You can use different units of measurement for the horizontal and vertical rulers. Your choices in the drop-down list box next to each option include Inches, Inches Decimal, Picas, Points, Millimeters, Centimeters, and Ciceros. Table 4-1 shows how Quark breaks down ruler markings according to the current unit of measurement.

Note   Table 4-1 shows the number of ruler markings per unit when the current view percentage is 100 percent (actual size). As you increase the view percentage, the number of ruler markings per unit increases. Decreasing the view percentage causes the number of ruler markings per unit to decrease.

TABLE 4-1

Ruler Markings per Unit of Measurement

Unit of Measurement	Ruler Markings per Unit
Inches	16 per inch
Inches Decimal	20 per inch
Picas	24 per inch (each marking = 1/2 pica, 12 pt, or 1/6 inch)
Points	24 per inch (each marking = 12 pt)
Millimeters	1 per 2 mm
Centimeters	5 per cm
Ciceros	4 per cicero

The unit of measurement you choose affects more than the rulers. It also determines the default unit of measurement that Quark displays for many (though not all) dialog box settings. In most cases, however, you can enter values using any unit of measurement, regardless of the current default. For example, you can enter page size in terms of picas, even if the current unit of measurement is inches. Quark converts the values you enter into the current unit of measurement. Table 4-2 lists the abbreviations you use when entering values for specific units of measurement and gives examples.

 Tip   To change the existing measurement of an item, add or subtract values from an existing value in a field. Assume, for example, that the left endpoint of a line is located exactly at the 4-inch mark, but that you

TABLE 4-2

Acceptable Abbreviations for Various Units of Measurement

Unit of Measurement	Valid Abbreviation	Example(s)
Inches, Inches Decimal	"	3.5"
Picas	p	3p6 (3 picas, 6 points)
Points	pt (or no abbrev. with picas)	8 pt, 3p6
Millimeters	mm	33 mm
Centimeters	cm	33 cm
Ciceros	c	3 c

want to shift it a few hundredths of an inch to the left. Using the Modify command in the Item menu, you might notate the new Left Endpoint measurement like this:

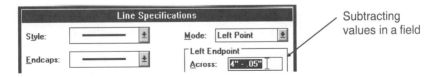

Subtracting values in a field

Auto Page Insertion

Use this option to determine whether and where to insert document pages automatically when a text box overflows. The drop-down list contains four possible settings—Off, End of Story, End of Section, and End of Document—as shown here:

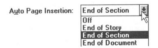

See the "Setting Up an Automatic Text Chain" section of Chapter 3 for applications-oriented advice on how to set this option.

Framing

The Framing option applies only to text and picture boxes to which you assign *frames* (outlines) using the Frame command in the Item menu. This option tells Quark whether to place frames inside items (the default setting) or outside items. Figure 4-7 shows, in an exaggerated way, the effect of each setting on the appearance and content of a picture box. The next sections explain the differences you see in Figure 4-7.

Note Changes made to the Framing setting during the current Quark session affect only text and picture boxes that you create from that point on. Existing items retain their original framing.

The placement of a frame (inside or outside) affects picture cropping and
overall picture box size

Framing: Inside
Frame width: 8 pt
W = 1.76" (126 pt)
H = 1.18" (85 pt)

Framing: Outside
Frame width: 8 pt
W = 1.982" (142 pt)
H = 1.402" (101 pt)

Inside

A frame that falls *inside* a text box or picture box does not change the
overall size of that item. Instead, it encroaches on the space used by the
content (text or graphics) of the item. In the case of a text box, you can
set the amount of space between frame and text through the Text Inset
option in the Text Box Specifications dialog box (Modify command, Item
menu). A frame inside a picture box simply crops the picture; to avoid
cutting off any part of a picture, increase the size of picture boxes to
compensate for the width of their frames.

Outside

If you choose the Outside option, Quark places frames outside the text
or picture box and does not encroach on space inside the item. While the
picture is seen in its entirety, this placement results in a slight increase

in the overall size of the item. Frames cannot extend past the eight selection handles or *bounding box* of the item.

 Remember Unless you use picture box frames that are wider than one or two points, the Framing option you choose will not make much of a visible difference to your graphics.

Guides

You use the Guides option to tell Quark where to place margin, ruler, and baseline grid guides relative to items in a document. If you use the In Front setting (the default), guides lie on top of text boxes, picture boxes, and lines so you can select and move the guides quickly. If you set the Guides option to Behind, you can conveniently select and move items without moving the guides accidentally.

Item Coordinates

The Item Coordinates option determines where Quark places the zero point on the horizontal ruler. With the default setting of Page, the horizontal ruler begins at zero at the upper-left corner of every page in a document. For facing-pages documents or multiple-page spreads, however, you might prefer to set Item Coordinates to Spread. Choosing the Spread setting results in continuous ruler increments all the way across facing pages or all the pages in a spread. Figure 4-8 shows how Quark numbers the horizontal ruler for a three-page spread when the Item Coordinates option is set to Spread.

Auto Picture Import

When you import a picture into a Quark document, what you see is only a representation or *placeholder* of that picture. The Auto Picture Import option determines whether Quark updates the placeholder if you edit a picture file in its original drawing or image editing program after

FIGURE 4-8

Document rulers for a three-page spread when Item Coordinates is set to Spread

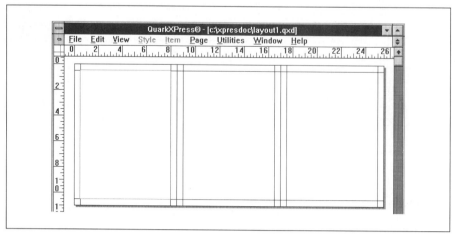

importing it into a Quark document. Three options are available: Off, On, and On (Verify).

Off

If Auto Picture Import is set to Off (the default setting) Quark does not update the placeholder of a picture the next time you open the document.

On

If Auto Picture Import is set to On, Quark automatically updates placeholders for any modified pictures the next time you open their documents.

On (Verify)

Select the On (Verify) option if you want to have a choice about whether to update the placeholders of modified pictures. If you modify a picture from an open Quark document, close the document, and then open it again, Quark displays a dialog box asking if you want to update the view of the modified picture as well, as shown here:

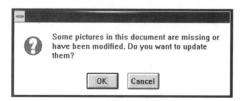

If you click Yes, Quark displays the Missing/Modified Pictures dialog box shown here:

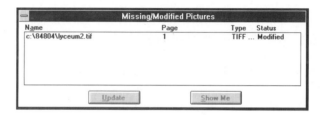

You can use this dialog box to preview and update the view of modified pictures.

Master Page Items

As you saw in Chapter 3, you can easily apply different master page designs to a given document page. Quark deletes unmodified master items from the old master page and replaces them with the master items from the new master page. If you have modified any master items directly on the document page, however, Quark does not update those items automatically when you apply a new master page. You control what happens to locally modified master items through the Master Page Items option, as shown here:

Keep Changes

Choose Keep Changes (the default) if you want locally modified master items to remain on a document page even after you apply a different master page.

Delete Changes

Select Delete Changes if you want Quark to delete *all* previous master items (both modified and unmodified) when you apply a new master page to a document page. Quark replaces all master items from the previous master page with the ones from the new master page.

Points/Inch, Ciceros/Cm

In traditional typography, one inch is equal to exactly 72 points, and one pica equals 12 points or 1/6 inch. Using the Points/Inch option in the General Preferences dialog box, you can specify a points-per-inch conversion ratio ranging from 72 to 73 in .01-point increments. The number you specify forms the basis for all point and pica measurements in Quark as well as all point-to-inch and pica-to-inch conversions.

The *cicero* is a French typesetting unit of measurement based on the metric system. Traditionally, one centimeter equals precisely 2.1967 ciceros, but you can specify a custom value between 2 and 3 using the Ciceros/Cm option. You can enter values in increments of .0001 ciceros.

Snap Distance

The value you enter in the Snap Distance field controls the distance, measured in pixels, at which items snap to margin, ruler, and baseline grid guides. The default is 6 pixels, but you can enter any value from 0 to 100. This option takes effect only when the Snap to Guides command in the View menu has a check mark in front of it.

Vector Above

QuarkXPress can display screen fonts in a document in two different ways: as bitmaps and as outline (vector) fonts. Both bitmap and outline fonts look fine at small point sizes, but bitmap fonts begin to look jagged as font size increases, as this example illustrates:

Outline fonts, on the other hand, look smooth at any point size.

The Vector Above option in the General Preferences dialog box tells Quark whether and at what point size to display screen fonts in outline format in order to minimize "jaggies." This option is turned off when you first install QuarkXPress. To turn it on, click in the check box. Once this option is active, you can specify a value from 2 to 720 points at which to display screen fonts as smooth vectors. The default value is 72 points. On some systems, screen redraw may be slightly slower if you specify a low point size. If you use Adobe Type manager, fonts will look smooth whether you turn Vector Above off or on.

Greek Below

As font size decreases, text characters look less and less legible, especially on small monitors at low pixel resolutions. Extremely small characters may be so hard to read that it is preferable to *greek* them—to substitute gray bars for the actual text characters. Greeking small characters also speeds screen redraw and affects only the display of text.

The Greek Below option lets you specify the point size below which Quark greeks all text. If you prefer something other than the default value of 7 points, you can enter a value from 2 to 720 points in increments as small as .001 point. If you have a large monitor that can display text clearly even at tiny point sizes, you may prefer to turn off the Greek Below option by clicking in the check box.

Note   The current view percentage affects the point size at which greeking occurs. At actual size (100 percent), Quark greeks text at the exact point size you have specified. Greeking occurs at higher point sizes than specified when the view percentage is below 100 percent and at smaller point sizes when the view percentage exceeds 100 percent.

Greek Pictures

Pictures in a document—especially bitmaps such as paint images or photographs—can slow screen redraw considerably for the pages in which they appear. To improve productivity in a document that contains many pictures, activate the Greek Pictures check box in the General Preferences dialog box. Pictures in that document will henceforth appear either as gray silhouettes or as solid gray picture boxes, as in Figure 4-9. If you click a picture box that contains a greeked picture when the Item, Content, or Rotation tool is active, Quark will display the picture normally so you can manipulate it.

Accurate Blends

The Accurate Blends option affects the appearance of gradient fills on systems that can display no more than 256 colors. If you leave this option unchecked, transitions between colors in a gradient fill are sharp and may show banding, as shown here:

FIGURE
4-9

Greeked pictures appear as solid gray picture boxes or as gray silhouettes.

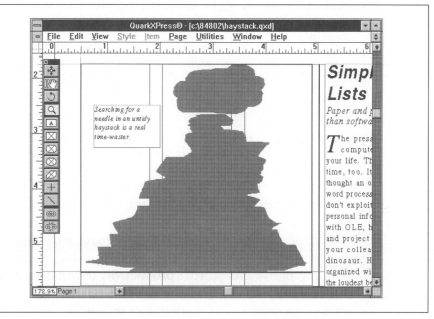

When this check box is activated, Quark *dithers*, or smooths, color transitions in a gradient fill so that little or no banding is visible. Color dithering slows screen redraw somewhat, but may be important if you require WYSIWYG color display. This setting does not affect the printing of color blends.

If your system can display 32,000 or 16 million colors, you will automatically see smooth transitions in all color blends and should leave the Accurate Blends option unchecked. See Chapter 10 to find out more about creating linear color blends in Quark.

Auto Constrain

Have you ever opened a set of Russian Easter dolls one after another, finding inside each doll a tinier version of the same doll? If so, you already understand something about the hierarchical relationship of constrained items in Quark. By activating the Auto Constrain option in the General Preferences dialog box, you can force a series of lines, text boxes, and picture boxes to fit within one another in sequence as you create them.

Here is a simple example of how Auto Constrain might work. Suppose you are designing a logo in which a series of picture and text boxes appear inside one another as Figure 4-10 shows. To force each new item to fit inside the one previously created, turn on the Auto Constrain option. The first text or picture box would have to be the largest, the second smaller, the third smaller yet, and so on. You would not be able to move any constrained item beyond the boundary of the item created just before it. If you rotate, size, or otherwise manipulate any item in the series, you would affect every item in the group. You would need to use special commands in the Item menu to free individual items from their constraining groups.

When Auto Constrain is unchecked (the default setting), newly created items in a document have no relationship to items created previously. You can move items anywhere on the page and size them without

FIGURE 4-10 Auto Constrain active: items fit within one another in the order in which they are drawn

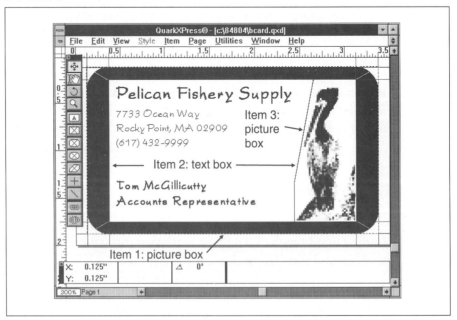

restrictions. Chapter 11 tells you more about grouping, constraining, and locking items.

Setting Typographic Preferences

The Preferences/Typographic command accesses the Typographical Preferences dialog box shown in Figure 4-11. This dialog box controls special text formatting and other typesetting conventions throughout a document. Chapters 5 and 6 provide more in-depth information on Quark's sophisticated typographic controls.

Just as it did with general preferences, Quark saves typographic preferences in one of two ways: with the active document and as defaults for new documents.

Saving Preferences with the Active Document   If you choose the Preferences/Typographic command when a document window is open, Quark saves your settings with that document. When multiple documents are open, the active document window is the one to which the new preferences apply. The name of the active document always appears in the title bar of the dialog box.

Saving Preferences as Defaults for New Documents   If you choose the Preferences/Typographic command when no document windows are open, the title bar of the Typographic Preferences dialog box contains no

FIGURE 4-11   The Typographical Preferences dialog box

Typographical Preferences			
Superscript	**Subscript**	**Baseline Grid**	
Offset: 33%	Offset: 33%	Start: 0.5"	
VScale: 100%	VScale: 100%	Increment: 12 pt	
HScale: 100%	HScale: 100%	Auto Leading: 20%	
Small Caps	**Superior**	Flex Space Width: 50%	
VScale: 75%	VScale: 50%	☒ Auto Kern Above: 10 pt	
HScale: 75%	HScale: 50%	☒ Maintain Leading	
Hyphenation Method: Enhanced			
Leading Mode: Typesetting		OK Cancel	

reference to a document file. This means that Quark will save any new settings as defaults for future new documents.

Superscript, Subscript

The Superscript and Subscript areas of the Typographic Preferences dialog box control the placement and sizing of superscript and subscript characters in a document. The same three options—Offset, VScale, and HScale—define the typographic features of both types of characters. For all three options, you can specify values from 0 percent to 100 percent in increments of one-tenth percent (.1 percent).

Offset

The Offset options determine the placement of superscript and subscript characters relative to the baseline of normal text. As Figure 4-12

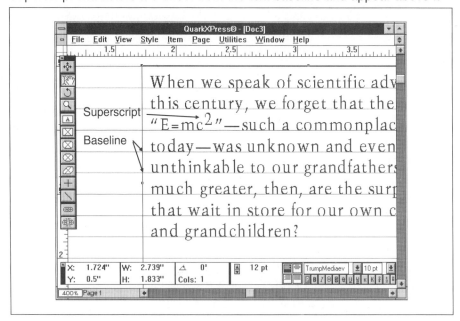

| FIGURE 4-12 | Superscript characters are offset from the text baseline and appear above it |

shows, the *baseline* is the normally invisible line along which the lower edges of the characters a, c, e, i, m, n, o, r, s, u, v, and x align. In the Superscript area of the dialog box, the Offset value determines how high above the baseline of normal text Quark places any superscript characters. The Offset value in the Subscript area of the dialog box specifies how far below the baseline Quark places the bottom edges of subscript characters. Quark expresses baseline offset as a percentage of font size.

VScale, HScale

The VScale and HScale values control the height (vertical scale) and width (horizontal scale), respectively, of superscript and subscript characters in a document. Quark measures vertical scale and horizontal scale as a percentage of normal font size. At the preset value of 100 percent, superscript and subscript characters are the same width and height as normal characters in surrounding text. However, you can easily make them smaller or change their proportions.

Small Caps, Superior

Desktop publishers and traditional typesetters commonly use small capital letters to represent abbreviations, computer keyboard commands, and for other special purposes. Typical superior characters include quotation marks, apostrophes, and footnote reference numbers or symbols. The Small Caps and Superior sections of the Typographical Preferences dialog box contain fields for specifying the height (VScale) and width (HScale) of these types of special characters relative to normal text characters.

VScale, HScale

The default VScale (height) and HScale (width) values for small caps are 75 percent of normal text size; for superior characters, the preset values are 50 percent of normal text size. The available range of values is from 0 percent to 100 percent in increments of .1 percent.

Baseline Grid

The Baseline Grid section of the Typographical Preferences dialog box defines the origin and increments of the baseline grid throughout a document. The baseline grid is normally invisible, but you can display it by choosing the Show Baseline Grid command in the View menu. If the Lock to Baseline Grid check box in the Paragraph Formats dialog box (Formats command, Paragraph menu) is active for a particular paragraph, Quark locks text baselines for that paragraph to the grid. Figure 4-12 shows a document page in which the baseline grid has been displayed.

Start

The value in the Start field defines the origin of a document's baseline grid relative to the top of the page. The preset value is 0.5 inches. You can enter a value using any unit of measurement, but Quark translates your entry back into the equivalent in inches (or whatever unit of measurement you have currently selected for Horizontal Measure in the Application Preferences dialog box).

Increment

The value in the Increment field tells Quark how far apart to locate the lines in a baseline grid. The preset value is 12 points; if you enter a value using a different unit of measurement and then leave the dialog box, Quark translates that value into the equivalent in points. The available range of values is from 5 to 144 points in .001-point increments.

Hyphenation Method

QuarkXPress can hyphenate paragraphs automatically if you specify Auto Hyphenation for them in the Edit Hyphenation and Justification dialog box (H&Js command, Edit menu). When you set a paragraph for Auto Hyphenation, Quark uses either a Standard or an Enhanced method. You choose between these methods using the Hyphenation

Method drop-down list in the Typographical Preferences dialog box, shown here:

Leading Mode

The term *leading* refers to the amount of vertical space between lines of type in a paragraph. This term usually has one meaning in desktop publishing packages and another in word processing packages. Using the Leading Mode option, you can choose which of the two leading methods—typesetting or word processing—you want to use based on the kinds of documents you create in Quark.

Typesetting

Typesetting is the default leading mode. In this mode, Quark measures leading from the baseline of one line upward to the baseline of the next. This is the mode to choose if you usually produce documents for commercial print uses such as books, periodicals, and brochures.

Word Processing

The word processing leading mode measures leading downward from the top of the ascenders on one line of text to the top of the ascenders on the following line. Choose Word Processing mode only if you usually produce letters, memos, and other short interoffice documents and if you do not use Quark for professional page layout.

Auto Leading

Whereas the Leading Mode option defines the *method* Quark uses to apply leading in a given document, the Auto Leading option defines the *amount* of leading to use. Actually, the Auto Leading option applies only to paragraphs to which you have assigned automatic leading using the Measurements Palette or the Leading or Formats command in the Style menu. Auto leading is preset for all paragraphs in a new document.

To determine an auto leading amount for a paragraph, Quark begins with the size of the largest font on each line and adds to it the value you specify in the Auto Leading field. Auto Leading is therefore *relative leading*, because the specific amount varies with the size of the font in a given paragraph. Auto leading is even more flexible in that you can enter values either as a percentage of font size or as an increment in points, picas, inches, millimeters, centimeters, or ciceros.

The examples given in the following sections should illustrate the difference between auto leading based on a percentage value and auto leading based on an incremental value.

Auto Leading Based on Percentage Values

Auto Leading based on percentage values results in proportional leading for all auto leaded paragraphs in a document. When you first install Quark, the Auto Leading option in the Typographical Preferences dialog box is preset to a percentage value of 20 percent. Using this value, an auto leaded paragraph containing 10-point text would feature 12 points of space between each line.

This formula shows how we reached that number:

10 points + [10 x 20%] = 10 points + 2 points = 12 points

You can specify any percentage value from 0 percent to 100 percent in 1-percent increments.

Auto Leading Based on Incremental Values

You also can base auto leading on a specific incremental value rather than on a percentage of font size. Leading specified this way will not be proportional for all auto leaded paragraphs in a document. Instead,

Quark will add the *same* set number of points (or other unit of measurement) between lines in all auto leaded paragraphs.

To specify auto leading in terms of incremental values, enter a plus (+) or minus (–) sign followed by the number of points to add or subtract from the font sizc. For example, a value of +3 tells Quark to add three extra points of space between every line in an auto leaded paragraph. Each paragraph of 10-point text would then have 13 points of leading, as this formula shows:

10 points + 3 points = 13 points

Flex Space Width

Until recently, QuarkXPress did not feature an en space among its special characters (see Chapter 5 for more about using special characters in Quark). Now, however, QuarkXPress for Windows and Quark 3.1 for the Macintosh let you define a *flex space*—a variable-size en space. When you specify the size of the flex space in the Typographical Preferences dialog box you'll get the same size flex space every time you use it in the current document.

In traditional typography, an en space is 50 percent of a standard em space for a given typeface and type size. Quark therefore presets the Flex Space Width value to 50 percent. You can enter any value from 0 percent to 400 percent in increments of .1 percent.

Auto Kern Above

Most outline fonts include kerning tables to control spacing between character pairs. The Auto Kern Above option in the Typographical Preferences dialog box tells Quark whether and at what point size to let these kerning tables handle intercharacter spacing automatically. By default, Auto Kern Above is turned on for all fonts larger than 10 points. You can specify any font size from 2 to 720 points in increments of .001

of any measurement system. If you wish, you can even turn off automatic kerning by clicking the Auto Kern Above check box to deactivate it.

Maintain Leading

The Maintain Leading option applies only to cases in which a line of text falls slightly below something else that lies in its way, such as a graphic overlaid on a text box. When the Maintain Leading check box is active (the default setting), Quark places the line of text normally according to its current leading value. This may result in a visible overlap between the line of text and the interfering item. If you deselect the Maintain Leading check box, the ascender of the line of text falls below the item that obstructs it. The distance by which the text falls below the obstructing item depends on the current Text Outset value for that item (Runaround command, Item menu). Chapter 12 gives more information about using runarounds to integrate graphics with text.

Setting Tool-Related Preferences

The Preferences/Tools command accesses the Tool Preferences dialog box shown here:

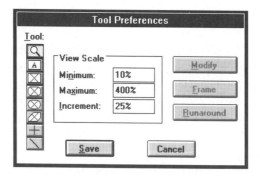

The Tool Preferences dialog box controls the behavior of eight of the tools in the Tool palette: the Zoom tool, the Text Box tool, the four Picture Box tools, and the two Line drawing tools.

Quark saves tool preference settings in one of two ways: with the active document and as defaults for new documents.

Saving Preferences with the Active Document If you choose the Preferences/Tools command when a document window is open, Quark saves your settings with that document. When multiple documents are open, the active document window is the one to which the new preferences apply. The name of the active document always appears in the title bar of the dialog box.

Saving Preferences As Defaults for New Documents If you choose the Preferences/Tools command when no document windows are open, the title bar of the Tool Preferences dialog box contains no reference to a document file. This is your clue that Quark will save any new settings as defaults for future new documents.

Setting Preferences for a Specific Tool

Not all of the options in the Tool Preferences dialog box are available for every tool. To set preferences for a specific tool, click the tool icon in the dialog box. The options that apply to that tool become highlighted; other options are grayed.

Magnification Tool Preferences

 To set preferences for the behavior of the Zoom tool in a document, click the Magnification tool's icon in the Tool Preferences dialog box. The Minimum, Maximum, and Increment options in the View Scale area of the dialog box become available.

Minimum, Maximum

The Minimum and Maximum values determine the lowest and highest viewing magnifications that you can obtain in the current document. The preset values are already at the extremes of the allowable range: 10 percent for Minimum and 400 percent for Maximum.

Increment

Each time you click in a document window while the Zoom tool is active, the viewing magnification changes by a specific increment. For example, if you assign the default Increment value of 25 percent to a document and the current view percentage is 100 percent, clicking once changes the view percentage to 125 percent. You may specify an increment value anywhere from 10 percent to 400 percent in increments as small as .1 percent.

Text Box Tool Preferences

 When you click the Text Box Tool icon in the Tool Preferences dialog box, the Modify, Frame, and Runaround buttons become available. Each of these buttons lets you access a dialog box in which you set default attributes for all the text boxes in a given document. Newly created text boxes in the document will be "preformatted" according to these settings.

Modifying Text Box Specifications

Click the Modify button to display the Text Box Specifications dialog box shown in Figure 4-13. This is essentially the same dialog box that

The Text Box Specifications dialog box for setting document-wide tool preferences

you see when you choose the Modify command in the Item menu with a text box selected, with two important differences:

☐ When you access this dialog box from inside the Tool Preferences dialog box, you are setting up formatting for *all* text boxes in a given document. Only those attributes that you can apply to text boxes document-wide are available in the Text Box Specifications dialog box; other attributes are grayed out.

☐ If you access this dialog box from the Modify command in the Item menu, all the options in the dialog box are available. However, their settings apply to the currently selected text box only.

The following sections give brief descriptions of how each available option in the Text Box Specifications dialog box functions. For thorough descriptions, see Chapter 5.

Columns   Enter the default number of columns per text box in this field. The preset value is 1.

Gutter   Enter the default amount of space between text box columns in this field. You can enter values in any unit of measure, but Quark translates them into the current unit of measure specified for Horizontal Measure in the General Preferences dialog box.

Text Inset   Entering a Text Inset value is equivalent to setting a default margin for the text boxes in a document. Use points to specify the amount of space between text and the edges of text boxes.

Suppress Printout   Activate this check box only if you do not want text boxes in a given document to print.

First Baseline, Offset and Minimum   Use this section of the dialog box to specify the default placement of the first line of text in text boxes document-wide.

☐ *Offset* tells Quark how much space there should be between the top of a text box and the first baseline. You can enter values in increments of .001 using any unit of measurement, but Quark translates your settings into the current unit of measurement as specified in the General Preferences dialog box.

☐   *Minimum* gives you three choices for defining placement of the first line of text at the top of a text box. Choose Cap + Accent for foreign-language documents; Ascent when using fonts in which the ascenders sometimes extend beyond normal cap heights; and Cap Height for most other documents.

Vertical Alignment, Type   Choose the option that defines how to align text vertically in text boxes document-wide. Top is the preset option. Other choices include Centered, Bottom, and Justified.

Background, Color   Use the Color drop-down list to specify the default background color for all text boxes in a document. If you have added custom colors to a document using the Colors command in the Edit menu, you will have more than the standard eight colors at your disposal.

Text Box Frame Specifications

When you click the Frame command button in the Tool Preferences dialog box, the Frame Specifications dialog box appears, as shown here:

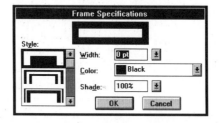

This is essentially the same dialog box that appears when you choose the Frame command in the Item menu with a single text box selected. There are two important differences, however:

☐   The Frame Specifications dialog box that you access from the Tool Preferences dialog box sets default frame attributes for text boxes throughout a document.

☐   The dialog box that you access through the Item menu defines frame attributes for the selected text box only.

Use the options in this dialog box to define the default outline Style, Width, Color, and Shade for text boxes document-wide.

Text Box Runaround Specifications

The term *runaround* in Quark refers to the methods by which you can control text flow when text boxes, lines, and/or picture boxes overlap. When you click the Runaround button in the Tool Preferences dialog box, the Runaround Specifications dialog box appears, as shown here:

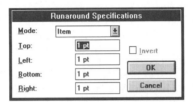

This is essentially the same dialog box you see when you choose the Runaround command in the Item menu with a specific text box selected, but the functions of the two dialog boxes are slightly different:

☐   The Runaround Specifications dialog box that you access from within the Tool Preferences dialog box lets you predefine runaround settings for all text boxes in a document.

☐   The settings in the dialog box that appears when you choose the Runaround command in the Item menu controls runaround for the selected text box only.

Mode   Two runaround modes are available for text boxes: None and Item.

☐   *None* If you choose None, the contents of items that lie behind text boxes in a document remain visible. Figure 4-14 shows a picture box behind a text box for which Runaround is set to None.

☐   *Item* If you choose Item, the contents of pictures behind text boxes are visible only beyond the boundaries of the text box. Figure 4-15 shows an overlapping text and picture box in a document in which Runaround has been set to Item as a Text Box tool preference. The overlapping parts of the picture in the background are no longer visible through the foreground text box.

FIGURE 4-14   Items in background show through a foreground text box for which Runaround mode is set to None

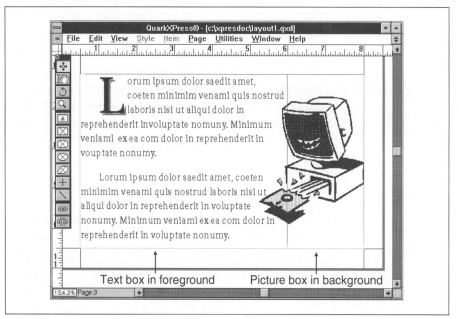

FIGURE 4-15   Overlapping items in the background remain invisible when the Runaround mode for a foreground text box is set to Item

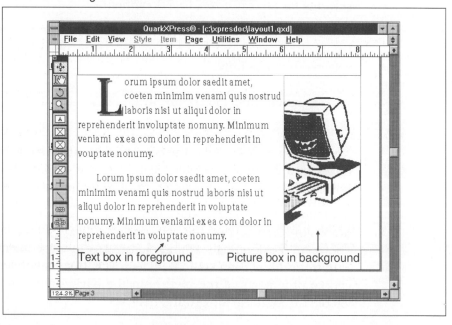

Note If you choose Item and two text boxes overlap, text in the background text box moves out of the way of the foreground text box by the amount of space you specify in the Top, Bottom, Left, and Right fields of the Runaround Specifications dialog box.

Top, Bottom, Left, and Right Runaround Amounts The Top, Bottom, Left, and Right runaround values define the amount of space by which overlapping items run around text boxes throughout a document. These fields are available only when the Item tool is selected.

Picture Box Tool Preferences

 When you click any of the four Picture Box tool icons in the Tool Preferences dialog box, the Modify, Frame, and Runaround buttons become available. Each of these buttons lets you access a dialog box in which you set default attributes for all the picture boxes of that type in a given document.

Modifying Picture Box Specifications

Click the Modify button to access the Picture Box Specifications dialog box shown in Figure 4-16. This is essentially the same dialog box as the one that appears when you choose Modify in the Item menu with a specific picture box selected, but its function is slightly different:

☐ When you access this dialog box from inside the Tool Preferences dialog box, you are setting up formatting for *all* picture boxes of the current type, document-wide. Only attributes that you can apply to picture boxes document-wide are available in the Picture Box Specifications dialog box; other attributes are grayed out.

☐ If you access this dialog box from the Modify command in the Item menu, all the options in the dialog box are available. However, their settings apply to the currently selected picture box only.

FIGURE
4-16

The Picture Box Specifications dialog box for setting document-wide Elliptical Tool Box preferences

> **Picture Box Specifications**
>
> Origin Across: Scale Across: `100%`
> Origin Down: Scale Down: `100%`
> Width: Offset Across: `0"`
> Height: Offset Down: `0"`
> Box Angle: Picture Angle: `0°`
> Corner Radius: `0.25"`   Picture Skew: `0°`
>
> Background
> ☐ Suppress Picture Printout   Color: `White`
> ☐ Suppress Printout   Shade: `100%`
>
> OK   Cancel

Corner Radius   The Corner Radius option, available for the Rounded Rectangle Picture Box tool only, defines the radius of the imaginary circles that form the corner of this type of picture box. You can specify any value from 0 inches to 2 inches using any unit of measurement; Quark translates your settings into the unit of measurement currently specified in the General Preferences dialog box.

Suppress Picture Printout, Suppress Printout   Activate the Suppress Picture Printout check box only if you do not want the *contents* of picture boxes of the current type to be printed in the document. The picture boxes themselves print unless you also activate the Suppress Printout check box.

Scale Across, Scale Down   The Scale Across and Scale Down options define the default sizing and scaling of pictures *within* picture boxes. The default values of 100 percent tells Quark to import all pictures in a document at their original sizes and in their original proportions. You can specify any percentage from 10 percent to 1000 percent.

The image in Figure 4-17 was imported with Scale Across and Scale Down each set at 100 percent as a Picture Box tool preference. Figure 4-18 shows the same image imported with Scale Across and Scale Down set to 50 percent for the picture box tools. Note that in both cases, the upper-left corner of the picture falls at the upper-left corner of the picture

FIGURE
4-17

Importing a picture in a document for which default Scale Across and Scale Down values are 100 percent

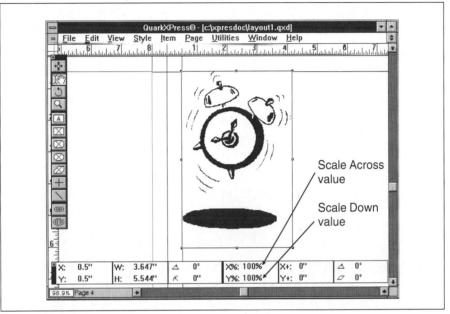

FIGURE
4-18

Importing a picture in a document for which default Scale Across and Scale Down values are 50 percent

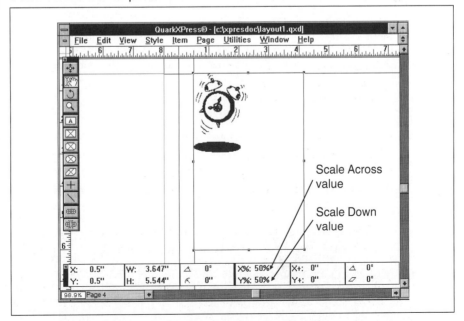

box. To set a different default *placement* of imported pictures, use the Offset Across and Offset Down options.

Offset Across, Offset Down The Offset Across and Offset Down options tell Quark where to position the upper-left corner of imported pictures relative to the upper-left corner of their picture boxes. At the default values of 0 inches, the upper-left corner of each picture coincides with the upper-left corner of the picture boxes that contain them, as seen in Figure 4-17. Here is how the values you enter affect the positioning of pictures within their picture boxes:

- *Positive value, Offset Across* The picture moves to the right.

- *Negative value, Offset Across* The picture moves to the left; the left edge of the picture is not visible within the picture box.

- *Positive value, Offset Down* The picture moves downward.

- *Negative value, Offset Down* The picture moves upward; the upper edge of the picture is not visible within the picture box.

You can enter values using any unit of measurement, in increments as small as .001 unit. Quark translates values into the unit of measurement currently specified in the General Preferences dialog box.

 Note In the cases of Rounded Rectangular, Elliptical, and Polygon picture boxes, Quark measures offset values from the upper-left corner of the bounding box, not from the edge of the picture box itself. With Offset values of zero, the extreme upper-left corners of pictures would not be visible in these non-rectangular picture boxes.

Picture Angle If you want all pictures in a document to be rotated at a specific angle, enter the angle here. You can enter angle values from –360 to 360 degrees in increments as small as .001 degree. The Picture Angle option affects pictures only; picture boxes themselves are not rotated.

Picture Skew If you want all pictures in a document to appear with a stylized slant as shown in Figure 4-19, enter the desired skew angle in this field. You can specify skew angles from –75 to 75 degrees in

FIGURE
4-19

Importing a picture in a document for which the default Skew angle is 35 degrees

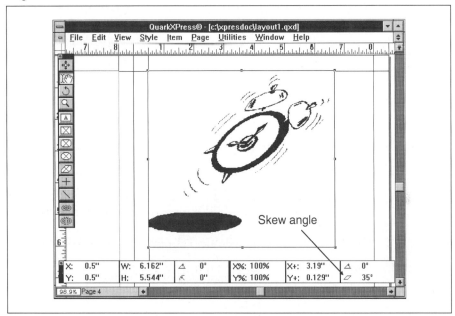

increments as small as .001 degree. The skew angle affects pictures only, not the picture boxes themselves.

Background Color   Use the Background Color drop-down list to specify a default background color for all picture boxes in a document, as shown here:

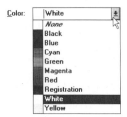

If you have added custom colors previously using the Colors dialog box (Colors command, Edit menu), the list box may contain more than the standard eight colors.

Picture Box Frame Specifications

When one of the picture box tools is active in the Tool Preferences dialog box, clicking the Frame button accesses the Frame Specifications dialog box (refer back to Figure 4-16). The options are identical for both picture boxes and text boxes. You can specify the default Style, Width, Color, and Shade of any outlines you wish to apply to picture boxes document-wide.

Picture Box Runaround Specifications

When you click the Runaround button with a picture box tool active, the Runaround Specifications dialog box appears. The options in this dialog box vary, depending on which type of Picture Box tool and which runaround mode are currently active. An example of a default Runaround Specifications dialog box for an Elliptical picture box is shown here:

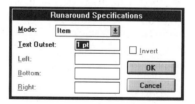

Mode Specifications   Three runaround modes are available for picture box tools: None, Item, and Auto Image.

☐   *None* Choose None if you want text to flow normally behind picture boxes of the current type.

☐   *Item* Choose Item (the default selection) if you want background text to flow around picture boxes by the amount you specify in the Top, Left, Bottom, and Right fields.

☐   *Auto Image* If you choose the Auto Image mode, text behind pictures in a document flows around the contours of *pictures* rather than around the edges of the picture boxes themselves. If pictures do not fill their frames entirely, text can flow into the blank spaces as shown in Figure 4-20. You define the default amount of space between picture contours and text in a document by specifying values in the Text Outset field.

When a picture box is set to Auto Image runaround, text in the background
wraps around picture contours.

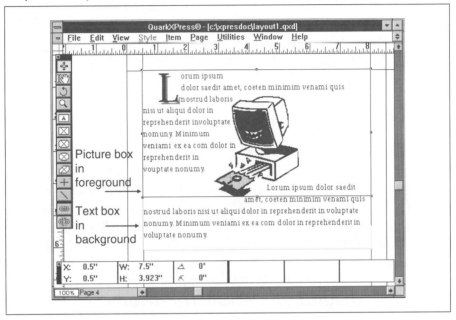

 Tip   An additional runaround mode, Manual Image, is available when
you specify runaround for a particular picture box. Refer to Chapter 12
for more information on specifying manual runarounds.

Text Outset   When the Auto Image mode is selected, the Text Outset
field becomes available, as shown here:

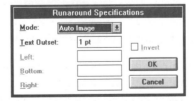

The value you enter in this field determines how much space falls between
picture contours and overlapping text in a document. The preset value
is 1 point, but you can enter any value in increments of .001 unit. Quark
translates your entries into their equivalents in points.

Top, Bottom, Left, and Right Runaround Amounts   When the Item mode is selected, the Top, Bottom, Left, and Right runaround values define the amount of space by which overlapping text runs around picture boxes throughout a document. You can specify different values for each field, using increments as small as .001 in any unit of measurement; Quark translates the values into points.

Line Tool Preferences

When you click one of the Line Tool icons in the Tool Preferences dialog box, the Modify and Runaround buttons become available. Each of these buttons lets you access a dialog box in which you set default attributes for all the lines you draw in a given document. Newly created lines throughout the document will be "preformatted" according to these settings.

Modifying Line Specifications

Click the Modify button in the Tool Preferences dialog box to display the Line Specifications dialog box shown in Figure 4-21. The options in this dialog box help you determine the default appearance of lines document-wide.

Style   Use the Style drop-down list to assign a default outline style for all the lines in a document, as shown here:

The eleven preset options include various solid, dotted, dashed, double, and triple line combinations. The default option is a solid line style.

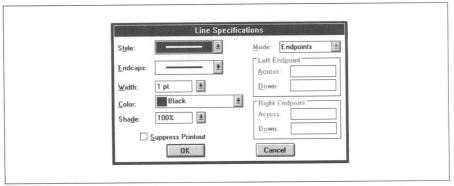

FIGURE 4-21 The default Line Specifications dialog box

End Caps   The End Caps drop-down list lets you choose the default appearance of line endings throughout a document. The preset option is a plain line ending, but five arrow end cap styles are also available, as shown here:

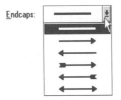

Width   There are two ways to specify a default line width. You can choose from among the preset options in the drop-down list or enter a custom width value in the field in increments of .001 unit. Quark translates the values you enter into points; the allowable range of widths is from 0 to 504 points. The preset line width is one point.

Color   To specify a default color for all lines in a document, choose a color from the Color drop-down list. If you have defined custom colors using the Colors dialog box (Colors command, Edit menu), more than the standard eight colors will be available.

Shade   Use the Shade drop-down list to assign a default shade of the specified color to all lines in a document. Alternatively, you can enter a custom shade percentage in this field in increments as small as .1 percent.

Suppress Printout   Activate the Suppress Printout check box only if you do not want any lines in a document to print out automatically.

Line Runaround Specifications

To define default runaround attributes for all the lines in a document, click the Runaround button when one of the Line tools is active in the Tool Preferences dialog box. The Runaround Specifications dialog box appears, as shown here:

All the options are grayed out here except for the Mode option, because Quark does not allow you to run text around a line by a specific number of points. If you select None as a mode (the default setting), background text flows behind all lines and may be obscured by them. If you select the Item mode, text flows to one side of lines, depending on which side has more horizontal space available.

Setting Other Document-Wide Defaults

Three additional commands in the Edit menu—Style Sheets, Colors, and H&Js—function like the document-specific commands in the Preferences submenu. If you set options for these commands when a document window is open, Quark saves them with that document. If you edit these options when no document is open, Quark saves them as default settings that apply to all new documents. This chapter provides a brief description of the uses of each command; for more detailed information, see the chapter or chapters to which each section refers.

Style Sheets

Choose the Style Sheets command in the Edit menu to access the Style Sheets dialog box shown here:

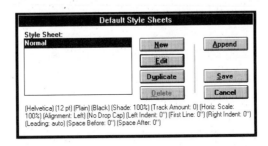

The options in this dialog box let you create or edit style sheets. As you will remember from Chapter 1, style sheets are comprehensive text formatting attributes that you can apply to entire paragraphs in a document.

If a document window is active when you choose the Style Sheets command, the document's name appears in the title bar of the dialog box. Quark saves style sheets and their attributes with that document. If no document window is open, the dialog box contains at least the Normal style sheet and bears the label "Default Style Sheets." Any style sheet attributes you edit or any new style sheets you create apply henceforth to all new documents.

The Style Sheets dialog box contains seven command buttons: New, Edit, Duplicate, Delete, Append, Save, and Cancel.

New   accesses a series of dialog boxes that you can use to name and define attributes for new style sheets.

Edit   opens a dialog box that you can use to edit attributes for existing style sheets.

Duplicate   lets you create a new style sheet based on the same attributes as an existing style sheet.

Delete   lets you delete the currently selected style sheet.

Append opens a dialog box that you can use to import all the style sheets from a different document.

Save tells Quark to save all style sheet changes you have made.

Cancel exits the Style Sheets dialog box without saving any changes.

Chapter 6 delves extensively into the process of designing and editing style sheets efficiently. Refer to that chapter for more information on the workings of the Style Sheet dialog box.

Colors

Choose the Colors command in the Edit menu to access the Edit Colors dialog box shown here:

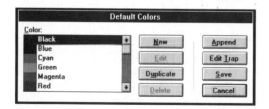

Use the options in this dialog box to add new colors to a document, edit existing colors, specify trapping parameters, or copy colors from another document.

If a document window is active when you choose the Colors command, the document's name appears in the title bar of the dialog box. Quark saves the current colors list with that document. If no document window is open, the dialog box bears the label "Default Colors" and contains at least the eight preset colors installed with QuarkXPress. Any changes you make to the default colors apply to all new documents you create later.

The Colors dialog box contains eight command buttons: New, Edit, Duplicate, Delete, Append, Edit Trap, Save, and Cancel.

New accesses a dialog box and color wheel that you can use to name and specify a new color.

Edit   opens a dialog box that you can use to redefine an existing color (Black, White, Cyan, Magenta, and Yellow excepted).

Duplicate   lets you add a new color based on the same attributes as an existing color (Registration excepted).

Delete   lets you delete the currently selected color (Black, White, Cyan, Magenta, and Yellow excepted).

Append   opens a dialog box that you can use to import all the colors from a different document.

Edit Trap   opens a dialog box in which you can specify default trapping relationships for individual colors in a document.

Save   tells Quark to save all changes you have made to the current document colors.

Cancel   exits the Colors dialog box without saving any changes.

Two other chapters in this book provide more information on working with the Colors dialog box. Chapter 10 steers you through the basics of specifying, using, and trapping color in QuarkXPress documents. Chapter 14 explores color-related issues you need to know about when preparing documents for commercial print output.

H&Js

Through the H&Js dialog box, QuarkXPress gives you precise typographical control over hyphenation and text justification rules used in a document. Choose the H&Js command in the Edit menu to access the Default H&Js dialog box, shown here:

The options in this dialog box help you to add new sets of hyphenation and justification rules, edit or copy existing sets, or copy sets of H&Js from another document to the current one.

If a document window is active when you choose the H&Js command, the document's name appears in the title bar of the dialog box. Quark saves the current set of H&Js with that document. If no document window is open, the dialog box bears the label "Default H&Js" and contains at least the Standard H&Js set installed with QuarkXPress. Any changes you make to the default colors apply to all new documents you create later.

The H&Js dialog box contains seven command buttons: New, Edit, Duplicate, Delete, Append, Save, and Cancel.

New   accesses a dialog box that you can use to name and specify a new set of automatic hyphenation and justification methods.

Edit   opens a dialog box that lets you redefine an existing set of H&Js.

Duplicate   lets you add a new set of H&Js based on the same attributes as an existing set (Standard, for example).

Delete   lets you delete the currently selected set of H&Js (the Standard set excepted).

Append   opens a dialog box that you can use to import all the H&J sets from a different document.

Save   tells Quark to save all changes you have made to the current sets of H&Js.

Cancel   exits the H&Js dialog box without saving any changes.

Chapter 6 includes substantial information on using and specifying hyphenation and justification rules in Quark.

Preferences and default values are important parts of the way Quark and its documents work. If you make a habit of checking and editing preset values whenever you set up a new document, you can make the layout and production process more efficient.

PART III

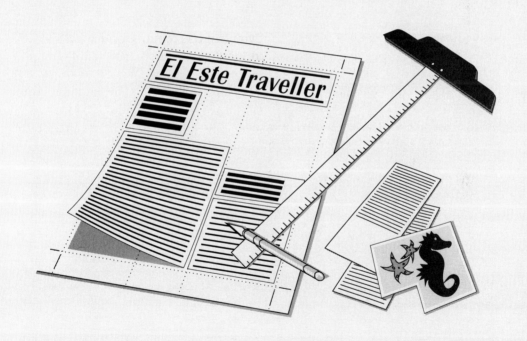

Editing and
Formatting Text

CHAPTER

Using Quark as a Word Processor

You have heard this before, but we will say it again: QuarkXPress does it all. That statement is never more true than when it applies to word processing functions. Quark's features stand up well against even the most sophisticated word processing packages. You can enter text directly on the pages of your documents; select and format characters, words, lines, paragraphs, or an entire document; search and replace words or even text attributes; check spelling; and create your own auxiliary dictionaries for specific documents.

As a word processor, QuarkXPress is as flexible as it is powerful. You can carry out most word processing tasks using your choice of several available techniques: often you can select between menu commands, the Measurements palette, and keyboard and mouse shortcuts to reach the same goal. Simply choose the technique that seems most intuitive to you; Quark never forces you to do it "their" way.

This chapter explores Quark's basic word processing and text editing functions, concentrating on text that you enter or edit directly within Quark documents. As your knowledge of QuarkXPress advances, you may begin formatting text at the paragraph level, using style sheets to format text automatically, and exploring advanced typographic controls; Chapter 6 gives more information on those subjects. If you usually import text into Quark from another word processor, be sure to read Chapter 7.

Text Boxes and Text

In order to enter or import text in QuarkXPress, you must first create a text box. Text boxes are more than empty rectangular frames for holding text; they also help you format and position the text they contain. The following sections review text boxes as they relate to word processing functions.

Creating a Text Box

To create a text box into which you can type or import text, follow these steps:

1. Open an existing document (CTRL-O) or create a new one (CTRL-N).

2. If necessary, adjust the page view so you can see as much of the page as you need for the text box. Use the View Percentage indicator, commands in the View menu, or the Page Grabber hand (ALT + mouse button) as desired.

3. Activate the Text Box tool in the Tools palette by clicking it. The pointer takes on the shape of a crosshair (+), indicating that you can draw an item on the page.

4. Position the crosshair pointer where you want to locate the upper-left corner of the text box. If the Measurements palette is visible, use its X and Y values to position this corner precisely.

5. Press and hold the mouse button and drag diagonally downward and to the right. As shown in Figure 5-1, a dotted rectangular outline follows the pointer, expanding or contracting according to your mouse movements. If the Measurements palette is visible, refer to the W and H values to view the current dimensions of the text box as you draw it.

Drawing a text box

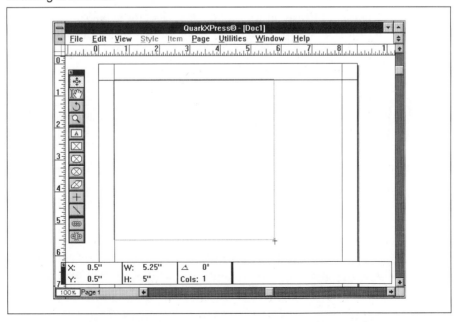

The completed text box immediately becomes active

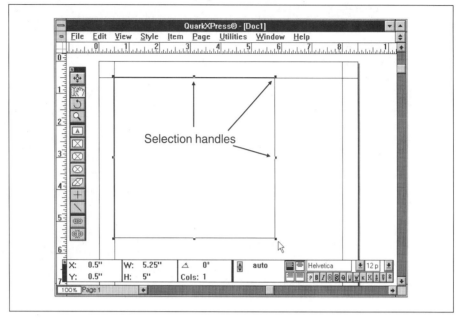

6. When the text box is the size you want, release the mouse button. The outline of the text box becomes solid, and eight selection handles appear around it as shown in Figure 5-2. These selection handles show that the text box is active; you can enter or import text into it immediately.

 The Content tool always becomes active as soon as you finish creating a text box, picture box, or line. This tool must be active in order for you to type, import text, or edit existing text.

 Tip If you plan to draw more than one text box in sequence, press ALT briefly as you activate the Text Box tool. Pressing and releasing this key tells Quark to keep the Text Box tool active rather than switch to the Content tool. When you have finished drawing text boxes, press ALT alone to release the repeating tool function, or simply select another tool.

 Tip To draw a perfectly square text box, press and hold SHIFT as you draw.

Activating a Text Box

A text box must be active (showing selection handles) in order for you to work with it. A text box that you have just created becomes active immediately, but if you change tools or manipulate a different item, it becomes inactive again.

There are two ways to activate an inactive text box: with the Content tool and with the Item tool. To activate an existing text box for *word processing* purposes, click the Content tool in the Tools palette and then click anywhere within the boundaries of the text box.

Note   Only one text box at a time can be active when the Content tool is selected.

To activate a text box for *layout* purposes, use the Item tool.

Sizing and Moving Text Boxes

Once you have created a text box, you can resize it or move it to another location. Three different techniques are at your disposal: you can use the mouse, the Measurements palette, or the Modify command in the Item menu.

Using a Mouse (Freehand Method)

To change the size of a text box using the mouse, follow these steps:

1. Activate the text box when either the Item tool or the Content tool is selected.

2. Position the mouse pointer at one of the eight selection handles surrounding the text box. The pointer turns into a hand with an extended index finger, as shown here:

1. If necessary, display the Measurements palette by choosing the Show Measurements command from the View menu.

2. With the Content tool or Item tool selected, activate the text box you want to resize.

3. Double-click the value in the W field of the Measurements palette, as shown in this example:

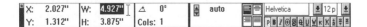

    Replace the current value with one that represents the desired width of the text box.

4. Press TAB to highlight the value in the H field. Replace the current value with one that represents the desired height of the text box.

To change the location of a text box using the Measurements palette, follow these steps:

FIGURE 5-3   Resizing a text box with the Content or Item tool

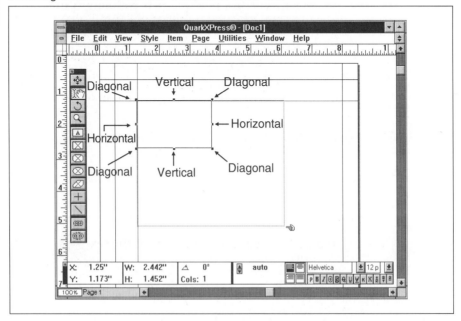

4. Release the mouse button. The dotted outline disappears and the solid outline and selection handles of a normal text box take its place.

Using the Measurements Palette

The Measurements palette is an intuitive yet precise tool for resizing and moving text boxes and other items. To change the size of a text box using the Measurements palette, follow these steps:

1. If necessary, display the Measurements palette by choosing the Show Measurements command from the View menu.

2. With the Content tool or Item tool selected, activate the text box you want to resize.

3. Double-click the value in the W field of the Measurements palette, as shown in this example:

Replace the current value with one that represents the desired width of the text box.

4. Press TAB to highlight the value in the H field. Replace the current value with one that represents the desired height of the text box.

To change the location of a text box using the Measurements palette, follow these steps:

1. Display the Measurements palette if it is not already visible.

2. Activate the text box with either the Content tool or the Item tool selected.

3. To change the horizontal position of the text box, double-click the value in the X field of the Measurements palette, as shown here:

4. Change the value as desired. Increasing the value moves the text box to the right; decreasing the value moves it to the left. Entering a negative number moves the text box beyond the page margins.

5. To change the vertical position of the text box, double-click the value in the Y field of the Measurements palette and replace it with a different value. Increasing the value moves the text box downward; decreasing the value moves it upward. Entering a negative number moves the text box beyond the page margins.

Using the Modify Command

When a text box is active, choose the Modify command in the Item menu (keyboard shortcut: CTRL-M) to access the Text Box Specifications dialog box shown in Figure 5-4. This dialog box has several functions, most of which are fully covered in the "'Formatting' a Text Box" section following this one. Four of the fields in this dialog box contain values that you can change to move or resize the active text box:

☐ *Origin Across* The Origin Across value controls the horizontal position of the upper-left corner of the text box. Reduce this value to move the text box to the left; increase it to move the text box to the right.

☐ *Origin Down* The Origin Down value controls the vertical position of the upper-left corner of the text box. Reducing this value moves the text box upward; decreasing the value moves it downward.

☐ *Width* The Width value controls the width of the active text box.

☐ *Height* The Height value controls the height of the active text box.

FIGURE 5-4

The Text Box Specifications dialog box

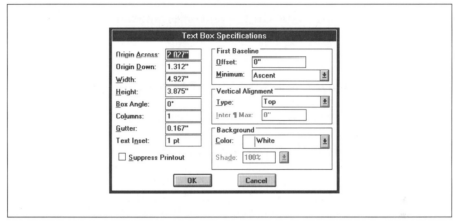

"Formatting" a Text Box

A text box is more than just an empty frame. In a very real sense, you can "format" text boxes to prepare them for receiving text. With the help of the Text Box Specifications dialog box shown in Figure 5-4, you can set text box margins, specify the number of columns and the width of gutters, and adjust the positioning of text in other ways. We will review only the dialog box options that pertain to the word processing functions of a text box. Chapters 10 and 11 give details on those options that don't relate to word processing.

To access the Text Box Specifications dialog box, activate a text box when either the Item tool or the Content tool is selected. Choose the Modify command in the Item menu or use the keyboard shortcut CTRL-M. You can also access this dialog box at any time by double-clicking on a text box when the Content or Item tool is active.

Specifying the Number of Columns

The value in the Columns field determines the number of columns in the active text box.

Specifying Gutter Width

The value in the Gutter field determines the amount of space between each column specified in the Columns field.

Specifying Margins with Text Inset

When you create a new document, you define margins for the entire page. By entering a value in the Text Inset field of the Text Box Specifications dialog box, you can also define a separate margin for the active text box. The *text inset* refers to the amount of space Quark places between text and all four edges of a text box.

Figure 5-5 shows examples of framed text boxes with different inset values. At 0 points, text bumps up against the edges of a text box—acceptable in some cases, but not when the text box has a visible frame or outline. At the default value of 1 point, text stops just short of the edges of its text box. A text box with a text inset value of 12 points (1 pica) features a wide margin on all four sides.

FIGURE 5-5   How Text Inset affects text box margins

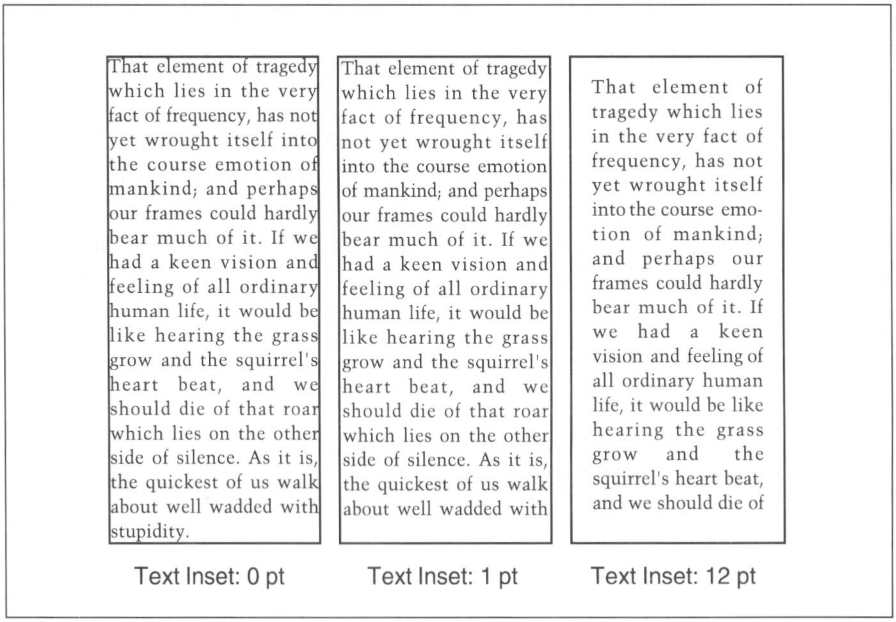

That element of tragedy which lies in the very fact of frequency, has not yet wrought itself into the course emotion of mankind; and perhaps our frames could hardly bear much of it. If we had a keen vision and feeling of all ordinary human life, it would be like hearing the grass grow and the squirrel's heart beat, and we should die of that roar which lies on the other side of silence. As it is, the quickest of us walk about well wadded with stupidity.

Text Inset: 0 pt

That element of tragedy which lies in the very fact of frequency, has not yet wrought itself into the course emotion of mankind; and perhaps our frames could hardly bear much of it. If we had a keen vision and feeling of all ordinary human life, it would be like hearing the grass grow and the squirrel's heart beat, and we should die of that roar which lies on the other side of silence. As it is, the quickest of us walk about well wadded with

Text Inset: 1 pt

That element of tragedy which lies in the very fact of frequency, has not yet wrought itself into the course emotion of mankind; and perhaps our frames could hardly bear much of it. If we had a keen vision and feeling of all ordinary human life, it would be like hearing the grass grow and the squirrel's heart beat, and we should die of

Text Inset: 12 pt

Adjusting the First Baseline

As you'll remember from Chapter 4, the baseline of text is the normally invisible line along which the bottoms of most letters are aligned. Figure 5-6 shows how setting the baseline can affect text placement. The Offset and Minimum options in the Text Box Specifications dialog box determine where Quark places the baseline of the first line of text in each column of the active text box. Quark always uses the larger of these two measurements.

Offset The Offset value tells Quark how much space to add between the top edge of the active text box and the first baseline. This is an absolute measurement that ignores and overrides any text inset value you may already have defined. If a text box has a text inset value of one-quarter inch and a baseline offset value of one inch, for example, the first baseline falls one inch below the top edge of the text box, as shown in Figure 5-7.

Minimum The Minimum setting you choose determines the *least* amount of space between the first text baseline and the top margin

FIGURE 5-6

Typographic factors to consider when adjusting the baseline position

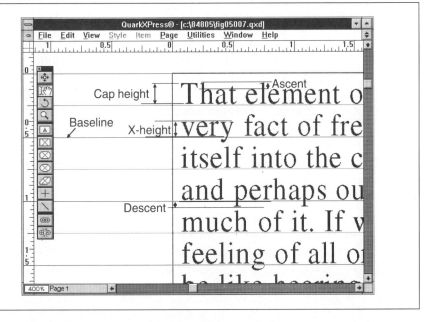

FIGURE
5-7

Baseline offset determines the total amount of space between top of text box and first baseline

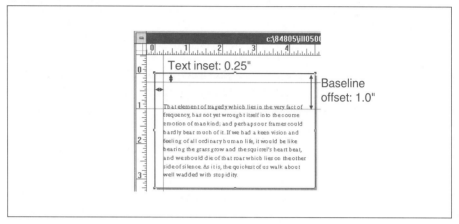

of the text box as defined by the text inset value. Three options are available in the drop-down list box: Cap Height, Cap + Accent, and Ascent.

Cap Height   When you choose this option, the tops of capital letters in the first line of text fall even with the top margin of the text box (see Figure 5-6).

If some fonts on the first line are larger than others and Cap Height is selected, the tallest capital letters lie flush against the top margin as shown in Figure 5-8.

Cap + Accent   Foreign words and phrases often include accent marks: *Élan* or *Ärger*, for example. Accented capital letters are taller than other capital letters in a font. If your document contains accented capitals, choose Cap + Accent to prevent accent marks from falling above the top margin of the text box.

Ascent   Ascent is the default Minimum setting because it applies to most fonts. The ascent of a font is the area in which letters such as h, f, and l rise above the x-height of other letters (see Figure 5-6). In many

FIGURE 5-8 Baseline minimum determines the minimum amount of space between text inset and the first baseline

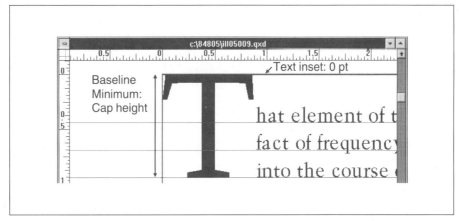

fonts, the ascent of lowercase letters rises even higher than the tops of capital letters, as shown here:

When using fonts like these in a text box, set baseline Minimum for that text box to Ascent. Quark will position the tops of ascenders (not the tops of capital letters) against the top margin of the text box.

 Remember   Quark measures baseline Offset relative to the top edge of the text box and Minimum relative to the top margin of the text box.

Setting Vertical Alignment

The Vertical Alignment options determine how text aligns relative to the top and bottom of the active text box. Figure 5-9 shows examples of how text aligns when you set Vertical Alignment Type to Top, Center, Bottom, and Justified. The Inter Paragraph Max. option, available only when you select Justified, tells Quark the maximum amount of space it

FIGURE 5-9

How the Vertical Alignment setting affects the position of text in a text box

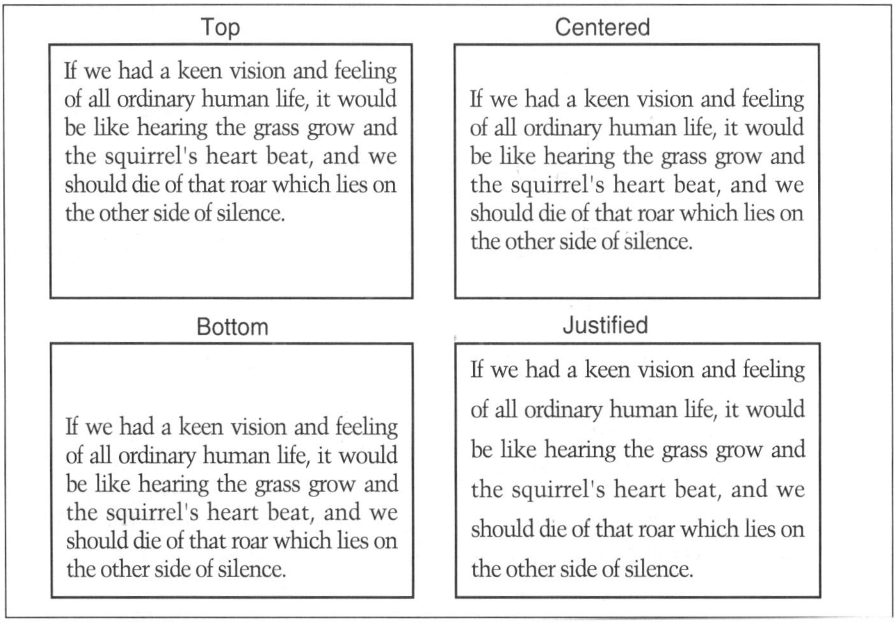

Top

If we had a keen vision and feeling of all ordinary human life, it would be like hearing the grass grow and the squirrel's heart beat, and we should die of that roar which lies on the other side of silence.

Centered

If we had a keen vision and feeling of all ordinary human life, it would be like hearing the grass grow and the squirrel's heart beat, and we should die of that roar which lies on the other side of silence.

Bottom

If we had a keen vision and feeling of all ordinary human life, it would be like hearing the grass grow and the squirrel's heart beat, and we should die of that roar which lies on the other side of silence.

Justified

If we had a keen vision and feeling of all ordinary human life, it would be like hearing the grass grow and the squirrel's heart beat, and we should die of that roar which lies on the other side of silence.

can add between paragraphs before it begins adding space arbitrarily between lines.

Tip   Do you want all or most of the text boxes in a document to have a specific formatting? If so, you can define preferences for the Text Box tool so that all the new text boxes you create will have the same number of columns, gutter width, text inset margin, and so forth. Immediately after creating the document, choose the Preferences/Tools command in the Edit menu and set defaults for the Text Box tool using the Modify button in the Tool Preferences dialog box. See Chapter 4 for details about setting tool defaults.

Placing Text in a Text Box

Once you have formatted a text box, how do you get text into it? There are three possibilities. You can import a text file from a word processing package, paste text from another Quark document or from another Windows application, or enter text directly in QuarkXPress.

Importing a Text File from a Word Processor

QuarkXPress for Windows accepts text files from Microsoft Word for Windows 1.0 or later, Microsoft Write, or any word processor that can save a file in ASCII (.TXT), XPress Tags (.XTG), or Rich Text Format (.RTF). To import a text file into QuarkXPress, follow these steps:

1. With the Content tool selected, activate the text box into which you want to import the text file.

2. Choose the Get Text command from the File menu (keyboard shortcut CTRL-E). The Get Text dialog box appears, as shown here:

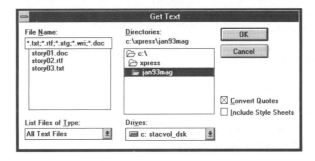

3. Select the desired file format from the List Files of Type list box.

4. If necessary, use the Drives and Directories list boxes to locate the text file.

5. Double-click the name of the desired text file in the File Name list box. Quark displays the progress of the import operation in the page number area at the bottom of the document window. When Quark has imported 100 percent of the file, text flows visibly into the active text box. If you have set up an automatic text box or an automatic text chain, text that overflows this first text box will flow into

additional text boxes or pages automatically. (See the section called "Creating an Automatic Text Chain" in Chapter 3.)

Chapter 7 offers a number of tips and tricks for preparing word processed text files that save you time and effort after you import them into Quark.

Pasting Text from the Clipboard

Another way to bring text into a Quark text box is to paste it from the Windows clipboard. You can paste text from another Windows application, from a non-Windows application, or from another Quark document. The amount of formatting that pasted text retains depends on the kind of application in which it originated.

Tip You may be able to use Object Linking and Embedding (OLE) to paste data from a Windows-based spreadsheet or database application into a Qaurk *picture* box with all formatting intact. See Chapter 8 for details.

Typing in a Text Box

Since Quark is a self-sufficient word processor, you can enter text directly into a text box.

To type in a text box, follow these steps:

1. With the Content tool active, click the text box in which you want to enter text. Selection handles appear around the text box, and a blinking text cursor appears in its upper-left corner.

2. Begin typing. Text appears in the text box in the current attributes for the Normal style sheet.

3. Format text as you type using the commands in the Style menu, the Measurements palette, or the Style Sheets palette described in Chapter 6.

What to Do When a Text Box Overflows

As you enter or edit text, the current text box may become full. If you already have set up an automatic text chain for your document in either master or document pages, text will flow automatically into the next box in the link. However, if you have not yet established any links, a small rectangle containing an x appears in the lower-right corner of the text box, indicating that text has overflowed, as shown here:

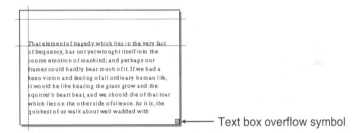

Text box overflow symbol

When you see this overflow indicator, you have several options. You can resize the text box. You can reformat the text so that it fits in the current text box. You could create an automatic text chain in the document's master pages. You might even decide to manually link the current text box to another one on the same or a different document page. See the "Modifying Text Links" and "Controlling Copy Flow Locally" sections of Chapter 3 for assistance on linking text boxes to control copy flow automatically.

Deciding Whether to Use Quark as Your Sole Word Processor

Sometimes it is preferable to enter all your text directly in Quark. At other times it is more convenient to use an external word processing package. The determining factor in deciding whether to use an external word processor is the number and types of graphics used in a document.

Text-Only Documents   For documents that contain mostly text, Quark is an ideal word processor, complete with spell checking and search and replace functions. Quark also gives you the advantages of a sophisticated page layout package. Text entry is speedy in these types of documents.

Graphics-Intensive Documents   Text entry is slower in documents that contain graphics, due to the added time Quark needs to redraw the screen after every text edit. The larger the number of graphics in a document, the less advisable it is to use Quark as your primary word processor—unless you greek the pictures using the Greek Pictures option in the General Preferences dialog box.

Entering and Editing Text

QuarkXPress makes it convenient for you to enter and edit text. Compared to other desktop publishing packages, Quark offers an exceptionally large number of keyboard and mouse shortcuts for moving the cursor and selecting the text you want to format.

Displaying "Invisible" Symbols

Activate the Show Invisibles command in the View menu (keyboard shortcut: CTRL-I) whenever you are using Quark as a word processor. This command causes Quark to display symbols for spaces, tabs, and paragraph end marks on your screen, as shown in Figure 5-10—a big help during text editing. When you no longer want to see these symbols, choose the Hide Invisibles command from the View menu.

Activating the Text Box and Choosing an Insertion Point

The first step in editing or entering text is to activate a text box and choose an *insertion point*—the point at which you want to begin editing. To activate a text box for editing purposes, simply click on it when the Content tool is selected. Quark responds in one of two ways:

☐   If the text box is empty, or if this is the first time you have worked in it since opening the document, Quark places a blinking text cursor at its upper-left corner.

FIGURE 5-10 Displaying spaces, tabs, and paragraph end marks with the Show Invisibles command

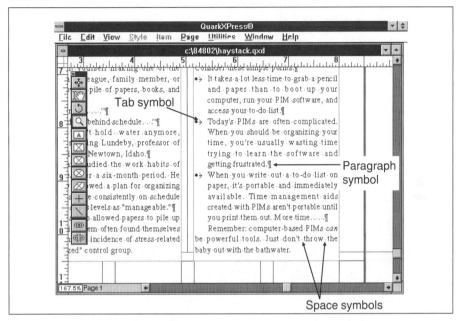

Space symbols

☐   If you already have worked in this text box during the current Quark session, the text cursor appears where you last left it. This handy "memory" feature can save you time during the layout process, when you often have to jump back and forth between text boxes or between text and picture boxes.

Perhaps the point at which the cursor appears is not where you want to begin editing. If so, click again in front of the desired character to select the correct insertion point.

Moving the Text Cursor

Quark provides a number of shortcuts for moving the text cursor during editing. You can quickly jump between characters, words, lines, paragraphs, or even linked text boxes using the key combinations given in Table 5-1.

TABLE
5-1

Moving the Text Cursor: Keyboard Shortcuts

To Move the Text Cursor	Press
Backward one character	LEFT ARROW
Forward one character	RIGHT ARROW
To the previous word	CTRL-LEFT ARROW
To the next word	CTRL-RIGHT ARROW
To the previous line	UP ARROW
To the next line	DOWN ARROW
To the previous paragraph	CTRL-UP ARROW
To the next paragraph	CTRL-DOWN ARROW
To the start of current line	HOME or CTRL-ALT-LEFT ARROW
To the end of current line	END or CTRL-ALT-RIGHT ARROW
To the start of current story	CTRL-HOME or CTRL-ALT-UP ARROW
To the end of current story	CTRL-END or CTRL-ALT-DOWN ARROW

Moving the Text Cursor Between Text Boxes

Newsletters, magazines, newspapers, and other periodicals usually contain multiple stories. A typical story occupies multiple text boxes, which are linked either manually in document pages or automatically through master pages (see Chapter 3). Often, the next or previous text box in the linked chain of a story is on a different page. No problem! You can move the text cursor between linked text boxes using the same keyboard shortcuts you use when a story fits in a single text box. You can even use Quark's shortcuts to help you *find* the next link in the story chain.

For example, suppose the cursor is located on the last line of a text box, but the story continues on another page. If you press DOWN ARROW, Quark jumps automatically to the page and text box where the story continues.

TABLE 5-2 Selecting Text with Multiple Clicks

To Select	Click
One word (including punctuation)	Twice
The current line	Three times
The current paragraph	Four times
The current story	Five times

Selecting Text

In order to format a character, a word, a line, or an entire paragraph, you must first select the characters by highlighting them. Once again, Quark proves its flexibility by letting you choose between mouse techniques and keyboard shortcuts. Table 5-2 lists the mouse techniques for selecting blocks of text. As Figure 5-11 shows, one click places the text cursor, two clicks selects a word, three clicks selects an entire line, four clicks selects the current paragraph, and five clicks selects all of the text in the current story. Table 5-3 gives the keyboard shortcuts for extending a text selection.

FIGURE 5-11 Selecting characters automatically with the mouse

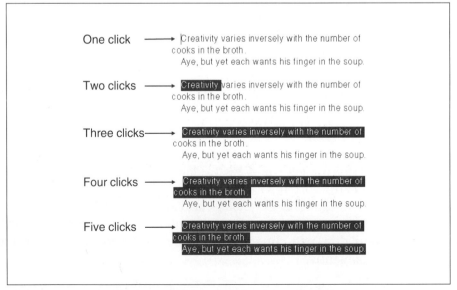

Extending Text Selection: Keyboard Shortcuts

To Extend the Current Selection to	Press
The previous character	SHIFT-LEFT ARROW
The next character	SHIFT-RIGHT ARROW
The previous word	CTRL-SHIFT-RIGHT ARROW
The next word	CTRL-SHIFT-RIGHT ARROW
The start of the current line	SHIFT-HOME or CTRL-ALT-SHIFT-LEFT ARROW
The end of the current line	SHIFT-END or CTRL-ALT-SHIFT-RIGHT ARROW
The previous line	SHIFT-UP ARROW
The next line	SHIFT-DOWN ARROW
The previous paragraph	CTRL-SHIFT-UP ARROW
The next paragraph	CTRL-SHIFT-DOWN ARROW
The beginning of the current story	CTRL-SHIFT-HOME or CTRL-ALT-SHIFT-UP ARROW
The end of the current story	CTRL-SHIFT-END or CTRL-ALT-SHIFT-DOWN ARROW
All the text in the current story	CTRL-A

Tip You can combine keyboard and mouse techniques to select text more quickly. For example, you might triple-click to select all the text on the current line and then press SHIFT-DOWN ARROW for each additional line that you want to select.

Deleting Text

There are several ways to delete text in Quark. Table 5-4 presents keyboard shortcuts for deleting a single character or a single word. If you need to delete larger blocks of text, first select them using any of the techniques pointed out in the previous section, "Selecting Text," and then press CTRL-X to cut the text to the clipboard or DEL to delete the text permanently.

TABLE 5-4   Deleting Text: Keyboard Shortcuts

To Delete	Press
The previous character	BACKSPACE
The next character	DELETE
The previous word	CTRL-DELETE
The next word	CTRL-SHIFT-DELETE
All highlighted text	DELETE

Typing Special Characters in Quark

Besides numbers and the familiar English alphabet, you can enter many additional characters in a text box. TrueType or Adobe Type 1 fonts that you install under Windows or Adobe Type Manager support the Windows character set, which includes many common symbols and foreign-language characters. Quark also directly supports a set of special typographical characters.

Using the Windows Character Set

It used to be that if you wanted to type a special foreign-language or symbol character in a Windows application, you had to press ALT and type a sequence of four numbers on your numeric keypad. Typing ALT-**0201** in most fonts, for example, yielded the foreign-language character É. This system worked fine, but all those characters were difficult to memorize, and having to frequently refer to command cards was tedious and time-consuming.

You can still use this method to enter characters from the Windows character set, but there is an easier way in Windows 3.1. Using Character Map, a little application in the Accessories group window, you can select a special character visually, copy it to the Windows clipboard in the desired font, and paste it directly into a Quark document. Character Map shows you the equivalent keystrokes for each character you select, so you no longer have to memorize to insert special characters. Here you see the Character Map window displaying the character set for the Times font; the Ä character is currently selected:

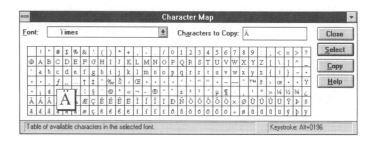

Consult Chapter 12 of your *Microsoft Windows User's Guide* to learn more about using Character Map to insert special characters into a Quark document.

Entering Quark Typographical Characters

QuarkXPress offers keyboard shortcuts for entering common typesetting characters such as the copyright symbol, bullets, and typographically correct single and double quotation marks. Table 5-5 lists these characters.

TABLE 5-5 Quark Typographical Characters

Character	Appearance	Key Combination
Open double quote	"	ALT-SHIFT-[
Close double quote	"	ALT-SHIFT-]
Open single quote	'	ALT-[
Close single quote	'	ALT-]
Registration mark	®	ALT-SHIFT-R
Copyright symbol	©	ALT-SHIFT-C
Section mark	§	ALT-SHIFT-6
Paragraph symbol	¶	ALT-SHIFT-7
Bullet	•	ALT-SHIFT-8

Entering Quark Formatting Characters

In addition to typesetting characters, you can also enter special formatting characters directly into a Quark text box. *Formatting characters* are spaces, hyphens, dashes, and invisible marker characters that help you fit copy and format text as you type. Table 5-6 lists these characters and the key combinations that you use to enter them. This section includes brief definitions of formatting characters with which you might not be familiar.

Indent Here   Inserting an Indent Here character (visible only when the Show Invisibles command in the View menu is active) causes all remain-

TABLE 5-6   Entering Formatting Characters: Keyboard Shortcuts

Formatting Character	Key Combination
Indent here	CTRL-\
New paragraph	ENTER
Discretionary new line	CTRL-ENTER
New line	SHIFT-ENTER
Jump to new column	Numeric keypad ENTER
Jump to new text box	SHIFT-numeric keypad ENTER
Right-indent tab stop	SHIFT-TAB
Nonbreaking hyphen	CTRL-SHIFT- -
Discretionary (soft) hyphen	CTRL- -
Nonbreaking en dash	CTRL-=
Em dash	CTRL-SHIFT-=
Nonbreaking em dash	CTRL-ALT-SHIFT-=
Nonbreaking space	CTRL-SPACEBAR
En space	CTRL-SHIFT-6
Nonbreaking en space	CTRL-ALT-SHIFT-6
Flex space	CTRL-SHIFT-5
Nonbreaking flex space	CTRL-ALT-SHIFT-5
Punctuation space	SHIFT-SPACEBAR
Nonbreaking punctuation space	CTRL-SHIFT-SPACEBAR

ing lines in the current paragraph to left-align at the location of the indent. Use this formatting character together with a nonbreaking en or em space to create an outdented head (Figure 5-12 shows an example of this).

New Line, Discretionary New Line   Entering the new line code causes the current line to break. Entering a discretionary new line character tells Quark to break the line at that point only if necessary for copyfitting purposes.

Right-Indent Tab Stop   Insert this invisible character to align the rest of the text on the same line with the right indent for the current paragraph.

Nonbreaking and Discretionary Hyphens   Entering an invisible nonbreaking hyphen character tells Quark not to break the word at that point, even for copyfitting purposes. The discretionary hyphen, on the other hand, tells Quark exactly where to break a word if necessary to fit copy.

FIGURE 5-12   Creating an outdented head using invisible formatting characters

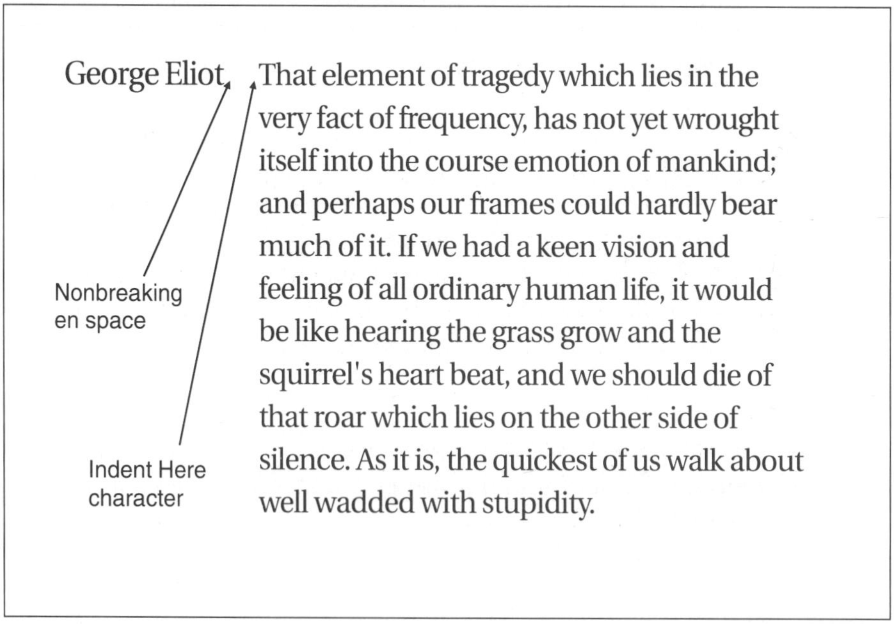

Em Dash, Nonbreaking Em Dash, Nonbreaking En Dash   An *em dash* is a dash that is as wide as two zeros (00) in the current font. Em dashes commonly appear as punctuation marks in the midst of sentences—here, for instance. Enter a nonbreaking em dash if you do not want to let Quark break a line at that point.

An *en dash* is half the width of an em dash, but visibly wider than a hyphen. Use it instead of a hyphen to label figure numbers, table numbers, and page numbers in books and manuals (examples: Figure 3–17, Page 3–12). An en dash in Quark is always nonbreaking; Quark does not break a word at that point, even if it falls at the end of a line of text.

Nonbreaking Space   Insert a nonbreaking space character between two words that you do not want Quark to separate at the end of a line. Titles and place names, for example (Dr. Dogood, New York), should always remain together.

En Space, Nonbreaking En Space, Em Space   An *en space* is equal to the space taken up by a zero (0) in the current font. Use it to separate two words on the same line by a visible amount. A nonbreaking en space prevents Quark from breaking a line where the en space occurs.

Quark provides no special character for entering an em space, which equals the width of two zeros in the current font. To enter the equivalent of an em space manually, simply type the code for an en space twice.

Flex Space, Nonbreaking Flex Space   In addition to all the fixed-width spaces used by traditional typographers, QuarkXPress lets you define and enter a variable-size space known as a *flex space*, or flexible space. You define the width of a flex space for the current document in the Typographical Preferences dialog box (Preferences/Typographic command, Edit menu). By entering a nonbreaking flex space, you tell Quark to not break the line at that point.

Punctuation Space, Nonbreaking Punctuation Space   A *punctuation space* separates a punctuation mark from the character immediately before it. A nonbreaking punctuation space does not break if it falls at the end of a line.

Formatting Text: An Overview

There are three ways to format text in QuarkXPress:

- ☐ *On the character level*, by editing specific attributes of selected characters only

- ☐ *On the paragraph level*, by editing specific attributes of a selected paragraph

- ☐ *Automatically*, by applying style sheets that affect *all* the attributes of an entire paragraph

This chapter focuses on techniques for locally formatting selected text on the character level—a common word processing operation. Chapter 6 shows you how to format text on the paragraph level and how to create, edit, and apply style sheets.

In formatting text as in other areas, Quark gives you a choice. You can change most character attributes using various commands in the Style menu, the Character Attributes dialog box, controls in the Measurements palette, or key commands. Each of these methods has special advantages, listed here:

- ☐ Use individual commands in the upper part of the Style menu (Font, Size, Style, and so on) when you want to alter only one type of character attribute at a time. As shown in Figure 5-13, the commands above the dividing line apply to selected characters only, while the commands in the lower part of the menu apply to an entire paragraph.

- ☐ Choose the Character command in the Style menu (keyboard shortcut: CTRL-SHIFT-D) when you want to edit several character attributes at once. The following shows the Character Attributes dialog box that you use for this purpose:

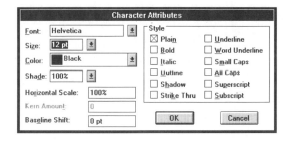

☐   Use the Measurements palette when you want controls to be always visible and easy to reach.

☐   Use key commands to carry out character formatting operations quickly without the use of the mouse.

Try each to see which technique seems most intuitive to you and then use it regularly.

     Note   Style menu commands are available for text only when a text box is active and the Content tool is selected.

FIGURE
5-13
Style menu commands for character and paragraph formatting

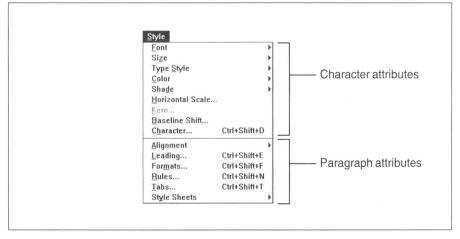

Formatting Text at the Character Level

The Font, Size, Type Style, Color, Shade, Horizontal Scale, Kern, Baseline Shift, and Character commands in the Style menu affect the appearance of only those characters that are currently selected (as opposed to the commands in the lower part of the Style menu, which affect the formatting of entire paragraphs in which text is selected).

In most cases, menu commands are not your only options for editing character attributes. You can also use the Measurements Palette, the Character Attributes dialog box, and keyboard shortcuts.

Changing the Font

To change the font in which selected text appears, use the Font command, the Character Attributes dialog box, or the font field in the Measurements palette.

Using the Font Command To change the font of selected text, choose the Font command in the Style menu. A submenu of the fonts currently installed in your system appears with the current font checked, as shown in Figure 5-14. If there are more fonts installed than will fit in the first list, highlighting the More command brings into view additional submenus.

 Note QuarkXPress for Windows supports both TrueType and Adobe Type 1 fonts. If you have some of each, all font names appear in the Font submenu and in the Measurements palette.

Using the Character Attributes Dialog Box To change the font of selected text using the Character Attributes dialog box, press CTRL-SHIFT-D. When the dialog box appears, use the Font drop-down list box to select the new font.

Using the Measurements Palette To change the font of selected text using the Measurements palette, click the drop-down list symbol next to the font field. The list of currently available fonts pops up, as shown here:

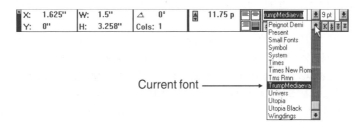

Highlight the desired font and then release the mouse button.

Changing Point Size

Quark lets you change the point size of selected text using the Size command, the Character Attributes dialog box, the Measurements palette, or special keyboard shortcuts.

The pop-out Font submenu

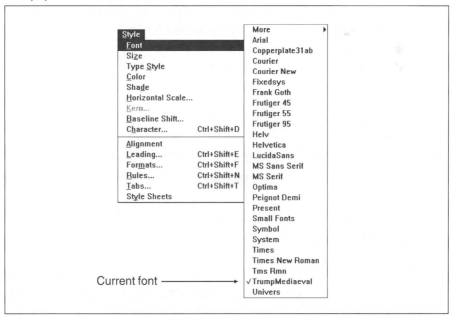

Using the Size Command   To change the point size of selected text using menu commands, choose the Size command in the Style menu. A submenu of preset font sizes pops out, as shown in Figure 5-15.

Click the desired font size. If you want to specify a font size that does not appear in the list, choose the Other option or press CTRL-SHIFT-\. The Font Size dialog box appears, as shown here:

Type the desired size (in points) in the Font Size field and press ENTER.

Using the Character Attributes Dialog Box   To change the point size of selected text using the Character Attributes dialog box, press CTRL-SHIFT-D to access the dialog box. Choose a preset font size from the Size drop-down list, or type a specific point size in the Size field.

Using the Measurements Palette   Two techniques are available for changing the point size of selected text using the Measurements palette. To choose a preset point size, click the drop-down list arrow in the

FIGURE 5-15   The pop-out Size submenu

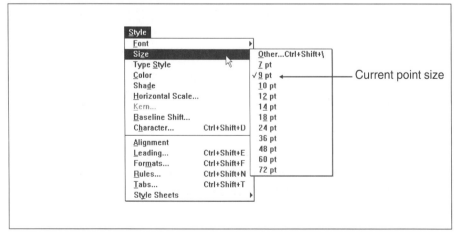

Measurements palette and highlight the desired point size from the list that appears, as shown here:

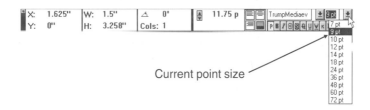

Current point size

To specify a point size that does not appear in the list, double-click the current number in the Point Size field and type a new value in its place.

Using Key Commands to Change Point Size   Quark lets you change the point size of selected text while you watch. Use the key commands in Table 5-7 to change point size either one point at a time or in preset increments. If the Measurements palette is visible, the font size value changes each time you invoke the keystrokes.

Applying Type Styles

QuarkXPress makes 13 different type styles available: Plain, Bold, Italic, Underline, Word Underline, Strike Thru, Outline, Shadow, All Caps, Small Caps, Superscript, Subscript, and Superior. Figure 5-16 shows examples of each type style's appearance. Apply a type style using either menu commands, the Measurements palette, or keyboard shortcuts.

TABLE
5-7

Changing the Point Size of Selected Text Interactively: Keyboard Shortcuts

If You Want To	Press
Increase font size in preset increments	CTRL-SHIFT->
Decrease font size in preset increments	CTRL-SHIFT-<
Increase font size 1 point at a time	CTRL-ALT-SHIFT->
Decrease font size 1 point at a time	CTRL-ALT-SHIFT-<

Quark Type Styles

Plain text	<u>Word Underline</u>
Bold text	Sᴍᴀʟʟ Cᴀᴘꜱ ᴛᴇxᴛ
Italic text	ALL CAPS TEXT
Outline text	Superscript ᵗᵉˣᵗ
Shadow text	Subscript ₜₑₓₜ
~~Strikethrough text~~	Superior ᵗᵉˣᵗ
<u>Underlined text</u>	

Tip   To remove styling from text to which you have already applied one or more style attributes, apply the Plain style.

Using the Type Style Command   To change the type style of selected text using a menu command, choose the Type Style command in the Style menu. A submenu containing a list of available type styles pops out, as shown in Figure 5-17.

A check mark appearing in the Type Style submenu indicates that all the selected characters share that style. Click the desired style name to apply it.

Applying Multiple Type Styles with the Character Attributes Dialog Box   When you want to apply more than one style at a time to selected text, use the Character Attributes dialog box. Press CTRL-SHIFT-D

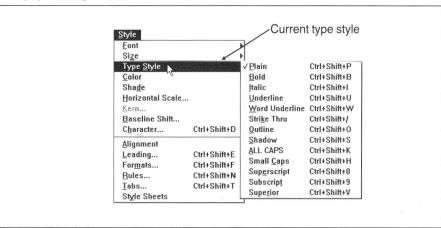

FIGURE	The pop-out Style submenu
5-17	

to display the dialog box, and then activate each check box in the Style area that represents a style you want to apply.

Using the Measurements Palette   Along the lower-right edge of the Measurements palette is a series of *style buttons* (shown in Figure 5-18); when you click a style button it becomes highlighted and applies that style to selected text. If you click a style button that is already highlighted, Quark removes that style attribute from selected text.

Using Keyboard Shortcuts   Table 5-8 lists the keyboard shortcuts for applying various type styles to selected text. These shortcuts also appear in the Type Style submenu next to each style name.

Changing Text Color

Change the color of currently selected characters by choosing the Color command in the Style menu or applying a color from the Colors palette. Chapter 10 gives more information about defining and applying color in QuarkXPress.

FIGURE
5-18

Style buttons in the Measurements palette

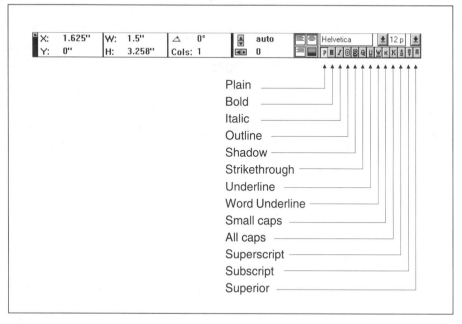

Plain
Bold
Italic
Outline
Shadow
Strikethrough
Underline
Word Underline
Small caps
All caps
Superscript
Subscript
Superior

TABLE
5-8

Applying Type Styles: Keyboard Shortcuts

To Apply This Style	Press
Plain (nullifies all styles)	CTRL-SHIFT-P
Bold	CTRL-SHIFT-B
Italic	CTRL-SHIFT-I
Underline (words and spaces)	CTRL-SHIFT-U
Word Underline (words only)	CTRL-SHIFT-W
Strike Thru	CTRL-SHIFT-/
Outline	CTRL-SHIFT-O
Shadow	CTRL-SHIFT-S
All Caps	CTRL-SHIFT-K
Small Caps	CTRL-SHIFT-H
Superscript	CTRL-SHIFT-0
Subscript	CTRL-SHIFT-9
Superior	CTRL-SHIFT-V

Using the Color Command   To change the color of selected text characters, choose the Color command in the Style menu. A submenu of the currently available colors pops up; click the desired color to apply it.

Using the Colors Palette   To apply a color to selected characters using the Colors palette, follow these steps:

1. Display the palette by choosing the Colors command in the Edit menu.

2. Click the text icon in the Colors palette to switch to text color mode. A list of the currently available colors appears, as shown here:

3. Click the color you want to apply. If it is not visible in the list, use the vertical scroll bar until it comes into view.

Changing the Shade of Text

In addition to applying a color to selected text, you can vary the *shade* or tint of that color. Use either the Shade command in the Style menu or the Colors palette. Chapter 10 gives more information about shading text and other items.

Using the Shade Command   To alter the shade of currently selected text in the current color, choose the Shade command in the Style menu. A submenu pops out containing preset shades in 10-percent increments; a check mark appears in front of the current shade, as shown in Figure 5-19.

Click the desired increment to apply that shade immediately.

The pop-out Shade submenu

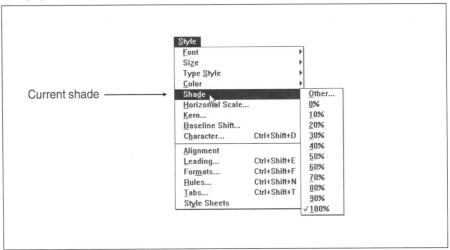

Current shade ─────────────→

If you want to apply a shade in a custom percentage, click the Other command in the Shade submenu. The Shade dialog box appears, with the current shade highlighted, as shown here:

Enter the desired percentage in the Shade field and click OK.

Using the Colors Palette   To change the current shade of selected characters using the Colors palette, follow these steps:

1. Display the palette by choosing the Show Colors command in the Edit menu.

2. Click the text icon in the Colors palette to switch to text color mode.

3. Click the Shades drop-down list box to make a list of preset shades appear, as shown here:

4. Click the desired shade percentage. If you prefer to specify a custom percentage, double-click the current value in the shades field and enter a replacement value.

Horizontal Scale: Expanding or Condensing Character Width

Every text character has a predefined width based on its font and point size. Quark's *horizontal scaling* feature lets you alter that width—expanding or condensing selected characters in terms of a percentage of normal character width. Just imagine the special effects you can create in headlines and advertisements!

Using the Horizontal Scale Command To expand or condense the horizontal scale of selected text, choose the Horizontal Scale command in the Style menu. The Horizontal Scale dialog box pops up, as shown here:

Type a percentage between 25 percent and 400 percent, using increments as small as .1 percent, and then press ENTER. The selected characters expand or condense as you have specified. Figure 5-20 shows examples of the same text at 100 percent (normal), 150 percent, and 50 percent horizontal scaling.

FIGURE
5-20

Expanding and contracting character widths with Horizontal Scaling

100% Horizontal Scaling

50% Horizontal Scaling

150% Horizontal Scaling

Using the Character Attributes Dialog Box When you want to edit more than one character attribute at a time, you can expand or condense selected characters using the Character Attributes dialog box. Press CTRL-SHIFT-D to access this dialog box, double-click the current value in the Horizontal Scale field, and enter a new value to replace it.

Adjusting Letter Spacing

Traditional typography has two closely related methods for adjusting letter spacing. *Kerning* means adjusting the amount of space between two text characters; *tracking* involves adjusting letter spacing among two or more characters by expanding or condensing the amount of space to the right of each character.

When using Quark as a word processor, most users focus on adjusting letter spacing for small numbers of selected characters—at the end of a line or after a drop cap, for example. What many don't realize is that QuarkXPress offers some of the most sophisticated kerning and tracking controls of any page layout package. See the "Advanced Typographic Controls" section of Chapter 6 to learn more about customizing kerning and tracking values for specific fonts, point sizes, and letter pairs.

To adjust letter spacing for selected text, use the Kern/Track command in the Style menu, the Kern Amount field in the Character Attributes dialog box, or the kerning and tracking controls in the Measurements palette. You can also adjust letter spacing interactively with keyboard shortcuts.

Using the Kern/Track Command   The Kern/Track command in the Style menu toggles according to the placement of the text cursor. When the cursor is *between* two characters with no text selected, the Kern command is available. When one or more characters are highlighted, the available command is Track. Choosing this command brings up the Kern Amount or Tracking dialog box (Tracking is shown here) with the current letter spacing value highlighted:

The default value of 0 indicates spacing defined by the characteristics of the current font. You can type an alternate value ranging from –100 to 100. Negative values decrease the amount of space between characters, while positive values increase it.

 Note   One kerning or tracking unit equals 1/200 of an em space. Quark defines an em space as the width of two zeros in a given font and at a given point size.

Using the Character Attributes Dialog Box   The Kern Amount field is available in the Character Attributes dialog box only when the blinking text cursor is positioned in a text box without any characters selected. To adjust kerning with this dialog box, click the space between letters that you want to adjust, and then press CTRL-SHIFT-D to access the Character Attributes dialog box. Double-click the current value in the Kern Amount field and enter a replacement value.

Using the Measurements Palette   The kerning and tracking control in the Measurements palette features a set of arrows, as shown here:

Kerning and tracking control

Clicking the right scroll arrow increases the kerning or tracking value in increments of ten (1/20 of an em space); clicking the left scroll arrow decreases the value in increments of ten. If you prefer to specify a smaller incremental change, double-click the current value and enter a new one in its place.

Using Key Commands   When the text cursor is between two letters or between a letter and a space, you can adjust kerning with the while-you-watch keyboard commands listed in Table 5-9. These key combinations also adjust tracking values when you select multiple characters.

Shifting the Baseline of Selected Text

Normally, the bottoms of text characters or their serifs align along an invisible baseline. With Quark, however, you can shift selected characters above or below their baseline to create special effects like the one shown in Figure 5-21. You can use the Shift Baseline command in the Style menu, the Character Attributes dialog box, or keyboard shortcuts.

TABLE 5-9

Adjusting Kerning and Tracking Values: Keyboard Shortcuts

To Adjust Letter Spacing By This Amount	Press
Increase by 1 unit (1/200 em)	CTRL-ALT-SHIFT-]
Increase by 10 units (1/20 em)	CTRL-SHIFT-]
Decrease by 1 unit (1/200 em)	CTRL-ALT-SHIFT-[
Decrease by 10 units (1/20 em)	CTRL-SHIFT-[

Shifting the baseline of text characters to create special effects

Using the Shift Baseline Command   To shift the baseline of currently selected characters, choose the Baseline Shift command in the Style menu and enter a value in the Baseline Shift dialog box that appears:

Negative values shift text below the baseline, while positive values move text above it.

Using the Character Attributes Dialog Box   Another way to shift the baseline of selected text is to type a point value in the Baseline Shift field of the Character Attributes dialog box (accessed by pressing CTRL-SHIFT-D).

Shifting Baselines Interactively   You can also shift the baseline of selected text interactively: just press CTRL-ALT-SHIFT-) to shift characters upward one point at a time and CTRL-ALT-SHIFT-(to shift characters downward one point at a time.

Accessing Character Formatting Commands: Keyboard Shortcuts

You can invoke several of the most important character formatting commands in the Style menu commands using key combinations. Table 5-10 lists these commands and the keyboard shortcuts that access the dialog boxes associated with them.

Using Quark's Search and Replace Features

The ability to find or find and replace words, characters, and blocks of text in a document is a primary feature of any word processor worth its salt. QuarkXPress takes this ability several steps further than most word processors. With the Find/Change command in the Edit menu (keyboard shortcut: CTRL-F), you can search and replace not only text, but also text attributes. You can search for specific or general instances of a font, a point size, or a type style, either in conjunction with text or independently of it. Quark also lets you specify *where* to search: on master pages, from the text cursor to the end of the current story, throughout the entire current story, or throughout the document.

TABLE 5-10 Character Formatting Commands in the Style Menu: Keyboard Shortcuts

To Invoke This Style Menu Command	Press
Size/Other	CTRL-SHIFT-\
Style	see Table 5-8
Character	CTRL-SHIFT-D

Telling Quark Where to Search

Although options in the Find/Change dialog box tell QuarkXPress *what* to search for, you can speed the search by determining *where* Quark will search even before you display the dialog box. You have four choices: the entire document, the current story, from a given point to the end of the current story, and master pages.

Searching the Entire Document

To search the active document from beginning to end, make sure no text box is currently selected.

Searching the Entire Story

Documents that contain multiple stories usually contain one or more automatic text chains that link several text boxes together (see Chapter 3). In order to search an entire story, the Content tool should be active and the text cursor should be blinking in front of the very *first* character in the first text box of the chain.

Searching from Cursor to End of Story

To have Quark search from a certain point onward, have the Content tool active and place the text cursor where you want the search to begin. Quark searches from that point forward to the end of the current story—that is, to the end of the last text box in the current text chain.

Searching Master Pages

QuarkXPress can search and replace text found on master pages as well as on document pages. Since master page text is repeating text, any changes will take effect in all associated document pages (there are a few exceptions; see Chapter 3). To prepare Quark for searching master page text, display the first master page in the document using either the Display command in the Page menu or the Document Layout palette in master page mode. If you want Quark to search all available master pages, make sure no text box is selected when you invoke the Find/Change command. To search a specific text box, display the desired master page and select the text box with the Content tool.

The Find/Change Dialog Box

To begin a search and replace operation after determining where Quark should search, choose the Find/Change command in the Edit menu or use the keyboard shortcut, CTRL-F. If this is the first time you have performed a search, the Find/Change dialog box appears as shown here:

The Find/Change dialog box can wear many different faces. Quark "remembers" the options you selected the last time you used the dialog box and presents those options again the next time you display it. If this is your first search and replace operation, the default options are the ones shown in the previous illustration.

Note   The Find/Change dialog box has more in common with a palette than with a normal dialog box. It remains on the screen until you double-click its control menu icon to close it.

Finding or Replacing Text Only

The simplest thing you can do in the Find/Change dialog box is to find or search and replace occurrences of text, without regard to font, point size, or style.

Finding Text Only

To find a character, word, or block of text when you do not care about attributes, follow these steps:

1. Make sure that the Ignore Attributes check box is active.

2. In the Find What field, enter the text string you want to locate (up to 80 characters). If the number of characters in the text string exceeds the visible area of the Find What field, text scrolls automatically so you can see the last 32 characters.

3. If you want to locate the text string only if it is a complete word without letters or other characters on either side, activate the Whole Word check box. Choose this option if, for example, you are looking for the word "able" and do not want to locate words like "constable" or "agreeable," in which "able" is part of a larger word.

4. If you do not care whether the text that Quark finds has the same combination of uppercase and lowercase letters as the search string, make sure that the Ignore Case check box is active. Deactivate this check box if you want the case to match exactly—for example, "QuarkXPress" rather than "Quarkxpress."

5. Click the Find Next button to locate the next occurrence of the text string. Depending on how you opened the dialog box, Quark begins the search at the text cursor location, the beginning of the story, or at the beginning of the active document. Quark highlights the text string in the document as shown in Figure 5-22.

Note If no text box was selected when you displayed the Find/Change dialog box, the Find Next button is not available. Click the Document check box to confirm that you want to search from the beginning of the document. This action activates the Find Next button.

Tip To find the very first occurrence of a text string in a story (or document, if the Document check box is active), press CTRL as you click the Find Next button. The button changes to Find First, as shown here:

Find First

FIGURE
5-22

Quark displays and highlights the search string in the document

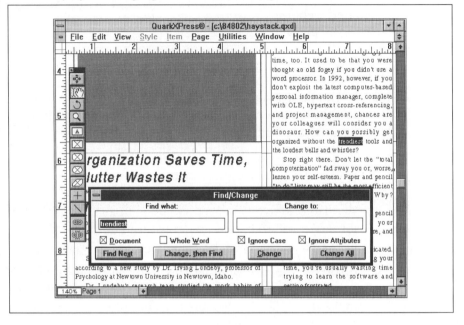

6. Continue clicking Find Next until you have located the text string you are seeking.

7. To close the dialog box, either double-click its control menu icon or click the icon once and choose Close.

Searching and Replacing Text Only

To search and replace a text string without regard for font, point size, or type style attributes, follow these steps:

1. Make certain that the Ignore Attributes check box is active.

2. In the Find What field, enter the text string you want to locate. The Find Next button becomes available.

3. Activate the Whole Word and Ignore Case check boxes, if desired.

4. In the Change To field, enter the replacement text string. This can be of any length. If you want to delete the search string, leave the Change To field blank.

5. Click the Find Next button (or Find First, if you press the CTRL key). As soon as Quark locates the search string, the three remaining command buttons in the dialog box—Change, Then Find, Change, and Change All—become available.

6. If the text highlighted in the document is not the instance you were looking for, click Find Next again. Otherwise, select one of these change options:

☐ *Change, then Find* causes Quark to replace the search string and then immediately find and display its next occurrence in the document.

☐ *Change* causes Quark to locate and highlight the search string and then change it to the replacement string while you watch. You do not move on to the next occurrence of the text string.

☐ *Change All* causes Quark to replace every occurrence of the search string. When all replacements have been made and there are no more occurrences of the search string, the three Change buttons become unavailable.

7. If you chose the Change option, continue clicking Find Next until you have replaced as many instances of the search string as necessary. If you chose the Change, then Find option, continue clicking Change, then Find, until you no longer wish to replace the search string.

8. Close the dialog box by double-clicking its control menu icon.

Finding or Replacing Text Attributes

When you deactivate the Ignore Attributes check box, the Find/Change dialog box expands to look like Figure 5-23. Use this "face" or mode of the dialog box to perform any of these tasks:

☐ Find or replace only those instances of a text string that appear in a specific font, point size, and/or type style

FIGURE
5-23

The Find/Change dialog box in attributes mode

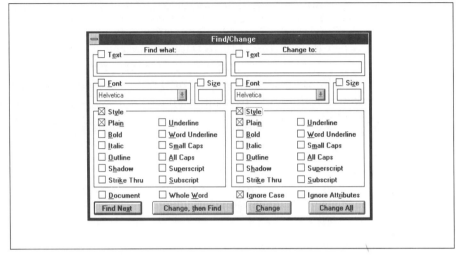

☐ Change both the content and the formatting of characters in a text string

☐ Reformat a text string without changing its content

Take a moment to become familiar with the dialog box in this configuration, and then go on to explore some examples of how to search and replace text attributes.

Text: The Find What and Change To Fields

Whoa! In attributes mode, the Find/Change dialog box no longer contains simple Find What and Change To fields. Instead, you can specify exactly what to find and to change. The Text field on the Find What side of the dialog box lets you specify the text string (if any) that you want to locate. To enter a search string here, first activate the Text check box. If you want to locate character attributes only (for example, instances of any text at all in boldface), leave the Text check box blank; the Text entry field then remains grayed and unavailable.

Use the Text field on the Change To side of the dialog box to specify the text string (if any) with which you want to replace the current Find What search string. You can enter a replacement text string here only if you first activate the Text check box. If you want to replace character attributes only, without changing the content of the text string on the Find What side of the dialog box, leave the Text check box blank and specify only a replacement font, point size, and/or type style. For example, if you wanted to locate a boldfaced company name and reformat it as bold italic in a different font, your options might look like the ones in Figure 5-24.

Font: The Find What and Change To Fields

To specify a font for Quark to locate, activate the Font check box on the left side of the Find/Change dialog box and then choose a font from the drop-down list box beneath. Notice that the list includes only the

FIGURE 5-24

Reformatting a search string without changing its content

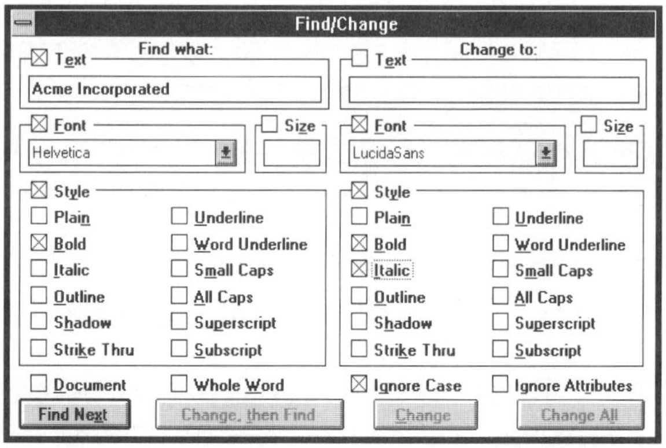

fonts used in the active document. A list box like the following, for example, indicates that only Helvetica, Times, and Symbol occur in the active document:

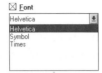

The Font list box on the Change To side of the dialog box behaves a little differently from its Find What counterpart. Activate this Font check box to specify a font that should reformat the current search string or replace the attributes on the Find What side of the dialog box. Then, choose a font from the drop-down list box beneath. Unlike the list box on the Find What side, this one includes all the fonts in your system. If you do not want to change any of the fonts on the Find What side of the dialog box, leave the Font check box on the Change To side of the dialog box blank.

Size: The Find What and Change To Fields

If the point size of the search string is important to you (or if you are looking for any text at all in a specific point size), activate the Size check box in the Find What area of the dialog box. Enter the exact point size in the field beneath this check box. If you leave the Size check box blank, you are telling Quark that point size is irrelevant in the search string.

The Size check box on the Change To side of the dialog box functions similarly. Activate it and enter a specific point size if you want to reformat the search string. If you do not want to alter the size of text in the search string, leave the Size check box blank.

Style: The Find What and Change To Fields

The check boxes in the Style areas of the dialog box let you find or replace instances of various type styles: bold, outline, shadow, and so on. If the Style check box on the Find What side of the dialog box is active, Quark will search out occurrences of any type styles next to which an x appears. If the Style check box on the Find What side of the dialog box is blank, type style is not a criterion in the search.

On the other hand, if the Style check box on the Change To side of the dialog box is active, Quark will reformat text in the search string according to the type styles that display an x. If the Style check box on the Change To side is blank, no reformatting of type styles takes place.

The various type style check boxes in the Style area behave a little differently from other check boxes in Quark. If you click a blank check box once, it turns gray. Click it again, and it turns into an x. Click it a third time, and it becomes blank again. These visual changes correspond to one of three different functions: Checked, Blank, and Solid Gray.

Checked—Find Me, Apply Me If a type style check box on the Find What side of the dialog box contains an x, Quark locates text with that style attribute. If a type style check box on the Change To side of the dialog box is checked, Quark applies that text style.

Blank—Don't Find Me, Unformat Me A blank type style check box on the Find What side of the dialog box indicates that Quark should *not* find text in that style. So far, so good. If a type style check box on the Change To side of the dialog box is blank, however, Quark will actually *remove* any such formatting in text that conforms to the search string.

For example, look at the options in Figure 5-25. Here, you are telling Quark to look for all instances of the word "zebra" that appear in italic. The Bold style check box in the Change To area of the dialog box is blank. This means that if Quark finds any instances of the word "zebra" that are bold as well as italic, the bold formatting will actually be removed.

Solid Gray—Ignore Me If a type style check box in the Find What area of the dialog box appears in solid gray, you are telling Quark to ignore that type style when searching for a text string. A gray type style check box in the Change To area of the dialog box indicates that Quark should likewise ignore that style when reformatting the search string. Quark will neither remove the type style nor apply it.

Look again at the example in Figure 5-25. On the Find What side of the dialog box, the Outline and Shadow type style check boxes are gray.

FIGURE 5-25

Gray style option check boxes indicate that Quark should ignore those style attributes when searching

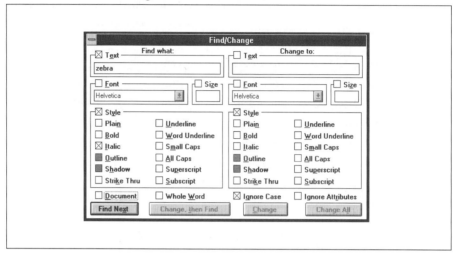

If any instances of the word "zebra" appears in one or both of these type styles, Quark will find it anyway. The Outline and Shadow type style check boxes on the Change To side of the dialog box are gray, too. Quark will not remove these type styles from any instances of the word "zebra" that it finds. Nor will Quark apply those type styles to instances that do not feature them already.

To summarize: if you want Quark to find something—be it a text string, a specific font, point size, or type style—make sure an x appears in the associated check box(es). If you want Quark *not* to find a certain attribute, leave its check box blank. And if you don't care whether a particular style attribute is present, click its check box until it is solid gray.

Searching and Replacing Special Characters

Quark can find and replace special formatting characters as well as "normal" text. Special characters include tabs, end of paragraph marks, and other such formatting symbols. Table 5-11 lists the characters you

| TABLE 5-11 | Finding and Replacing Special Characters in the Find/Change Dialog box |

To Enter This Character	Type
Tab	\t
New line symbol	\n
End of paragraph symbol	\p
New column symbol	\c
New text box symbol	\b
Previous text box page no.	\2
Current text box page no.	\3
Next text box page no.	\4
One-character wild card (Find what only)	\?
Backslash	\\

can enter in the Find What/Text and Change To/Text fields and how you should represent them. And, yes, you can search for the font, point size, and type style of these characters, too.

Condensing and Expanding the Find/Change Dialog Box

If you have anything smaller than a 20-inch monitor, you probably prefer to have palettes and dialog boxes take up as little room as possible. The developers at Quark had this in mind when they designed the Find/Change dialog box. Its control menu contains a toggle command that lets you shrink the dialog box down to size or expand it again with a single click.

To shrink the Find/Change dialog box when it looks like either Figure 5-22 or 5-25, click the control menu box and then the Condense command:

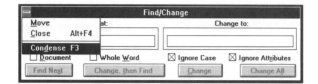

The dialog box collapses to a tiny rectangle in which nothing remains but the four find/change command buttons shown here:

When the dialog box is condensed, you cannot change any of your current search and replace options. The best time to shrink it, then, is when you intend to reuse the current options again and again. Of course, you can easily restore the dialog box to its former size if you need to edit your options. Simply click the control menu again and choose the Expand command.

Using the Spell Checker

No word processor should be without a spell checking dictionary. Quark has one—80,000 words worth, in fact—and you can create and edit up to 127 additional auxiliary dictionaries for specific document projects.

To check spelling, choose the Check Spelling command in the Utilities menu. A pop-up submenu appears, as shown here:

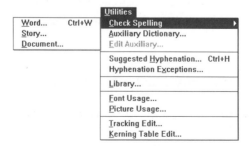

You can check the spelling of the currently selected word, the current story, or the entire document.

Checking the Spelling of a Word

To check the spelling of a single word, follow these steps:

1. Select the word, either by highlighting it or by placing the text cursor anywhere within the word.

2. Choose the Check Spelling/Word command from the Utilities menu, or use the keyboard shortcut, CTRL-W. The Check Word dialog box appears, displaying all the words in the Quark dictionary that are similar to the selected "Suspect" word:

3. If the selected word appears in the list and is highlighted, Quark recognizes it as the correct word. Click Cancel or press ESC to exit the dialog box.

4. If the selected word does not appear in the list, scroll through the list until you find a replacement that fits. Click that word to highlight it and then click the Replace button. The Check Word dialog box disappears from the screen.

5. If the dictionary contains no words similar to the one you have selected, a "No similar words found" message appears in the dialog box. Click Cancel to close the dialog box.

Checking Spelling for a Story

As you already know from Chapter 3, a story is any series of linked text boxes. To check spelling for a single story in a document that contains more than one text file, follow these steps:

1. Activate any text box in the story using the Content tool.

2. Choose the Check Spelling command in the Utilities menu and click the Story option, or use the keyboard shortcut, CTRL-ALT-W. After a moment, the Word Count dialog box appears, showing the total number of words in the story, the number of unique (different) words, and the number of words with questionable or suspect spellings, as shown here:

3. Click OK. If there are any suspect words in the story, the Check Story dialog box appears, with the first suspect word (and the number of times it appears, if it appears more than once) at the top of the dialog box like this:

Quark also highlights the suspect word in the active document window.

4. You now have four options.

   ❏ If you know the proper spelling for the suspect word, enter it in the Replace With field and then click the Replace button. Quark substitutes the word into the story, and the Check Story dialog box disappears.

   ❏ If you do not know the correct spelling of the word, click the Lookup button to have Quark present a list of similar alternatives in the list box. Choose one of the alternative spellings by highlighting it in the list and then clicking the Replace button.

☐   To save the suspect word in an auxiliary dictionary (see "Creating Custom Dictionaries" near the end of this chapter), click the Keep command button. This option is available only if an auxiliary dictionary is already open.

☐   To move on to the next suspect word without correcting this one, click the Skip command button.

If there are additional suspect words in the story, Quark displays them one by one. You can continue checking these words until no more suspect words remain. At that point, the Check Story dialog box disappears.

Checking Spelling Document-Wide

To check spelling throughout a document, no matter how many dependent stories it contains, choose the Check Spelling command from the Utilities menu and click the Document option. As with the Check Story option, Quark displays the Word Count dialog box and then checks all suspect words. The Check Document dialog box used for this purpose closely resembles the Check Story dialog box.

Checking Spelling on Master Pages

To check the spelling of all text on master pages, display a master page using either the Display command in the Page menu or the Document Layout palette. After making sure that the Content tool is active, choose the Check Spelling command from the Utilities menu and click the Masters option, which replaces the Document option, as shown here:

Quark checks both word count and all suspect words, just as when spell checking a story or document pages.

Creating Custom Dictionaries

Quark does not allow users to alter the standard dictionary. Instead, you can create *auxiliary dictionaries* and save specialized words in them. Only one auxiliary dictionary can be open at a time. However, Quark remembers which auxiliary dictionary you last used with a particular document, and opens that dictionary with the document until you create or begin using a different auxiliary dictionary.

Creating or Opening an Auxiliary Dictionary

To create a new auxiliary dictionary, follow these steps:

1. Open the document with which you want to associate a new dictionary.

2. Choose the Auxiliary Dictionary command from the Utilities menu. The dialog box in Figure 5-26 appears.

3. Use the Drives and Directories list boxes to locate the drive and directory where you want to store the new dictionary file. It is usually best to store it with the document file so Quark can locate it for future sessions.

FIGURE 5-26   The Auxiliary Dictionary dialog box

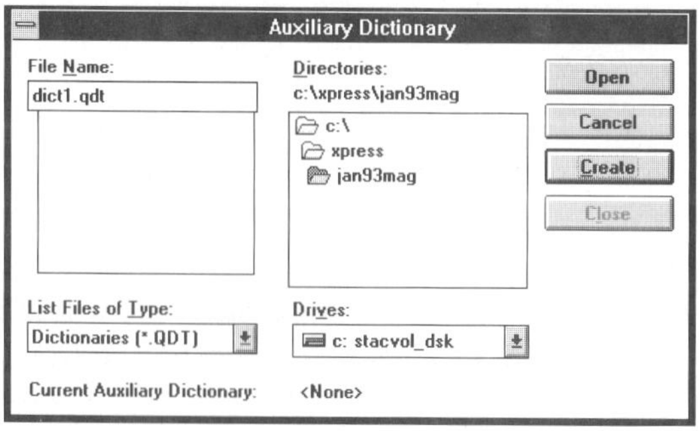

4. In the Files list box, type the name of the new dictionary and then press ENTER. Quark adds the identifying extension .qdt automatically.

A new auxiliary dictionary file contains no words. You add words either by clicking the Keep button while in the Check Story, Check Document, or Check Masters dialog box, or by choosing the Edit Auxiliary command in the Utilities menu.

To open an existing auxiliary dictionary follow these steps:

1. Choose the Auxiliary Dictionary command in the Utilities menu to display the Auxiliary Dictionary dialog box.

2. Locate the drive and directory where the desired dictionary file (.qdt) is stored.

3. Double-click the filename to open it.

Editing an Auxiliary Dictionary

To edit an existing auxiliary dictionary directly, make sure the dictionary is open and then choose the Edit Auxiliary command from the Utilities menu. The Edit Auxiliary Dictionary dialog box appears, as shown here:

Adding a New Word   To add a new word to the current auxiliary dictionary, type the word in the blank text field and then click the Add button.

Deleting a Word from the Auxiliary Dictionary   To delete a word from the current auxiliary dictionary, use the scroll list until the desired word comes into view. Highlight it with the mouse and then click the Delete button.

Saving the Dictionary   When you are finished editing the dictionary, click the Save button to retain your changes.

 Caution   Quark cannot accept certain characters in an auxiliary dictionary. If a word contains accented foreign-language characters (é or ä, for example), hyphens, punctuation marks, or blank spaces, Quark will highlight the offending character and refuse to accept the word into the dictionary.

If you think Quark is full-featured as a word processor, just wait until you get a feel for the magic of automatic formatting through style sheets. Chapter 6 contains a wealth of information on formatting paragraph attributes, developing and editing style sheets, and achieving typographical special effects.

CHAPTER

Style Sheets and Typographic Controls

The format of text in a document is inseparable from design and layout issues. In QuarkXPress, you can format text either locally—at the character or paragraph level—or automatically using style sheets. Chapter 5 dealt with text formatting at the character level during the normal course of word processing.

In this chapter, you will explore more sophisticated text formatting techniques: local paragraph formatting, style sheets, and advanced hyphenation, justification, kerning, and tracking options. If you prefer to format text locally, you can always assign attributes such as leading, alignment, tab stops, and rules to the currently selected paragraph or paragraphs. If you use Quark regularly, take advantage of style sheets, which assign *sets* of character and paragraph attributes to text automatically. You'll learn how to master stylesheets in this chapter.

Formatting Text on the Paragraph Level

Text attributes such as alignment, linc spacing, tab stops, and indents affect an entire paragraph, not just the characters that are highlighted. To select a paragraph in order to assign attributes to it, either position the text cursor anywhere in the paragraph or highlight one or more characters in the paragraph. If characters in more than one paragraph are highlighted when you edit paragraph attributes, Quark applies new formatting to all paragraphs in which at least some text is selected.

Quark provides several alternative techniques for applying most paragraph attributes. The Alignment, Leading, Rules, and Tabs commands in the Style menu let you change single attributes of the currently selected paragraph(s). The Paragraph Formats dialog box, accessed through the Formats command in the Style menu, is handy when you need to edit several attributes of a paragraph at one time. The Measurements palette is convenient if you prefer to have controls always visible.

Setting Indents

An *indent* in QuarkXPress is the distance by which you offset a paragraph or line of text from the margin of the text box. To set indents for the currently selected paragraph, choose the Formats command in the Style menu (keyboard shortcut: CTRL-SHIFT-F) to access the Paragraph Formats dialog box shown in Figure 6-1. You can use either the ruler or the Left Indent, First Line, and Right Indent options in this dialog box to specify indents. The ruler is an intuitive visual aid, while the three indent options let you specify indent values precisely.

Left Indent, First Line, and Right Indent Options

To set indent values precisely for the currently selected paragraph(s), follow these steps:

1. Choose the Formats command from the Style menu or use the keyboard shortcut, CTRL-SHIFT-F. The Paragraph Formats dialog box appears, with the Left Indent field already highlighted.

2. To replace the current Left Indent value, enter a new one in the Left Indent field. You can enter positive values in increments as small as .001 of any unit of measurement. Quark translates your value into the unit of measurement currently specified for Horizontal Measure in the General Preferences dialog box.

The Paragraph Formats dialog box

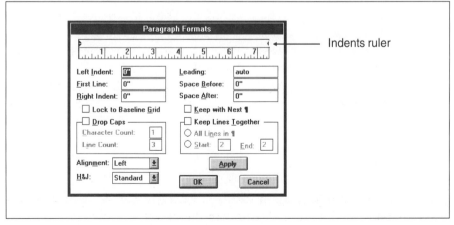

3. To change the top line indent, double-click the current value in the First Line field and replace it. Keep these guidelines in mind:

❑ With a first line indent of zero, the first line of the paragraph aligns with all the other lines in the paragraph, as shown in the first paragraph in Figure 6-2. There is no indent.

❑ A positive first line indent value indents the first line to the *right* of the other lines in the paragraph, as shown in the second paragraph in Figure 6-2. This is a common setting for body text paragraphs in periodicals and long documents.

❑ A negative first line indent value creates a *hanging indent*: the first line of the paragraph falls to the left of the other lines in the paragraph, as shown in the third paragraph in Figure 6-2. A negative first line indent value cannot exceed the current Left Indent value, because you cannot place text outside the text box.

FIGURE 6-2   Creating block paragraphs, paragraph indents, and hanging indents with the First Line indent option

First line indent: 0" ⟶   If we had a keen vision and feeling of all ordinary human life, it would be like hearing the grass grow and the squirrel's heart beat, and we should die of that roar which lies on the other side of silence. As it is, the quickest of us walk about well wadded with stupidity.

First line indent: 0.5" ⟶   If we had a keen vision and feeling of all ordinary human life, it would be like hearing the grass grow and the squirrel's heart beat, and we should die of that roar which lies on the other side of silence. As it is, the quickest of us walk about well wadded with stupidity.

First line indent: −0.5" ⟶   If we had a keen vision and feeling of all ordinary human life, it would be like hearing the grass grow and the squirrel's heart beat, and we should die of that roar which lies on the other side of silence. As it is, the quickest of us walk about well wadded with stupidity.

4. To offset a paragraph from the right margin of its text box, double-click the Right Indent field and enter a new positive value there.

Setting Indents Interactively with the Ruler

The ruler at the top of the Paragraph Formats dialog box represents the width of the text box in which the cursor or currently selected paragraph is located. If the text box is so wide at the current viewing magnification that the ruler does not fit completely within the dialog box, a scroll arrow appears at either end of the ruler, as shown here:

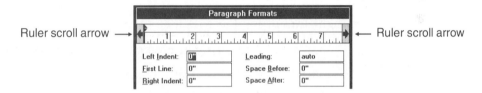

You can view areas of the ruler that are out of range by clicking or pressing the scroll arrow that points in the direction you want to view.

This ruler contains three triangle-shaped markers that you can move to set a left indent, first line indent, and right indent for the currently selected paragraph(s), as shown here:

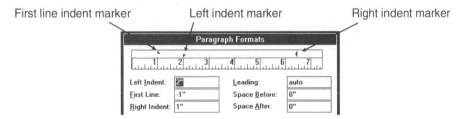

To set indents for a paragraph using the ruler in the Paragraph Formats dialog box, follow these steps:

1. With one or more paragraphs selected, press CTRL-SHIFT-F to access the Paragraph Formats dialog box.

2. Set the left indent first by dragging the lower-left triangle to the desired position. The upper-left triangle marker moves with it automatically. As you drag, the precise position of the indent appears in the Left Indent field of the dialog box.

3. Next, set the first line indent (if any) by dragging the upper-left triangle marker to the desired position. The First Line field in the dialog box displays the position of the indent as you drag.

Tip   If you later adjust the left indent, you will need to readjust the first line indent, too, because the first line indent marker always moves with the left indent marker. You can always adjust the first line indent marker by itself, though.

4. Finally, set the right indent (if any) by dragging the large triangle at the right edge of the ruler to the desired position. The value in the Right Indent field of the dialog box changes as you drag the marker.

Note   To align all remaining text in a paragraph at the location of the text cursor while typing, enter the Indent Here character (CTRL-\). The Indent Here character (described in the "Entering Formatting Characters" section of Chapter 5) lets you quickly create outdented heads and hanging indents in the current paragraph.

Specifying Leading

You will remember from Chapter 4 that leading is the amount of space between lines in a paragraph. Along with kerning and tracking, leading is the attribute that determines whether text in a paragraph looks well spaced, too tight, or too loose. Figure 6-3 shows examples of paragraphs set in the same font and at the same point size, but with different leading increments.

Let the design of a document and the font you are using for a particular paragraph determine what looks right in each case.

Quark's Leading Modes

Quark measures leading in one of two modes, depending on the current setting in the Typographic Preferences dialog box (see Chapter 4):

Paragraphs with different leading

Solid leading: 10/10
If we had a keen vision and feeling of all ordinary human life, it would be like hearing the grass grow and the squirrel's heart beat, and we should die of that roar which lies on the other side of silence. As it is, the quickest of us walk about well wadded with stupidity.

Auto leading: 10/12
If we had a keen vision and feeling of all ordinary human life, it would be like hearing the grass grow and the squirrel's heart beat, and we should die of that roar which lies on the other side of silence. As it is, the quickest of us walk about well wadded with stupidity.

Wide leading: 10/16
If we had a keen vision and feeling of all ordinary human life, it would be like hearing the grass grow and the squirrel's heart beat, and we should die of that roar which lies on the other side of silence. As it is, the quickest of us walk about well wadded with stupidity.

Typesetting Mode   In typesetting mode, the default, Quark measures the space between lines from baseline to baseline. This mode is the standard in commercial publishing.

Word Processing Mode   In word processing mode, Quark measures the space between lines from ascent to ascent—for example, from the top of a lowercase "h" in one line to the top of another "h" on the next.

Setting Leading for Best Results

Quark lets you specify leading as an absolute value, as an automatically adjusted value, or relative to the point size of the current font. Each method is best for certain kinds of documents.

Absolute Leading   Absolute leading means specifying interline spacing as an exact point size, such as 14 points. An absolute leading value is independent of the point size used in a paragraph. This can be a problem if you have to tweak point sizes frequently during the layout process, because the leading value does not change automatically with point size. Use this rule of thumb: describe leading in absolute terms for style sheets that you set up in advance and for which you expect few changes during the layout process. If you anticipate on-the-fly typography for a document, try auto leading or relative leading instead.

Auto Leading   *Auto leading*—Quark's default—expresses interline spacing as a percentage over and above the largest font used in a line of text. At Quark's preset auto leading value of 20 percent, a paragraph containing 10-point text would feature 12 points of space between each line, while paragraphs containing 20-point text would have 24 points of leading, and so on. The advantage of using auto leading is that you can change point sizes without having to readjust leading yourself; Quark does it for you.

Auto leading has two disadvantages, though. First, uneven line spacing can occur when some lines of text in a paragraph include in-line graphics or much larger fonts, as shown in Figure 6-4. More important, auto leading adds a *fixed* percentage to every font size—a real hindrance if you prefer to vary the proportions of leading for some paragraphs in a document.

Note   To change the current auto leading percentage throughout a document, open the document and choose the Preferences/Typographic command in the Edit menu. Edit the current percentage value in the Auto Leading field and click OK.

Relative Leading   Use *relative leading* for documents that are likely to require many formatting changes on the fly—you do not have to remember to adjust leading every time you change point size in a paragraph. To describe leading in relative terms, type a plus (+) or minus (–) sign before the leading value, like this:

In effect, you are adding a fixed number of points to the font size in the selected paragraph (or subtracting a fixed number of points from it). If

FIGURE 6-4 With auto leading, interline spacing adjusts for in-line graphics or larger fonts automatically

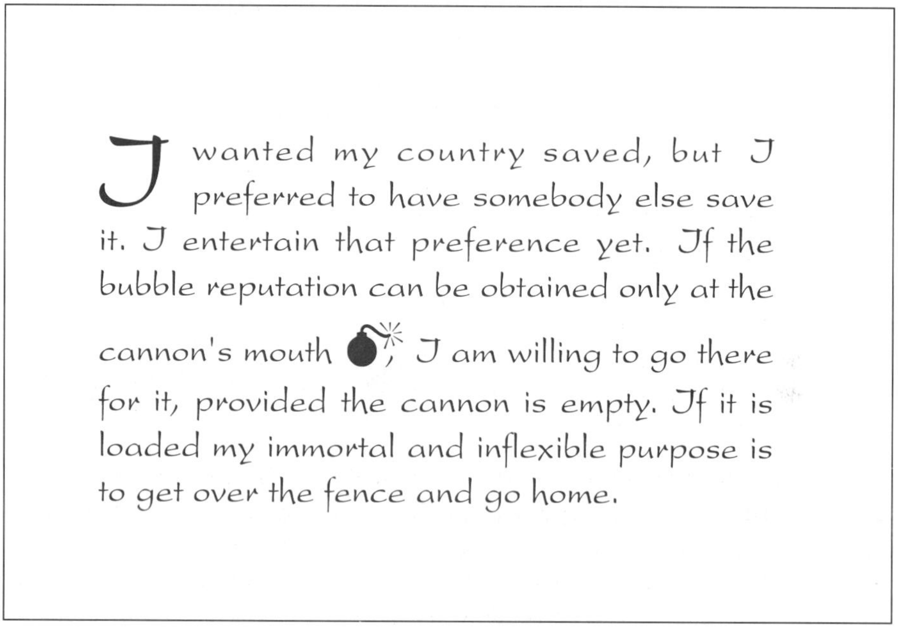

> J wanted my country saved, but J preferred to have somebody else save it. J entertain that preference yet. Jf the bubble reputation can be obtained only at the cannon's mouth 💣, J am willing to go there for it, provided the cannon is empty. Jf it is loaded my immortal and inflexible purpose is to get over the fence and go home.

you specify a leading value of +4 for 20-point text, for example, there will be 24 points of space between each line in the paragraph. Change the point size in that paragraph to 24 points, and interline spacing equals 28 points (24 + 4).

Quark lets you specify leading through the Leading command in the Style menu, the Paragraph Formats dialog box, the Measurements palette, and a group of keyboard shortcuts.

Using the Leading Command

Choose the Leading command in the Style menu (keyboard shortcut: CTRL-SHIFT-E) to specify leading for the currently selected paragraph(s). The Leading dialog box appears, with the current leading value highlighted, as shown here:

Type a replacement value in the Leading field and then click OK.

Using the Paragraph Formats Dialog Box

When editing more than one paragraph attribute at a time, you can specify leading in the Paragraph Formats dialog box. Press CTRL-SHIFT-F to access this dialog box, double-click the Leading field, and replace the current value with the desired one.

Using the Measurements Palette

The leading control in the Measurements palette lies just above the horizontal scaling control, as shown here:

Leading control

To increase leading one point at a time for the current paragraph(s), click the upper scroll arrow next to the leading field. To decrease leading one point at a time, click the lower scroll arrow. You can also specify a custom leading value (including auto) by double-clicking the current value and typing over it.

Note If more than one paragraph is highlighted and the leading field in the Measurements palette is blank, the selected paragraphs have different leading values.

Using Key Commands

Many people prefer to use keyboard shortcuts for just about everything. Fortunately, with Quark you can even specify leading using the keyboard. Table 6-1 lists the keyboard commands that let you adjust leading in preset increments.

Adjusting Spacing Between Paragraphs

Whereas leading controls the amount of space between lines of a paragraph, the Space Before and Space After options in the Paragraph Formats dialog box (CTRL-SHIFT-F) determine the amount of space between paragraphs. These values appear in the current unit of measurement; if you enter new values using a different measurement system, Quark translates them into the current system. Figure 6-5 shows interparagraph spacing when Space Before and Space After are at zero, contrasted with the same paragraphs when Space Before is set to 12 points.

Tip   The Space Before value does not affect the placement of a paragraph at the top of a column. To offset the first paragraph in a column from the top margin of the current text box, adjust the First Baseline value in the Text Box Specifications dialog box (CTRL-M).

Locking a Paragraph to the Baseline Grid

When activated, the Lock to Baseline Grid overrides any current leading values for the selected paragraph(s) and forces each line in the paragraph to align with the document's baseline grid. (You can display this grid by choosing the Show Baseline Grid command in the View menu.) If leading for the selected paragraph(s) is less than or equal to the

Adjusting Leading Interactively: Keyboard Shortcuts

To Adjust Leading This Way	Press
Increase leading in 1-point increments	CTRL-SHIFT-"
Increase leading in .1-point increments	CTRL-ALT-SHIFT-"
Decrease leading in 1-point increments	CTRL-SHIFT-:
Decrease leading in .1-point increments	CTRL-ALT-SHIFT-:

FIGURE
6-5

The Space Before and Space After settings control spacing between paragraphs

L orem ipsum dolor sit amet, consectetuer adipiscing elit, sed diam nonummy nibh euismod tincidunt ut laoreet dolore magna aliquam erat voluptat.

Ut wisi enim ad minim veniam, quis nostrud exerci tation ullamcorper suscipit lobortis nisl ut aliquip ex ea commodo consequat. Duis te feugifacilisi.

Lorem ipsum dolor sit amet, consectetuer adipiscing elit, nibh euismod.

Space before: 0 pt

L orem ipsum dolor sit amet, consectetuer adipiscing elit, sed diam nonummy nibh euismod tincidunt ut laoreet dolore magna aliquam erat voluptat.

Ut wisi enim ad minim veniam, quis nostrud exerci tation ullamcorper suscipit lobortis nisl ut aliquip ex ea commodo consequat. Duis te feugifacilisi.

Lorem ipsum dolor sit amet, consectetuer adipiscing elit, nibh euismod.

Space before: 12 pt

spacing of the baseline grid, each line of text locks to each grid line, as shown here:

If leading for the selected paragraph(s) is *greater* than the spacing of the baseline grid, Quark spaces lines in those paragraphs according to the nearest *multiple* of the baseline grid spacing. If baseline grid spacing in a document is only 18 points, for example, a paragraph with 24-point leading would lock to every second grid line, or at intervals of 36 points ($18 \times 2 = 36$), as shown here:

 Tip To adjust the placement of the baseline grid in a text box, edit the Baseline Grid Start and Increment settings in the Typographical Preferences dialog box (Preferences/Typographic command, Edit menu).

Creating Automatic Drop Caps

Drop caps are oversized capital letters that appear at the beginning of a paragraph and sink downward by a specified number of lines, as shown here:

> I candidly acknowledge that I ran away at the Battle of Gettysburg. My friends have tried to smooth over this fact by asserting that I did so for the purpose of imitating Washington, who went into the woods at Valley Forge for the purpose of saying his prayers. It was a miserable subterfuge. I struck out in a straight line for the Tropic of Cancer because I was scared. I wanted my

You can assign automatic drop caps to a paragraph through the Paragraph Formats dialog box, specifying the number of initial drop cap characters and the number of lines by which they sink.

To define drop caps for the selected paragraph(s), follow these steps:

1. With one or more paragraphs selected, press CTRL-SHIFT-F to access the Paragraph Formats dialog box.

2. Click the Drop Caps check box to activate it. The Character Count and Line Count fields become available, as shown here:

3. In the Character Count field, enter the number of initial characters in the paragraph that you want to format as enlarged drop caps. The maximum number is eight.

4. In the Line Count field, enter the number of lines by which you want the drop cap(s) to sink. The drop caps automatically increase in point size to fit this number of lines exactly.

Resizing a Drop Cap

You can always resize an automatic drop cap after having assigned it to a paragraph. Quark lets you specify the change in size either as a percentage of current drop cap size or as an absolute point size. Both the Measurements palette and a special keyboard command are available for this purpose.

Using the Measurements Palette   To resize a drop cap using the Measurements palette, follow these steps:

1. Highlight the drop cap and then click the scroll bar next to the Point Size field. A menu pops up, listing several preset percentage values.

2. To resize the drop cap according to a percentage of its current size, click the desired percentage value. To enter a custom percentage, double-click the current value in the Point Size field and enter a replacement value.

3. If you prefer to specify an absolute point size rather than a percentage value, double-click the current percentage value in the Point Size field and enter the new value followed by the abbreviation **pt**.

Using the Keyboard   To resize a drop cap using a keyboard command, highlight the drop cap and press CTRL-SHIFT-\ to access the Font Size dialog box. Enter the desired value either as a percentage of current size or as an absolute number of points, then click OK.

Don't Forget to Kern

When a drop cap sinks by several lines, you sometimes need to adjust the spacing between the drop cap and adjacent letters in those lines. Position the text cursor in the space after the drop cap and then use one of the kerning techniques discussed in Chapter 5. Reducing the kerning value brings the drop cap and adjacent letters closer together; increasing it spaces them further apart.

Keeping Paragraphs and Lines Together

Heads and subheads in books, manuals, newsletters, and magazines should appear together with the paragraphs that follow them. If a head falls at the bottom of a page or column, however, it could easily become separated from the text that follows—a typographic no-no. Equally bad are *widows*—the last line of a paragraph falling alone at the top of a column—and *orphans*—the first line of a new paragraph falling alone at the bottom of a column.

Quark helps you avoid these with the Keep with Next and Keep Lines Together options in the Paragraph Formats dialog box. These options ensure that lines and paragraphs that belong together do in fact stay together.

The Keep With Next Option

To keep subheads and text, step numbers and steps, and other mutually dependent paragraphs together, follow these steps:

1. With the Content tool active, position the text cursor in the first of two paragraphs that must stay together.

2. Press CTRL-SHIFT-F or choose the Formats command in the Style menu to access the Paragraph Formats dialog box.

3. Activate the Keep With Next check box and then click OK.

The Keep Lines Together Option

To control paragraph breaks so that widows and orphans do not occur, follow these steps:

1. Select the paragraph(s) in danger of breaking incorrectly, and then press CTRL-SHIFT-F to access the Paragraph Formats dialog box.

2. Activate the Keep Lines Together check box. Three other options—All Lines in Paragraph, Start, and End—now become available.

   ❑ If you do not want the current paragraph(s) to break at all, activate the All Lines in Paragraph check box. This setting is useful for two- or three-line paragraphs and heads that span multiple lines of text.

   ❑ If you want to keep a set minimum of lines in the paragraph(s) together, enter the desired numbers in the Start and End fields. The Start value determines how many lines in a new paragraph must remain together at the bottom of a column; the End value controls how many lines at the end of a paragraph must remain together at the top of a column.

Tip When Keep With Next and Keep Lines Together are active, heads, subheads, and even longer paragraphs will often jump to the top of the next page or column, leaving an unsightly gap at the bottom of the previous page. Not all documents require text to line up at the top and bottom of each page, but if you want pages to vertically justify in these situations, you have several options at your disposal. Experiment with Space Before and Space After settings for paragraphs on the offending pages (Paragraph Formats dialog box), or develop a vertical justification scheme using the Vertical Alignment: Justified and Inter Paragraph Max options in the Text Box Specifications dialog box.

Adjusting Alignment

The *alignment* of a paragraph has to do with its horizontal position in the text box. QuarkXPress permits four different types of alignment: Left, Centered, Right, and Justified. Figure 6-6 shows examples of each type of paragraph alignment.

Paragraphs set for Left, Centered, Right, and Justified alignment

Left

Set the centre of the sterre
upon the lyne meridionall, and
tak kep of thy zodiak, and loke
what degre of eny signe that
sitte upon the same lyne
meridionall at that same tyme,
and take there the degre in

Centered

Set the centre of the sterre
upon the lyne meridionall, and
tak kep of thy zodiak, and loke
what degre of eny signe that
sitte upon the same lyne
meridionall at that same tyme,
and take there the degre in

Set the centre of the sterre
upon the lyne meridionall, and
tak kep of thy zodiak, and loke
what degre of eny signe that
sitte upon the same lyne
meridionall at that same tyme,
and take there the degre in

Set the centre of the sterre
upon the lyne meridionall, and
tak kep of thy zodiak, and loke
what degre of eny signe that
sitte upon the same lyne
meridionall at that same tyme,
and take there the degre in

Right

Justified

You can assign alignment to a paragraph using your choice of the Paragraph Formats dialog box, the Alignment command in the Style menu, the Measurements palette, or keyboard commands.

Using the Paragraph Formats Dialog Box

When you want to specify several paragraph attributes at once, choose an alignment option within the Paragraph Formats dialog box (CTRL-SHIFT-F). Click the drop-down list box next to Alignment to display the four options (Left, Right, Centered, and Justified). Click the desired option to activate it.

Using the Alignment Command

To specify alignment for the currently selected paragraphs, choose the Alignment command in the Style menu. A submenu containing four options pops out, as shown here:

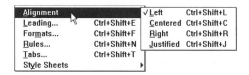

Click the desired alignment option to apply it to the paragraph(s).

Using the Measurements Palette

Quark provides four icons in the Measurements palette to let you specify alignment instantly, as shown here:

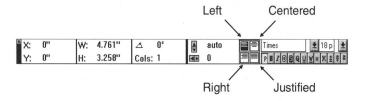

The icon that represents the current alignment setting is always highlighted. To select a new setting, click the desired icon.

Using Keyboard Commands

When you use one of the keyboard shortcuts listed in Table 6-2, Quark realigns the selected paragraph(s) instantly.

TABLE 6-2

Aligning Paragraphs: Keyboard Shortcuts

To Align a Selected Paragraph	Press
Left	CTRL-SHIFT-L
Centered	CTRL-SHIFT-C
Right	CTRL-SHIFT-R
Justified	CTRL-SHIFT-J

Choosing a Hyphenation and Justification Method

Quark's flexibility in typographic matters extends even to the rules governing word hyphenation and line justification for paragraphs. The H&Js option in the Paragraph Formats dialog box lets you choose a hyphenation and justification method for the currently selected paragraph(s), as shown here:

The Standard method—Quark's default—is always available. Other methods will also be available if:

☐ You have used the H&Js command in the Edit menu to define custom sets of hyphenation and justification rules for the current document, or

☐ You have used the H&Js command to define custom sets of H&Js that apply to all new documents.

See the "Customizing Hyphenation and Justification" section later in this chapter to learn more about adjusting hyphenation and justification rules, saving custom sets of these rules for specific documents, and editing Quark's hyphenation dictionaries.

Defining Rules for a Paragraph

Rules break up the monotony of paragraphs, drawing attention to text you want to emphasize and providing visual interest. Using Quark's Paragraph Rules dialog box, you can assign rules above and/or below any selected paragraph, controlling the placement and length of the rule, its distance from surrounding text, its width, color, and shade. Rules that you define this way travel with the paragraph automatically.

To define a rule for the selected paragraph(s), follow these steps:

1. With the Content tool active and the paragraph(s) to which you want to assign a rule selected, choose the Rules command from the Style menu (CTRL-SHIFT-N). The Paragraph Rules dialog box appears. If the selected paragraph contains no rules, the dialog box is in the unexpanded form shown here:

2. To begin defining a rule above the paragraph, click the Rule Above check box. To define a rule below the paragraph, click the Rule Below check box. In either case, the Paragraph Rules dialog box expands, displaying a list of options. Figure 6-7 shows these options with their default settings.

3. To specify the point relative to which Quark measures the length of the rule, choose an option from the Length drop-down list box. See the "Length" section following these steps.

4. To offset the rule horizontally from the current left and/or right margin of the paragraph(s), specify a value in the From Left and

The expanded Paragraph Rules dialog box

From Right fields. See the "From Left, From Right" section following these steps.

5. Specify the vertical distance of the rule from the selected paragraph using the Offset field. You can describe this value as an absolute number of points or as a percentage; see the "Offset" section following these steps.

6. Choose one of the preset line styles from the drop-down list box. Single, double, and triple line styles are available, as well as dotted, dashed, and dot-dash lines, as shown here:

7. Use the Width field or drop-down list box to define the width of the rule. To choose a preset width, click the desired width setting in the drop-down list box shown here:

If you prefer a custom line width, double-click the current value in the Width field and enter a replacement value.

Note A hairline rule is .25 points wide. It prints thicker on a 300 dpi laser printer, however, due to inherent limitations of such printers. If you use hairline rules in a document that you will eventually output to a high-resolution imagesetter, remember that only the final output will display such thin rules correctly.

8. Use the Color drop-down list box to define the color of the rule. If you have defined new default colors or custom colors for the current

document, they will appear in the Color drop-down list box; otherwise, only the preset Quark colors shown here appear:

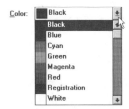

See Chapter 10 for information on defining custom colors.

9. Use the Shade field or drop-down list box to define the saturation of the rule color you have chosen. To choose a preset shade in increments of 10 percent, use the drop-down list box. To specify a custom saturation percentage, double-click the current value in the Shade field and enter a replacement value.

10. To preview the results of your settings before committing yourself, click the Apply button. You may have to move the dialog box if it is in the way of the selected paragraph(s) on your screen.

11. Click OK when you are satisfied with settings for the rule.

Four options in the Paragraph Rules dialog box—Length, From Left, From Right, and Offset—determine the length and placement of a rule. Each of these options affects some of the others, so a little clarification here may be useful.

Length

The Length option in the Paragraph Rules dialog box defines how Quark measures the length of a rule. Two choices are available: Indents and Text.

Indents If you choose Indents, Quark bases the length of the rule on the Left Indent and Right Indent values for the currently selected paragraph. You can find these values in the Paragraph Formats dialog box (CTRL-SHIFT-F). If the From Left and From Right values are both zero, a rule based on indents has the exact same line length as the paragraph to which you assign it, as shown here:

> Know by thin almenak the degre of the ecliptik of eny signe in which that the planete is rekned for to be, and that is clepid the degre of his longitude. And know also the degre of his latitude fro the ecliptik north or south. And by these ensamples folweynge in speciall maist thou worche forsothe in every signe of the zodiak.

Text If you select Text, Quark bases the length of a rule on the length of the first line in the paragraph (when you assign a Rule Above) or the last line in the paragraph (when you assign a Rule Below), as shown here:

> Know by thin almenak the degre of the ecliptik of eny signe in which that the planete is rekned for to be, and that is clepid the degre of his longitude. And know also the degre of his latitude fro the ecliptik north or south. And by these ensamples folweynge in speciall maist thou worche forsothe in every signe of the zodiak.

From Left, From Right

The From Left and From Right options let you further modify the length of a rule beyond what you specify in the Length option. When both the From Left and the From Right values are zero, the Length option determines the exact width and placement of the rule. When you begin altering these values, you can achieve interesting visual effects. For example:

☐   Specify a positive From Left value when you want to indent the rule from the left edge of a paragraph (Length: Indents) or from the left edge of the first or last line in the paragraph (Length: Text).

☐   Specify a negative From Left value when you want to outdent the rule from the left edge of a paragraph (Length: Indents)

Know by thin almenak the degre of the ecliptik of eny signe in which that the planete is rekned for to be, and that is clepid the degre of his longitude. And know also the degre of his latitude fro the ecliptik north or south. And by these ensamples folweynge in speciall maist thou worche forsothe in every signe of the zodiak.

or from the left edge of the first or last line in a paragraph (Length: Text). A rule may not extend beyond the text box margin, so a negative From Left value cannot be greater than the Left Indent value for the selected paragraph in the Paragraph Formats dialog box.

☐ Specify a positive From Right value when you want to indent the rule from the right edge of a paragraph (Length: Indents) or from the right edge of the first or last line in the paragraph (Length: Text).

☐ Specify a negative From Right value when you want to outdent the rule from the right edge of a paragraph (Length: Indents)

Know by thin almenak the degre of the ecliptik of eny signe in which that the planete is rekned for to be, and that is clepid the degre of his longitude. And know also the degre of his latitude fro the ecliptik north or south. And by these ensamples folweynge in speciall maist thou worche forsothe in every signe of the zodiak.

or from the right edge of the first or last line in the paragraph (Length: Text). A rule may not extend beyond the text box margin, so a negative From Right value cannot be greater than the Right Indent value for the selected paragraph in the Paragraph Formats dialog box.

Offset

The Offset value in the Paragraph Rules dialog box determines the vertical distance between a rule and the paragraph to which you assign it. You can specify this value either in absolute terms (as a specific number of points, inches, and so on) or as a percentage. Quark measures the offset distance differently in both cases.

Specifying Offset as an Absolute Value   Specify Offset as an absolute measurement when you want the rule to be at a fixed distance from the baseline of the first or last line of a paragraph. For a Rule Above, Quark calculates rule position *upward* from the baseline of the first line in a paragraph, as shown here:

Rule Above offset: 0.25"

K now by thin almenak the degre of the ecliptik of eny signe in which that
   the planete is rekned for to be, and that is clepid the degre of his   Baseline
longitude. And know also the degre of his latitude fro the ecliptik north or
south. And by these ensamples folweynge in speciall maist thou worche
forsothe in every signe of the zodiak.

For a Rule Below, Quark calculates rule position *downward* from the baseline of the last line in a paragraph. If the font in the selected paragraph has long descenders (the bottoms of letters such as g, p, and y), be sure to specify a large enough offset to avoid having the descenders touch the rule. Quark accepts only positive values when you specify rule offset in absolute terms.

   Tip   Quark does not adjust the distance between neighboring paragraphs to compensate for the position of a rule. When you specify Offset as an absolute value, adjust the Space Before and Space After values in the Paragraph Formats dialog box to control this distance yourself.

Specifying Offset as a Percentage   Specify Offset as a percentage when you want Quark to position a rule based on the *relative* distance between the selected paragraph and the one before it (Rule Above) or between the selected paragraph and the one after it (Rule Below). This way of measuring rule offset makes it easy to "guesstimate" an aesthetically pleasing position for a rule without first having to calculate exact interparagraph spacing. The total distance between a paragraph with a rule and a neighboring paragraph is always 100 percent.

For example, assume that you specify Offset for a Rule Below at 20 percent. Quark calculates the amount of space between the descent of the last line of the selected paragraph and the ascent of the first line of the paragraph following it. The top of the rule falls 20 percent of this distance below the selected paragraph, as shown here:

18. To knowe for what latitude in eny regioun the
almykanteras of eny table ben compowned.   Total interparagraph
                                               distance
Rule below offset: 20%

Rekene how many degrees of almykanteras in the meridionall lyne ben
fro the cercle equinoxiall unto the cenyth, or elles from the pool artyk
unto the north orisonte; and for so gret a latitude, or for so smal a
latitude, is the table compowned.

If you specify Offset for a Rule Above at 20 percent, Quark calculates the
amount of space between the ascent of the first line of the selected
paragraph and the descent of the last line in the paragraph above it. The
bottom of the rule then falls into position 20 percent of this distance
above the selected paragraph.

Setting Tabs

Forget about ever again using spaces to control columns in a table.
One hallmark of a good page layout package is its ability to use tabs to
control horizontal alignment of text within a line, and Quark has some
of the most sophisticated tab controls you are ever likely to see. Quark's
techniques for setting tabs can be precise or visually intuitive.

Tab Stop Attributes

Quark offers you extraordinary control over three attributes of tab
stops: alignment, position, and fill character. The concept of tab position
is straightforward, but tab alignment and fill character options open the
door to many creative applications.

Tab Alignment   You can set tabs to align in six different ways in Quark.
Each type of tab alignment is suited to specific uses.

☐   *Left Alignment* aligns text flush left against the tab stop. This type
of alignment is appropriate for tables that contain text only, or for
the second column in a table of contents, as shown in Figure 6-8.

☐   *Center Alignment* centers text relative to the tab stop. This type of
alignment is especially useful for headers and footers that contain

information at the left margin, in the center of the page, and at the right margin, as shown in Figure 6-9.

☐ *Right Alignment* aligns text flush right against the tab stop. Common uses for right-aligned tabs include the headers and footers just mentioned, as well as page numbers in a table of contents (see Figure 6-8).

Tip Regardless of the tab stops set for a given paragraph, you can enter a right-indent tab manually at any point by pressing SHIFT-TAB. Entering this character causes subsequent text to align with the right indent for the current paragraph.

☐*Decimal Alignment* aligns text against a decimal point (period). This is the best type of alignment to use in tables that contain numeric or financial data, or anywhere you want to align tab stops against a period as shown in Figure 6-8.

FIGURE 6-8 Left-, decimal, and right-aligned tab stops and tab leaders in a table of contents

CONTENTS

Chapter	Title	Page
1.	Doing It Naturally	3
2.	Civilization and its Malcontents	29
3.	Convention and Malarkey	52
4.	Malarkey and Convention	84
5.	Malarkey and Baloney	101
6.	Turkey Baloney and Cholesterol	135
7.	It's Not What You Eat, It's What Eats You	159
8.	Sifting the Wheat from the Chaff	172
9.	When Only a Grain Mill Will Do	193
10.	And Then There's Juicing	202

↑ Decimal tab stop   ↖ Left-aligned tab stop   ↗ Tab leader   ↑ Right-aligned tab stop

FIGURE
6-9

A header that makes use of a center-aligned tab stop

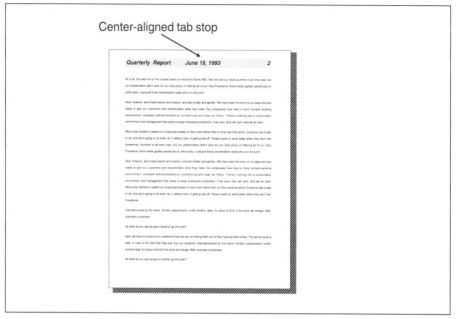

☐ *Comma Alignment* is useful for foreign-language tables containing monetary or fractional data. Some European languages other than English use commas rather than decimal points.

☐ *Align On* allows you to define any character as the character against which to align text. For example, imagine you want to construct a table in which each line contains a symbolic Zapf Dingbats character that has a special meaning in context. You could use the Windows Character Map utility to select the Zapf Dingbats character you want to use, and then copy and paste that character into both the Paragraph Tabs dialog box and the table. The special character would align in each line.

Tip Paste the contents of the clipboard into a dialog box field by pressing CTRL-V.

Tabs and Fill Characters A *fill character* is a repeating character that fills the space between one tab stop and the next. Not all tabs require fill characters; many tables, for example, should have plenty of blank space between tabs for clarity's sake. Typical fill characters include periods for tables of contents (see Figure 6-8) and underscore characters for fill-in-the-blanks entries in business forms, as shown in Figure 6-10.

When you feel like getting creative with design, keep in mind that Quark allows you to use any character in any font as a fill character. Fill characters can be decorative as well as purposeful. Consider this example, which uses Zapf Dingbat and Wing Ding fill characters:

Heart-Healthy Tips ♠ ♠ ♠ ♠ ♠ ♠ ♠ ♠ ♠ ♠ ♠ ♠ Dr. Vascomb ♠ ♠ ♠ ♠ 1:30

Managing Stress ☺ ☺ ☺ ☺ ☺ ☺ ☺ ☺ ☺ ☺ ☺ Dr. Stund ☺ ☺ ☺ ☺ 3:00

Tip To avoid a crowded appearance, space symbolic fill characters further apart by selecting the characters and increasing tracking interactively using the Measurements palette.

FIGURE 6-10

Using an underscore fill character to create business forms

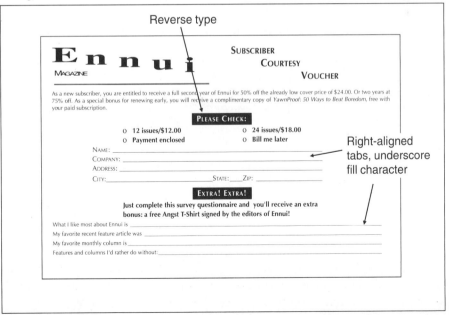

Quark's Tabbing Defaults

You can use tabs in a paragraph even if you have not customized its tab settings. Quark sets up default left-aligned tab stops every half inch. You could create a table without changing these defaults by simply pressing TAB multiple times to move between columns. However, this is not always the most efficient manner of desktop publishing. By choosing tab alignment, position, and fill character carefully, you can use tabs for a wide range of attractive typographic effects, from artfully arranging headers and footers to creating efficient business forms and fancy tables.

You can define tabs in Quark in one of two places: in the Paragraph Tabs dialog box (accessed through the Tabs command in the Style menu) or in the Paragraph Formats dialog box discussed earlier in this chapter.

Defining Tabs in the Paragraph Tabs Dialog Box

To define tab stops through the Paragraph Tabs dialog box, follow these steps:

1. With one or more paragraphs selected, choose the Tabs command in the Style menu (keyboard shortcut: CTRL-SHIFT-T) to access the Paragraph Tabs dialog box. If the current text box is wider than will fit in the dialog box at the current viewing magnification, the ruler displays scroll arrows at either end, like this:

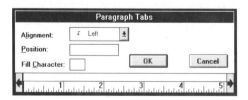

2. Click the Alignment drop-down list box and then one of the six tab alignment options shown here:

If you select the Align On option, a field appears into which you can enter the desired alignment character.

3. Specify a position for the new tab, either by entering a precise value or interactively.

☐ To specify a *precise* numerical position for the tab, enter a value in the Position dialog box. You can enter a value in .001 increments in any unit of measurement; a hooked arrow indicating the tab alignment appears at the corresponding position on the tab ruler.

☐ If you prefer to set a tab position interactively, simply click at the point on the tab ruler where you want to locate the tab. The tab location icon appears at the position you have chosen, and the Position field reflects the tab position to the nearest thousandth of a unit.

4. Decide whether you want the area between tab stops to have fill characters or remain blank. If you want the space to remain blank, leave the Fill Character field blank, too. If you want a repeating character to appear between tab stops, enter the character in the Fill Character field.

Tip To enter a character from Zapf Dingbats, Wing Dings, or other symbol font installed on your system, use the Windows 3.1 Character Map utility (located in the Accessories group window) to find out the ALT + keystroke that represents the equivalent character in the current font. Enter this keystroke into the Fill Character field. Once out of the dialog box, highlight the fill characters (which are still in the current font) and change them to the symbol font.

5. To set additional tab stops, repeat steps 2-5 for each additional tab. Quark represents each of the six types of tab alignments with a different tab symbol, as shown here:

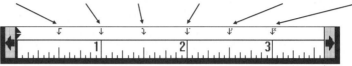

Left aligned   Center aligned   Right aligned   Decimal aligned   Comma aligned   Align on

6. When all the tab stops are to your liking, click OK.

Tip   To view tab characters on a document page, activate the Show Invisibles command in the View menu.

Tab Stops in the Paragraph Formats Dialog Box

A tab ruler appears in the Paragraph Formats dialog box as well as in the Paragraph Tabs dialog box. It displays the alignment types and positions of all the tabs you have already set for the selected paragraph(s), as shown here:

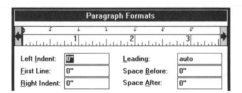

The primary function of this tab ruler is to let you conveniently view current tab stops. Although you can set tabs by clicking in the tab ruler, there is neither an Alignment nor a Position field in the Paragraph Formats dialog box. Consequently, all the tabs that you set interactively will be left-aligned tabs.

Deleting All Tab Stops

To erase all current tab stops in the Paragraph Tabs or Paragraph Formats dialog box, position the pointer over the tab ruler, press CTRL, and click. All the marker symbols indicating current tab stops disappear.

Using Keyboard Shortcuts

You can invoke several of the most important paragraph formatting commands in the Style menu using key combinations. Table 6-3 lists these commands and the keyboard shortcuts that access the dialog boxes associated with them.

Creating and Managing Style Sheets

The breakneck pace of today's business world demands that you format text in your documents as quickly as possible. While it may be fun to tweak characters and paragraphs one at a time, it is hardly practical to lay out an entire document using only local formatting.

Enter style sheets, the powerful, automatic way to apply an entire set of character and paragraph attributes to text in a Quark document. Style sheets make it possible to reformat an entire paragraph or series of paragraphs with a single click or keyboard shortcut.

TABLE 6-3   Style Menu Commands for Text: Keyboard Shortcuts

To Invoke this Style Menu Command	Press
Alignment/Left	CTRL-SHIFT-L
Alignment/Centered	CTRL-SHIFT-C
Alignment/Right	CTRL-SHIFT-R
Alignment/Justified	CTRL-SHIFT-J
Leading	CTRL-SHIFT-E
Formats	CTRL-SHIFT-F
Rules	CTRL-SHIFT-N
Tabs	CTRL-SHIFT-T

Style Sheet Basics

A style sheet is a collection of character and paragraph attributes that you can apply to any paragraph in a document. A document can contain up to 127 different style sheets, each with a unique name. Style sheets let you standardize and automate the formatting of text in periodicals and long documents.

Quark saves style sheets with the document in which you create them. Every new document contains at least two style sheets: Normal and No Style.

☐   *Normal* The Normal style sheet is the default style sheet for text that you enter in a new text box. You can edit the default attributes of the Normal style sheet differently in each document.

☐   *No Style* Applying the No Style style sheet to a paragraph is like turning automatic formatting off. Quark treats every edit you make to that paragraph as local formatting from that point forward.

Tip   If you edit style sheets when no documents are open, you can create additional default style sheets that will be available to every new document.

Two commands and one palette offer you a multitude of techniques for working with style sheets in QuarkXPress.

☐   The Style Sheets command in the Style menu, available when the Content tool and a text box are active, lets you apply an existing style sheet to the selected paragraph(s).

☐   The Style Sheets command in the Edit menu lets you create new style sheets, edit existing ones, and append style sheets from other documents.

☐   The Style Sheets palette is an intuitive aid to applying and editing style sheets.

The Style Sheets Palette

Many users find that Quark's Style Sheets palette is all they need to apply, create, and manage style sheets in a document. To display this palette (shown in Figure 6-11), choose the Show Style Sheets command in the View menu. To remove it from the screen, double-click the palette's control menu icon or choose Hide Style Sheets from the View menu.

Moving and Sizing the Style Sheets Palette

To move the Style Sheets palette, drag it by its title bar. If the palette for the active document contains so many style sheets that you cannot view them all, resize the palette by dragging one of its sides or corners outward.

Viewing the Current Style Sheet

To find out which style sheet applies to a particular paragraph, click within the paragraph when the Content tool is active and the Style Sheets palette is visible. The style sheet that currently applies to the paragraph will be highlighted in the Style Sheets palette.

FIGURE 6-11

The Style Sheets palette

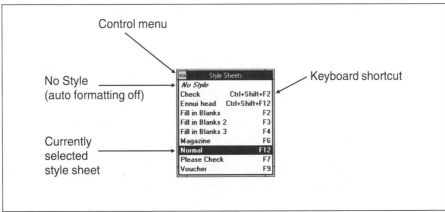

Applying a Style Sheet to a Paragraph

Applying a style sheet to a paragraph causes the paragraph to reformat instantly. Apply an existing style sheet to a paragraph with the Style Sheets command in the Style menu, the Style Sheets palette, or (in some cases) keyboard shortcuts.

Using the Style Sheets Command

To apply a style sheet to a paragraph using a menu command, with the Content tool active click anywhere in the paragraph, and then choose the Style Sheets command in the Style menu. A submenu pops out containing all of the existing style sheets in the document, as shown here:

Click the desired style sheet name to apply it.

Using the Style Sheets Palette

To apply a style sheet to a paragraph when the Style Sheets palette is visible, click anywhere in the paragraph with the Content tool active and then click the style sheet name in the palette. The new style sheet name becomes highlighted.

Using Keyboard Shortcuts

When you create or edit a style sheet using the Style Sheets dialog box, you have the option of assigning a keyboard shortcut to it. If the style sheet you want to apply has a keyboard shortcut, simply position the text cursor in the paragraph and then press the required keys.

Applying a Style Sheet to a Locally Formatted Paragraph

Local formatting takes precedence over style sheet formatting in Quark. If you have modified any text in a paragraph using Style menu commands or the Measurements palette (local formatting), that text does not reformat automatically when you apply a style sheet. To work around this, press SHIFT as you click the name of the style sheet you want to apply. This temporarily applies the No Style style sheet and *then* the style sheet you originally intended to use. The style sheet then overrides all of your local formatting.

Creating a New Style Sheet

All the work of creating and editing style sheets begins in the Style Sheets dialog box shown here:

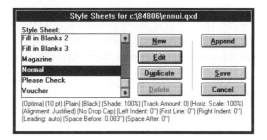

There are two ways to access that dialog box:

☐   Choose the Style Sheets command in the Edit menu.

☐   If the Style Sheets palette is visible, press CTRL and then click the name of the style sheet you want to edit (or the Normal style sheet, if you are creating a new one).

You have available several techniques for designing a new style sheet:

☐   Set all the attributes through the Style Sheets dialog box and dependent dialog boxes

☐ Duplicate an existing style sheet and then adapt some of its attributes

☐ Locally format a paragraph the way you want a new style sheet to look and *then* access the Style Sheets dialog box

Follow along to explore each of these techniques and find the one that best suits your style of working.

Creating a Style Sheet from Scratch

To define a fresh style sheet option by option, follow these steps:

1. Open the document to which you want to add the new style sheet. If you define a new style sheet when no documents are open, Quark saves it as a default style sheet that will be available for all future new documents.

2. Access the Style Sheets dialog box by choosing the Style Sheets command from the Edit menu. If you prefer to use the Style Sheets palette for this purpose, activate the Content tool, click in any text box, and then click any of the style sheets in the palette while pressing CTRL.

3. Click the New button in the Style Sheets dialog box. The Edit Style Sheet dialog box shown in Figure 6-12 appears. Note that the style attributes at the bottom of the dialog box match those of the Normal style sheet for the active document, and that the new style sheet is based on No Style.

4. Enter a name for the new style sheet in the Name field. The name should bear an easily recognizable relation to the function of this style sheet in your document: Head 1 or Caption, for example. This is especially important for workgroup publishing, when several different people may be working with the same document.

5. In the Keyboard Equivalent field, enter the desired keyboard shortcut (if any) by pressing the one-, two- or three-key sequence that you want to use for this style sheet. Here are some guidelines for choosing a key sequence:

FIGURE
6-12

The Edit Style Sheet dialog box

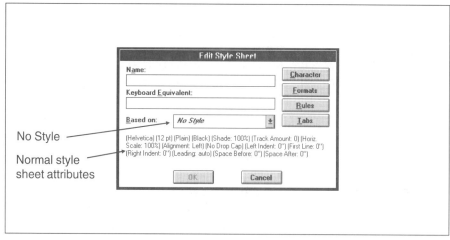

No Style

Normal style
sheet attributes

- [ ] All key sequences must include a function key (F2, for example). If you use a single-key shortcut, use a function key only.

- [ ] If you use a two- or three-key combination, use CTRL, SHIFT, and/or ALT plus a function key. Letter keys are not available for applying style sheets.

 Note If the key combination you enter is unavailable (used for some other function within QuarkXPress), the Keyboard Equivalent field remains blank. Try again with a different combination.

6. Click the command button (Character, Paragraph, Rules, Tabs) that represents the kinds of attributes you want to define for the new style sheet. The Character button accesses the Character Attributes dialog box discussed in Chapter 5. The Paragraph, Rules, and Tab buttons access the Paragraph Attributes, Paragraph Rules, and Paragraph Tabs dialog boxes, respectively. Review the "Formatting Text on the Paragraph Level" section at the beginning of this chapter if you need to brush up on the functions of various attributes.

7. After defining attributes in one of the four subdialog boxes, click OK to return to the Edit Style Sheet dialog box. Continue accessing other subdialog boxes and defining other attributes as desired.

8. When you have defined all the attributes for the new style sheet, review the list of attributes in the Edit Style Sheet dialog box to ensure that they are correct. Then, click OK to return to the Style Sheets dialog box.

9. Click Save to save the new style sheet and return to the active document. The new style sheet name now appears in the Style Sheets palette and in the submenu of the Style Sheets command in the Style menu.

If the text cursor is located in a paragraph when you exit the Style Sheets dialog box, Quark does not automatically apply the new style sheet to it. This is a safety measure that prevents you from applying style sheets unintentionally. You must click the style sheet name in the palette if you want to apply it to the current paragraph.

Duplicating an Existing Style Sheet

A time-saving technique for defining a new style sheet is to adapt it from an existing one. You do this in Quark by duplicating the attributes of one style sheet and then renaming it.

To create a new style sheet by adapting it from an existing one, follow these steps:

1. Open the document to which you want to add the new style sheet. If you define a new style sheet when no documents are open, Quark saves it as a default style sheet that will be available for all future new documents.

2. Access the Style Sheets dialog box by choosing the Style Sheets command from the Edit menu. If you prefer to use the Style Sheets palette for this purpose, activate the Content tool, click in any text box, and then click any of the style sheets in the palette while pressing CTRL.

3. In the Style Sheet list box, click the name of the style sheet you want to use as a model for the new one. Then, click the Duplicate button in the Style Sheets dialog box. The Edit Style Sheet dialog box appears, but this time the dialog box resembles Figure 6-13. The name "Copy of (style sheet name)" appears in the Name field. The

attributes of the model style sheet appear at the bottom of the dialog box, too.

4. Now, you must choose whether to link the new style sheet to the existing one.

☐ If you want Quark always to update the new style sheet automatically whenever you edit the style sheet you are using as a model, click the Based On drop-down list box and select the name of the model style sheet. Changing the point size, leading, or other attribute of the model style sheet in the future will result in Quark applying the same changes to the new style sheet.

☐ If you want the two style sheets to remain independent of each other regardless of future changes, leave the No Style option selected in the Based On list box. That way, Quark copies the current attributes of the existing style sheet to the new one on a one-time basis.

5. Edit the current attributes of the new style sheet as desired using the Character, Paragraph, Rules, and Tabs buttons.

6. After defining new attributes, click OK in the Edit Style Sheets dialog box to return to the Style Sheets dialog box.

Basing a new style sheet on an existing one

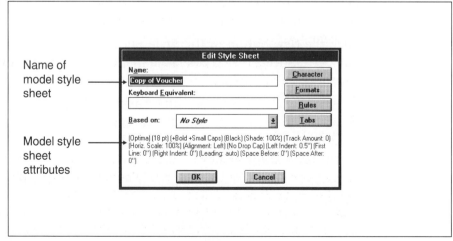

7. Click Save to save the new style sheet. It now appears in the Style Sheets palette as well as in the submenu of the Style Sheets command in the Style menu.

Basing a New Style Sheet on an Existing Paragraph

A third way to define a new style sheet is to apply local formatting to a paragraph until it looks just right, and only then to access the Style Sheets dialog box. The No Style style sheet comes in handy for this method.

To define a new style sheet based on the attributes of a paragraph, follow these steps:

1. With the Content tool active, click anywhere in the paragraph you want to use as a model and then click No Style in the Style Sheets palette. Any paragraph to which you apply the No Style style sheet accepts only local formatting.

2. Use the Measurements palette or commands in the Style menu to edit the attributes of the paragraph.

3. When the paragraph meets with your satisfaction, choose the Style Sheets command in the Edit menu, or press CTRL and click any style sheet name in the Style Sheets palette.

4. Click the New button in the Style Sheets dialog box to access the Edit Style Sheets dialog box. Note that all the current attributes of the paragraph you are formatting appear here.

5. Name the new style sheet and enter a keyboard equivalent, if desired, and then click OK. You do not need to define additional attributes at this time, because you already did that when formatting the paragraph locally.

6. Click Save to exit the Style Sheets dialog box and save the new style sheet.

Copying Paragraph Attributes from One Paragraph to Another

There may be occasions when you locally modify a few attributes of a paragraph to which you have already applied a style sheet. Quark makes it possible to copy both the style sheet and local paragraph-related attributes from one paragraph to another using a special key command.

To copy attributes from one paragraph to another, follow these steps:

1. Click anywhere in the paragraph whose attributes you want to change. You do not need to select any characters.

2. While pressing ALT-SHIFT, click in the paragraph that contains the attributes you want to copy. The first paragraph reformats instantly, taking on both the style sheet and locally modified paragraph attributes of the other paragraph.

The only drawback to this technique is that it does not copy locally modified *character* attributes such as font, point size, type style, and kerning values. If your purposes are met by copying paragraph attributes such as leading, indents, and tab stops, this could be a useful shortcut.

Editing an Existing Style Sheet

When you edit the attributes of an existing style sheet, Quark automatically reformats all paragraphs in the document to which that style sheet applies. To edit a style sheet, follow these steps:

1. Choose the Style Sheets command in the Edit menu, or press CTRL and click on a style sheet name in the Style Sheets palette. The Style Sheets dialog box appears.

2. In the Style Sheets list box, click the name of the style sheet you want to edit and then click the Edit button. When the Edit Style Sheets box appears, the Name field contains the name of the selected style sheet and is grayed out.

3. Add a keyboard equivalent or edit the existing one, if desired.

4. Edit attributes as desired using the Character, Paragraph, Rules, and Tabs buttons. When finished, click OK to return to the Edit Style Sheets dialog box.

5. Click OK in the Edit Style Sheets dialog box and Save in the Style Sheets dialog box. Quark reformats all the paragraphs to which you have assigned this style sheet.

Appending Style Sheets from Other Documents

Have you ever wished you could bring the style sheets from another document into the one you are working on now? With Quark, you can, thanks to the Append button in the Style Sheets dialog box. You can append all existing style sheets from another Quark document.

To append style sheets from another document, follow these steps:

1. Choose the Style Sheets command from the Edit menu or press CTRL and click on a style sheet name in the Style Sheets palette. The Style Sheets dialog box appears.

2. Click the Append button in the Style Sheets dialog box. The Append Style Sheets dialog box shown here appears:

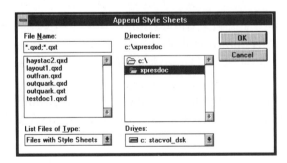

3. Using the List Files of Type drop-down list box, select the type of files you want Quark to recognize. You have four choices:

   ☐ *Files with Style Sheets* include all Quark document and template files.

    ☐   *Document Files* include only Quark files with the extension .qxd.

    ☐   *Template Files* are Quark files with the extension .qxt.

    ☐   *All Files* displays files of any extension in any directory. Keep in mind that Quark cannot append style sheets from all of these files.

  4. Using the Drives and Directories list boxes, locate the file that contains the style sheets you want to import.

  5. Click OK to append the style sheets.

Style sheets that you append from other Quark documents transfer with all their character, paragraph, rules, and tabs attributes intact.

There are two cases in which style sheets may not transfer quite as you expect. Quark will not append a style sheet that has the same name as a style sheet already in the active document, because doing so would overwrite the current style sheet. In addition, if a style sheet that you want to append uses the same keyboard shortcut as a style sheet in the active document, Quark appends it *without* its keyboard equivalent.

Deleting Style Sheets

From time to time, you should purge unneeded style sheets from your documents. Quark has a limit of 127 style sheets per document; even if you do not exceed this limit, many documents probably contain customized style sheets that you do not use regularly.

Quark assigns the No Style style sheet to paragraphs associated with a deleted style sheet. Those paragraphs retain their current formatting, but Quark no longer updates them automatically with any style sheet.

To delete one or more style sheets from a document, follow these steps:

  1. Access the Style Sheets dialog box using either the Style Sheets palette or the Style Sheets command in the Edit menu.

  2. In the Style Sheets list box, click the name of the first style sheet you want to delete.

3. Click the Delete command button. If you have applied this style sheet to any paragraph in the active document, Quark displays a warning message box, as shown here:

4. Click OK to delete the style sheet or Cancel to halt the process.

5. Continue deleting additional style sheets if desired. When finished, click OK to exit the Style Sheets dialog box and return to your document.

If the document contains any paragraphs to which you had previously applied the deleted style sheet(s), assign new style sheets to them. Otherwise, Quark treats the text in those paragraphs as locally formatted and no automatic updating occurs.

Mouse and Keyboard Shortcuts

Table 6-4 lists a few handy shortcuts to help you work more efficiently with style sheets and the Style Sheets palette.

Creating Typographic Special Effects

There are virtually no limits to the number and types of special effects you can create with text in Quark. What follows is a mere sampling of "how-to's" for commonly used typographic effects. Perhaps these suggestions will spark your own creativity.

TABLE 6-4 Working with Style Sheets: Mouse and Keyboard Shortcuts

To Do This	Do this
Access the Style Sheets dialog box	CTRL + click style sheet name
Apply a style sheet to selected paragraph	Click style sheet name
Reformat locally formatted text with a style sheet	SHIFT + click style sheet name
Copy locally modified paragraph attributes	Click in target paragraph, then ALT-SHIFT + click in model paragraph

Creating Fill-in-the-Blanks Forms with Tabs

Forms can be tedious to design with a page layout package unless you can automate the process. Thanks to Quark's tabbing options, designing fill-in-the-blanks questionnaires like the response card pictured in Figure 6-10 is a breeze. Two settings in the Paragraph Tabs dialog box enable you to create smooth blank lines that align perfectly:

☐ *Fill Character* Specify the underscore character (_) as the fill character for tabs in all the style sheets that contain fill-in lines.

☐ *Alignment* Use right-aligned tab stops to align the blank lines in a form.

Reversed Type

Figure 6-10 also contains an example of *reversed type*: white or light text against a dark gray, black, or colored background. To create a style sheet that features reversed type, follow these guidelines:

1. Set the text color either to white or a light shade of some other color in the Character Attributes dialog box.

2. In the Paragraph Rules dialog box, specify a Rule Above that is several points wider than the point size of the text in the style sheet. The rule should be black, dark gray, or a dark shade of another color.

3. Set Offset in the Paragraph Rules dialog box to a *negative* value that is equal to the difference between the point size of the current style sheet and the width of the rule. This positions the rule below the baseline, leaving two dark areas of equal size above and below the text itself.

If text for the current style sheet is 14 points, for example, you might specify 20 pt for Rule Above and give an Offset value of –0.083" (–6 pt). The resulting position of the rule leaves a three-point margin above and below the text as shown in Figure 6-10.

When assigning a reverse type style sheet to a one-line paragraph, add two invisible characters (you will see how shortly): one before the first text character and another after the last character on the line. Otherwise, the dark rule lies flush against the edge of text in an unsightly way. Contrast these two examples:

PLEASE CHECK: **PLEASE CHECK:**

In the first example, no invisible characters have been added to the line of text, and the resulting rule seems poorly designed. The first character in the second example is an en space (CTRL-SHIFT-6), while the last character is a single zero (Quark's definition of an en space). The zero is invisible because its color has been altered to match the color of the rule. You must enter actual characters at the end of a line, because invisible spaces do not cause the rule to extend further than the last text character.

Variable-Length Sets of Rules

Rules that you assign to a style sheet through the Paragraph Rules dialog box must all be the same length. However, you can create the illusion of multiple variable-length rules accompanying a single paragraph by using two different style sheets. There are several ways of doing this, but one useful technique is to specify the rule offset as a percentage for one tag and as an absolute number of points for the other.

In the example document shown in Figure 6-14, the paragraph before the outdented section number features a Rule Below, while the section number style sheet includes a Rule Above. Rule offset for the paragraph before the section number is one-quarter inch, a value that places the rule just slightly above the section number paragraph. Offset for the section number paragraph is 14 points above the baseline—two points above the text, which is 12 points. The result? The two rules lie flush against one another and look as though they both accompany the same paragraph. To achieve the same look in your own documents, juggle offset distance values and percentages in the Paragraph Rules dialog box and Leading, Space Before, and Space After values in the Paragraph Formats dialog box.

Pull Quotes

Newspapers, newsletters, and magazines often use *pull quotes* like the one shown in Figure 6-15 to highlight key remarks in an article. Pull quotes should be easy to spot, and there are any number of techniques you can use to make them stand out. For example:

☐ *Character Attributes* Set the pull quote style sheet in a different font from surrounding text, or assign it a different type style or larger point size.

☐ *Paragraph Attributes* Give the pull quote style sheet a different alignment setting from surrounding text (see Figure 6-15). It also helps to increase the Space Before and Space After values and to vary the leading and indents.

☐ *Paragraph Rules* Use rules above and below to set off a pull quote from the rest of the article, or try the reverse text technique just described.

Creating multiple rules of varying lengths and styles

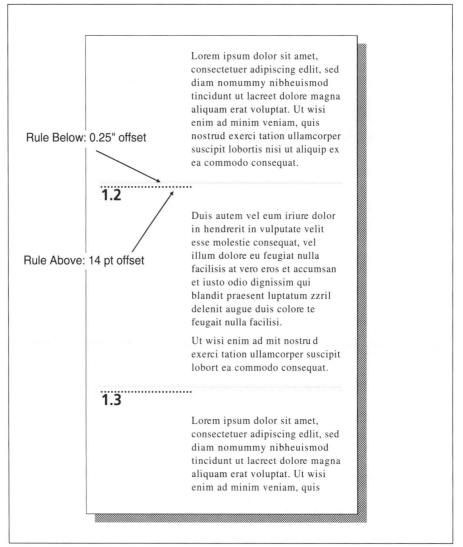

Enhancing Text-Only Documents

Not all documents require graphics, and not all companies or clients have the printing budget for them. QuarkXPress offers you so many ways

Creating pull quotes with rules and contrasting fonts, type style, and alignment settings

Haystackers' Herald

Clutterers Anonymous monthly   *Vol. 3 No. 9*   *September 1992*

Searching for a needle in an untidy haystack is a real time-waster.

Organization Saves Time, Clutter Wastes It
New study shows clutter works against timeliness

*H*ow often have you caught yourself making one of the following excuses when a colleague, family member, or friend remarked on that ever-growing pile of papers, books, and disks around your work area?

"I don't have time to get organized. . . ."

"If I put this mess in order, I'd fall behind schedule. . . ."

Sorry, but those excuses won't hold water anymore, according to a new study by Dr. Irving Lundeby, professor of Psychology at Newtown University in Newtown, Idaho.

Dr. Lundeby's research team studied the work habits of several hundred busy executives over a six-month period. He found that people who routinely followed a plan for organizing documents and other work items were consistently on schedule with their projects and described stress levels as "manageable."

On the other hand, executives who allowed papers to pile up and didn't take the time to organize them often found themselves behind schedule and suffered a higher incidence of stress-related health disorders than the "organized" control group.

Simple "To Do" Lists Serve Best
Paper and pencil more efficient than software time managers

*T*he pressure's on these days to let computers organize every task in your life. That goes for managing your time, too. It used to be that you were thought an old fogey if you didn't use a word processor. In 1992, however, if you don't exploit the latest computer-based personal information manager, complete with OLE, hypertext cross-referencing, and project management, chances are your colleagues will consider you a dinosaur. How can you possibly get organized without the trendiest tools and the loudest bells and whistles?

When you should be organizing your time, you're usually wasting time. . . .

Stop right there. Don't let the "total computerization" fad sway you or, worse, lessen your self-esteem. Paper and pencil "to do" lists may still be the most efficient way to organize your time. Why? Consider these simple points.

- It takes a lot less time to grab a pencil and paper than to boot up your computer, run your PIM software, and access your to-do list.
- Today's PIMs are often complicated. When you should be organizing your time, you're usually wasting time trying to learn the software and getting frustrated.

Pull quote

to enhance text-only documents that you need not be concerned about text looking boring. Keep in mind that even black-and-white text can exude "color," and that you can design a style sheet to maximize the variety of colors available to you. Here are some of the ways in which you can vary the "color" of text in a black-and-white document:

☐ *Use Contrasting Fonts* Each font varies in terms of height, ascent, descent, and character width. The same text string set in two different fonts can have an entirely different weight or color in each case, as shown here:

Please Check: **Please Check:**

☐ *Use Contrasting Type Sizes* Multiple point sizes can help readers find the information they seek.

☐ *Use Different Type Styles* Bold, Italic, Outline, and Shadow styles are especially useful for introducing variable "color" into text. However, don't overdo a variety of type styles, and be sure the styles you use are appropriate for the contents of text.

☐ *Vary the Leading of Different Style Sheets* The amount of space between lines of text in a paragraph can make text look lighter (airier leading) or darker (tighter leading).

☐ *Use Drop Caps* Drop Caps can vary text "color" within a single paragraph.

☐ *Exploit the Horizontal Scale, Tracking Amount, and Baseline Shift Settings in the Character Attributes Dialog Box* Horizontal scaling can give display type an airier look, while tracking can influence the relative tightness or roominess of text. As you have already seen in earlier sections of this chapter, altering baseline shift for some characters can enhance visual variety and fight monotony.

☐ *Use Rules* Use rules in various weights to draw attention to text.

☐ *Explore Different Shades of Gray* Use different shades of gray for text, drop caps, and rules. Including several different shades of gray in a document as shown in Figure 6-14 helps emphasize certain text and keeps the eye intrigued.

In short, balance contrast and variety with good taste, and text in your document need never look dull.

Customizing Hyphenation and Justification

Quark's control over hyphenation and justification (H&Js) in a document is legendary. You can customize rules for the Standard H&J set, create additional sets of rules, and assign your choice of H&J sets to each style sheet. Beyond this, you can hyphenate words manually using a special character, check Quark's suggested hyphenation for a specific word, and enter custom hyphenation exceptions that Quark will store for future use. Hyphenation and justification rules give you the maximum benefits of automation combined with flexibility.

Five different menu commands help you control hyphenation and justification at the document, paragraph, and word level:

☐   The H&Js command in the Edit menu lets you edit the Standard H&J set and create customized sets of H&Js.

☐   The Formats command in the Style menu and the Style Sheets command in the Edit menu give you access to the Paragraph Formats dialog box, in which you select a set of H&Js for a specific paragraph or style sheet.

☐   Use the Suggested Hyphenation command in the Utilities menu to view Quark's suggested hyphenation breaks for the currently selected word.

☐   With the help of the Hyphenation Exceptions command in the Utilities menu, you can customize Quark's hyphenation dictionary for special words in your documents.

Assigning an H&J Set to a Paragraph

To assign an available H&J set to a paragraph, use the H&Js drop-down list box in the Paragraph Formats dialog box. If you access this dialog box through the Style menu, the H&J you choose applies to the current paragraph only. If you access Paragraph Formats through the Style Sheets dialog box, the selected H&J applies to all paragraphs defined by the current style sheet.

Editing an Existing H&J

Quark comes shipped with a standard set of hyphenation and justification rules, known as the Standard H&J. All new documents contain the Standard H&J; if you create additional H&J sets when no document is open, these will be available for all future new documents. Custom H&Js that you create within a document are saved with that document. If you edit the Standard H&J when no documents are open, you change the default hyphenation and justification rules that apply to all future new documents.

To edit the Standard H&J or another H&J set that you have created previously, follow these steps:

1. Choose the H&Js command in the Edit menu to access the H&Js dialog box shown here. (If you have not created custom sets of H&Js previously, only the Standard set will appear in the dialog box.)

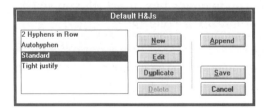

2. Choose the H&J you want to edit by clicking its name in the list box.

3. Click the Edit button to display the Edit Hyphenation and Justification dialog box pictured here. (The Name field is grayed out

because you are editing an existing H&J rather than creating a new one.)

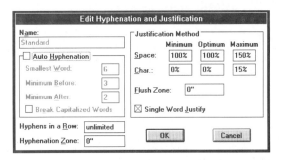

4. Edit the values in the various fields of the dialog box and then click OK. See the sections following this one for an explanation of each setting.

5. Click Save in the H&Js dialog box to save your changes to the H&J set.

Specifying Auto Hyphenation Rules

Use the Auto Hyphenation section of the Edit Hyphenation and Justification dialog box to turn automatic hyphenation on or off and to specify the rules by which automatic hyphenation occurs. When Auto Hyphenation is turned off (the default Standard H&J setting), no hyphenation occurs in a given paragraph unless you enter hyphens manually.

Remember Auto Hyphenation occurs on a paragraph-by-paragraph basis. The deciding factor is whether Auto Hyphenation is turned on for the H&J you specify in the Paragraph Formats dialog box.

Smallest Word The Smallest Word field tells Quark how many letters a word must contain in order for automatic hyphenation to occur. The default value is six letters.

Minimum Before When Auto Hyphenation is turned on, this field determines the minimum number of letters in a word that must precede a hyphen break. The default value is three letters.

Minimum After   The Minimum After field defines the minimum number of letters that must remain in a word after an automatic hyphen break. The default value is two letters.

Break Capitalized Words   The Break Capitalized Words option lets you choose whether to allow automatic hyphenation to occur in proper names and/or the first word in a line. This option is turned off in the default Standard H&J set.

Hyphens in a Row

The Hyphens in a Row option determines the number of lines in a row that can end in a hyphen, regardless of whether you use manual or automatic hyphenation. The default setting is unlimited. For aesthetic reasons, it is best that no more than three consecutive lines end in a hyphen.

Hyphenation Zone

The Hyphenation Zone is the area within which hyphenation can occur at the end of a line, relative to the right indent of the paragraph (Paragraph Formats dialog box). At the default setting of zero inches, other settings in the Edit Hyphenation and Justification dialog box determine whether and where Quark hyphenates a particular word. If you specify a positive distance value, Quark will hyphenate a word only if the previous word ends before the hyphenation zone and an appropriate break point is available within the word. Figure 6-16 illustrates how the hyphenation zone operates.

Defining a Justification Method

When you specify Justified alignment for a paragraph or style sheet, Quark must adjust spacing between words and letters slightly to force text to extend from the left to the right indent. The options in the Justification Method section of the Edit Hyphenation and Justification dialog box let you define the amount and range of spacing adjustment that occurs. The Minimum, Optimum, and Maximum options for word and character spacing apply to all paragraphs regardless of their align-

FIGURE 6-16 The Hyphenation Zone setting determines how far from the right indent hyphen breaks can occur

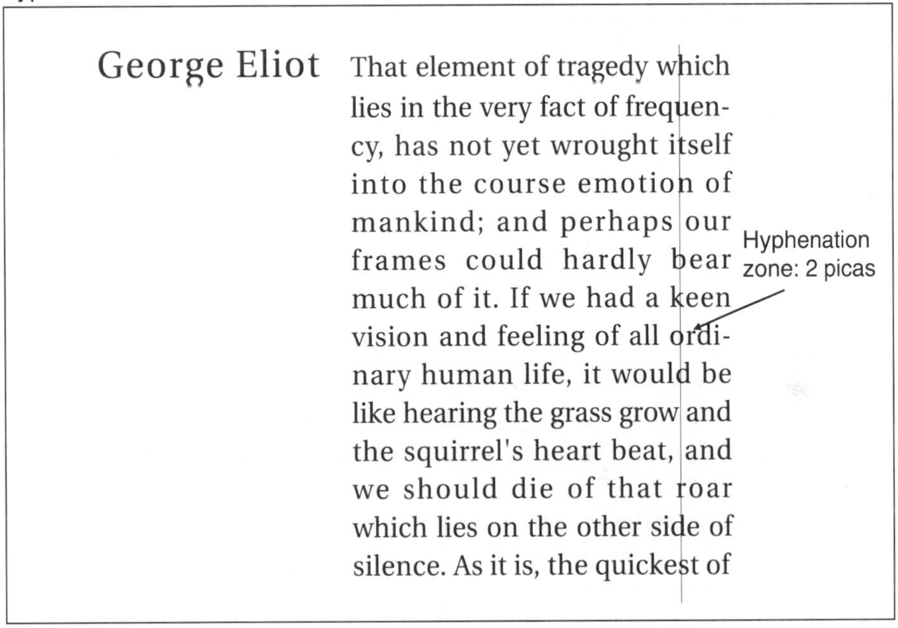

George Eliot That element of tragedy which lies in the very fact of frequency, has not yet wrought itself into the course emotion of mankind; and perhaps our frames could hardly bear much of it. If we had a keen vision and feeling of all ordinary human life, it would be like hearing the grass grow and the squirrel's heart beat, and we should die of that roar which lies on the other side of silence. As it is, the quickest of

Hyphenation zone: 2 picas

ment settings, but the other options apply only to paragraphs and style sheets featuring Justified alignment.

Space The Minimum, Optimum, and Maximum fields next to the Space option determine how much space Quark can add or remove between *words* in justified paragraphs. Quark expresses these values as a percentage of normal interword spacing. Quark always attempts to justify a line based on the Optimum value; if this fails, spacing can be adjusted within the range that falls between the Minimum and Maximum values. If nothing else works, Quark can exceed the Maximum interword spacing value.

Quark accepts Minimum, Optimum, and Maximum interword spacing values from 0 percent to 500 percent.

Character The Minimum, Optimum, and Maximum fields next to the Char. option determine how much space Quark can add or remove between *letters* in justified paragraphs. Like the Space values, these values also represent a percentage of normal letter spacing. The smallest allowable Minimum value is –50 percent, while the largest Maximum value is 100 percent.

Flush Zone   The Flush Zone option affects what happens to the last line of text in a justified paragraph. When Flush Zone is at zero inches (the default setting), Quark automatically justifies the last line of a justified paragraph, even if falls short and resulting intercharacter or interword spacing is too wide. You can prevent this from happening by adjusting the Flush Zone value.

Quark measures the flush zone relative to the right indent of a paragraph. As Figure 6-17 illustrates, Quark justifies only lines that end to the right of the Flush Zone value. If the last line in a paragraph ends to the left of this distance, it retains its normal word and letter spacing; Quark does not justify it.

Single Word Justify   When you check the Single Word Justify option, Quark forces a line containing a single word to justify, no matter how

FIGURE 6-17   The Flush Zone value determines whether Quark justifies the last line in a justified paragraph

George Eliot   That element of tragedy which lies in the very fact of frequency, has not yet wrought itself into the course emotion of mankind; and perhaps our frames could hardly bear much of it. If we had a keen vision and feeling of all ordinary human life, it would be like hearing the grass grow and the squirrel's heart beat, and we should die of that roar which lies on the other side of silence. As it is, the quickest of walk about well wadded with stupidity.

Flush zone: 3 picas

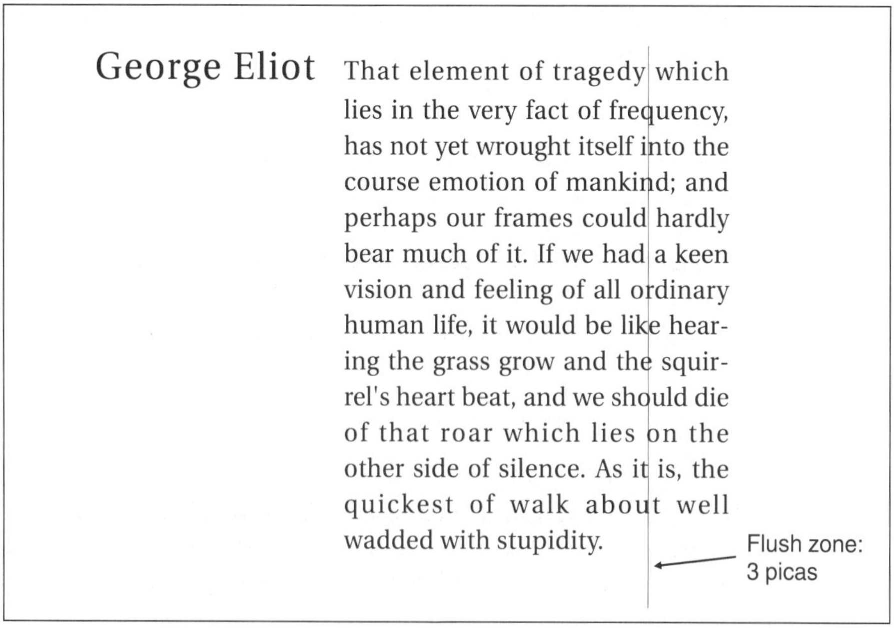

much space it has to add between words and letters. In most cases, text will look better if you leave Single Word Justify turned off.

Creating Custom H&Js

Every style sheet in a document has its own hyphenation and justification requirements. Consider the difference between body text and table cell data in a manual, for example. While automatic hyphenation might be desirable for body text paragraphs, it probably would not be advisable for information in a narrow table column. You can create up to 127 different sets of H&Js in a document to accommodate the needs of all your style sheets.

With H&Js, as with style sheets, you have options. You can define a new H&J from scratch or adapt a new H&J from an existing one.

Creating a New H&J

To define a new H&J, choose the H&Js command in the Edit menu and click the New button. The default options that you see in the Edit Hyphenation and Justification dialog box are those of the current normal H&J set. You can specify a name for the H&J that reflects its function in your document.

Creating an H&J by Example (Duplication)

To base a new H&J on an existing one, follow these steps:

1. Choose the H&Js command from the Edit menu to display the H&Js dialog box.

2. Click the H&J in the list box that you want to use as a model for a new one.

3. Click the Duplicate command button. When the Edit Hyphenation and Justification dialog box appears, enter a new name for the custom H&J set and adapt the existing values as desired.

Appending H&Js from Other Documents

You can append H&J sets from other Quark documents by clicking the Append button in the H&Js dialog box. The Append H&Js dialog box (shown here) closely resembles the Append Style Sheets dialog box and functions in the same way:

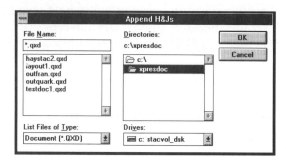

Deleting H&Js

To delete an existing set of H&Js (other than Standard), choose the H&Js command from the Edit menu, select the H&J set you want to delete, and then click the Delete button. If the active document contains any paragraphs to which this H&J applies, Quark responds with a warning message, as shown here:

Click OK to delete the H&J and apply the Standard H&J set to affected paragraphs. Keep in mind that line endings may change in the affected paragraphs, causing the copy in your document to reflow differently.

Editing Hyphenation Exceptions

Although Quark's hyphenation dictionary does not include every word in the English language, Quark can suggest hyphenation breaks for any word based on algorithms. When you are unsure about where Quark might hyphenate an unfamiliar or technical word, invoke the Suggested Hyphenation command in the Utilities menu. If Quark's suggested hyphenation breaks do not satisfy you, create your own dictionary of hyphenation exceptions (Quark will save this from one session to the next).

Viewing Suggested Hyphenation for a Word

To view Quark's suggested hyphenation breaks for any word in a document, follow these steps:

1. With the Content tool active and a document open, position the text cursor within or to the right of the word you want to check.

2. Choose the Suggested Hyphenation command in the Utilities menu. A small dialog box shows Quark's hyphenation breaks for the word, as shown here:

3. Click OK to exit the dialog box and return to the document. If you do not care for Quark's suggested breaks, use the Hyphenation Exceptions dictionary described in the next section.

Note The placement of the text cursor is very important when you choose the Suggested Hyphenations command. If more than one word is selected, Quark displays hyphenation breaks for the first word only.

Using Quark's Hyphenation Exceptions Dictionary

Many documents contain special words such as technical terms, jargon, or proper nouns peculiar to a specific field of interest. You can specify and save your preferred hyphenation breaks for these words using the Hyphenation Exceptions command in the Utilities menu. You can also edit the existing Hyphenation Exceptions dictionary at any time.

How Quark saves your preferred hyphenation exceptions depends on what you are doing when you choose the Hyphenation Exceptions command. To make the matter simpler, base your action on what you *want* Quark to do:

☐ If you want Quark to save hyphenation exceptions so that they will always be available for any document you create, choose the Hyphenation Exceptions command when no documents are open. Quark then saves your exceptions with its own xpress.prf preferences file.

☐ If you want hyphenation exceptions to be available in both the xpress.prf file and in a specific document, choose the Hyphenation Exceptions command when a document is open. When you next open the document, a dialog box will inform you that your preferences do not match Quark's. If you choose to accept Quark's preferences, the new hyphenation exceptions will become part of Quark's standard hyphenation dictionary.

☐ To save hyphenation exceptions with a specific document only, choose the Hyphenation Exceptions command when a document is open. The next time you open the document, Quark will inform you that your preferences do not match the standard ones. Choose the Keep Document Settings option in the dialog box that appears; Quark will retain your preferred exceptions separately from its standard hyphenation exceptions. This is a good option to choose when the words you hyphenate are extremely specialized and do not apply to most documents you produce.

To edit hyphenation preferences, follow these steps:

1. Choose the Hyphenation Exceptions command from the Utilities menu. The Hyphenation Exceptions dialog box appears, as shown here:

If you have entered hyphenation exceptions previously, the words you have entered appear in the list box. If the list contains no words, the message "No exceptions" appears instead.

2. To add a new word with hyphenation breaks, enter it in the text field at the bottom of the dialog box. Be sure to include all the potential hyphen breaks you want Quark to consider, as shown here:

The Add button becomes available when you begin typing. Click this button to add the word to the dictionary.

 Note You cannot enter capital letters or words with accented characters into this dialog box.

3. To delete an existing word with its hyphenation breaks, click the word in the list box and click Delete.

4. To save your edits and exit the dialog box, click the Save button.

Editing Kerning and Tracking Tables

Two additional commands in the Utilities menu give you unparalleled control over letter spacing on a font-by-font basis. Using the Tracking Edit command in the Utilities menu, you can plot a graph that links letter spacing to point size for any font installed in your system. The Kerning Edit command, also in the Utilities menu, lets you edit the built-in kerning values for specific letter pairs specified by font manufacturers. Both commands are available only if you installed the ktedit.xxt Quark XTension when you installed Quark.

How Quark saves your preferred tracking and kerning tables depends on what you are doing when you choose the Tracking Edit or Kerning Edit command.

❑ If you want your edited kerning and tracking tables to become the new defaults for all future documents, choose the Kerning Table Edit or Track Edit command when no documents are open. Quark then saves your font edits with its own ktedit.xxt file.

❑ If you want altered kerning and tracking tables to be available for both a specific document and all future new documents, choose the Kerning Table Edit or Track Edit command when a document is open. Later, when you next open the document, a dialog box will pop up to inform you that your preferences do not match Quark's. You can then choose to accept Quark's preferences, and the new kerning and tracking tables will become standard in your copy of Quark.

❑ To save edited kerning and tracking tables with a specific document only, choose the associated commands when a document is open. The next time you open the document, Quark will inform you that your preferences do not match the standard ones. Choose the Keep Document Settings option in the dialog box that appears; Quark will retain your edited kerning and tracking tables separately from its standard ones. Use this option when you are stylizing kerning and tracking values for a single document and unlikely to apply those values to every document you produce.

Editing and Managing Kerning Tables

Most fonts include a kerning table supplied by the font manufacturer. A *kerning table* lists many specific character pairs and a value for standard letter spacing between those pairs. Unfortunately, today's digital fonts rarely contain as many kerning pairs as their older electronic typesetting counterparts, with the result that kerning is somewhat less thorough and less elegant. QuarkXPress lets you edit any font's built-in kerning table, altering standard kerning values or even adding new kerning pairs to continue where the font manufacturer left off. You can then export the edited values for later use, or import and edit kerning values that you have stored previously.

Editing Kerning Tables

To edit kerning pair values for a specific font, follow these steps:

1. Choose the Kerning Table Edit command from the Utilities menu. The Kerning Table Edit dialog box shown here appears, listing all the fonts and weights of those fonts that are currently installed in your system.

2. Click the font and weight in the list box whose kerning table you want to edit. The Edit button becomes available.

3. Click the Edit button to access the Kerning Values dialog box for the chosen weight of the selected font. The following Kerning Values dialog box is for the Adobe Boatman font:

Letter pairs

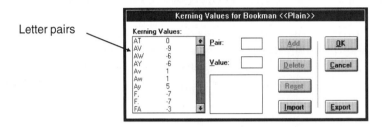

4. To edit existing values for a predefined kerning pair, click on the desired letter pair in the Kerning Values list box. The two characters appear in the Pair field, and their current kerning value appears in the Value field.

5. Enter a new value in the Value field and click the Replace button. The letter spacing between the sample characters in the display box changes as you watch.

Remember   Increasing or reducing a kerning value by 1 changes the distance between letter pairs by 1/200 of an em space. You can enter values ranging from –100/200 (–100) of an em space to 100/200 (100) of an em space.

6. Continue editing letter pairs in the same way. If you want to *add* a new kerning pair that the font manufacturer did not provide, enter the two characters in the Pair field and specify a kerning value in the Value field. Click the Add button (which appears instead of the Replace button) to add the new pair to the existing kerning table.

7. When finished editing or adding kerning pairs, click OK in the Kerning Values dialog box to return to the Kerning Table Edit dialog box.

8. Click Save to save changes to the current kerning table.

Managing Kerning Tables

If a document calls for specially edited kerning tables, you can export custom tables to separate files and import them again for later use. You can also delete existing kerning pairs from a kerning table.

To export a custom kerning table, follow these steps:

1. Choose the Kerning Table Edit command from the Utilities menu and edit or add kerning pairs as described in the previous section.

2. When ready, click the Export command button in the Kerning Values dialog box. The Save As dialog box appears as shown here, with Save File as Type set to Kern Tables (*.krn).

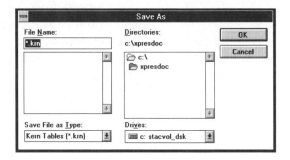

3. If you plan to use the custom kerning table with a specific document file, export the kerning table to the same directory. If you plan to use the custom kerning table with all Quark documents, export it to the xpress directory.

Importing a kerning table for further editing or use with the current document is a similar operation. Click the Import button in the Kerning Values dialog box and import the desired .krn file in the Open dialog box.

If you change your mind about a kerning value that you have edited, click the Reset button to change it back to its original value. Clicking Delete removes the selected kerning pair from the current kerning table.

Tip If you use a service bureau to output files from a document that contains one or more edited kerning tables, make sure you send the appropriate kerning files (with extension .krn) to the service bureau along with your document files. If you forget to do this, line endings and letter spacings may turn out differently from what you expect. The best safeguard might be to create your own output files.

Creating Custom Tracking Graphs

Whereas kerning has to do with spacing between two specific letters, you will remember from Chapter 5 that tracking deals with general letter spacing for a font. The Track Edit command in the Utilities menu gives you just as much refined control over tracking values as the Kerning Table Edit command does over kerning values. With the Track Edit command, however, you have a graphical interface in which you can create a custom tracking curve for any font at specific point sizes.

Many fonts look best if you decrease tracking (make letter spacing tighter) as font size increases. This is one useful application among many for the Tracking Values dialog box.

To edit tracking values for a given font, follow these steps:

1. Choose the Track Edit command in the Utilities menu to access the Tracking Edit dialog box shown here:

This dialog box lists all the fonts currently installed in your system.

2. Click the font whose tracking table you want to edit and then click the Edit button. The Tracking Values dialog box for the chosen font appears as Figure 6-18 shows. If you have not previously changed the tracking table, it appears as a straight line at a value of zero.

FIGURE 6-18   The Tracking Values dialog box with a default tracking curve

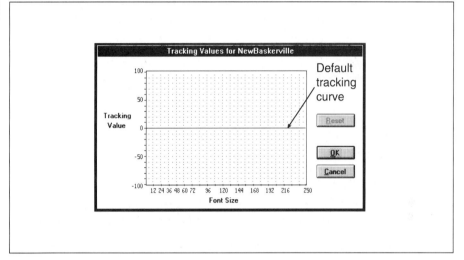

Tracking values appear along the vertical axis, while font sizes appear along the horizontal axis.

3. Modifying the tracking curve changes the tracking values at specific point sizes of the font. To modify the curve, click anywhere along its axis to create a handle. When you have created two handles, you can drag one to alter the slope of the curve. (Up to four handles are allowed.) Figure 6-19 shows a curve that represents tightened letter spacing as the point size of the font increases.

Remember   Increasing or reducing a tracking value by 1 changes letter spacing at a given point size by 1/200 of an em space. You can enter values ranging from –100/200 (–100) of an em space to 100/200 (100) of an em space.

4. If you change your mind about tracking values you have edited, click the Reset button to return the curve to its default horizontal line shape.

5. To save an edited tracking table, click OK in the Tracking Values dialog box and Save in the Tracking Edit dialog box. Quark saves the new tracking information as described at the beginning of the "Editing Kerning and Tracking Tables" section earlier.

FIGURE

6-19

An edited tracking curve showing tighter tracking as font size increases

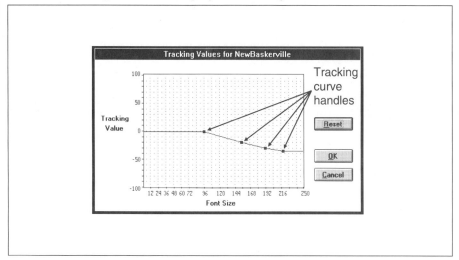

In Chapters 5 and 6, you have explored Quark's capabilities for stylizing text and automating typography. Chapter 7 takes your mastery of text handling one step further, into the realm of importing, exporting, and preformatting text from other word processors.

CHAPTER

Importing and Exporting Text

*I*n an ideal world, everyone would use QuarkXPress to enter text as well as to format it. In the real world, however, the author of a document is not always the person who lays it out. Some types of documents—newsletters, magazines, journals, or manuals, for example—have multiple authors, each with his or her own favorite word processor. The result? At layout time, you have to acquire external text files before you can edit them in Quark.

Quark offers you choices about how to acquire externally created text. You can import text, copy and paste it using the Windows clipboard, or—in the case of Microsoft Excel and some other databases—link it to or embed it in Quark using the OLE capabilities of Windows 3.1. If you place a high value on saving layout time, you can even learn how to precode text in a word processor so that it comes into Quark already formatted.

After editing or formatting text in Quark, you may sometimes need to re-export it back to its original application for further work. Here, too, you have options. You can export text to another file format or (if the text is linked or embedded) edit it in its original application without leaving Quark. This chapter explores how and when to use each of these options.

Text File Formats Supported

Quark can import and export text files in a variety of formats. Some of these are specific to popular word processors, while others are supported almost universally. The file format you choose when importing or exporting text determines how much formatting will survive intact the transfer between Quark and the word processor.

 Note Quark imports a *copy* of a text file, never the original. The imported text file becomes part of the Quark document. Any text editing you perform has no effect on the original text file.

Word Processor-Specific Formats

When you installed QuarkXPress, you had the option of installing several word processor filters at the same time. These filters, or XTensions, as Quark prefers to call them, let Quark translate character and paragraph attributes of a specific word processor with very little loss.

Tip As a general rule, the only formatting that transfers well between Quark and another word processor is the formatting that both programs share in common or describe in similar ways.

Word for Windows 1.0 and 2.0 (.doc)

QuarkXPress and Microsoft Word for Windows define character attributes, paragraph attributes, and style sheets in similar ways. This may explain why Quark can retain most character, paragraph, tab, and ruling line attributes from an imported Word for Windows 1.0 or 2.0 document.

One warning, though: Quark imports a Word for Windows document as locally formatted text with No Style assigned. If you apply existing Quark style sheets to any imported paragraphs, you will lose all those carefully preserved text attributes. The most painless way to retain these attributes intact is to create new style sheets based on paragraphs in the imported document. Refer to the "Basing a New Style Sheet on an Existing Paragraph" section of Chapter 6 to review how to do this.

Tip The Macintosh version of QuarkXPress 3.1 can import Microsoft Word files with their style sheets intact. If you are part of a publishing workgroup that includes Macintosh Quark users, you may want to take advantage of this feature.

Microsoft Write (.wri)

Microsoft Write, installed with Microsoft Windows 3.1 in the Accessories group window, is capable of assigning a broad variety of character and paragraph attributes to text. Quark imports text saved in Write with all formatting intact, but since Write does not support the use of style sheets, Quark assigns the entire text file to the style sheet in effect at the current text cursor position. In an empty text box, this is usually the Normal style sheet.

Quark treats all text attributes in the imported Write file as local formatting within the Normal style sheet. If you assign other Quark style sheets to the imported text, you lose the original Write formatting. You can retain the attributes in an imported Write document by basing new style sheets on the paragraphs in which they occur, as described in Chapter 6.

Word Processor-Independent File Formats

If you or your clients use a word processor other than Microsoft Word for Windows or Microsoft Write, no problem. Quark can accept text in several additional file formats that are not proprietary to any single word processing package. The three independent file formats that Quark supports for text import and export are Rich Text Format (.rtf), ASCII (.txt), and Quark's own XPress Tags (.xtg).

Rich Text Format (.rtf)

The past several years have seen the development of a few file formats that word processors can use to share formatting information with one another and with page layout software. Rich Text Format (with the extension .rtf) is the most well-known of these. Files saved in Rich Text Format retain their character and paragraph formatting information, which gets translated into generic instructions that many word processors can read.

Here are some of the more popular word processors that can save files in .rtf format:

- WordPerfect 5.1 for DOS
- WordPerfect for Windows
- Ami Pro 2.0
- Microsoft Word for DOS 5.0 or later
- Microsoft Word for Windows 1.x and later
- XyWrite III Plus

When Quark imports a text file saved in .rtf format, it assigns No Style to each of the paragraphs. In other words, it treats all imported attributes as local formatting. If you apply any Quark style sheet to the imported text, Quark overwrites the original formatting. Just as with Word for Windows and Microsoft Write files, you can get around this disadvantage easily by developing new Quark style sheets based on paragraphs in the imported text file.

ASCII Text (.txt)

Nearly every word processor can save text in ASCII format (extension .txt). ASCII text is the lowest common denominator of any text file format in terms of the amount of formatting it retains. Text saved in ASCII format retains no character attributes (font, point size, style, and so forth) and no information about indents, alignment, or other paragraph attributes. Tab stops become spaces and line breaks become paragraph breaks when you import a file saved in ASCII format.

If the only Quark-compatible format in which your or your clients' word processor can save text is ASCII, be sure to prepare the text with as little formatting as possible. The best strategy is to enter all text flush left with no special indenting, tabs, bold, or italic. If a text file contains tables, you or the author of the text file should insert a single space between each data entry in a row, without worrying about how data aligns in the word processor. That way, after importing text, you will have to spend less time weeding out extra spaces before you set up tab stops for the proper alignment.

XPress Tags Format (.xtg)

Quark's XPress Tags format (extension .xtg) is actually a heavily coded ASCII format that any word processor can read. XPress Tags allow you to define every kind of formatting—character, paragraph, and style sheet—that Quark can apply, and to import text into Quark without losing any formatting whatsoever.

You can generate an XPress Tags file in a word processor by entering XPress Tag codes with your text (see the "Preformatting Text with XPress Tags" section of this chapter) and then saving the file as an ASCII document with the .xtg extension before importing it into Quark. You can also export text in a Quark document to the XPress Tags format for further editing in a word processor.

Importing Text with the Get Text Command

In order to import text into a Quark document, you must first select a text box when the Content tool is active. The Get Text command in the File menu then becomes available.

To import a text file into a document, follow these steps:

1. Activate the Content tool and click anywhere in the text box into which you want to import the text file. If the text box already contains text, click to position the text cursor at the point where you want the imported copy to flow.

2. Choose the Get Text command from the File menu or press CTRL-E. The Get Text dialog box shown here appears:

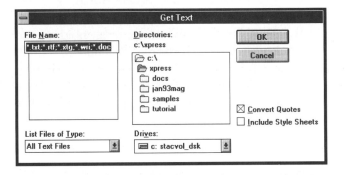

3. Use the List Files of Type drop-down list box to select the file formats you want to be able to view in the File Name list box. Your options are: All Text Files, ASCII Text, Rich Text Format, XPress Tags, Microsoft Write, Word for Windows 1.x, Word for Windows 2.x, and All Files. With the default All Text Files option selected, you can see text files of any compatible format.

Tip Choose the All Files option if you normally save text files with unusual file extensions.

4. Use the Drives and Directories list boxes to locate the file you want to import; highlight the filename in the Files list box.

5. If you want Quark to convert double dashes in the text file to em dashes (—) and foot and inch marks (' and ") to typographically correct quotation marks (" and "), check the Convert Quotes check box.

6. If you are importing an XPress Tags file and want existing style sheet information to transfer into Quark intact, remember to check the Include Style Sheets check box.

7. Click OK to import the text file.

Quark always imports a file at the current position of the text cursor. This feature is a boon to desktop publishers who need to combine multiple text files within a single text box or text chain. If the selected text box is linked to other text boxes, Quark sends any overflow copy to the next text box in the chain. If the selected text box is part of an automatic text chain and Auto Page Insertion in the General Preferences dialog box is turned on, Quark adds as many pages as are necessary to fit copy. Depending on the Auto Page Insertion setting, Quark may add the pages at the end of the current section, at the end of the story, or at the end of the document. See Chapter 3 for more information about setting up automatic text chains through master or document pages.

Exporting Text with the Save Text Command

During document layout and production, you may sometimes find it useful to export text in a Quark document back to an external word processor for further editing. This is especially desirable when documents contain so many graphics that screen redraw slows down unacceptably during text editing. The Save Text command in the File menu, available when the Content tool is active and a text box is selected, comes to your rescue for cases like these.

Quark can export its own text to the same file formats from which it imports (see "Text File Formats Supported" at the beginning of this chapter). Be forewarned, however, that only the XPress Tags format, which fully supports Quark style sheet information, is acceptable for exporting text that you plan to re-import into Quark later. If you export text to other supported file formats and then bring the text back into Quark, you lose all the links to Quark style sheets and will need to reapply them one paragraph at a time—ugh!

To export text from a Quark document to an external word processor, follow these steps:

1. Activate the Content tool and select the text box that contains the story or text you want to export. If you plan to export only a limited block of text, highlight it at this point.

Note If the active text box is part of a linked chain and you do not select any text in step 1, Quark will export text in all the text boxes that are linked to the current one.

2. Choose the Save Text command in the File menu. The Save Text dialog box shown here appears:

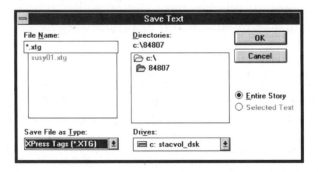

3. Use the Save File as Type list box to select the file format to which to export the text.

Note If you plan to export text to Word for Windows 2.0 format, the file extension Quark will assign to the file is .wrd.

4. Use the Drives and Directories list boxes to locate the directory in which to save the exported text file.

5. If any text is currently selected in the active text box, both the Entire Story and Selected Text buttons will be available. Click the button that describes the amount of text you want to export. If you did not select any text in step 1, only the Entire Story button is available; Quark will export all the text in text boxes linked to the active one.

6. Enter the name of the text file in the File Name entry box and click OK to generate the new text file.

See the "Preformatting Text with XPress Tags" section for more information on how to export text in XPress Tags format to an external word processor.

Preformatting Text with XPress Tags

If you have ever worked with Ventura Publisher, the notion of precoding text files to save layout time is probably not new to you. Precoding lets you embed style sheet and other page layout formatting information directly into a word processor text file. When you import the file into the layout program, text is formatted automatically.

XPress Tags, Quark's own precoding system, is a formatting powerhouse. XPress Tag codes are capable of specifying any Quark character or paragraph attribute, kerning text, entering special typographical characters, or defining and applying Quark style sheets. Files saved in or exported to Quark's XPress Tags file format (extension .xtg) are simply ASCII text files with embedded codes; you can edit and save these files in any word processor.

XPress Tags codes may not look pretty in a text file, but they are powerful. Advanced Quark users can generate original text files in the word processor, embed XPress Tags codes in them, and save the files as ASCII files with the extension .xtg for eventual import into Quark. If you find the idea of entering all those codes in a text file intimidating, keep in mind that Quark can do much of the work for you. After all, text exported from an existing Quark document in XPress Tags format (.xtg) already contains XPress Tag codes that you can view and edit in the word processor.

Taking a Peek Behind the Scenes

There is no better way to gain an overview of how XPress Tags work than to view tags from an existing Quark document that you have exported in XPress Tags format. Figure 7-1 shows a formatted Quark document featuring several different style sheets, various fonts, and locally formatted text. After exporting the text in this document to XPress Tags format, we re-imported it into a new Quark document, leaving the Include Style Sheets and Convert Quotes options unchecked. With these settings, Quark imported the text file as shown in Figures 7-2a and 7-2b, without converting the codes to actual formatting attributes. Comparing Figure 7-1 with Figures 7-2a and 7-2b gives you an idea of the anatomy of an XPress Tags document.

Refer to Figures 7-2a and 7-2b during the following examination of the structure of an XPress Tags file and the kinds of information it contains. The subsequent sections will teach you more about entering specific codes for character attributes, paragraph attributes, special characters, or style sheet definitions.

Quark Version and Character Set

The first line of an XPress Tags file always indicates the version of Quark that produced it and the character set used. Both of these codes appear between greater than (>) and less than (<) signs. Figure 7-2a shows that version 3.1 of QuarkXPress generated the file using the Windows character set (e1). This information can be useful for troubleshooting if you ever encounter problems working with XPress Tags files from different software versions or files transferred from the Macintosh version of QuarkXPress. The "Inserting Special Characters with XPress Tag Codes" section of this chapter contains a list of available character set codes.

FIGURE 7-1 A formatted Quark document featuring several different style sheets, various fonts, and locally formatted text

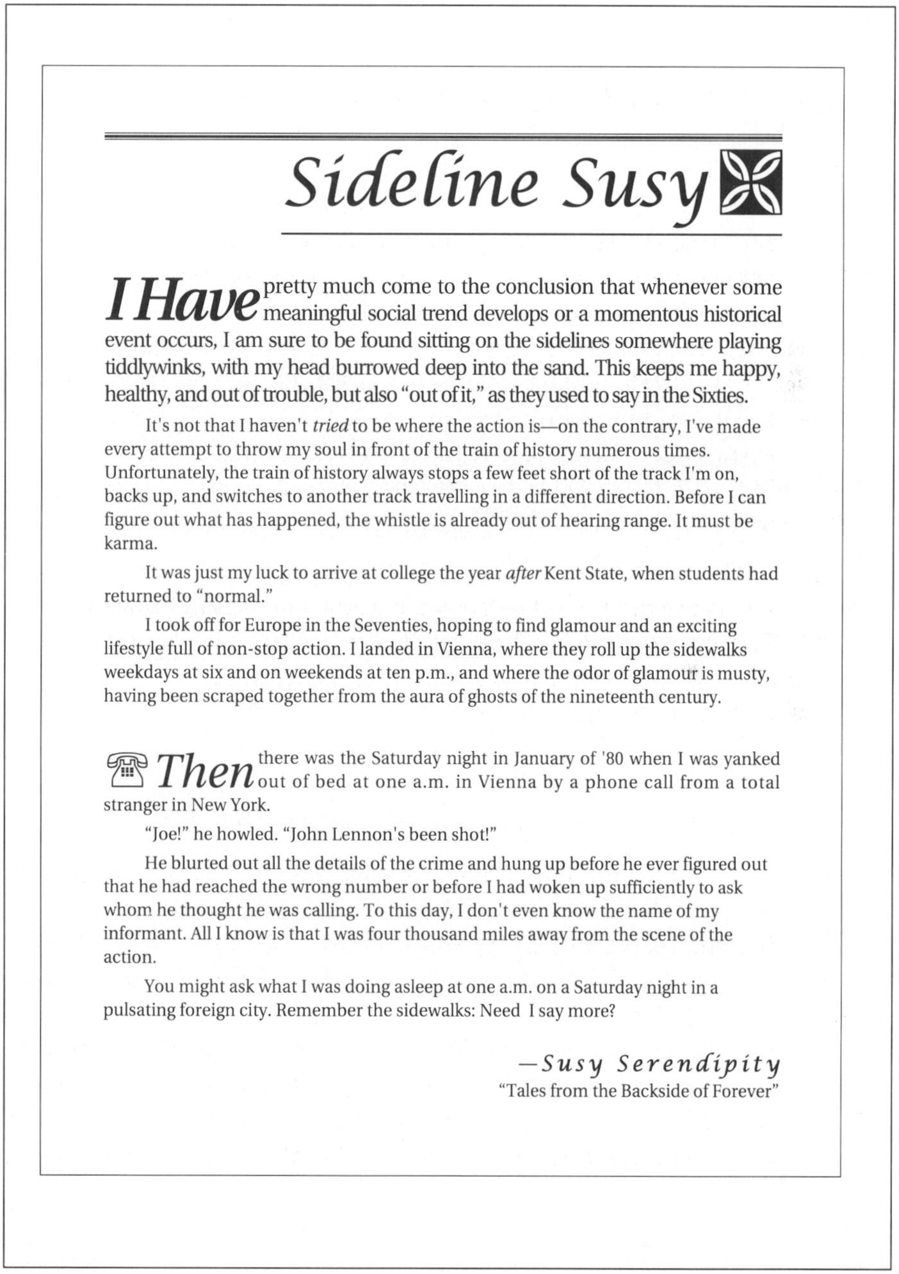

Sideline Susy

I Have pretty much come to the conclusion that whenever some meaningful social trend develops or a momentous historical event occurs, I am sure to be found sitting on the sidelines somewhere playing tiddlywinks, with my head burrowed deep into the sand. This keeps me happy, healthy, and out of trouble, but also "out of it," as they used to say in the Sixties.

It's not that I haven't *tried* to be where the action is—on the contrary, I've made every attempt to throw my soul in front of the train of history numerous times. Unfortunately, the train of history always stops a few feet short of the track I'm on, backs up, and switches to another track travelling in a different direction. Before I can figure out what has happened, the whistle is already out of hearing range. It must be karma.

It was just my luck to arrive at college the year *after* Kent State, when students had returned to "normal."

I took off for Europe in the Seventies, hoping to find glamour and an exciting lifestyle full of non-stop action. I landed in Vienna, where they roll up the sidewalks weekdays at six and on weekends at ten p.m., and where the odor of glamour is musty, having been scraped together from the aura of ghosts of the nineteenth century.

Then there was the Saturday night in January of '80 when I was yanked out of bed at one a.m. in Vienna by a phone call from a total stranger in New York.

"Joe!" he howled. "John Lennon's been shot!"

He blurted out all the details of the crime and hung up before he ever figured out that he had reached the wrong number or before I had woken up sufficiently to ask whom he thought he was calling. To this day, I don't even know the name of my informant. All I know is that I was four thousand miles away from the scene of the action.

You might ask what I was doing asleep at one a.m. on a Saturday night in a pulsating foreign city. Remember the sidewalks: Need I say more?

—*Susy Serendipity*
"Tales from the Backside of Forever"

FIGURE
7-2a

The "Sideline Susy" document in XPress Tags format

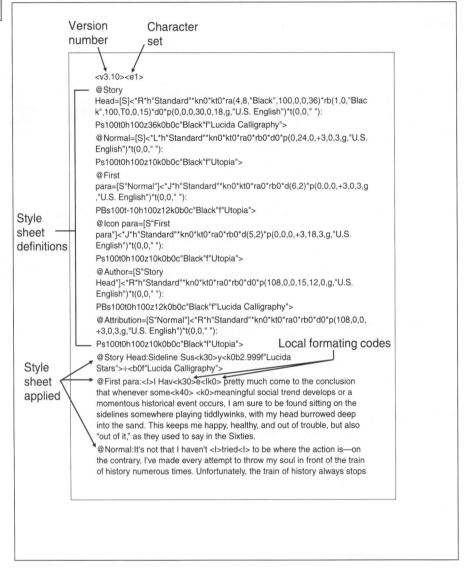

FIGURE 7-2b

More of the "Sideline Susy" document in XPress Tags format

a few feet short of the track I'm on, backs up, and switches to another track travelling in a different direction. Before I can figure out what has happened, the whistle is already out of hearing range. It must be karma.

It was just my luck to arrive at college the year <I>after<I> Kent State, when students had returned to "normal."

I took off for Europe in the Seventies, hoping to find glamour and an exciting lifestyle full of non-stop action. I landed in Vienna, where they roll up the sidewalks weekdays at six and on weekends at ten p.m., and where the odor of glamour is musty, having been scraped together from the aura of ghosts of the nineteenth century.

@Icon para:<f"Lucida Icons">/<If"Utopia">The<k20>n<Ik0> there was the Saturday night in January of '80 when I was yanked<k30> <k0>out of bed at one a.m. in Vienna by a phone call from a total stranger in New York.

@Normal:"Joe!" he howled. "John Lennon's been shot!"

He blurted out all the details of the crime and hung up before he ever figured out that he had reached the wrong number or before I had woken up sufficiently to ask whom he thought he was calling. To this day, I don't even know the name of my informant. All I know is that I was four thousand miles away from the scene of the action.

You might ask what I was doing asleep at one a.m. on a Saturday night in a pulsating foreign city. Remember the sidewalks: Need <\p>I say more?

@Author:—Susy Serendipity

@Attribution:"Tales from the Backside of Forever"

Style sheet applied

Consecutive paragraphs using same style sheet

Style Sheet Definitions

The next section of an XPress Tags file (see Figure 7-2a) lists all the style sheets used in the current document, together with their character, paragraph, rule, and tab attributes. This part of the file may be shorter or longer depending on the number of style sheets a document contains. See the "Defining and Applying Style Sheets with Codes" section for more specific information.

 Tip You also can define a style sheet just before the first paragraph in which you use it in a text file. However, placing all style sheet definitions at the head of a text file is a more efficient way to encode the file and makes it easier to find style sheet attributes.

Style Sheets Applied to Paragraphs

After the style sheet definitions come the actual text paragraphs in the document. At the beginning of most paragraphs in Figures 7-2a and 7-2b, you can see the @ symbol followed by a name and a colon (:). These sequences are codes for the style sheet applied to the current paragraph and always appear at the very beginning of a paragraph.

If two or more paragraphs in a row have the same style sheet applied to them, only the first paragraph in the series contains the style sheet code (see the example in Figure 7-2b). Paragraphs continue without style sheet codes until Quark encounters a paragraph to which a different style sheet applies.

Local Formatting Codes

Remember, locally applied character and paragraph attributes always take precedence over style sheet formatting in Quark. If you alter the font, type style, kerning, tracking, or other attributes of selected characters within a paragraph, Quark inserts codes to show the type of formatting and where it begins and ends. Figure 7-2a shows examples of changes to font, point size, kerning values, and baseline shift applied to some characters in the second paragraph in the text file. Refer back to Figure 7-1 to see how Quark translates those codes into formatting. You can find more detailed listings of local formatting codes and their uses in the "Character Attribute Codes and Conventions" and "Paragraph Attribute Codes and Conventions" sections of this chapter.

Character Attribute Codes and Conventions

As you saw in Chapter 5, you can apply character attributes—font, point size, color, shade, style, and so on—to any number of selected characters in a Quark document. Quark's XPress Tags codes for character attributes appear in Table 7-1. To enter these codes correctly, you need to follow certain conventions, given in the table.

Recognizing Character Attribute Codes

Figure 7-3 shows a paragraph that includes several locally formatted changes in character attributes, side by side with its equivalent in XPress Tags format. As you can see from this example, character attribute codes are always enclosed by a less than and greater than sign (<>). Each code includes a letter or character that helps you remember the function of the code. For example, the code <k40> indicates that you are applying a kerning value of 40 between two characters as local formatting (see Table 7-1).

You can combine multiple codes within a single enclosure. For instance, the code sequence

<s30f"Utopia Black">

signifies the beginning of a text string to which you have applied both a 30 percent shade and the Utopia Black font.

Positioning Character Attribute Codes

You must position a character attribute code immediately before the first character to which it applies. As shown in Figure 7-4, the attribute

TABLE 7-1   XPress Tags Codes for Character Attributes

To Set This Character Attribute	Enter This Code
Style Attributes	
Plain style	<P>
Bold style	<B>
Italic style	<I>
Outline style	<O>
Shadow style	<S>
Underline style	<U>
Word Underline style	<W>
Strikethru style	</>
All Caps style	<K>
Small Caps style	<H>
Superscript style	<+>
Subscript style	<->
Superior style	<V>
Turn off current local style attribute	Repeat attribute code or use <P> for plain
Revert to style of current style sheet	<$>
Other Character Attributes	
Change font	<f"fontname">
Change point size	<z###.##> where # represents number of points
Change text color (spot color)	<c"colorname">
Change text color (process color)	<cC###,cM###,cY###,cK###> where # represents value
Change text shade	<s###> where # represents percentage
Horizontal scale value	<h###.##> where # represents scale percentage

TABLE 7-1   XPress Tags Codes for Character Attributes (*continued*)

To Set This Character Attribute	Enter This Code
Kern the next two characters	<k###.##> where # represents 1/200 cm space
Track selected characters	<t###.##> where # represents 1/200 em space
Change baseline shift	<b###.##> where # represents number of points
Reset attributes to current style sheet	Include $ in code string (e.g., <c$> resets color)

or attributes described in the code remain in effect until Quark encounters another set of codes that either resets the attributes or changes them to another set of attributes.

Cancelling or Resetting Character Attributes

There are several ways to tell Quark that you no longer want locally formatted character attributes to be in effect. The coding you use depends on the character attribute currently applied and whether you are using style sheets to format the document.

Cancelling Style Attributes   To cancel a style attribute code when you are applying local formatting, repeat the character attribute code *after* the last character to which it applies. For example, the sequence

<BI>I have<BI> just about come to the conclusion

tells Quark to format the words "I have" in bold and italic styles and then to turn those styles off for the remaining text.

FIGURE
7-3

Local character formatting in Quark format and in XPress Tags codes

just about come to the conclusion that whenever some meaningful social trend develops or a momentous historical event occurs, I am sure to be found sitting on the sidelines somewhere playing tiddlywinks, with my head burrowed deep into the sand. This keeps me happy, healthy, and out of trouble, but also "out of it," as they used to say in the Sixties.

```
@First para:<s30f"Utopia
Black">I
Hav<k40>e<s100k0f"Utopia">j
ust about come to the
conclusion that whenever
some meaningful social trend
develops or a momentous
historical event occurs, I am
sure to be found sitting on the
sidelines some<\h>where
playing tiddly<\h>winks, with
my head burrowed deep into
the sand. This keeps me
happy, healthy, and out of
trouble, but also "out of it," as
they used to say in the Sixties.
```

Shade and font changes

Kerning value

Reset to default shade, kerning, and font

Another way to achieve the same end (if plain text is the default) would be to insert the code <P> to cancel the bold and italic and revert to plain text, as shown with this coding:

<BI>I have<P> just about come to the conclusion

To change to a *different* style rather than just cancel the current formatting, you can specify the style directly. For instance,

<OS>I have<U> just about come to the conclusion

tells Quark to use the outline and shadow styles for the first few characters and then the underline style thereafter.

FIGURE
7-4

Using the $ character to revert to default attributes (here, point size) for the current style sheet

I Have Just About come to the conclusion that whenever some meaningful social trend develops or a momentous historical event occurs, I am sure to be found sitting on the sidelines some-where playing tiddly-winks, with my head burrowed deep into the sand.

Style changes

@Normal:<lOS>I Have Just About <$>come to the conclusion that whenever some meaningful social trend develops or a momentous historical event occurs, I am sure to be found sitting on the sidelines some<\h>where playing tiddly<\h>winks, with my head burrowed deep into the sand.

Revert to default style for style sheet

If a document uses style sheets, you have a fourth option in addition to the three just described. To cancel a style attribute and reset it to whatever style attribute the current style sheet is using, insert the <$> code after the last character to which the local formatting applies. Figure 7-4 shows an example paragraph formatted with a Normal style sheet that uses italic text. After the code sequence <lOS> applies the plain, outline, and shadow styles to the first few words in the paragraph, the XPress Tags code <$> reverts text back to the italic style assigned to the style sheet.

Cancelling or Resetting Other Character Attributes   Character attributes other than style require that you specify a name or value in addition to the code. A font name, for example, must be enclosed within quotation marks as in the following example:

<f"Utopia Black"> I have

Cancelling a locally applied font or color is as simple as substituting another font name or color in the code string:

<f"Utopia Black"> I have<f"Utopia"> just about come

Remember to spell font and color names exactly as they appear under Adobe Type Manager, or else Quark will not recognize them.

Cancelling point size, kerning increments, or other character attributes that specify values is a matter of stipulating the new values after the locally formatted text, as shown here:

I hav<k40>e<k0> just about come to the conclusion

In the foregoing example, the codes tell Quark to increase kerning between the letter "e" and the space following it by 40 units, and then to return to a kerning value of zero.

To revert to the assigned values for the current style sheet, substitute a dollar sign ($) after a code letter instead of a specific value. Thus, the sequence

I hav<k40>e<k$> pretty much made up my mind

tells Quark to return to the default kerning value after applying 40 units of kerning between the "e" and the space that follows it.

Color shading is another example of an attribute that requires you to specify a value. For example, the code sequence

<s30>I Have<s100> just about come to the conclusion

tells Quark to format the words "I have" as 30 percent gray and then revert to a 100 percent shade of black for the remaining text in the paragraph, as shown here:

I Have **just about come to the conclusion**

Paragraph Attribute Codes and Conventions

XPress Tags' paragraph attribute codes are a little more complex than character attribute codes, in that they consist of specifications for several attributes strung together. Figure 7-5 shows an example of a locally formatted paragraph as it appears in Quark and in XPress Tags format. The paragraph attributes cluster together in the first few lines of the text file, followed by character attributes coding on separate lines. Table 7-2 lists the code sequences you should use when entering paragraph attribute codes in a text file.

Recognizing Paragraph Attribute Codes

A cluster of paragraph attribute codes always begins with a less than sign (<). An asterisk appears in front of each code in the series to distinguish it from character attribute codes. The code character or characters help you remember the function of the attribute (ra for rule above, for instance). Most paragraph attribute codes (except alignment codes) can be complex, consisting of multiple attribute specifications enclosed by parentheses and separated by commas. Consider this specification for a rule above:

<*ra(3,3,"Black",100,0,0,18)>

This rule is defined as three points wide, using the third style in the Style drop-down list box, 100 percent black, with no left or right indent, and offset by 18 points. The result looks like this:

Unfortunately, the train of history always stops a few feet short of the track I'm on, backs up, and switches to another track travelling in a different direction.

FIGURE 7-5

A locally formatted paragraph in Quark and as it appears in XPress Tags codes

I have just about come to the conclusion that whenever some meaningful social tre nd develops or a momentous historical event occurs, I am sure to be found sitting on the sidelines somewhere playing tiddlywinks, with my head burrowed deep into the sand.

Paragraph attribute codes

<*C*h"Standard"*kn0*kt0*ra(1,0,"Black",100,0,0,15)*rb(1,0,"Black",100,0,0,6)*d(1,3)*p(12,0,12,+5,0,0,g,"U.S. English")*t(0,0," "):

Pls100t0h100z12k0b0c"Black"f"Bookman">I have just about come to the conclusion that whenever some meaningful social trend develops or a momentous historical event occurs, I am sure to be found sitting on the sidelines some<\h>where playing tiddly<\h>winks, with my head burrowed deep into the sand.

Character attribute codes

Note Remember not to add any spaces between commas when you enter these codes yourself in a word processor!

Codes for Tab Stops Table 7-2 describes the function of the three values that make up the XPress Tags code for any tab stop. Here are a few more tips to help you edit existing Quark codes or define your own:

❑ Specify the Position value using the unit of measurement currently set for Horizontal Ruler in the General Preferences dialog box. For example, use " for inches and pt for points.

❑ The Alignment value is a number that represents the order in which alignment options appear in the drop-down list within the Paragraph Tabs dialog box. Thus, 1 specifies Left, 2 Centered, 3 Right, 4 Decimal, 5 Comma, and 6 Align On.

❑ The Fill Character value appears between quotation marks. If you do not want any fill character for a given tab stop, press the SPACEBAR to add a blank space between the quotation marks (" ").

TABLE
7-2

XPress Tags Codes for Paragraph Attributes

To Set This Paragraph Attribute	Enter This Code
Alignment Attributes	
Left-align paragraph	<*L>
Center paragraph	<*C>
Right-align paragraph	<*R>
Justify paragraph	<*J>
Other Paragraph Attributes	
Tab stops	<*t(##.#,#,"character")> First value represents position Second value specifies alignment number "character" specifies fill character
Paragraph formats	<*p(##.#,##.#,##.#,##.#,##.#,##.#,G or g, "Language")> First value specifies Left Indent Second value specifies First Line Indent Third value specifies Right Indent Fourth value specifies Leading amount Fifth value specifies Space Before Sixth value specifies Space After Seventh value specifies Lock to Baseline Grid (G=on, g=off) Eighth value specifies hyphenation dictionary language
Hyphenation and Justification	<*h"specification name">
Paragraph Rule Above	<*ra(##,#,"color name",#,## or T##,## or T##,## or ##%)> First value specifies rule Width Second value specifies rule Style "color name" specifies color of rule Fourth value specifies Shade percentage Fifth value specifies Indent From Left or Text Indent (T) Sixth value specifies Indent From Right or Text Indent (T) Seventh value specifies rule Offset as absolute value or percent

TABLE

7-2

XPress Tags Codes for Paragraph Attributes (*continued*)

To Set This Paragraph Attribute	Enter This Code
Paragraph Rule Below	<*rb(##,#,"color name",#,##,##,## or ##%)> First value specifies rule Width Second value specifies rule Style "color name" specifies color of rule Fourth value specifies Shade percentage Fifth value specifies Indent From Left or Text Indent (T) Sixth value specifies Indent From Right or Text Indent (T) Seventh value specifies rule Offset as absolute value or percent
Drop Cap	<*d(character count,line count)>
Keep with Next	<*kn1> to keep with next paragraph or <*kn0> to *not* keep with next paragraph
Keep Together	<*kt(A)> to keep all lines in paragraph together or <*kt(#,#)> to specify start line number, end line number

Codes for Paragraph Formats   You may recall from Chapter 6 that the Paragraph Formats dialog box contains many settings that define paragraph attributes. The equivalent in XPress Tags codes consists of a series of eight values whose functions appear in Table 7-2. Remember to use the correct case when specifying a lock to baseline grid setting: whereas a capital "G" locks the paragraph to the grid, a lowercase "g" has just the opposite effect. Unless you use a foreign-language version of QuarkXPress, the default hyphenation dictionary "Language" code will be "U.S. English".

Codes for Rules Above and Below   The eight values that define every paragraph rule in XPress Tags have their equivalents in the Paragraph Rules dialog box described in Chapter 6. Table 7-2 describes the function of each value; to help you find your way when entering or editing codes in your own XPress Tags text files, here are some additional tips:

☐   Always express rule width and rule indent values in terms of points.

☐   Express the Shade value (the fourth in the series) as a percentage.

☐   If you want to base the length of the ruling line on text length rather than indent values, place a capital "**T**" in front of the From Left and From Right indent values as in this example defining a rule below:

      <*rb(2,5,"Red",10,T00,T00,20%)>

☐   To turn a ruling line off for a paragraph whose style sheet normally contains a Rule Above, enter the code **<*ra0)**. To turn off a ruling line for a paragraph whose style sheet normally contains a Rule Below, enter the code **<*rb0>**.

Positioning Paragraph Attribute Codes

Paragraph attribute codes must appear at the very beginning of a paragraph as shown in Figure 7-5. The attributes you define through these codes remain in effect until you reset them to the defaults for the current style sheet, specify other codes at the beginning of a later paragraph, or apply a different style sheet code at the beginning of a new paragraph.

Specifying Current Style Sheet Values in Paragraph Attribute Codes

Using paragraph attribute codes, you can specify that a given paragraph include all the default attributes for the current style sheet *except* the ones for which you state a fixed value. Suppose, for instance, that several paragraphs in a row follow the Normal style sheet, and that in one paragraph, you want to change only the default Space Before value to 6 points. You would still need to specify all eight values for paragraph formats in XPress Tags coding (see Table 7-2), but you could use the following shortcut:

<*p($,$,$,$,6,$,$,"$")>

To indicate that Quark should reset *all* paragraph format attributes to the ones specified for the current style sheet, enter a series of eight dollar signs at the beginning of a paragraph, as shown here:

<*p($,$,$,$,$,$,$,"$")>

Defining and Applying Style Sheets with Codes

If you export the text from a Quark document in XPress Tags format and then open the resulting .xtg file in your word processor, you will notice that XPress Tags code address style sheets in three different ways. There is one syntax for defining a style sheet from scratch, a second for defining a style sheet based on another style sheet, and a third syntax for applying an existing style sheet. Table 7-3 summarizes the codes and syntax used in defining and applying style sheets.

TABLE 7-3   XPress Tags Codes for Defining and Applying Style Sheets

To Define or Apply a Style Sheet	Use This Syntax
Applying a Style Sheet	
Apply the Normal style sheet	@$:paragraph text
Apply No Style (locally formatted paragraph)	@:paragraph text
Apply an already defined style sheet	@Stylesheetname:paragraph text
Defining a Style Sheet	
Define an original style sheet	@Stylesheetname=[S] <paragraph attributes definition>: (hard return) Character attributes definition
Define a style sheet based on another	@Stylesheetname= [S"Othername"]=<paragraph attributes definition. :(hard return) Character attributes definition

Defining a Style Sheet with XPress Tags Codes

Style sheets must be defined only once in an XPress Tags text file: either at the beginning of the file (see Figure 7-2a) or immediately before their first use. Having all style sheet definitions at the head of a text file makes it easy to find them if you need to edit them. Typically, the Normal style sheet definition appears first in the list.

The "ingredients" of a style sheet definition in XPress Tags coding are the same character and paragraph attributes you have already read about. Only the syntax is new. A style sheet definition, to be complete, must specify every paragraph and character attribute that Quark supports. Figure 7-6 shows a magnified example of several style sheet definitions and the standard order in which the attribute codes appear.

Paragraph Attributes   The first part of a style sheet definition includes the at sign, the style sheet name, an equal sign, and the [S] indicator, as shown in this example:

@First para=[S]

The next character is the less than sign, which signifies the beginning of the attributes definitions. The paragraph attribute codes, each preceded by an asterisk symbol (*), continue in the following order:

☐ Alignment

☐ Hyphenation and Justification

☐ Keep with Next setting

☐ Keep Together setting

☐ Rule Above settings

☐ Rule Below settings

☐ Drop Cap settings

☐ Paragraph Formats settings (all eight of them)

☐ Tab stop settings

FIGURE
7-6

Magnified example of several style sheet definitions and the standard order
in which the attribute codes appear

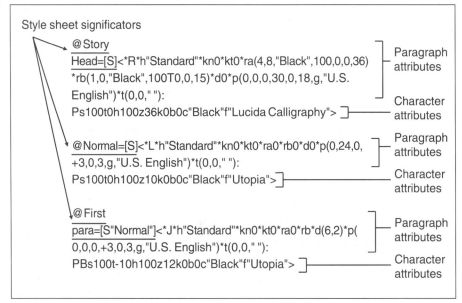

Refer to Figure 7-6 and note that specific definitions can be more or
less elaborate, depending on whether you specify something other than
the standard setting for each attribute. When you leave values at their
default settings, each attribute code is followed by a zero (for example,
*ra0 when you do not specify any Rule Above). If you specify a rule above,
rule below, or tab stops, the settings for those attributes are enclosed
within parentheses.

A colon (:) and a hard return follow the end of the paragraph attributes
definitions. These codes indicate that the definitions of character attributes follow on a new line.

Character Attributes   The last line of a style sheet definition consists
of all the character attributes, without any spaces or punctuation
separating them. The character attribute codes and any values attached
to them appear in the following sequence:

☐   Style

☐   Shade percentage

☐   Tracking value

☐   Horizontal Scaling percentage

☐   Point size

☐   Kerning value

☐   Baseline Shift amount

☐   Text color

☐   Font name

A less than sign (<) follows the last of the character attributes codes to indicate that this is the end of the style sheet definition. A hard return separates the current style sheet definition from the next one or from the next text paragraph.

Defining a Style Sheet Based on Another   The definition for a style sheet that you have based on a different style sheet follows the format just described. The only difference is that the name of the model style sheet appears at the beginning of the definition, as shown here:

@First para=[S"Normal"]

Applying a Style Sheet Using XPress Tags Codes

Once an XPress Tags text file contains a style sheet definition, applying the style sheet is easy. Simply insert the following code at the beginning of the paragraph to which you want to apply a style sheet, substituting the desired style sheet name:

@Stylesheetname:

The text of the paragraph should begin immediately after the colon, without any spaces in between (as shown in Figures 7-2a and 7-2b). Quark applies the designated style sheet to all subsequent paragraphs until it encounters a paragraph with another style sheet assignment.

Applying the No Style Code   Insert the following code at the beginning of a paragraph that you want Quark to treat as hard-coded local formatting to which no style sheet is assigned:

@:

Applying the Normal Style Sheet   A shortcut for applying the Normal style sheet to a paragraph is to insert the following code at the beginning of the paragraph:

@$:

The $ symbol, as you have already seen in the codes for character and paragraph attributes, tells Quark to reset to the default—in this case, the Normal style sheet.

Inserting Special Characters with XPress Tags Codes

Special character codes are like local character attribute codes in that you insert them exactly where you want them to appear in the text. Table 7-4 lists the XPress Tags codes for special characters; you can see some examples of them in Figures 7-3 and 7-4. Note that the ! symbol indicates a nonbreaking character.

Tips for Using XPress Tags Codes

You can work with XPress Tags codes at various levels of expertise. If you tend to define style sheets within Quark documents, your encounters with XPress Tags will probably be casual. In that case, familiarize yourself with them only for the purpose of editing them in a word processor. Power Quark users, on the other hand, may relish the challenge of precoding even original text files with XPress Tags, creating macros that insert codes

TABLE 7-4

XPress Tags Codes for Special Characters

To Insert This Special Character	Enter This Code
Mac character set (first line of text file)	<e0>
Windows character set (first line of text file)	<e1>
ISO Latin 1 character set (first line of text file)	<e2>
New line (soft return)	<\n>
Discretionary soft return	<\d>
Hyphen	<\->
Discretionary hyphen	<\h>
Nonbreaking discretionary hyphen	<\!h>
Indent Here	<\i>
Right indent tab	<\t>
Standard space	<\s>
Nonbreaking standard space	<\!s>
Figure space	<\f>
Nonbreaking figure space	<\!f>
Punctuation space	<\p>
Nonbreaking punctuation space	<\!p>
1/4 em space	<\q>
Nonbreaking 1/4 em space	<\!q>
Display page number of previous text box in chain	<\2>
Display page number of current text box	<\3>
Display page number of next text box in chain	<\4>
Go to new column	<\c>
Go to new text box	<\b>

automatically. Whatever your skill or interest level, the following tips may make your acquaintance with XPress Tags more rewarding.

Avoiding Character Drop-Out

In any XPress Tags text file, Quark recognizes the characters @, \, <, and > as code characters. If you want Quark to recognize these as text characters instead, encode them using the conventions given in Table 7-5.

Use the Right Case

XPress Tags are case sensitive. If you enter a capital "B" as in <B>, for example, Quark changes subsequent text to boldface. If you enter a lowercase "b" as in <b>, Quark expects you to set a new baseline shift value. Make sure your case is correct when entering or editing attribute codes.

Watch Blank Space and Punctuation Marks

XPress Tags are also finicky about spaces between attribute codes and punctuation marks between attribute codes in a series. Avoid adding spaces between attribute codes when the tables do not indicate any, and do not substitute periods or exclamation marks for commas.

Check Your Colors and H&Js

When specifying colors in an XPress Tags text file, be sure that you have already defined those colors for the current document through the Colors command in the Edit menu. If you specify a color that is not available to the document into which you import the file, Quark sets the color to black instead.

TABLE 7-5 Entering XPress Tags Code Characters as Normal Text Characters

To Use This Character as a Text Character	Enter This Code
@	<\@>
<	<\<>
>	<\>>
\	<\\>

Similarly, if you specify a set of Hyphenation and Justification rules (H&Js) that you have not defined for the target document, Quark substitutes the Standard set when you import the XPress Tags file.

Use Word Processor Macros to Store Favorite XPress Tags

If you are the kind of power user who prefers to define all style sheets and attribute codes within a word processor rather than in Quark, you may want to use macros to insert long XPress Tags codes automatically. There are many ways to handle this task. On a basic level, you could set up a macro that inserts a full generic style sheet definition with default attributes at the beginning of a paragraph. Such a "generic" style sheet definition might look like this:

```
@Normal=[S]<*L*h"Standard"*kn0*kt0*ra0*rb0*d0*p(0,0,0,auto,0,0,g,
"U.S. English")*t(0,0," "):
Ps100t0h100z12k0b0c"Black"f"Helvetica">
```

You could then edit the style sheet name and default attributes after inserting the code string. Word for Windows 2.0 features an outstanding, intuitive macro utility and would be an excellent word processor in which to simplify the entry and editing of XPress Tags.

You can also use macros to insert and edit more customized attribute and style sheet codes than the one just described. Typically, a text file that you export from Quark in .xtg format already contains codes for previously defined text attributes and style sheet definitions. You can copy these existing codes in the word processor and save them as macros that you can apply at will—all without memorizing a single code.

Sharing Text: The Clipboard and OLE

While importing text files is one way to acquire text for a Quark document, it is not the only way. The Windows clipboard offers you several options for importing text. You can copy and paste text between Quark documents or between other word processing applications and

Quark. Thanks to the Object Linking and Embedding (OLE) functions supported by Windows 3.1 and by a growing number of other Windows applications, you can also paste formatted database or spreadsheet tables into a Quark document and update them from within QuarkXPress. See Chapter 8 for a discussion of linking and embedding data from other applications.

Copying and Pasting Text Between Quark Documents

The most reliable way to transfer text into Quark using the clipboard is to copy and paste text from one Quark document to another. When you use the Copy and Paste commands in the Edit menu to transfer text this way, you copy not only the text, but also its style sheet and any local formatting attributes.

To copy text between two Quark documents, follow these steps:

1. Open the document that contains the text you want to copy.

2. With the Content tool active, activate the text box that contains the text to be copied and highlight the text.

3. Choose Copy from the Edit menu or press CTRL-C.

4. Open the document into which you want to paste the text, or switch to its document window if it is already open.

5. Position the text cursor at the point where you want to paste the text and then choose the Paste command from the Edit menu or press CTRL-V. The text appears at the cursor location. If the Style Sheets palette is visible, you can verify that you have pasted both the text and its style sheet(s) into the active document.

Copying Text from Other Word Processors

When you use the clipboard to copy text from a Windows-based or DOS-based word processor into a Quark document, you lose both local formatting and style sheet information assigned within the original word processor. Quark assigns the style sheet that is in force at the text cursor location.

 Note   In order to copy text from a DOS-based word processor into the Windows clipboard, you need to be running it in a window. Review your *Microsoft Windows User's Guide* for more information.

PART

Graphics, Color, and Layout Power

CHAPTER

Importing and Working with Pictures

uarkXPress is legendary for the creativity-inspiring control it gives you over graphics in a document. When was the last time you worked with a page layout package that offered the perfect combination of precision, design savvy, and intuitive flexibility in the handling of pictures? Quark has all three:

☐ *Precision* Quark lets you create picture boxes and crop and size pictures to the nearest thousandth of a unit of measurement. Using Quark's runaround controls, you can define the exact relationship between a picture and any surrounding text.

☐ *Design savvy* You can rotate pictures and their picture boxes independently of one another, skew pictures, and combine picture manipulation techniques for special effects. If your documents contain photographic or other bitmapped images, you can also experiment with contrast settings, apply colors and tints, and invert existing colors. These kinds of image enhancement capabilities are usually available only in dedicated image processing packages.

☐ *Intuitive flexibility* You can use your choice of tools to accomplish the foregoing tasks. Menu commands and dialog boxes, the Measurements and Colors palettes, and a number of interactive keyboard shortcuts are all at your disposal.

Picture management is easy with Quark, too. With the help of the Picture Usage command, Links command, and the General Preferences dialog box, you can keep track of and update the pictures in your documents at any time.

This chapter focuses on what you need to know to import pictures successfully, manipulate pictures and picture boxes, and manage picture files. Turn to Chapter 9 when your primary interest is enhancing photographs and other bitmaps, and to Chapter 10 to learn more about handling color in both pictures and text.

Creating and Editing Picture Boxes

Do you want a picture in your document? You need a picture box to contain it. That is a fundamental Quark law, but it is hardly a restrictive one. In fact, the Quark "picture frame" can be as much of a design element as the artwork you put into it. Unlike other page layout packages, Quark lets you choose from four different picture box shapes. And since the fourth shape is a define-it-yourself polygon, your choice of shapes is almost infinite.

Four different tools in the Tools palette represent the basic types of picture boxes you can create in Quark.

 ☐ The Rectangular Picture Box tool creates four-sided, angular picture boxes. If you press and hold SHIFT while using this tool, you constrain a picture box to a perfect square.

 ☐ The Rounded Rectangular Picture Box tool creates picture boxes with rounded corners. Press and hold SHIFT while using this tool to create a rounded picture box with equilateral sides.

 ☐ The Elliptical Picture Box tool creates oval or circular picture boxes. To constrain an elliptical picture box to a circle, press SHIFT as you draw it.

 ☐ The Polygon Picture Box tool lets you design a picture box with any number of sides. Pressing SHIFT as you draw this type of picture box forces each side to a perfectly horizontal or vertical 90-degree angle.

The techniques for creating rectangular, rounded rectangular, or elliptical picture boxes are similar. Drawing a polygon picture box is a slightly different process worth covering separately.

Creating a Fixed-Shape Picture Box

To create a rectangular, rounded rectangular, or elliptical picture box, follow these steps:

1. With a document open, activate the picture box tool of your choice. If you want to draw multiple picture boxes of the same type, press ALT briefly while you activate the tool. This leaves the tool selected until you press ALT again or activate a different tool.

2. Move the pointer onto the page area, where it takes on the shape of a crosshair pointer (+).

3. Position the pointer where you want the upper-left corner or edge of the picture box to be. For greater precision, use the Measurements palette or a guideline to define this location. If you want to constrain the shape of the picture box as described earlier, press and hold SHIFT.

4. Drag downward and to the right. A dotted outline representing the picture box follows the pointer, as shown here:

5. When the picture box is the desired size (again, use the Measurements palette or a guideline as an aid), release the mouse button. The completed picture box now appears with a solid outline and is surrounded by eight selection handles that indicate it is active. An "x" fills the picture box to indicate that it is empty. Figure 8-1 shows a completed circular picture box.

Note that the selection handles of any type of picture box fit within a rectangular area. This area is known as the *bounding box.*

Creating and Shaping a Polygon Picture Box

Drawing a polygon picture box is similar to creating a polygon in a drawing or illustration program. To create a free-form picture box with the Polygon Picture Box tool, follow these steps:

1. With a document open, activate the Polygon Picture Box tool. If you want to draw multiple picture boxes of this type, press ALT briefly while you activate the tool. This leaves the tool selected until you press ALT again or activate a different tool.

2. Move the pointer onto the page area, where it takes on the shape of a crosshair (+).

3. Click to establish a starting point for the picture box.

4. Move the crosshair to where you want to establish the end of the first line segment and then click again. A dotted outline follows the crosshair to mark the first line segment of the polygon.

5. Continue placing additional line segments by moving the crosshair pointer and clicking. If you press and hold SHIFT while placing a line segment, you constrain that segment to a 90-degree angle.

6. To close the polygon, position the crosshair pointer over the starting point (where it momentarily assumes a rectangular shape) and click. The completed picture box becomes active immediately; surrounded

FIGURE
8-1

A completed circular picture box

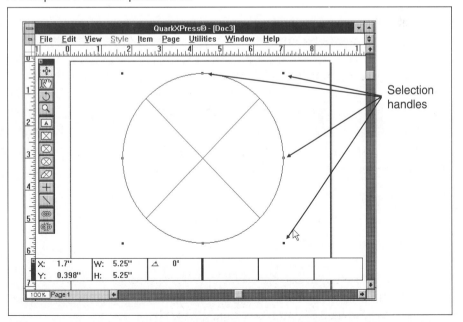

Selection handles

by the selection handles that describe its bounding box, it now appears with a solid outline. Figure 8-2 shows a polygon picture box as it is being closed and after being completed.

Another way to close a polygon is to double-click from the current crosshair position. Quark automatically generates a final line segment that extends from the crosshair position to the starting point.

 Tip Using solid colors, tints, and/or color blends, you can turn a polygon picture box into a free-standing design element in a Quark document—even if it contains no picture.

Changing Picture Box Shape

Not only can you create picture boxes in a variety of shapes, you can also change the shape of an existing picture box on the spur of the moment. Simply activate the Content or Item tool, select the picture box you want to change, and then choose the Picture Box Shape command

FIGURE
8-2

A polygon picture box being closed and after completion

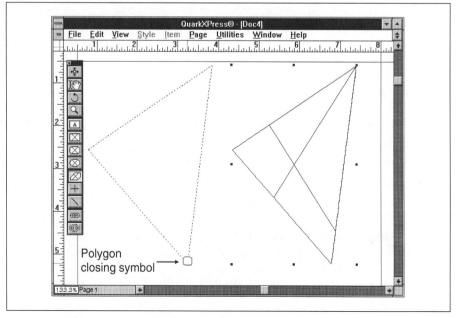

from the Item menu. A submenu of six picture box shapes appears, as shown here:

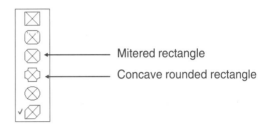

Mitered rectangle

Concave rounded rectangle

Note that two additional picture box shapes are available beyond the ones you can create with the toolbox. Click the shape you want the current picture box to assume. Quark fits the new picture box shape within the bounding box of the previous shape, so the total area occupied by the picture box remains approximately the same.

When you change a fixed-shape picture box into a polygon, the apparent shape of the picture box or its bounding box remains unchanged. Figure 8-3 shows a mitered corner rectangular picture box that has been transformed into a polygon picture box. If the Reshape Polygon command in the Item menu is currently checked, however, *corner points* appear wherever there were corners or curves in the previous picture box shape, as in Figure 8-3(b). You can drag, subtract, or add corner points to reshape the polygon. The next section describes how to do this.

Reshaping a Polygon Picture Box

After you initially shape a polygon picture box, it might seem that its form is written in stone. Not so! You can always reshape the currently selected polygon if you first activate the Reshape Polygon command in the Item menu.

The Reshape Polygon command works like a toggle: it is either on or off. When no check mark appears in front of it, polygon picture boxes display a normal bounding box like the first example in Figure 8-3, and you cannot reshape them. When the Reshape Polygon command is active, any polygon picture box you select displays corner points instead of the usual bounding box, as the second example in Figure 8-3 shows.

FIGURE

8-3

The appearance of a polygon picture box changes when the Reshape Polygon command is active

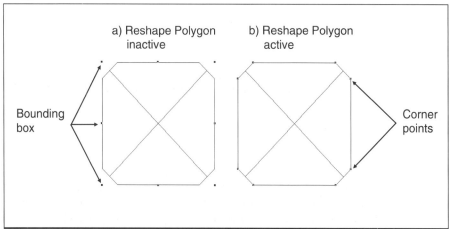

Three techniques are available for reshaping a polygon when the Reshape Polygon command is active:

☐   You can drag an existing corner point

☐   You can subtract unwanted corner points

☐   You can add new corner points

Dragging a Corner Point

To reshape a polygon picture box by dragging one or more corner points, follow these steps:

1. With the Content or Item tool active, click on the polygon you want to reshape.

2. Activate the Reshape Polygon command in the Item menu. Corner points appear at the end of each line segment of the polygon.

3. Move the pointer over the corner point you want to reshape. Here, the pointer takes on the appearance of a resizing hand.

4. Drag in the desired direction. A dotted outline indicating the change in shape follows the pointer, as shown here:

5. Release the mouse button when the corner point is in the desired location.

Subtracting a Corner Point

You can remove excess line segments from a polygon picture box by subtracting one or more corner points. To subtract a corner point when the Reshape Polygon command is active, follow these steps:

1. With the Content or Item tool active, click on the polygon picture box to display the corner points.

2. Press and hold CTRL and move the pointer directly over the first corner point you want to remove. The pointer turns into a corner point subtraction symbol, as shown here:

Corner point subtraction symbol

3. Click to remove the selected corner point.

You can continue removing additional corner points in the same way.

Adding a Corner Point

If a polygon picture box does not contain enough corner points for you to reshape it as you would wish, you can add new ones. To add one or more corner points to a polygon when the Reshape Polygon command in the Item menu is active, follow these steps:

1. With the Item or Content tool active, click on the polygon picture box you want to reshape.

2. Move the pointer to the place where you want to add a new corner point and press CTRL. The pointer turns into a corner point addition symbol, as shown here:

Corner point
addition symbol

3. Click to add the new corner point. You can now drag this corner point to reshape the polygon.

Figure 8-4 shows an example of how you might reshape a simple polygon into a stylized letter. The following suggests a creative use for such a reshaped polygon: filling it with an imported bitmap pattern for ornamental effects in a document:

Creating and Editing Picture Boxes: Shortcuts

For handy reference, Table 8-1 lists the mouse and keyboard combinations that you can use when creating picture boxes of all types or reshaping polygon picture boxes.

FIGURE
8-4

Reshaping a simple polygon picture box into a stylized letter and filling it with an imported bitmapped pattern file

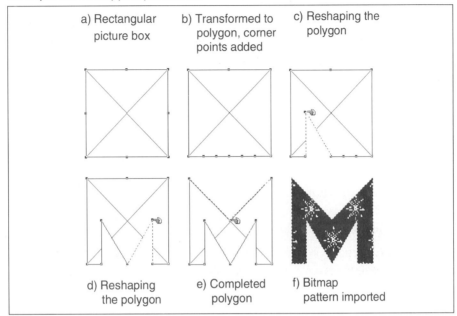

a) Rectangular picture box

b) Transformed to polygon, corner points added

c) Reshaping the polygon

d) Reshaping the polygon

e) Completed polygon

f) Bitmap pattern imported

Activating a Picture Box

A picture box must be active in order for you to size or move it, import a picture into it, or edit an existing picture. A picture box is always active immediately after you create it. Inactive picture boxes have dotted outlines and no selection handles. To activate an inactive picture box, click anywhere within the picture box outlines. If the Item tool is selected, you can activate multiple picture boxes by pressing and holding SHIFT as you click.

Tip To select a picture box that lies beneath one or more other items, activate the Content or Item tool, press CTRL-ALT-SHIFT, and click in the area of the picture box. Each time you click while pressing CTRL-ALT-SHIFT, Quark activates the item on the next layer.

TABLE
8-1

Creating and Shaping Picture Boxes: Mouse and Keyboard Shortcuts

To Do This	With This Tool Selected	Press
Creating Picture Boxes		
Constrain rectangle to square	Rectangle	SHIFT
Constrain rounded rectangle to equilateral	Rounded rectangle	SHIFT
Constrain ellipse to circle	Ellipse	SHIFT
Constrain polygon segments to 90-degree angles	Polygon	SHIFT
Keep current picture box tool selected		ALT while activating tool
Reshaping a Polygon		
Subtract a corner point	Item, Content	CTRL + click corner point
Add a corner point	Item, Content	CTRL + click blank area of line segment

Sizing and Moving Picture Boxes

If you decide to change the size or position of a picture box after you create it, don't worry. Quark lets you do so using your choice of a freehand technique, the Measurements palette, keyboard shortcuts, or (as you will see later in the chapter) a dialog box.

Using the Freehand Method

You can resize or reposition an active picture box with the mouse when the Content or Item tool is selected. To change the size of a picture box, follow these steps:

1. With the Content or Item tool active, click a picture box to activate it.

2. Position the mouse pointer at the selection handle that corresponds to the direction in which you want to size the picture box (horizontal, vertical, or diagonal). The pointer takes on the shape of a resizing hand, as shown here:

3. Drag the selection handle in the desired direction. A dotted outline of the picture box follows the pointer, as this example shows:

4. Release the mouse button when the picture box is the size you want.

Note Changing the size of a picture box has no effect on the size of any picture it contains.

Tip To maintain the current aspect ratio (proportions) of a picture box as you resize it, press and hold ALT-SHIFT as you drag.

Keep in mind that the status of the Reshape Polygon command in the Item menu determines what happens when you resize a polygon picture box. When this command is active, you can drag a polygon by its individual corner points, reshaping it as you resize it. When Reshape Polygon is *inactive*, you must drag the polygon by its bounding box handles, which allow you to resize but not reshape the picture box.

To move a picture box using the mouse, activate the Item tool and position the mouse pointer anywhere within the outlines of the picture box. Drag the picture box to a new location. If a tool other than the Item tool is active, you can still move the active picture box by pressing and holding CTRL as you drag.

Using the Measurements Palette

When the Content or Item tool is selected and a picture box is the active item, you can change picture box size by editing the values in the W (width) and H (height) fields of the Measurements palette. To change the position of the active picture box, edit the values in the X (horizontal position) and Y (vertical position) fields of the Measurements palette.

Using Picture Box Specifications

The Picture Box Specifications dialog box (see "Defining Picture and Picture Box Attributes" in this chapter) includes options for changing the size and position of the active text box. To access this dialog box, choose the Modify command in the Item menu (keyboard shortcut: CTRL-M) or double-click the picture box when the Item tool is active. Edit the Origin Across and Origin Down fields to move the picture box and the Width and Height fields to resize it.

Activating, Sizing, and Moving Picture Boxes: Shortcuts

As you might expect from Quark, you can use the keyboard to move the active picture box in one-point or one-tenth point increments. Table 8-2 lists the key combinations available for this purpose, as well as shortcuts for activating, sizing, and moving picture boxes.

Defining Picture and Picture Box Attributes

Before or after you import a picture, you can define picture and picture box attributes using the Modify, Frame, and Runaround commands in the Item menu. These commands are available for a selected picture box when either the Content or the Item tool is active.

TABLE 8-2 Activating, Sizing, and Moving the Active Picture Box: Mouse and Keyboard Shortcuts

To Do This	With This Tool Active	Press
Activating Picture Boxes		
Activate multiple picture boxes	Item, Content	SHIFT + click
Activate hidden/overlapping picture box	Item, Content	CTRL-ALT-SHIFT + click
Sizing Picture Boxes		
Maintain current aspect ratio	Item, Content	ALT-SHIFT + drag handle
Moving the Active Picture Box		
Move picture box, Item tool inactive	Any tool except Item	CTRL + drag
Nudge left in 1-point increments	Item, Content	LEFT ARROW
Nudge left in 1/10 point increments	Item, Content	ALT + LEFT ARROW
Nudge right in 1-point increments	Item, Content	RIGHT ARROW
Nudge right in 1/10 point increments	Item, Content	ALT + RIGHT ARROW
Nudge up in 1-point increments	Item, Content	UP ARROW
Nudge up in 1/10 point increments	Item, Content	ALT + UP ARROW
Nudge down in 1-point increments	Item, Content	DOWN ARROW
Nudge down in 1/10 point increments	Item, Content	ALT + DOWN ARROW

Tip If you want to standardize attributes for all the pictures and picture boxes in a document, define those attributes through the Tool Preferences dialog box (Preferences/Tools command, Edit menu) soon after you create a new document. Use this dialog box to set up default specifications for each of the picture box tools.

Defining Picture and Picture Box Specifications

The Picture Box Specifications dialog box shown next is Quark's one-stop command post for determining most of the attributes of the active picture box and its contents. The options in this dialog box control the position, size, color, shade, and angle of the active picture box as well as the position, scaling, angle, and skew of any picture it contains. There are also options for suppressing the printout of a picture, its picture box, or both.

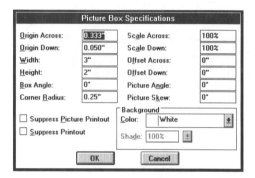

When the Content or Item tool is active and a picture box is selected, you can access the Picture Box Specifications dialog box by choosing the Modify command in the Item menu or using the keyboard shortcut, CTRL-M. Another quick way to access the dialog box is to double-click anywhere within the outline of a picture box when the Item tool is active.

The following sections give the attributes you can define through the Picture Box Specifications dialog box, together with brief descriptions of their functions.

Origin Across, Origin Down The Origin Across and Origin Down fields let you define the position of the active picture box by specifying the location of its upper-left corner. For a polygon picture box, the upper-left corner of the bounding box marks the origin point.

Width, Height　The values in the Width and Height fields define the size of the active picture box.

Box Angle　The Box Angle option controls the *angle of rotation* of the picture box. This is independent of any angle you might assign to the picture itself.

Corner Radius　The *corner radius* value of a picture box describes the roundness of its corners. Imagine a circle touching the corner of a picture box as shown in Figure 8-5. The radius of that circle is equivalent to the amount of rounding in the corners. As the measurement value in the Corner Radius field increases, so does the amount of rounding.

Tip　Any type of picture box except a polygon can have rounded corners. To round the corners of a picture box interactively, specify a value in the Corner Radius field of the Measurements palette, as shown here:

Corner radius field

Suppress Picture Printout　If you print the active document when the Suppress Picture Printout option is checked, Quark prints the picture box, but without the picture it contains.

Suppress Printout　Check the Suppress Printout option to keep Quark from printing both the picture and the picture box.

Background Color, Shade　The Background Color and Shade options let you apply a solid color or tint to the picture box. A background color is visible only in areas of the picture box not occupied by a graphic; using this option does not affect picture color. A useful design application for this feature, illustrated in Figure 8-6, is to generate a separate background color for the blank areas in a polygon picture box.

FIGURE
8-5

The radius of a circle tangent to the corner of a picture box describes the amount of rounding

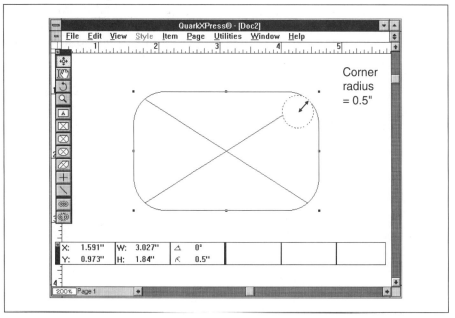

Scale Across, Scale Down   The values in the Scale Across and Scale Down fields define the proportion or *scaling* of a picture relative to its original size before importing. See the "Sizing Pictures" section later in this chapter.

Offset Across, Offset Down   The Offset Across and Offset Down options let you control the position of a picture within its picture box. See the "Cropping and Positioning Pictures" section later in this chapter.

Picture Angle, Picture Skew   The Picture Angle value defines the angle of rotation of a picture. Quark lets you specify different angles for the picture and its picture box, which can lead to some pretty interesting visual effects. See "Rotating Pictures and Picture Boxes" later in this chapter. The Picture Skew value defines the degree of slant or *skew* of a picture, another useful technique for creating special effects.

FIGURE 8-6 Applying a background color or tint to blank areas of a picture box

Picture box background: 15 percent gray

Defining Frame Specifications

By default, picture boxes that you create in Quark have no visible outlines. To define outline attributes for the active picture box, choose the Frame command in the Item menu or use the keyboard shortcut, CTRL-B. The Frame Specifications dialog box shown here appears:

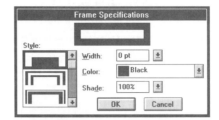

Use the options in this dialog box to define an outline style, width, color, and shade for the active picture box. The sample frame at the top of the dialog box lets you preview your choices.

Defining Runaround Specifications

The term *runaround* in QuarkXPress refers to how overlapping text and graphics relate to one another. Managing runaround in document layout can be an art unto itself, especially when the layering of items is involved, so we will reserve a more thorough discussion of it until Chapter 12. Here, the important point to remember is that you control runaround specifications for the active picture box through the Runaround command in the Item menu. Choosing this command, available when the Content or Item tool is active and a picture box is selected, accesses the Runaround Specifications dialog box shown next. You can also reach this dialog box by using the keyboard shortcut CTRL-T.

Runaround Mode

The Mode option determines the type of runaround that applies to the active picture box. Your choices are None, Item (the default for picture boxes), Auto Image, and Manual Image.

None   Selecting None causes text in an underlying text box to flow through the picture box as though it were transparent, like this:

> *Pitying I drop'd a tear;*
> *But I saw a glow-worm near:*
> *Who replied, What wailing wight*
> *Calls the watchman of the night.*
>
> *I am set to light the ground,*
> *While the beetle goes his round:*
> *Follow now the beetles hum,*
> *Little wanderer hie thee home.*

Item   This is the default mode. It causes text to flow around the contours of the active picture box, no matter what its shape, as shown here:

Text outset: 6 pt

> *Pitying I drop'd a tear;*
> *But I saw a glow-worm near:*
> *Who replied, What wailing wight*
> *Calls the watchman of the night.*
>
> *I am set to light the ground,*
> *While the beetle goes his round:*
> *Follow now the beetles hum,*
> *Little wanderer hie thee home.*

The Text Outset value you specify tells Quark the minimum amount of space to allow between the edges of the picture box and any surrounding text.

Note   When you choose Item mode, text flows to one side of the active picture box—the side with the most horizontal space.

Auto Image   Choose Auto Image if you want text to flow around the contours of the picture. Text can flow into any blank spaces in the picture box, as long as the minimum Text Outset space is maintained, as shown here:

> *Pitying I drop'd a tear;*
> *But I saw a glow-worm near:*
> *Who replied, What wailing wight*
> *Calls the watchman of the night.*
>
> *I am set to light the ground,*
> *While the beetle goes his round:*
> *Follow now the beetles hum,*
> *Little wanderer hie thee home.*

If the active picture box contains only a background color and no picture, text flows around the contours of the picture box itself.

Manual Image In Manual Image runaround mode, Quark generates a dotted outline called the *runaround polygon*, which hugs the contours of the picture, as Figure 8-7 shows. You determine how much space to allow between the picture and text by adjusting the selection handles of the runaround polygon at various points. You can even add handles to or subtract them from the runaround polygon in much the same way as you add and subtract nodes from a polygon picture box. The runaround polygon gives you precise control over text flow, making Manual Image the most flexible runaround mode. Refer to Chapter 12 for more detailed information on manipulating a runaround polygon in this mode.

FIGURE 8-7

A runaround polygon hugs picture contours when a picture box is in manual runaround mode

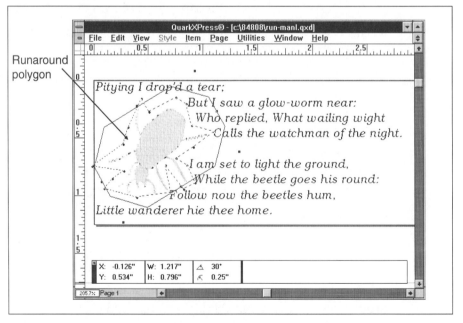

Auto Image and Manual Image runaround modes have one important limitation of which you should be aware. When you assign these modes to a picture box containing an .EPS picture, a runaround that looks perfect on your monitor may not be accurate when you print. This is because Quark bases an auto or manual runaround on the preview header for the .EPS file, which is never WYSIWYG and usually smaller than the graphic it represents. As a result, text that seems to run perfectly around the .EPS header on screen may actually overprint part of the picture. Don't let this inconvenience keep you from using .EPS picture files—after all, .EPS and .TIF are the most reliable formats for obtaining high-quality PostScript printing results. Instead, try one of the following workarounds that will help you avoid potential printing surprises:

☐   When using Auto Image runaround, assign a higher Text Outset value than the visual .EPS header seems to warrant, and then print a draft version of the page. These measures should ensure that no text overlaps with the picture.

☐   When defining a Manual Image runaround, temporarily substitute a second copy of the picture saved in a different format—.DRW or .CGM for object-oriented pictures, or .BMP or .PCX for bitmapped pictures, for example. These formats may be somewhat less ideal for printing purposes, but they will display the image with realistic sizing and contours. Edit the runaround polygon while the substitute picture is in the picture box and then re-import the .EPS picture. The picture box will retain the runaround polygon you have defined.

Text Outset

The value you specify in the Text Outset field determines the minimum amount of space that must lie between the picture box and text (Item mode), the picture contours and text (Auto Image mode), or the runaround polygon and text (Manual Image mode).

Invert

The Invert check box, available only when you select Manual Image runaround mode, allows text to flow *inside* a runaround polygon. As you will see in Chapter 12, inverting text flow can be an exciting way to create word pictures in a document, shaping text to the contours of an image.

Defining Picture Box Attributes: Shortcuts

Table 8-3 lists the keyboard commands for accessing the Picture Box Specifications, Frame Specifications, and Runaround Specifications dialog boxes.

Importing Pictures

You can bring a picture into a picture box in one of three ways: import it, paste it normally through the clipboard, or link or embed it using the OLE (object linking and embedding) features available under Microsoft Windows 3.1. QuarkXPress uses the term picture to refer to two different kinds of visuals: object-oriented graphics and bitmapped images.

Object-oriented graphics are line art pictures created by a drawing or illustration program such as CorelDRAW!, Micrografx Designer, or Adobe Illustrator. These types of programs create artwork that you can resize in Quark without loss of quality, because they are composed of mathematically defined objects. They typically have small file sizes of less than 100K (kilobytes) each.

TABLE 8-3 Defining Picture Box Attributes: Keyboard Commands

To Define These Attributes For The Active Picture Box	Press
Picture Box Specifications	CTRL-M
Frame Specifications	CTRL-B
Runaround Specifications	CTRL-T

On the other hand, *bitmapped images*—scanned digital photographs, paintings, and some clip art—consist of large numbers of separate pixels that cannot be described or manipulated in any way other than one pixel at a time. As a result, the file sizes of bitmapped images are generally much larger than those of their line art brethren—several megabytes larger is not uncommon, especially for color images.

Note For the sake of maintaining image quality, it is important not to resize bitmapped images arbitrarily within Quark. You should either import them at their original size, or else resize them proportionally outside of Quark using an image-editing program such as Aldus PhotoStyler or Micrografx Picture Publisher.

Note Certain file formats, collectively referred to as metafiles, can save pictures that contain object-oriented graphics, bitmaps, or both in the same file.

Quark lets you import, link, and embed both object-oriented and bitmapped pictures. This chapter deals with both types of pictures, concentrating on object-oriented graphics. Chapter 9 delves into techniques for enhancing and handling bitmapped images in a document.

Picture Formats Supported by QuarkXPress

Among the XTensions supplied with the release version of QuarkXPress for Windows are import filters for several types of picture formats. If you installed these filters with your software, you should be able to import pictures saved in all the formats described in this section.

Keep in mind that your choice of which image file formats to use in a document should depend on how you plan to output the document in final form. If you plan to output your documents to a PostScript imagesetter, the best image file formats to use for consistent results are TIFF (.tif) for bitmapped images and Encapsulated PostScript (.eps) for object-oriented graphics. (You will learn all about .tif and .eps files shortly.)

Tip   If you link or embed a picture in a document using OLE, you can import still other types of pictures whose formats otherwise might not be compatible with QuarkXPress. See the "Linking and Embedding Pictures" section later in this chapter.

Note   Text that you have shaped in a graphics package such as CorelDRAW! or Adobe Illustrator must be imported into Quark as a picture. You must place it in a picture box, not a text box.

Object-Oriented Picture Formats

Quark permits the import of several different types of object-oriented picture files. Chances are that your favorite drawing or illustration package supports one or more of these file formats. The following gives brief descriptions of each file format type and recommendations for when to use it.

Encapsulated PostScript (.eps)   The Encapsulated PostScript file format, often referred to simply as EPS, is a standard in the desktop publishing industry. It includes the most information about the imported graphic, and service bureau operators tend to have experience in outputting such files successfully. Files saved in EPS format usually have *headers* that display a coarse representation of the image for placement purposes only; the digital image prints out at much higher quality.

If you import an EPS image that has been saved without a header, Quark represents it as a gray area containing the words "PostScript Picture." You can verify that the active picture box does indeed contain an image by choosing the Picture Usage command in the Utilities menu.

Computer Graphics Metafile (.cgm)   The Computer Graphics Metafile file format originated with Harvard Graphics, but many other graphics programs now support it, and several variants of the format are available. Files in .cgm format can contain bitmaps as well as object-oriented graphics. You can import .cgm files only if you installed the special filter supplied with your QuarkXPress software. When you import a .cgm file, a dialog box containing several options pops up. Use the options to determine whether to ignore the background color of the source file, convert bitmapped fonts to scalable object-oriented fonts, retain dotted lines, and use the standard Harvard Graphics color table.

HPGL Graphics (.plt)   The HPGL Graphics file format was developed for use with pen-driven graphics plotters. In order to import a file in this format, you must have installed the HPGL filter along with QuarkXPress. A dialog box appears during the import process, letting you select paper size, the number of pens (up to a maximum of eight), and the color used for each pen in the source file. Files in this format can contain bitmaps as well as line drawings.

Macintosh PICT (.pct)   This popular Macintosh graphics format is useful for importing graphics from Macintosh drawing and image-editing applications. It can contain both object-oriented and bitmapped graphics in a single file.

PICT is another metafile format that can include both bitmaps and objects peacefully coexisting in the same file. PostScript-based imagesetters sometimes encounter difficulties with PICT files during output, though, so images of this type may be more suitable for documents for which the ultimate output device is non-PostScript.

Micrografx Designer (.drw)   You can import Micrografx Designer artwork if you installed the .drw filter along with QuarkXPress. A dialog box appears during the import process; you can use its options to determine whether to ignore the background color of the source file and convert bitmapped fonts to scalable object-oriented fonts. Files in this format can contain both object-oriented and bitmapped artwork.

Windows Metafiles (.wmf)   When you copy an object-oriented or bitmapped graphic to the Windows clipboard, Windows translates it into its own metafiles (.wmf) format. Many Windows applications can also save files in this format.

Bitmapped Picture Formats

You can import several different types of bitmapped files into a Quark picture box. Most image scanning, editing, and painting programs support several of these formats. In addition, some of the file formats described under "Object-Oriented Graphics Formats" can save bitmaps, too. The following gives brief descriptions of each bitmap file format and recommendations for when to use it.

Tagged Image File Format (TIFF, .tif) The TIFF file format, originally developed by Aldus Corporation, is the industry standard for image files, just as EPS is the preferred standard for object-oriented graphics. It supports 24-bit color, grayscale, and black-and-white images.

Windows Bitmap (.bmp, .dib, .rle) The .bmp file format used by Microsoft Paintbrush is becoming a standard among Windows applications. The .dib and .rle formats are formats used by earlier versions of Windows clipboard files.

CompuServe GIF (.gif) The CompuServe file format was developed so that graphic artists working on various platforms (DOS, Macintosh, Amiga) could share color artwork files through on-line services such as CompuServe. This format does not yet support the high number of digital colors (16 million) required for commercial-grade color print publishing.

Paintbrush (.pcx) The Paintbrush file format, one of the oldest and most familiar on the DOS platform, evolved from the ZSoft Paintbrush family of products. Most paint, scanning, and image-editing packages support it, but be aware that many variations of this standard exist. Newer versions of this format support 24-bit color as well as grayscale and black-and-white images.

Scitex (.ct) Service bureaus specializing in color work often cater to advertisers and commercial magazine publishers—markets that require even higher color quality than popular flatbed and slide scanners can deliver. Many such service bureaus have dedicated systems available for scanning the multi-megabyte images that can produce this kind of superior color, and the Scitex family of color systems is the most well-known of these. However, the color images generated by Scitex systems translate into files so huge that importing these files into a Quark document would slow down the page layout process unnecessarily. To circumvent this problem, Quark users who need Scitex-generated color images typically obtain lower-resolution image files in .ct format at the same time. They place these "for position only" images in their documents until output time, when the service bureau substitutes the original high-resolution color files and generates camera-ready film through the Scitex system.

Importing a Picture with the Get Picture Command

The Get Picture command in the File menu, available only when the Content tool is active, is the normal means by which you import a picture file into the currently selected picture box. To import a picture, follow these steps:

1. With the Content tool active and a picture box selected, choose the Get Picture command from the File menu or press the keyboard shortcut CTRL-E. The Get Picture dialog box appears as shown next, with the List Files of Type list box set to All Picture Files. Any picture files in the current directory that Quark can import appear in the Files list box.

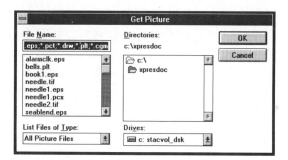

2. Using the Drives and Directories list boxes, change to the drive and directory where the file you are seeking is located. If you want to view only files in a certain format, choose that format in the List Files of Type drop-down list box.

3. Double-click the chosen filename in the Files list box to import the picture.

Normally, Quark aligns the upper-left corner of a newly imported picture with the upper-left corner of the picture box. (The exception is if you have already modified the Offset Across and Offset Down options in the Picture Box Specifications dialog box.) If you cannot see all of your picture when you first import it, you may need to resize either the picture or the picture box. Refer to the sections on "Sizing Pictures" and "Cropping and Positioning Pictures" later in this chapter.

Importing a Picture of a Document Page

The Save Page as EPS command in the File menu is a boon to graphic designers who like to showcase documents within documents as shown in Figure 8-8. Using the Save Page as EPS command, you can create an Encapsulated PostScript "snapshot" of a Quark document page and then embed it into another document as a picture.

FIGURE
8-8

This document within a document is an EPS page picture

To create a picture from a Quark document page and import it into a picture box, follow these steps:

1. Open the desired document and choose the Save Page as EPS command from the File menu. The Save Page as EPS dialog box appears as shown here, with the List Files of Type list box already set to .EPS:

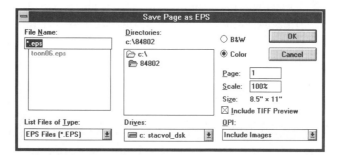

2. Locate the drive and directory where you want to save the file and then enter a name in the File Name entry box.

3. Choose either the BW or Color radio button depending on whether you want to create the page picture in grayscale or in color.

4. In the Page field, enter the number of the page you want to capture as a PostScript file. You can capture only one page at a time.

5. In the Scale field, enter the percentage of actual size at which you want to reproduce the page. An indicator underneath this field shows you the resulting dimensions.

Tip Don't worry about getting the size wrong; you can always scale EPS files up or down later without loss of quality. The Scale value affects only the size of the TIFF preview header that represents your picture.

6. Check the Include TIFF Preview option if you want to have a visible representation of the PostScript file when you import it into a picture box. TIFF preview headers tend to be memory hogs, so omitting the TIFF header could reduce the size of an EPS file by several hundred kilobytes. If you forego a TIFF preview header, though, the picture box into which you import the EPS page will appear blank or gray.

7. Choose an OPI (Open Prepress Interface) option from the drop-down list box according to the way you plan to print the final document that contains the page picture. You should choose the Include Images option unless you use a high-end, dedicated color prepress system as a final output device. See Chapter 14 for more about color image output.

8. Click OK to create the EPS page picture.

9. Open the document into which you want to import the EPS page. Import the EPS file into a picture box normally.

Page pictures are like other object-oriented graphics in that you can scale them to any size without loss of image quality. The important thing to remember about page pictures is that at printing time, Quark requires the font and picture files used in the original page. As long as these are available to the document into which you import the page picture, text and pictures in the embedded page reproduce perfectly. If Quark cannot find the fonts, text in the page picture will print as Courier. If you do not maintain links to pictures in the original page, Quark substitutes low-resolution versions of these for printing. See the "Managing Picture Files in a Document" section later in this chapter.

Pasting a Picture from the Clipboard

The Windows clipboard offers another way to import pictures into a QuarkXPress document. If you have already copied a graphic into the clipboard from another Windows application, you can import it into the active picture box by choosing the Paste command from the Edit menu. The Content tool must be active in order for this command to be available.

Windows stores clipboard graphics in one of its own metafile formats, which may or may not transfer all picture attributes exactly as they were in the original application. Pictures pasted from the clipboard are also harder to track than pictures saved as files, because Quark does not reference them in the Picture Usage dialog box. See the "Managing Picture Files in a Document" section later in this chapter.

Linking and Embedding Pictures and Other Data

Basically, Windows applications that participate in the OLE scheme are either servers or clients. *Server* applications can provide data to other applications, while *client* applications can receive data in its original format from servers. Quark acts as a client application that can receive data from any Windows application capable of playing the role of server.

While most of the server applications that can provide data to Quark documents are graphics packages, some spreadsheet or database programs can act as servers as well. This means that you can paste formatted spreadsheet cells or tables from, say, Microsoft Excel into a Quark picture box and then edit and print the tables from within Quark. Database publishing will never be the same!

Embedded Versus Linked Data Exchanges

There are two ways to exchange data in the OLE scheme: linking and embedding.

☐ When you *embed* data, you are making a separate copy of the data from the source application and placing it within a Quark document. When you edit an embedded picture or table, you change only the data in the Quark document, not the original file from the server application.

☐ When you *link* pictures or data, on the other hand, you merely create a reference to the source file in the Quark document. Only one file exists—the one in the server application. Whenever you edit linked data, you update both the source file and the data in the Quark document.

Linking Pictures and Data

When you *link* a picture to a Quark document, you import a graphic representation of the source file rather than the source file itself. Quark generates a reference to the source file within the document to keep track of it. You can edit a linked picture either in the source application or from within Quark, and since only one "original" exists, you update its content in both places at once.

Three commands help you link and manage linked pictures. You use the Paste Link or the Paste Special command in the Edit menu to create a link to a picture. And the Links command in the Edit menu lets you define how and when to update the display of a specific linked picture that has been modified.

To link a picture to a Quark document, follow these steps:

1. Create or open a picture file in the graphics application you want to use. This application must support OLE and be capable of acting as a server.

2. Copy the picture or part of the picture to the clipboard using the Copy command in the Edit menu.

3. Switch to or open QuarkXPress and then open the document to which you want to link the picture.

4. Activate the Content tool and the picture box that is to contain the linked picture.

5. Choose Paste Link from the Edit menu. The picture appears, aligned with the upper-left corner of the picture box.

Another way to link a picture file is to use the Paste Special command. This command accesses a dialog box that lets you either link or embed a picture, depending on which of several available data formats you choose. To link a picture using this command:

1. From the server application, copy a picture or part of a picture to the clipboard.

2. Switch to or open QuarkXPress and then open the document to which you want to link the picture.

3. Activate the Content tool and the picture box that will contain the linked picture.

4. Choose the Paste Special command from the Edit menu. The Paste Special dialog box appears as shown next, with information about the picture source and filename appearing at the top of the dialog box. The Data Type list box displays two or more ways in which Microsoft Windows can translate the data in the picture file.

5. Highlight the data type that includes the word "Object." This is the only format that includes all the information in the original program's file, with no data loss. The Paste Link button becomes available.

6. Click Paste Link to link the picture and import it into the picture box.

Editing and Updating Linked Pictures

Once you have linked a picture to a Quark document, you can edit it from within Quark or from within the server application. Editing the data is not necessarily the same as updating it. Quark updates the data (displays it with changes) according to the options you choose through the Links command in the Edit menu.

To edit a linked picture from within the server application, simply open the server application, open the source file, make your changes, and save the file. To edit linked data from within a Quark document, follow these steps:

1. With the Content tool active, double-click the picture box that contains the linked picture. The server application opens along with the source file.

2. Edit the file and save it.

3. Close the application to return to the Quark document. The commands you use to do this may vary from one application to another.

At this point, you have already changed the linked picture in both the server application and the Quark document. Whether or not you have updated the display of the picture depends on the current settings in the Links dialog box.

Controlling Picture Updates with the Links command   The Links command in the Edit menu helps you determine how and when Quark updates the display of linked pictures that have been modified. You can instruct Quark to update pictures automatically or only when you request an update. You can also use this command to break the link between a picture and its server application, or to relink the document with a different picture or graphics application.

To control picture links in a document using the Links command:

1. Activate the Content tool and choose the Links command in the Edit menu. The Links dialog box shown next appears. The Links area of the dialog box lists the filenames, file formats, and the current link type (automatic or manual) of all the linked pictures in the current document.

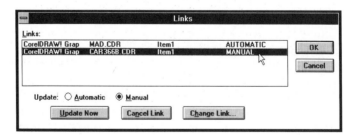

2. Highlight the row of information on the linked picture whose update options you want to change.

3. Below the Links field, activate the button that tells Quark how you want to update the selected picture.

☐ *Automatic* updates the display of linked pictures in real time as they are modified, either in the original application or from within Quark. This is the default setting.

☐ *Manual* updates the display of linked pictures only when you save them in the server application, when you exit the server application after modifying a picture, or when you request an update by clicking the Update Now button.

☐ *Update Now* is available only for linked pictures that you have set to Manual update. Clicking this button updates the display of the selected linked picture upon request.

☐ *Change Link* accesses a dialog box that you can use to link a different picture or a different server application. You can also use this button to reestablish the link to an original picture file that has been moved to a different drive or directory.

☐ *Cancel Link* permanently breaks the link between the picture you have selected and the server application. The picture remains in your document, but you can no longer edit it, just as you cannot edit a picture that you have pasted normally from the Windows clipboard.

4. Click OK to exit the dialog box with your changes in effect.

Embedding Pictures

When you *embed* a picture, you are taking a *copy* of the source picture file in its native format and placing it within a Quark document. When you edit an embedded picture, you update only the copy in the Quark document, not the original file from the server application. You use the Paste Special command to embed a picture in Quark.

To embed a picture within a Quark document, follow these steps:

1. Open the server application and the graphics file that contains the picture you want to embed in Quark.

2. To place a copy of the picture in the clipboard, select the picture or the part of it you want to embed and then choose the Copy command in the Edit menu.

3. Switch to or open QuarkXPress and then open the document in which you want to embed the picture.

4. With the Content tool and the desired picture box active, choose the Paste Special command from the Edit menu. The Paste Special dialog box shown next appears. This dialog box presents all the different formats in which the picture data in the clipboard is available.

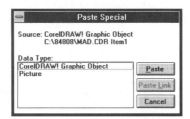

5. To embed the picture in its native format (the format used by the server application), choose the option that includes the word Object. This is the only option that guarantees no picture data will be lost.

6. Click the Paste button to embed the picture and return to your document.

Updating Embedded Pictures   An embedded picture is an independent copy of the picture in the original source file. Once you embed a picture within a Quark document using the Paste Special command, you can no longer update or edit it from the server application. Instead, you double-click the picture box when the Content tool is active, and Quark opens the server application so that you can edit the embedded picture from within Quark. When you have finished editing the picture, choose Exit and Return or Update from the File menu of the server application. Quark updates the display of the embedded picture immediately.

Managing Picture Display

How an imported picture appears on the screen depends on the current settings for several options in the Application Preferences and General Preferences dialog boxes. As you may recall from Chapter 4, application preferences affect all documents, while Quark saves general preferences with specific documents.

Low Resolution TIFF

The Low Resolution TIFF check box in the Application Preferences dialog box (Preferences/Application command, Edit menu) affects the onscreen display of any TIFF format images you import into in a document. When this option is checked, TIFF images appear at half the monitor's display resolution as you import them—for instance, at 48 dpi if your monitor and display adapter support a standard VGA display resolution of 96 dpi. To display all TIFF images at full-screen resolution, deselect the check box. Keep in mind that full-resolution display tends to slow screen redraw.

Tip   You can toggle the display resolution of a specific TIFF image by pressing SHIFT as you import it. For example, if Low Resolution TIFF is currently checked, pressing SHIFT as you import the picture causes Quark to display it at full-screen resolution. Other TIFF images in the document continue to be displayed at low resolution.

8-Bit TIFF

The 8-Bit TIFF option in the Application Preferences dialog box affects the onscreen appearance of color TIFF images that contain 256 or 16 million colors. Check this option to represent such images with a 256-color palette rather than Quark's standard 16-color palette. Again, screen redraw may be slower when this option is active. If your monitor can display 16 million colors, leaving 8-Bit TIFF unchecked causes 24-bit color pictures to appear in their original colors.

256 Levels of Gray

The 256 Levels of Gray option in the Application Preferences dialog box affects the display of grayscale images containing 256 different shades of gray. Check this option if you want all 256 shades to appear on the screen (and your monitor supports it). Leave this option unchecked if you want to represent such images with only 16 levels of gray for faster screen redraw.

Auto Picture Import

The Auto Picture Import option in the General Preferences dialog box (Preferences/General command, Edit menu) determines whether and when Quark updates the display of pictures that have been modified since the last time you opened the active document. See the "Controlling Picture Updates with Auto Picture Import" section earlier in this chapter for more information.

Greeking Pictures

To speed screen redraw in a document that contains many pictures, check the Greek Pictures option in the General Preferences dialog box. When pictures are greeked, their picture boxes appear solid gray on the monitor.

Sizing Pictures

Quark lets you change the size of a picture independently of its picture box. In general, you should avoid resizing bitmapped or photographic images after importing them, because there is an intricate relationship between the number of pixels in an image, image width in a document, and eventual print quality (more about that in Chapter 9). Object-oriented pictures from drawing programs don't present this problem, so you can scale them up or down without any worries.

Sizing a Picture with the Picture Box Specifications Dialog Box

Double-clicking a picture box when the Item tool is active brings up the Picture Box Specifications dialog box described earlier in this chapter. (When the Content tool is active, display this dialog box by pressing CTRL-M.) Use the Scale Across and Scale Down fields to enter the new picture size as a percentage of current size. To maintain the current aspect ratio (proportions) of a picture, enter the same value for both Scale Across and Scale Down. Entering different values distorts the picture, which can sometimes be useful for special effects. The four images shown in Figure 8-9 depict a graphic at original size, scaled down to 50 percent in both dimensions, and resized to create a distorted effect.

FIGURE 8-9

Changing horizontal and vertical scaling to resize and/or distort a picture

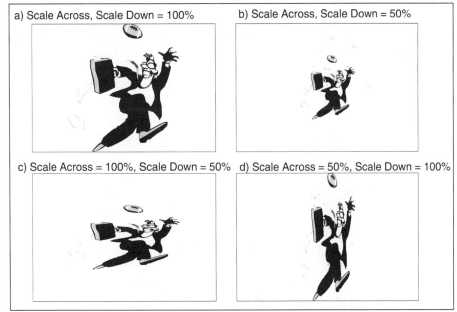

a) Scale Across, Scale Down = 100%

b) Scale Across, Scale Down = 50%

c) Scale Across = 100%, Scale Down = 50%

d) Scale Across = 50%, Scale Down = 100%

Sizing a Picture with the Measurements Palette

When the Content tool is active and a picture box is selected, the right side of the Measurements palette displays information about the picture, as shown here:

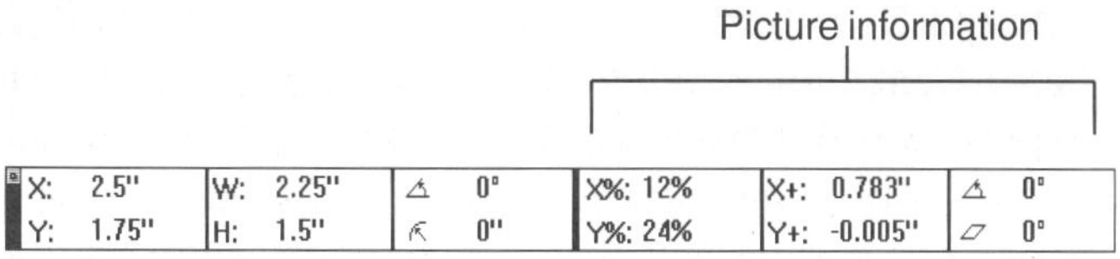

Picture information

| X: | 2.5" | W: | 2.25" | △ | 0° | X%: 12% | X+: | 0.783" | △ | 0° |
| Y: | 1.75" | H: | 1.5" | ⟲ | 0" | Y%: 24% | Y+: | -0.005" | ⟋ | 0° |

To change picture size with the Measurements palette, edit the values in the X% and Y% fields. The values you enter should be equal unless you deliberately choose to distort the picture.

Sizing Pictures with the Keyboard

When the Content tool is active and a picture box selected, you can increase the scale of a picture in 5-percent increments by pressing CTRL-ALT-SHIFT->. To decrease the scale of a picture by the same amount, press CTRL-ALT-SHIFT-<.

Simultaneously Scaling a Picture and Its Picture Box

To scale a picture and its picture box at the same time, activate the picture box when the Content or Item tool is active, press CTRL, and drag the selection handle of your choice. To ensure that the aspect ratio of both the picture and its picture box remain the same, press CTRL-ALT-SHIFT as you drag.

Cropping and Positioning Pictures

The art of fitting and/or positioning a picture within its picture box is known as *cropping*. Quark's flexibility in cropping pictures is unparalleled. You can reposition or center pictures using your choice of mouse, keyboard, palette, and dialog box techniques.

 Caution If you want only a small area of a picture to be visible, you may wish to edit out the unwanted portions using an image-editing or drawing program. Otherwise, Quark still has to process the entire picture file when you print the document, and that could waste valuable time and memory.

Cropping Pictures Interactively

For a hands-on, WYSIWYG method of repositioning a picture within its picture box, activate the Content tool, select the picture box, and start dragging. As shown in Figure 8-10, the pointer takes on the shape of a hand that "pushes" the picture in the direction of your mouse movement.

Cropping Pictures with the Picture Box Specifications Dialog Box

The Picture Box Specifications dialog box contains two fields—Offset Across and Offset Down—that precisely define the position of a picture relative to the upper-left corner of its picture box. To access this dialog box when a picture box is selected, press CTRL-M when the Content or

FIGURE
8-10

Positioning a picture with the cropping pointer when the Content tool is active

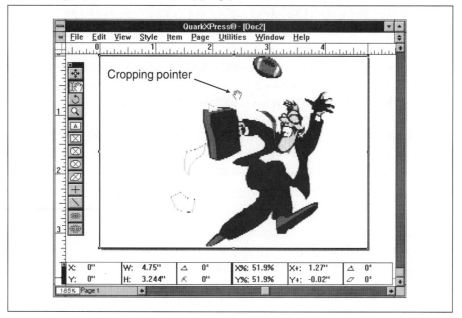

Item tool is active, or double-click the picture box when the Item tool is active.

☐ The value in the Offset Across field specifies the *horizontal* position of the upper-left corner of the picture. Increasing the value moves the picture to the right; decreasing the value moves it to the left. A negative value indicates that the left edge of the picture extends beyond the left edge of its picture box.

☐ The value in the Offset Down field specifies the *vertical* position of the upper-left corner of the picture. Increasing this value moves the picture upward, while decreasing it moves the picture downward. A negative value indicates that the upper edge of the picture extends beyond the upper edge of its picture box.

Cropping Pictures with the Measurements Palette

The X+ and Y+ fields in the Measurements palette indicate the current position of the active picture relative to the upper-left corner of its picture box. These fields are visible only when the Content tool is active and a picture box is selected. To edit one or both of these values, double-click in the desired field and enter a new value.

"Nudging" Pictures with the Keyboard

If a picture is almost but not quite where you want it, you can use the cursor and/or ALT keys to nudge it up, down, left, or right in one- or one-tenth point increments. Table 8-4 shows the keyboard shortcuts to use.

Centering and Fitting a Picture

Several keyboard shortcuts are available in Quark for automatically centering and resizing the active picture relative to its picture box. To

TABLE
8-4

Nudging a Picture in Small Increments: Keyboard Shortcuts

To Nudge a Picture	Press
Left in 1-pt increments	LEFT ARROW
Right in 1-pt increments	RIGHT ARROW
Up in 1-pt increments	UP ARROW
Down in 1-pt increments	DOWN ARROW
Left in .1-pt increments	ALT-LEFT ARROW
Right in .1-pt increments	ALT-RIGHT ARROW
Up in .1-pt increments	ALT-UP ARROW
Down in .1-pt increments	ALT-DOWN ARROW

center a picture without changing its current size, press CTRL-SHIFT-M. To make a picture fit precisely within its picture box—even at the price of distorting the picture—press CTRL-SHIFT-F. To center and fit a picture to the picture box without distorting it, press CTRL-ALT-SHIFT-F. Figure 8-11 shows examples of a picture imported at current size, centered at current size, resized and centered with distortion, and scaled to fit the picture box without distortion.

 Caution Avoid automatically resizing bitmaps and photographic images unless you're sure that the result won't degrade the print quality of the image. See Chapter 9.

Rotating Pictures and Picture Boxes

Not only can you move and size pictures and picture boxes independently of one another, you can rotate them independently, too. As usual, Quark provides a plethora of techniques for getting the results you want.

**FIGURE
8-11**

Centering and resizing the picture relative to its picture box

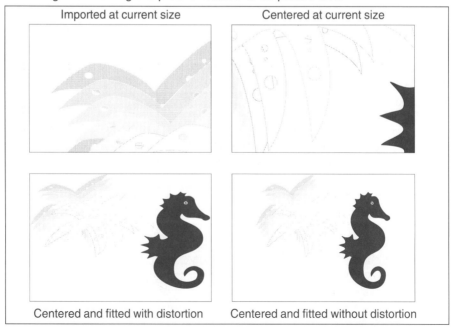

Rotating Interactively

    The Rotation tool in the Tools palette lets you rotate a picture box interactively using the mouse. If a picture box already contains a picture, using this tool rotates both at the same time. Unlike other techniques, using the Rotation tool offers the great advantage of letting you choose the *axis of rotation*—the point around which the picture box turns. To rotate a picture and its picture box with the Rotation tool, follow these steps:

1. Activate the Rotation tool by clicking its icon in the Tools palette. If you plan on rotating an image more than once without pausing, press ALT briefly as you select the tool. This keeps the tool active for further use.

2. Move the pointer over the picture box you want to rotate and position it where you want to define the axis of rotation. The pointer takes on the appearance of a crosshair surrounded by a circle, as shown here:

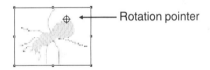

3. Your next step depends on whether you want to see the picture as you rotate it.

   ☐ To rotate the picture box quickly, press and hold the mouse button and drag in the desired direction. The original picture box and picture remain in place, and you see only a dotted outline as you rotate, as shown here:

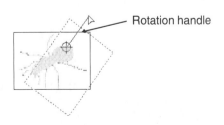

☐   To see the picture as you rotate it, press and hold the mouse button for about half a second before you begin dragging. The picture box rotates a little more slowly this way, but it helps if you need to see exactly what is happening:

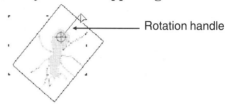

Rotation handle

4.   Release the mouse button when the picture box is in the desired position.

Rotating with the Picture Box Specifications Dialog Box

For those who value numerical precision above WYSIWYG interaction, the Picture Box Specifications dialog box offers a tidy way to rotate pictures and picture boxes. Unlike the Rotation tool, this dialog box lets you rotate the picture and its picture box independently of one another. The Box Angle value defines the angle of rotation of the picture box, while the Picture Angle value defines the angle of rotation of the picture itself. Figure 8-12 shows an example of a picture that is at a different angle of rotation from its picture box.

Rotating with the Measurements Palette

When you select a picture box with the Content tool, the Measurements palette includes fields that let you define the angle of rotation for both the picture box and the picture inside it, as shown here:

Picture box angle   Picture angle

X:	0.236"	W:	3.5"	△	15°	X%: 38.5%	X+:	0.734"	△	-20°
Y:	0.817"	H:	2.5"	⋔	0.25"	Y%: 38.5%	Y+:	-0.316"	⊘	0°

FIGURE 8-12

Rotating a picture and its picture box independently from one another

Picture box: 15°

Picture: −20°

To change either value, double-click the appropriate field and overtype the desired angle value. If the numbers seem confusing, think of angles of rotation as points on an imaginary compass. As Figure 8-13 shows, positive numbers define angles that increase counterclockwise from east to west, while negative values define angles that increase clockwise from east to west.

Skewing a Picture

Skewing a picture involves slanting it for a distorted effect as Figure 8-14 shows. You can skew a picture (but not its picture box) to the left or right at angles of up to 75 degrees. To skew a picture from within the Picture Box Specifications dialog box, edit the value in the Picture Skew field. When the Content tool is selected, you can skew the active picture box by editing the value in the skew field:

| X: | 0.236" | W: | 3.5" | △ | 15° | X%: | 38.5% | X+: | 0.973" | △ | -20° |
| Y: | 0.817" | H: | 2.5" | ⋉ | 0.25" | Y%: | 38.5% | Y+: | -0.229" | ⟋ | 15° |

Picture skew angle

FIGURE 8-13

How Quark measures positive and negative angles of rotation

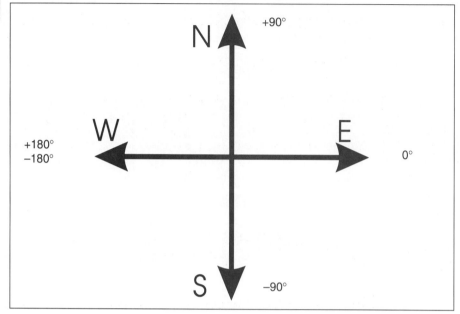

FIGURE 8-14

A skewed picture

A positive angle skews the picture to the right, while a negative angle skews it to the left.

If a picture already fills its picture box before you skew it, it may extend beyond the picture box boundaries. To compensate, you may need to resize either the picture or its picture box after skewing.

Tip To simulate a skewed picture box to match a skewed picture, change the picture box shape to a polygon and then slant the angles of the picture box. See "Reshaping a Polygon Picture Box" earlier in this chapter.

Importing and Manipulating Pictures: Shortcuts

Table 8-5 is a list of handy shortcuts you can use when importing, resizing, centering, and fitting pictures within their picture boxes. The Content tool must be active in order for you to manipulate a picture with these key commands.

Importing and Manipulating Pictures: Keyboard Shortcuts

To Do This	Press
Import Picture into current picture box	CTRL-E
Toggle between low and high display resolution	SHIFT while importing
Increase picture size in 5% increments	CTRL-ALT-SHIFT->
Decrease picture size in 5% increments	CTRL-ALT-SHIFT-<
Center picture at current size	CTRL-SHIFT-M
Fit picture to box, with distortion	CTRL-SHIFT-F
Center and fit picture to box, maintain aspect ratio	CTRL-ALT-SHIFT-F

Managing Picture Files in a Document

If you were already out of diapers in the 1970s and '80s, the television news slogan, "It's ten o'clock. Do you know where your children are?" is probably familiar to you. With QuarkXPress, the phrase to remember is, "It's time to print. Do you know where your pictures are?" They are *not* in your document. Those low-resolution images you see in picture boxes are only placeholders for the actual picture files, which can be anywhere on your hard drive. Keeping track of and updating the links to those picture files is one of the most important tasks you accomplish in Quark.

When you first import a picture, Quark "remembers" the location of the picture file and expects to find it there every time you open the document. If you delete or move a picture file and then print the document that refers to it, the picture will print out at the lower screen resolution you used to represent it (see the "Low Resolution TIFF" section of this chapter).

Fortunately, Quark provides several tools to ease the pain and strain of picture management. The Auto Picture Import option in the General Preferences dialog box, discussed in the "Linking and Embedding Pictures" section of this chapter, can be set to warn you that a picture is no longer where Quark expects to find it. The Links dialog box, also discussed earlier in this chapter, handles file management for OLE-linked pictures. You don't have to worry about pictures copied through the clipboard or embedded in a document, because they don't exist outside the document. That leaves pictures imported with the Get Picture command in the File menu—the Picture Usage dialog box helps you keep track of those.

The Picture Usage Dialog Box

If you're the type who has trouble staying organized (digitally speaking), be sure to choose the Picture Usage command in the Utilities menu periodically to check the status of imported pictures in the active document. Or, if you think you might forget to do this, be sure to set Auto Picture Import in the General Preferences dialog box to On (Verify). That way, if you open a document in which one or more picture files have been moved, modified, or deleted, Quark displays the following message box:

Click OK to display the Missing/Modified Pictures dialog box shown here:

This dialog box, which is based on the Picture Usage dialog box, displays all the imported picture files (except linked, embedded, and clipboard files) used in the current document. The name and location of each picture file, the page(s) on which it appears, the file format, and the current status (OK, Modified, or Missing) appear here.

To see a picture listed in the Missing/Modified pictures or Picture Usage dialog box, click the name of the picture and then click Show Me. Quark scrolls to the page on which the picture is located. To update the display of a picture listed as Modified, click the Update button. If you click Update when a picture listed as Missing is selected, Quark displays a "Find" dialog box, similar to a standard file management dialog box. You can use this dialog box to locate the drive and directory of the missing picture.

Picture Management Dos and Don'ts

Since picture files are separate from Quark document files, it's important to keep track of them. Here are some suggestions for managing pictures and documents; Chapter 14 offers additional tips.

☐ Store all the picture files for a document in the same directory as the document files.

☐ Don't delete a picture file that is part of an existing document unless you want an unpleasant surprise at printing time.

☐ Avoid moving picture files to different directories after placing them in a document.

☐ When printing a draft document using your own printer, check the Picture Usage dialog box and Links dialog box prior to choosing the Print command.

☐ If you need to use the services of an off-site service bureau for printing, create your own PostScript output files if at all possible. If you can't create your own output files, be sure to give the service bureau all the picture files that go with the document.

☐ Be sure to set up the proper trapping for all the pictures in a document before you print the final copy (or create final output files). See Chapter 10 for more information on trapping.

This chapter has covered the basics of importing, manipulating, and tracking all types of pictures in your Quark documents. The next chapter explores techniques for working with a very special class of pictures—bitmaps and photographic images.

CHAPTER

Enhancing
Photographs and
Other Bitmaps

*P*icture boxes in a Quark document can contain either object-oriented or bitmapped pictures. If a picture box contains bitmapped artwork—a digital painting, scanned photograph, or bitmapped clip art piece—and the Content tool is active, the commands in the Style menu become available. These commands let you enhance bitmapped pictures in a variety of ways. You can

- Apply a color or tint to a grayscale or black-and-white bitmap

- Invert the colors or gray shades in a color, grayscale, or black-and-white bitmap

- Modify brightness and contrast levels in grayscale bitmaps

- Define preset or custom halftone screens that determine how Quark prints grayscale bitmaps

This chapter introduces you to each of these enhancement techniques. Along the way, you'll also learn how to prepare, size, and manipulate bitmapped artwork in Quark for best results.

Why Bitmaps Are Special

Bitmapped pictures—which we'll refer to in this chapter as *images*—require more fussy handling than their object-oriented siblings. This is because the two types of artwork have very different components. Whereas an electronic drawing consists of mathematically defined objects that you can size up or down without loss of quality, an image consists of a fixed number of *pixels* or dots. The enlargement in Figure 9-1 shows the individual pixels from the boxed section of the complete image. Thanks to those little pixels, you must be concerned about the size, resolution, and pixel depth of every bitmapped image—characteristics that determine how an image will print and affect the way you work in Quark.

FIGURE 9-1

A bitmapped image consists of a fixed number of individual pixels

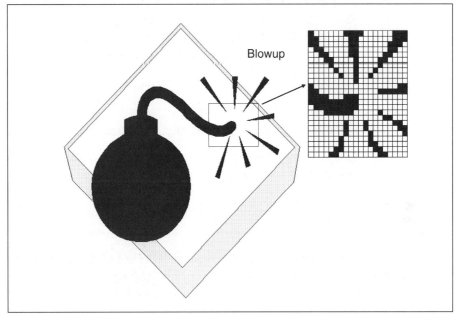

Blowup

Determining Optimum Image Size and Resolution

Images, unlike object-oriented pictures, print well only at specific sizes. If you enlarge an image too much, the printed version looks grainy because the pixel density or *resolution* is too low—the pixels are too far apart. Reducing the size of an image makes it look sharper, but only up to a certain point. If you increase resolution too much, thereby reducing image size too far, the printed version loses detail and its colors or shades of gray become compacted. Figure 9-2 illustrates the inverse relationship between image size and resolution.

Several factors determine the size at which a given image will print with the greatest degree of sharpness or clarity. These factors are

- The *print width* or width of the image in the document layout

- The width of the undigitized *source image*—the hard-copy photograph or artwork before it is scanned (this doesn't apply to original artwork created on the computer)

- The total number of pixels in the width of a scanned or other digital image

- The image resolution or density, measured in pixels or dots per inch

- The type of printing device (laser printer, imagesetter, and so on) you plan to use for final output

If you know the parameters for at least two or three of these factors, you should be able to come up with an image of just the right size.

Suppose, for example, that you have a clear understanding of your layout and your output requirements but need to find out how many pixels wide your picture should be to look good. You know you need a photograph that will take up four horizontal inches in your document,

FIGURE 9-2   Image size decreases as resolution increases

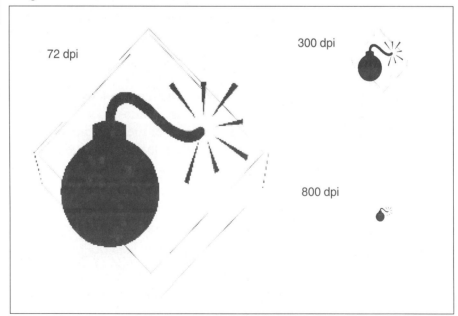

and you know that your service bureau will output the document to film using a PostScript imagesetter at a halftone screen frequency of 150 lpi (*lines per inch*—more about that in the "Defining Halftone Screens" section later in this chapter). PostScript devices need about two pixels for every halftone dot in order to create good output. Armed with this knowledge, you can use the following formula to derive the necessary pixel width for the photograph:

Halftone screen frequency (lpi) × print width × 2 = optimum number of pixels
150 lpi × 4 inches × 2 = 1200 pixels

If you then have to scan a source image, your work becomes easier because you know you must choose a scanning resolution that will yield a digital image 1200 pixels wide. You can obtain the best possible scanning resolution by using this formula:

Optimum pixel width ÷ source image width = ideal scanning resolution

Assuming that the source image in the example is four inches wide, you would scan the image at 300 dpi to obtain enough pixels for high-quality printed output (1200 pixels ÷ 4 inches = 300 dpi). Substitute your own measurements for the real-world images you encounter every day.

As the layout person on a project, however, you're not always in control of your image sources. Let's look at another example in which you receive an image file that someone has already scanned or painted; in this case how do you arrive at a picture size (print width) in Quark that will give you the best output results? Assume you have viewed the image in your scanning or image editing software and know that the image is 1800 pixels wide. You also know that your final output device will be an imagesetter using a 150 lpi halftone screen frequency. You can determine the optimum print width using this formula:

Image width in pixels ÷ (halftone screen frequency × 2) = optimum print width
1800 pixels ÷ 300 = 6 inches width

If the document requires that your image take up less space than this, you can always *resample* the image in your scanning or image editing package, cutting out some unnecessary pixels before you even bring it into Quark. If the document requires a *larger* print width than what the pixel density of the image supports, you'll either have to scan the image at a higher resolution (to obtain more pixels) or sacrifice print quality.

The moral of the story is to know as much as you can about your project or your images before you start creating, scanning, or importing images into a document. "Guesstimating" image size or pixel width could lead to unprofessional-looking printed images later on. Thus, you should avoid arbitrarily resizing bitmapped images using the CTRL-ALT-SHIFT-F keyboard command described in Chapter 8. Instead, match the picture box size to the print width of each image, or change the image's resolution using your favorite image editing package.

Color (Pixel) Depth

Color depth, also known as *pixel depth*, is another important characteristic of bitmapped images, one that impacts image file size and the speed of screen redraw in Quark. Color depth, measured in bits, is related exponentially to the total number of different colors an image can contain as well as how much information it takes to describe the color of each pixel in the image. Most of the images you'll use in Quark will be black and white, grayscale, or color. Black-and-white images are 1-bit (2^1) images because the pixels they contain are either black or white, off or on. Grayscale or 8-bit images can contain up to 256 (2^8) different shades of gray. The 24-bit color images possible with today's scanners and paint programs can contain up to 16 million (2^{24}) different colors, although some color images contain only 16 or 256 colors.

As the number of bits and colors in an image increases, so does its file size. Images saved in a 24-bit color format gobble up several times the disk space of an equivalent grayscale image. Even though Quark displays only a rough representation of images on your monitor, rest assured that the bigger the image file, the longer its placeholder will take to redraw on your screen. You should probably opt to greek pictures in documents that contain several grayscale or 24-bit color images.

 Tip   To reduce the number of on-screen colors in a 24-bit color image to 256 and speed screen redraw, check the 8-bit TIFF option in the Application Preferences dialog box (Preferences/Application command, Edit menu).

Color Separations and Image File Formats

If you produce color documents that will be printed commercially, you know that Quark can create *color separations*—separate films or plates for each of the four standard process colors used on printing presses (this process is explained more fully in Chapters 10 and 14). Don't assume, though, that if you import a color bitmap into a document, Quark will automatically create color separations for it at printing time. Quark won't. QuarkXPress for Windows can create automatic color separations for TIFF images only. You can import other types of color bitmapped images into a Quark document, but unless you use a third-party color separation utility (see Chapter 14 and Appendix A), you will obtain only grayscale versions of those images from any imagesetter or black-and-white laser printer. Equally important, Quark will color separate a TIFF image automatically only in one of the following cases:

☐   You have saved the image in the CMYK TIFF format supported by some Macintosh-based image editing programs. This format is just beginning to be supported by Windows-based image editing packages.

☐   You have used a third-party color separation utility that creates five output files for each color TIFF image.

☐   You import the TIFF image into an object-oriented drawing program such as CorelDRAW! or Adobe Illustrator, save the image as an EPS file, and then import this EPS picture into a Quark picture box.

Of course, not everyone requires commercial printing for color documents. With today's crop of color laser printers and continuous-tone color printers by Iris, Kodak, and others, Quark users who produce documents for corporate circulation in-house can print any type of color bitmap in color. Just remember that your options for professional-quality color printing through commercial print processes are more limited.

Images and the Style Menu

As you may recall from Chapter 1, the Style menu wears different faces depending on the type of item currently selected in a document. When the Content tool is active and you have selected a picture box that contains a bitmap, the Style menu looks like this:

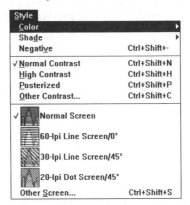

Not all of the options in the Style menu are available for every type of bitmapped image. Table 9-1 provides a quick reference to what you can and cannot do with each image type.

Note   File formats known as *metafiles*—.cgm, .drw, .pct, .plt, and .wmf—can save bitmapped graphics as well as object-oriented ones. You can apply contrast and halftone screens to grayscale and black-and-white bitmaps saved in these formats, but you may not always get a visible or WYSIWYG onscreen representation of them. You'll just have to trust that Quark will print such images according to your Style menu specifications. (Refer to Chapter 8 for more information on metafiles.)

Changes that you make to bitmapped images using Quark's Style menu commands affect only how the images print. They do not alter the

---

TABLE 9-1   Image Enhancement Techniques Available for Each Image Type

Enhancement Technique	Color Images	Grayscale Images	Black-and-White Images
Apply color	no	yes	yes
Apply tint (shade)	no	yes	yes
Invert colors (negative)	yes	yes	yes
Define contrast levels	no	yes	no
Apply halftone screens	no	yes	yes

TABLE 9-2   Style Menu Commands for Images: Keyboard Shortcuts

To Apply This Command	Press
Negative	CTRL-SHIFT--
Normal	CTRL-SHIFT-N
High Contrast	CTRL-SHIFT-H
Posterized	CTRL-SHIFT-P
Other Contrast	CTRL-SHIFT-C
Other Screen	CTRL-SHIFT-S

original picture files. Table 9-2 lists the keyboard shortcuts that you can use to invoke some of the image enhancement commands in the Style menu.

Applying a Color or Tint to an Image

The Color and Shade commands in the Style menu let you apply a color or tint to the black or gray areas of black-and-white and grayscale images. Quark applies color and tint for display and printing purposes only and does not actually change the tonal values in the original image files.

Note   You can use the Colors Palette to apply colors and tints to images, too. See Chapter 10.

To apply a color to a grayscale or black-and-white bitmap, follow these steps:

1. With the Content tool active and the desired picture box selected, choose Color from the Style menu. A submenu appears containing all the colors that you have defined for the current document, as this example shows:

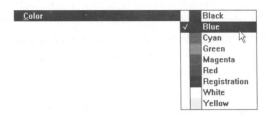

The position of the check mark shows which color is currently applied to the image.

2. Click the option that represents the color you want to apply.

For black-and-white images, Quark applies the solid color to all black areas of the image. If the current image is a grayscale one, Quark applies the color at varying levels of saturation, matching the gray levels in the image.

In some cases, you may not want to apply the most saturated shade of a specific color. To apply a lighter tint of the current color, follow these steps:

1. With the Content tool active and the desired picture box selected, choose the Shade command from the Style menu. A submenu of shades in 10 percent increments appears, as shown here:

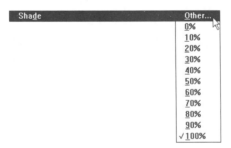

2. Click the shade you want to apply. To specify a custom shade, click the Other command in the submenu and specify a percentage in the Shade dialog box. You can specify any shade in increments of one-tenth of a percent.

A useful application for the Shade command is to apply a very light (10-20 percent) tint of a color to a black-and-white or high-contrast grayscale image that you want to use as a background graphic. Place the picture box behind the text box using the commands in the Arrange menu, and assign a runaround setting of None to the text box (Runaround command, Item menu). Text will flow through the image but will still be readable because of the light tint you have applied. Figure 9-3 shows an example of this technique.

Inverting the Colors of an Image

The Negative command (keyboard shortcut: CTRL-SHIFT- –) is the only command in the Style menu that works with all types of bitmapped images—color, grayscale, and black-and-white. When you apply this command to a color image, Quark inverts the original colors—making the image look like a photographic "negative" of the original. When you apply it to a grayscale image, Quark assigns the complementary gray

FIGURE 9-3 A lightly tinted black-and-white or high-contrast grayscale image can serve as a background graphic

By the Sea, by the Sea, by the Beautiful Sea

Why is so-called Greek text always in Latin? This is one even the experts can't answer. Praesent luptatum delenit augue duis dolore te feugait nulla facilisi. Consequat duis aute ver eum iriure dolor in hendrerit in vulputate velit esse. Pablum rostrum nostrum, scube dube du, exchangus glancus.

Supercalifragilisticexpialidocious, praesent luptatum delenit augue duis dolore te feugait nulla facilisi. Consequat duis aute ver eum iriure dolor in hendrerit in vulputate velit esse. Pablum rostrum nostrum, scube dube du, exchangus glancus.

Ad nauseam, et alia. Ipso facto, mea culpa, youa culpa, we all scream for ice cream in flagrante delicto. At vero enos et accusan et iusto idio dignissim qui blandit.

Why is so-called Greek text always in Latin? This is one even the experts can't answer. Praesent luptatum delenit augue duis dolore te feugait nulla facilisi. Consequat duis aute ver eum iriure dolor in hendrerit in vulputate velit esse. Pablum rostrum nostrum, scube dube du, exchangus glancus. Supercalifragilistic. . .

shades as shown in Figure 9-4. When you apply the Negative command to a black-and-white image, black areas become white and white areas become black. Turning an image into a negative affects only the way the image displays and prints and does not actually change the colors or tones in the original image file.

The Negative command acts like a toggle switch. Choosing the Negative command a second time causes the image to revert to its original colors or tones.

Changing the Contrast of Grayscale Images

The Normal Contrast, High Contrast, Posterized, and Other Contrast commands in the Style menu are available when the Content tool is active and the currently selected picture is a grayscale image. These commands

FIGURE 9-4   Creating a negative of an image inverts its original colors or gray shades

let you manipulate the *contrast* within the image—the relationships between the *highlights* (light grays), *midtones* (medium grays), and *shadows* (dark grays). These commands affect only the way that the currently selected image displays and prints and do not overwrite the original grayscale values in the digital source file. You can only change contrast levels for images imported using the Get Picture command. The contrast-related commands are not available for images that you have copied from the clipboard or that you have linked or embedded using OLE (see Chapter 8).

The Normal Contrast Command

A check mark in front of the Normal Contrast command (keyboard shortcut: CTRL-SHIFT-N) indicates that Quark has not altered the original contrast relationships in the selected grayscale image. You can activate this command to undo any contrast alterations you make through the other contrast-related commands in the Style menu.

The High Contrast Command

The High Contrast command (keyboard shortcut: CTRL-SHIFT-H) reduces all the gray shades in a grayscale image to either black or white. Pixels lighter than 30 percent gray become white, while pixels darker than 30 percent gray turn black. Figure 9-5 shows what happens to a grayscale image to which you apply this command.

The distribution of grays in every grayscale image is different, so Quark's preset 30 percent threshold for assigning black or white may result in an image that lacks detail. If you need to stylize a grayscale image with high contrast but want more control over detail, try choosing the Other Contrast command and using the Hand tool to vary the threshold value, as described in the "Defining Custom Contrast Levels" section later in this chapter.

FIGURE
9-5
The High Contrast command reduces all gray shades in a grayscale image to either black or white

The Posterized Command

When you apply the Posterized command to a grayscale image, Quark reduces the total number of gray levels to six: black (100%), white (0%), 20%, 40%, 60%, and 80%. As Figure 9-6 shows, this type of reduction allows for more detail than the High Contrast command, while still retaining a fairly high level of contrast.

Defining Custom Contrast Levels

Quark always lets you do things your way, and changing contrast levels in a picture is no exception. You're not stuck with the preset gray levels that the Normal Contrast, High Contrast, and Posterized commands assign to an image. Choose the Other Contrast command in the

FIGURE
9-6

The Posterized command reduces the number of gray shades in a grayscale image to six

Style menu (keyboard shortcut: CTRL-SHIFT-S) to access the Picture Contrast Specifications dialog box shown here:

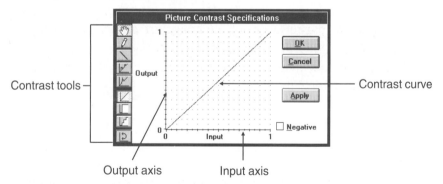

The nine tools and the contrast curve contained in this dialog box let you correct for poorly scanned images, create all types of special effects, and alter contrast relationships in an infinite number of ways. You can

preview your modifications to an image at any time by pressing the Apply button or pressing CTRL-A.

Understanding the Contrast Curve

The focal point of the Picture Contrast Specifications dialog box is the *contrast curve*. The contrast curve is a graph of the original gray values in an image compared to any modifications you have made. For an unmodified grayscale image, the contrast curve is a diagonal line at a 45-degree angle as shown in the previous illustration. Such a line indicates that *input*—the original contrast values represented by the horizontal axis—equals *output*—the modified contrast values represented by the vertical axis.

Reading and interpreting the contrast curve as you modify it is easy if you keep a few basic concepts in mind:

- Input and Output values can range from zero (white) to one (black). The 20 tick marks along both axes of the graph mark off gray values in five percent increments: 5 percent, 10 percent, 15 percent, and so on, right up to 100 percent or one.

- The *slope*, or angle, of the curve indicates the range of contrast in the modified image. A steep slope indicates a wide spectrum of contrast, while a shallow slope indicates that the gray shades fall within a narrow range. Here is an example of a contrast curve in which darker areas of the image are spread across a good range of grays but lighter areas lack contrast:

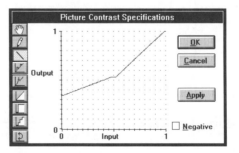

☐ Flat (perfectly horizontal) areas of the contrast curve indicate that a certain range of gray shades have been deleted and assigned to a single gray value. In this contrast curve, very light grays and very dark grays have been remapped to 35% gray and 80% gray, respectively:

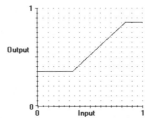

☐ Downward dips in the curve represent gray shades in the original image that you have brightened, while upward spikes represent gray shades that you have darkened:

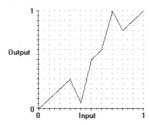

Above all, when making modifications to the contrast curve, remember that you don't have to use just one tool. You can combine several tools to create the desired effect.

The Hand Tool: Shifting the Curve

 The Hand tool in the Picture Contrast Specifications dialog box lets you move the entire contrast curve at one time by dragging. This tool can produce several effects, depending on how you drag. For example, you can

☐ Move the curve straight up to darken the image as a whole while remapping the darker shades to black. Move the curve straight down to brighten the image as a whole while remapping the lighter shades to white. (Pressing SHIFT as you drag constrains movement horizontally or vertically.)

◻ Move the curve diagonally upward and to the left to increase contrast in the shadows as you darken the image; move it diagonally upward and to the right to increase contrast in the highlights while darkening the rest of the image.

◻ Move the curve diagonally downward and to the right to increase contrast in the highlights as you brighten the image; move it downward and to the left to increase contrast in the shadows as you brighten the rest of the image.

◻ Move the curve straight left to increase contrast in the shadows and straight right to increase contrast in the highlight areas of the image. If you drag the curve first left, then right, you increase contrast at both extremes. (Pressing SHIFT as you drag constrains movement of the tool horizontally or vertically.)

Figure 9-7 shows an unmodified image, a contrast curve in which the Hand tool has increased contrast in the highlights and brightened the shadows, and the modified image represented by the new curve.

| FIGURE 9-7 | Brightening highlights and shadows with the Hand tool |

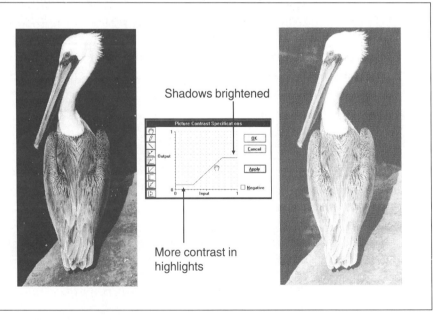

Using the Pencil Tool

The Pencil tool lets you draw a freehand contrast curve by dragging. You can use this tool to create special effects like the one shown in Figure 9-8 or to modify a contrast curve that you have already manipulated using another tool. The Pencil tool is especially effective in smoothing out problem gray shades in an imperfectly scanned grayscale image.

Line Tool

The Line tool lets you modify a curve by creating sharp peaks and valleys or by altering the slope at the points of your choice, as shown here:

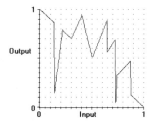

Wherever you increase the slope of the curve, contrast increases and gray shades get deleted. Wherever you decrease the slope of (flatten) the curve, contrast decreases and gray shades *beyond* the slope get deleted (see Figure 9-7). If you press SHIFT while dragging the curve with the Line tool, you constrain movement to zero, 45, or 90 degrees.

Posterizer Tool

When you select the Posterizer tool, Quark adds ten nodes or handles to the contrast curve, as shown here:

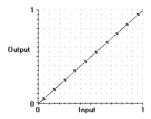

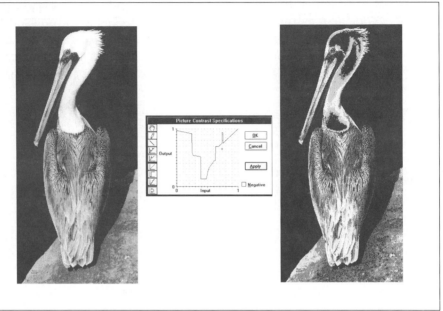

FIGURE 9-8

Drawing a freehand contrast curve with the Pencil tool can yield special effects

These nodes fall at 10 percent grayscale increments along the curve. Dragging a node flattens the curve for that entire 10 percent increment, reducing all the gray shades in that spectrum to a single one. By aligning the nodes horizontally with one another, you can reduce the number of gray shades in the current image to any number between two and ten.

Spike Tool

The Spike tool works somewhat like the Pencil tool in that you can use it to shift gray shades dramatically at specific points in the curve. However, selecting the Spike tool causes handles to appear at 10 percent increments along the curve, and you can create spikes or dips only at these 10 percent increment marks. Use the Spike tool to darken or lighten *specific* gray shades sharply, as shown in Figure 9-9.

FIGURE
9-9

The Spike tool lets you shift specific ranges of gray shades precisely

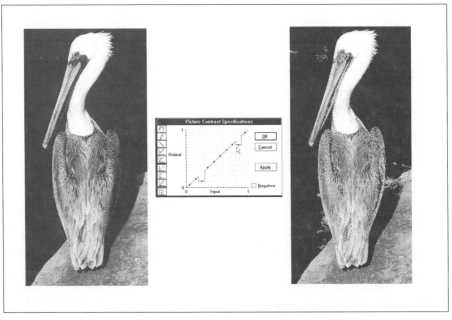

Normal Contrast Tool

Select the Normal Contrast tool to reset the contrast curve to its default 45-degree angle. Activating this tool has the same effect as choosing the Normal Contrast command in the Style menu.

High Contrast Tool

Activating the High Contrast tool has the same effect as choosing the High Contrast command in the Style menu. Both ends of the high contrast curve are flat, indicating that Quark has remapped all shades of gray to either black or white. The default threshold value is a 30 percent gray, as shown here:

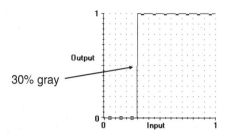

30% gray

As mentioned in "The High Contrast Command" section, earlier in this chapter, a 30 percent threshold is not necessarily the best choice for the average image. High-quality photographic images often show better detail if you set the high-contrast threshold at a value somewhere between 50 percent and 70 percent. To do this, activate the High Contrast tool and then select the Hand tool, shifting the curve to the right until the vertical line falls somewhere between the 50 percent and 70 percent tick marks.

 Remember You can always preview the effects of your settings by pressing CTRL-A or clicking the Apply button. Try out different high-contrast threshold values until you find one that yields just the right amount of detail for the image at hand.

Posterized Tool

 The Posterized tool and the Posterizer tool have similar names, but their effects are slightly different. The Posterized tool reduces the current image to six preset shades of gray, just as the Posterized command in the Style menu does. Quark represents this graphically by a contrast curve that looks like an ascending stairway:

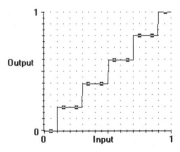

Use the Hand, Pencil, or Line tool to modify the default contrast curve for a posterized image.

Inversion Tool, Negative Check Box

The Inversion tool and the Negative check box may seem similar, but they perform quite different functions. The Negative check box, when active, inverts the gray shades in the original unmodified image, producing the same effect as the Negative command in the Style menu. The Inversion tool, on the other hand, inverts the gray shades in the *current* contrast curve, whatever shape that may be. If you have already edited the contrast curve using other tools, activating the Inversion tool simply flips the existing curve upside down.

Defining Halftone Screens

The last five commands in the Style menu let you apply preset or custom halftone screens to bitmapped images to enhance printing. Before delving into the uses of each command, let's look at what halftone screens represent and why they are important for bitmapped images.

About Halftone Screens

Graphic artists and commercial printing professionals often refer to grayscale bitmaps as *continuous-tone images*, because the gradations from one shade to the next are usually far more subtle than with object-oriented drawings. Laser printers and high-resolution imagesetters, however, can reproduce only black and white. How, then, can we account for the many apparently continuous shades of gray that we "see" in a printed image? Halftone screens are the key to this mystery.

The term *halftone screens* has its origin in traditional print technologies, in which commercial printers reproduced multiple shades of gray by photographing images through a screen of fine lines. Three components of a halftone screen—its frequency, shape, and angle—determined how the final image would look when it came off the printing press.

Laser printers and PostScript imagesetters do things a little differently than traditional methods, but the essential concepts and their functions remain the same. In order to simulate multiple shades of gray, laser printers and PostScript imagesetters—the chief printing devices for most of us—group fixed-size dots together in clusters known as *halftone cells*. Each halftone cell contains a specific number of such dots (also called *spots*), and each spot within a cell is either on (black) or off (white). By varying the number of spots within a halftone cell, these printing devices create the illusion that some cells are "more" gray than others. You specify halftone screen characteristics—varying the frequency, shape, and angle of a halftone screen—for each bitmapped image in a Quark document so that it will print as sharply and with as much detail as possible using the printing device you have selected. The following sections show you how to do this.

Screen Frequency

The *frequency* of a halftone screen, measured in lines per inch (lpi), determines the amount of detail and the level of contrast in a printed image. The higher the screen frequency, the sharper the image. On printers with resolutions lower than 1200 dots per inch (dpi), there is always a trade-off between the screen frequency you can specify and the number of gray shades you can reproduce. Laser printers with 300 dpi output resolutions, for example, can reproduce only 32 shades of gray at a screen frequency of 60 lpi.

You can increase the screen frequency for output to a low-resolution laser printer, but only at the cost of reducing the number of gray shades still further. High-resolution laser printers can reproduce 100-120 gray shades at screen frequencies adequate for newspapers and mass-market books, but it takes a PostScript imagesetter to reproduce 256 shades of gray for higher-quality publications. Newer-model imagesetters can reproduce a full 256 shades of gray starting at 1200 dpi output resolution; check with your service bureau to find out their output capabilities.

Screen Pattern

Every halftone cell in a given grayscale image has the same basic *shape* or pattern. Quark lets you choose among several shapes that are commonly used in the printing industry—dot, ellipse, line, square, and ordered dither. Most commercial print vendors recommend the dot or ellipse shape for grayscale images because this shape does not interfere with the eye's perception of image content. Quark lets you choose among these and other commonly used halftone screen patterns.

Note   Screen patterns are not supposed to be noticed unless you are aiming for special effects. At the screen frequencies used by high-resolution imagesetters, screen patterns are too small to be noticed casually by the naked eye.

Screen Angle

The purpose of a screen angle, like the purpose of a halftone screen shape, is to keep the eye focused on the content of a printed image rather than on the halftone screen itself. Printing industry conventions have determined that halftone screens placed at a 45-degree angle usually work well with grayscale images. Quark offers you several preset screen angle options, and you can always define custom screen angles using the Other Screen command in the Style menu.

Normal Screen

Unless you choose a different halftone screen command for a bitmapped image, Normal Screen is the default setting. An image to which you assign Normal Screen prints using a dot pattern at a 45-degree angle—tried and true standards for grayscale images. The screen frequency represented by the Normal Screen command depends on the current setting for Halftone Screen in the Printer Setup dialog box (Printer Setup command, File menu). Figure 9-10(a) shows an image printed on an imagesetter that specifies a 106 lpi halftone screen frequency.

60-lpi Line Screen/0°

Choose the 60-lpi Line Screen/0° command to print the active image using a screen frequency of 60 lines per inch, a line-shaped screen

FIGURE 9-10 An image printed with different halftone screen settings

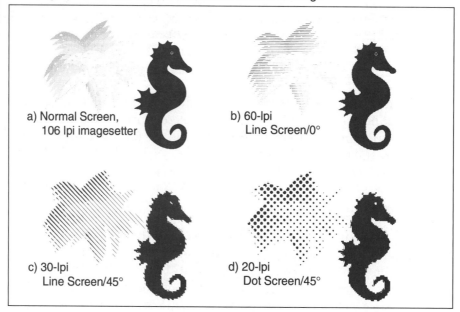

a) Normal Screen,
106 lpi imagesetter

b) 60-lpi
Line Screen/0°

c) 30-lpi
Line Screen/45°

d) 20-lpi
Dot Screen/45°

pattern, and a screen angle of zero degrees. A screen frequency of 60 lpi is typical for 300 dpi laser printers. Figure 9-10(b) shows an image printed using these parameters.

30-lpi Line Screen/45°

Choose the 30-lpi Line Screen/45° command to print the active image using a screen frequency of 30 lpi, a line-shaped screen pattern, and a screen angle of 45 degrees. Figure 9-10(c) shows an example of an image printed at these settings. Screen frequencies of 30 lpi are fairly coarse, generally suitable for silk-screening but not for commercial printing unless you are aiming for special effects.

20-lpi Dot Screen/45°

Applying the 20-lpi Dot Screen/45° command prints the active bitmap-ped image at a very coarse 20 lpi dot-shaped halftone screen using an angle of 45 degrees. At such a low screen frequency, it becomes difficult to see the content of an image because the halftone screen patterning itself is so obvious, as Figure 9-10(d) shows.

Defining a Custom Screen

Choose the Other Screen command (keyboard shortcut: CTRL-SHIFT-S) when you want to define a custom screen frequency, pattern, and/or angle for the currently selected bitmapped image. This Picture Screening Specifications dialog box appears when you select this command:

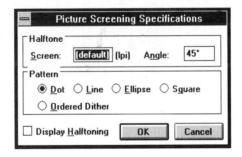

Screen

Use the Screen entry field to specify a halftone screen frequency in lines per inch. The setting "default" prints images at the current Halftone Screen setting specified in the Printer Setup dialog box. You can enter any value from 15 to 400.

Angle

Use the Angle field to specify an angle for the halftone screen you are defining. The default value is 45 degrees, but you can enter custom values ranging from –360 degrees to 360 degrees.

Pattern

Quark offers five commonly used halftone screen patterns: dot, line, ellipse, square, and ordered dither, exaggerated examples of which are shown in Figure 9-11. The dot pattern works well with many grayscale images, but check with your print vendor to confirm the best specifications for a given document. The ordered dither option, designed especially for low-resolution laser printer output, makes the dots in images produced by such printers less obvious than they normally would be.

Display Halftoning

Activate this check box if you want to be able to see the halftone screen for the current image on your monitor. Turning this option on or off does not affect how the image prints.

 Tip The halftone screen settings you specify for a particular image override the default halftone screen settings for your printer. You can even assign separate halftone screen settings to different images on the

---

| FIGURE 9-11 | The five screen patterns available for a bitmapped image |

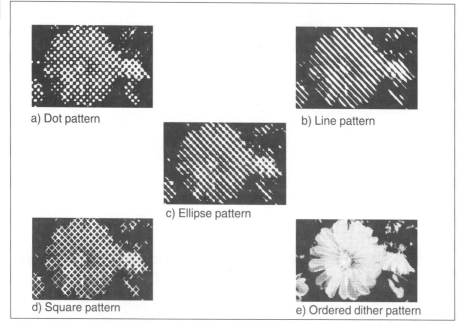

a) Dot pattern

b) Line pattern

c) Ellipse pattern

d) Square pattern

e) Ordered dither pattern

same page and print them together on a single piece of paper or film—a feat not possible with most other page layout packages.

Bitmapped images and printing devices are so closely linked that it's impossible to discuss the two subjects separately. This chapter has given you the basics on the relationship between halftone screens and the output quality of grayscale images. Chapters 10 and 14 contain even more information useful for printing both grayscale and color images in Quark documents.

CHAPTER

Working with Color

QuarkXPress is one of the ringleaders in what desktop publishers are calling "the Desktop color revolution." Color has been around in desktop publishing for awhile, but until recently, most of it involved single colors applied to rules, picture box frames, or text. Anything more complicated, such as color photographs or preparing multiple color plates for the printing press, required manual stripping at the print vendor's place of business.

Those days are gone forever. With QuarkXPress, you can add color to your documents and make a bigger impact on your readers. Quark lets you specify colors using your choice of several industry-standard color sets and assign them to almost anything in your documents. You can integrate full-color TIFF photographs and EPS graphics into a document electronically and output them—along with other colored elements—in a camera-ready format that saves money on your company's or client's printing budget. Equally important, you can do all this with a degree of precision that reduces the margin for error and yields printed results as professional as the ones only a top-notch specialist used to be able to achieve.

Desktop color has a learning curve, and it isn't always easy to implement. There are multiple standards for displaying, specifying, and printing color, and it is vital to communicate clearly with your service bureau and/or print vendor. But with QuarkXPress, you have all the necessary tools at your disposal—a more complete set of such tools than any other page layout package can provide.

What Can You Color?

You can assign color to almost any element in a Quark document, including:

- ☐   The background of a text box
- ☐   The frame of a text box
- ☐   Style sheets
- ☐   Selected text characters
- ☐   The background of a picture box

- ☐ The frame of a picture box

- ☐ A grayscale or black-and-white picture

- ☐ A line

An imported color drawing or photograph is a slightly different case. Although you cannot assign color to a color picture, QuarkXPress can prepare camera-ready output for it, as you will see in Chapter 14. Figure 10-1 shows grayscale examples of each type of element that can accept color.

Translating Color into Print

"Why do I need software to assign color to anything?" you may ask. Why not just tell the print vendor to use blue for all the heads (or ruling lines, or picture frames, and so on) and be done with it?

Document elements that can accept color

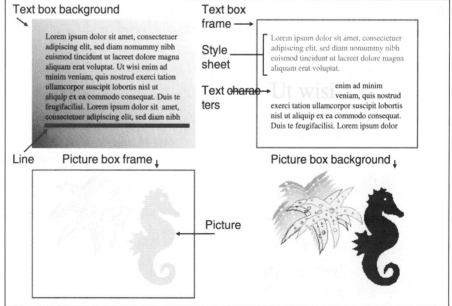

You can, in fact, handle your color printing requirements in just this way, but you probably wouldn't want to unless you have an unlimited printing budget. Because commercial printers need to make a separate *plate* for each color on a page in order to ready the page for the printing press, adding color this way is costly.

If you want to print an extra color in your document—say, blue in addition to black—and you give your printer only one sheet of paper or one piece of film per page, the printer must go through several intermediate steps to create the additional plate and prepare for printing. That can become needlessly expensive, especially if you require more than two colors per document.

Using QuarkXPress' color controls, on the other hand, you can cut out some of those intermediate steps and give your print vendor something much closer to the *camera ready output* he or she needs to create color plates. In the process, you save money. You also reduce the possibility of error in communication between designer and printer, because Quark can define color using the same sets of standards that print industry professionals are already familiar with. To translate color into print effectively using Quark, you need to carry out only three basic tasks:

☐   Build a color palette that contains all the colors you want to use in a given document.

☐   Assign color to document elements during layout.

☐   At printing time, generate *color separations* so that all the document elements that share a given color print on a separate piece of paper or film for each page.

Before you can assign color to your documents, you must first build a palette that makes the colors of your choice available to them. The next few sections describe how to define, edit, and manage colors for the active document or for all new documents.

Building a Custom Color Palette

In the real world, color simply exists; you don't have to analyze it much. Color on computers, however, is a more involved matter. A digital color comes into existence and becomes usable only after you define it by numeric values and give it a name. Graphic designers call this process *specifying color.*

You can specify an independent set of colors for each document in QuarkXPress. When you first install Quark, a default set of nine colors—Black, Blue, Cyan, Green, Magenta, Red, Registration, White, and Yellow—is available. The current default colors automatically become the startup palette of each new document you open. At any time, you can edit the color set for a specific document or the default palette that applies to all new documents.

Tip   Items to which you assign Registration color print out on every plate of a document for which you create color separations. Suggested uses for Registration color include custom crop marks or references that identify the document, the client, or other job-specific information.

The Colors Dialog Box

The Colors dialog box, shown here, is Quark's "Grand Central Station" for every kind of task related to defining, editing, and managing color:

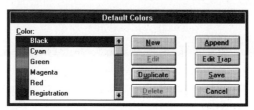

Here you will find options for specifying new colors, editing and duplicating specifications for existing colors, copying colors between documents, and managing trapping parameters for specific colors (you will learn what this means shortly). You can access the Colors dialog box in one of two ways:

☐ Choose the Colors command in the Edit menu.

☐ Display the Colors palette (Show Colors command, View menu) and press CTRL while clicking on one of the currently available colors. See "The Colors Palette" section later in this chapter for details.

To change the default colors—the colors that automatically become the palette of new documents—display the Colors dialog box when no document is open. The dialog box then bears the title "Default Colors" as shown in the previous illustration, and any colors you define will be available to all new documents you create from that point on. To change the color set for a specific document only, access the Colors dialog box when that document is open and active. The title bar of the Colors dialog box will include the filename of the current document as shown here:

Defining, Editing, and Duplicating Colors

Three of the command buttons in the Colors dialog box—New, Edit, and Duplicate—open onto the Edit Color dialog box where you specify color. These three command buttons correspond to the three different techniques Quark makes available for specifying color: defining a new color from scratch, editing an existing color, or duplicating an existing color.

Defining a New Color

To define a new color independently of other colors currently in the palette, click the New button in the Colors dialog box. Quark opens the Edit Color dialog box with the current color set to white.

Editing an Existing Color

To change the definition of an existing color that appears in the Colors dialog box, click the name of the color in the Colors list box and then click the Edit button. This button is not available for Cyan, Magenta, or Yellow, because these are standard colors for the printing industry. Quark does not allow you to edit Black or White, either.

Duplicating an Existing Color

To base a new color on the definition of an existing one, in the Colors dialog box click the name of the color you want to duplicate in the Colors list box; then click the Duplicate command button. Quark opens the Edit Color dialog box with the values for the selected color already displayed.

 Note Trapping color is a specialized subject. You will find more information about trapping in the "Trapping Color in Quark" section later in this chapter.

Specifying Color in the Edit Color Dialog Box

Specifying color in QuarkXPress can be as intuitive as clicking in a visual color wheel or as precise as entering percentage values. The work of defining color takes place in the Edit Color dialog box (shown in Figure 10-2), which you access by clicking the New, Edit, or Duplicate buttons in the Colors dialog box. There are basically four steps to defining or editing any color:

1. Choose a color model from the Model drop-down list box.

2. Select a color by using the scroll bars to specify numerical values (HSB, RGB, and CMYK models, explained in the next section), clicking on a color in the color wheel (HSB and RGB models), or clicking on a color in a predefined visual catalog (Pantone, Trumatch, and Focoltone models, discussed shortly).

3. Name the color (HSB, RGB, and CMYK models). The Pantone, Trumatch, and Focoltone colors have predefined names that appear in the Name field of the dialog box automatically.

4. Activate or deactivate the Process Separation check box based on how you plan to output the document in preparation for color printing. See the "Process Separation" and "Screen Values" sections later in this chapter.

FIGURE 10-2

The Edit Color dialog box

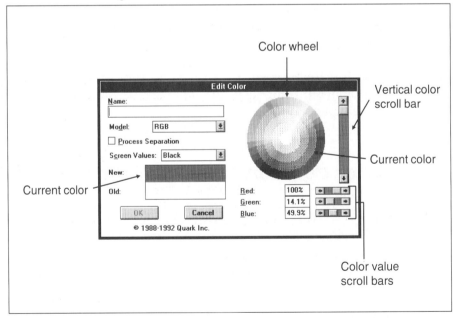

Choosing a Color Model

The human eye *perceives* light one way, computer monitors *transmit* it in another, and printers' inks *reflect* it in yet a third way. The printing industry itself has developed a number of competing standards for specifying color precisely. That, in a nutshell, is why there are multiple *color models*, or systems for describing and defining colors in a standardized way.

The Model drop-down list box in the Edit Color dialog box lets you base your color specifications on one of six different color models—HSB, RGB, CMYK, Pantone, Trumatch, or Focoltone, as shown here:

QuarkXPress supports this many color models so that you can match your color definitions to the standards required by your clients, your service bureau, or your print vendor. Ultimately, you should base your choice of color model on consultations with these parties.

HSB Color The HSB color model describes every color in terms of three values: hue, saturation, and brightness, all expressed in percentages. The *Hue* value describes the essential color in terms of its position on a circular color wheel, with colors arranged in the order red (0 percent), orange, yellow, green, cyan, blue, violet, magenta, pink, and back to red. The *Saturation* value describes the intensity of a color, with 0 percent indicating a shade of gray and 100 percent the most brilliant intensity of the color possible. *Brightness* describes the amount of black a color contains; a 0 percent brightness value indicates pure black, while a color with a 100 percent brightness value contains no black at all. Many graphic artists and designers feel that the HSB color model is intuitive because it is based on the way the human eye perceives color.

When you choose the HSB color model, the Edit Color dialog box looks like this:

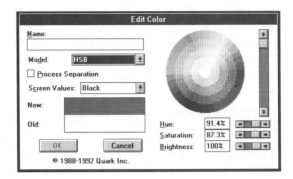

If you prefer to select colors visually, use the vertical scroll bar to view a limited spectrum of color in the color wheel and then click on the desired point in the wheel. To specify color values numerically, use the Hue, Saturation, and Brightness scroll bars or enter values directly in the corresponding fields. Keep in mind that when you use the HSB color model, the colors you select will probably look brighter onscreen than in the final printed piece. This is due to inherent limitations in the way computer monitors display color.

RGB Color Computer monitors do not represent color in the same way that the eye perceives it. Monitors transmit light using a combination of red, green, and blue phosphors—the initials of the RGB color model.

When you choose the RGB color model, the Edit Color dialog box looks like this:

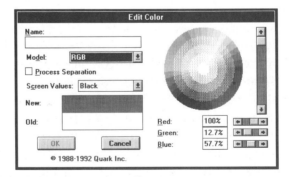

To select RGB colors visually, adjust the vertical scroll bar so you can see the desired part of the spectrum on the color wheel, and then click a color on the wheel itself. To specify RGB colors numerically, adjust the Red, Green, and Blue scroll bars or enter values in the corresponding fields. You see black when all three RGB percentages are set to zero, white when all three are set to 100 percent, and shades of gray when all three RGB values are equal. The brightness of colors in the RGB model increases with the percentages of each color.

CMYK Color   CMYK stands for Cyan, Magenta, Yellow, and Black, the four *process colors* mixed on the printing press in varying percentages to reproduce a much larger number of colors. The CMYK color model is a printing industry standard with which you should become familiar if your documents contain multicolored artwork that requires commercial printing. Cyan, Magenta, and Yellow are actually the complementary colors of Red, Green, and Blue, respectively. Due to the nature of printing inks, it is necessary to add a fourth color, black, to reproduce colors accurately and with sufficient richness on paper.

When you choose the CMYK color model, the Edit Color dialog box looks like this:

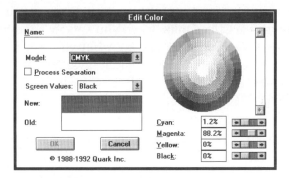

In CMYK mode, you must specify colors numerically rather than through the color wheel, because there is no way to match onscreen colors exactly to printers' inks. You can define colors either by adjusting the Cyan, Magenta, Yellow, and Black scroll bars or by entering values directly in the corresponding fields.

There are so many variables in process color printing that getting the CMYK colors you specify to match their printed output is not always an easy task. If predictable process color matching is critical for your documents, consider specifying color using either the Trumatch model or the Focoltone model, discussed later in this chapter.

Caution   Due to technological limitations, computer monitors are not completely accurate in representing colors as they will appear when printed. If you specify colors using the Pantone, Trumatch, or Focoltone color matching systems, be sure to have the corresponding hard-copy color guide handy as a reference. Use the hard-copy guide, not the screen-based color, as the ultimate standard.

Note   Always check with your print vendor before you start work to make sure you each use the same system to specify and match colors.

Pantone Colors   The Pantone Color Matching System is a color standard developed by the Pantone Corporation and widely used by commercial print vendors. Whereas the CMYK color model is appropriate for process color printing jobs, Pantone colors are often preferable for documents that contain only a handful of discrete colors—say, one- or two-color rules or pictures tinted with a single color. Documents like these are more economical to produce using *spot color* printing, in which a separate page or plate prints out for each color. Pantone inks are premixed, meaning that there is no experimenting with imprecise percentages of CMYK inks; when you specify a Pantone color, the color that prints out on press is exactly what you ask for every time. Hard-copy Pantone color guides are readily available wherever you purchase art supplies.

When you choose the Pantone color model, the Edit Color dialog box looks like this:

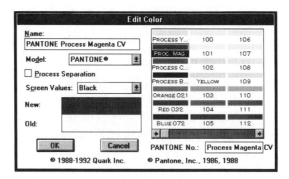

To select a color from the onscreen catalog, adjust the scroll bar until the desired color appears and then click it. The color's name appears both in the Pantone No. field beneath the catalog and in the Name field.

Trumatch Colors   The Trumatch color system uses CMYK color values to specify exact combinations of process colors for the printing press. Designed to take advantage of electronic imagesetters' ability to adjust halftone screens in one-percent increments, the TruMatch system lets designers specify lighter or darker values of a given color in small, even increments, without changing the actual hue. Since they translate easily into CMYK specifications that you can give to a print vendor, TRUMATCH colors lighten the burden of achieving predictable color output.

When you choose the TRUMATCH color model, the Edit Color dialog box looks like this:

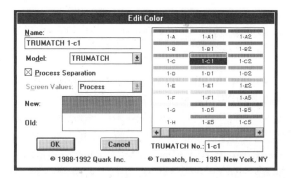

Select a color by adjusting the scroll bar under the onscreen catalog and then clicking the color. The color name appears in both the TRUMATCH No. field beneath the catalog and in the Name field. You can see the equivalent CMYK percentages of a TRUMATCH color by selecting the color and then changing the color model to CMYK.

TRUMATCH's hard-copy swatchbooks represent the TRUMATCH colors more accurately than the onscreen catalog does. Registered users of QuarkXPress can obtain printed TRUMATCH color guides at a discount.

Focoltone Colors Focoltone is another color system created to help designers and commercial printers achieve predictable printed results when specifying CMYK colors. Focoltone's onscreen catalog of 763 colors represents the entire spectrum of colors that CMYK inks can reproduce.

When you choose the Focoltone color model, this is how the Edit Color dialog box appears:

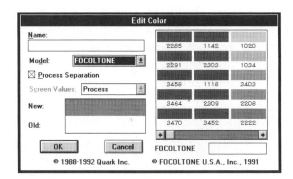

To choose a Focoltone color, select Focoltone in the Model drop-down list box, adjust the scroll bar under the catalog, and click the color. To see the equivalent CMYK percentages of a Focoltone color that you have selected, temporarily change the color model to CMYK using the Model drop-down list box.

Focoltone U.S.A., Inc. also makes available a printed swatchbook, a large-format chart that includes CMYK percentages and formulas for mixing CMYK inks as single spot colors, and software that helps commercial printers reduce *dot gain*—ink spreading due to the enlargement of halftone dots on the press.

Tip   When editing an existing color, you can use any color model to redefine it, regardless of which color model you used to specify it originally. The exceptions to this rule are fluorescent and metallic Pantone colors, which have no counterparts in other color models.

Naming a Color

If you are specifying color using the HSB, RGB, or CMYK color models, you can enter a custom name for the color in the Name field of the Edit Color dialog box. (The Pantone, TRUMATCH, and FocolTone color models include predefined color names.) Naming a color is useful if you need to share colors with other QuarkXPress users or with other Quark documents. To name a new color or rename an existing color, enter any combination of words or characters (up to 62 characters total) in the Name field of the Edit Color dialog box. If you are duplicating an existing

color, the name "Copy of. . ." appears in this field when you open the
dialog box, as shown here:

 Tip For HSB, RGB, and CMYK colors, choose names that convey
information about the color values you have assigned. For example,
C100M00Y30K05 might indicate a color composed of 100 percent Cyan,
0 percent Magenta, 30 percent Yellow, and 5 percent Black. Standardiz-
ing color names this way prevents you from having to reenter the Edit
Color dialog box to find out component values for a specific color.

New and Old Color Indicators

The New and Old color indicators are useful if you are editing or
duplicating an existing color. These indicators show you, in real time,
the visual changes between the original (Old) color and the adjusted (New)
color.

Process Separation

As we mentioned earlier, you can prepare a document for commercial
printing by having Quark generate color separations from it using the
Make Separations option in the Print dialog box (see Chapter 14). The
exact number of color separations you obtain per page depends on how
many colors you are using in a document and whether you have defined
them as spot colors or process colors. When you check the Process
Separation option in the Edit Color dialog box, you are defining the
current color as a process color; when you leave this option unchecked,
you are defining it as a spot color. In spot color printing, you generate as
many separations per page as there are different colors used. If a
document is to contain only two or three discrete colors, you will probably
save on the printing budget by defining all colors as spot colors. In
process color printing, on the other hand, you generate exactly four
separations per page—one each for cyan, magenta, yellow, and black—
and individual colors are broken down into their four CMYK components.
Defining colors as process colors is more economical if a document is to

contain color photographs or more than three separate colors. It is possible to mix both spot colors and process colors in a single document, though most desktop publishers use one system or the other for reasons of economics.

Screen Value

The Screen Value drop-down list box is available only when you have defined a color as a spot color by leaving the Process Separations option unchecked. It affects a special case: the halftone screen settings that Quark assigns when you use a given spot color as a tint for a bitmapped picture.

As you may recall from the discussion of bitmapped pictures in Chapter 9, halftone screens have three components: frequency, angle, and pattern. The Screen Value option most directly affects the halftone screen *angle* used to print a given color. Conventional screen angles in the printing industry are 75 degrees for Magenta, 105 degrees for Cyan, 90 degrees for Yellow, and 45 degrees for Black. The default Screen Value setting for any spot color is Black, but you can substitute one of the other three colors instead.

 Tip   Many imagesetter models that have appeared since late 1991 can output color separations using even more exact angles for high-quality color printing. Consult with your service bureau to find out your options.

To control the default halftone screen frequency used when you output all colors in a document (including any spot color), adjust the Halftone Screen value in the Printer Setup dialog box (Printer Setup command, File menu). To define a custom halftone screen frequency and pattern for a tinted bitmap, choose the Other Screen command in the Style menu when a picture box containing a bitmap is active.

Appending Colors from Other Quark Documents

Defining a complete set of custom colors from scratch for every document can be time-consuming. Fortunately, if an existing document already uses the colors you want, you have a shortcut available. The Append button in the Colors dialog box lets you copy the color definitions from one document to another.

To copy all the colors from another document into the active document, follow these steps:

1. Open the document into which you want to copy the colors and make it the active document.

2. Access the Colors dialog box either by choosing the Colors command in the Edit menu or by clicking a color name in the Colors palette as you press CTRL.

3. Click Append. The Append Colors dialog box shown here appears:

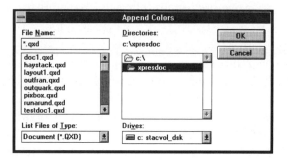

4. To append colors from a Quark document, set List Files of Type to Document (.QXD). To append colors from a template, set List Files of Type to Template (.QXT).

5. Locate the drive and directory of the Quark document or template whose colors you want to copy into the active document. Double-click the desired filename to append the colors and return to the Colors dialog box.

 Tip   To append a single color from another document, use the clipboard to copy an item containing the desired color and paste that item into the active document. The color specifications for the item transfers through the clipboard, and Quark updates the Colors palette and Colors dialog box immediately.

Deleting Colors

When a color palette for a given document starts getting cluttered, you can prune unneeded colors using the Delete button in the Colors dialog box. To delete a color, click the color name in the Color list box and then click Delete. Black, White, Cyan, Magenta, Yellow, and Registration are essential for printing industry conventions, so Quark does not allow you to delete them.

Saving Changes to the Color Set

To save any changes you have made to the current color set and return to the active document, click the Save button in the Colors dialog box.

Applying Color in a Document

Every document includes at least the default color palette; if you have defined custom colors through the Colors and Edit Color dialog boxes, even more colors will be available. You can apply any available color to text and picture box backgrounds, frames, lines, text, or grayscale and black-and-white pictures.

Quark offers a variety of techniques for applying color, including the Colors palette, Style menu commands, and Item menu commands. The item to which you are assigning color determines which tool or technique is the most appropriate to use. For most elements in a document, the Colors palette is an especially intuitive tool for applying color.

The Colors Palette

The Colors palette, pictured here, lets you assign color to the active document element simply by pointing and clicking.

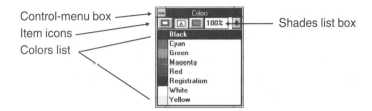

Control-menu box — Item icons — Colors list — Shades list box

If you need to define or edit colors, access the Colors dialog box from the Colors palette by pressing CTRL and then clicking on any color or color name.

Displaying, Moving, and Sizing the Colors Palette

To display the Colors palette, choose Show Colors from the View menu. To hide the palette again, either double-click its control menu box or choose Hide Colors from the View menu. You can move the palette to any location by dragging its title bar. If the list of colors for the current document is longer than will fit in the visible area of the palette, you can use the scroll bar to view additional colors. You can also resize the palette by dragging any corner or outline.

The appearance of the Colors palette varies depending on which tool and document element are currently selected. The following is a brief overview of Colors palette components that will make your work with the palette even more intuitive.

Item Icons

At the top of the Colors palette is a row of icons that varies according to the active tool and the currently selected item. The icon that is currently highlighted shows the item to which you can apply color.

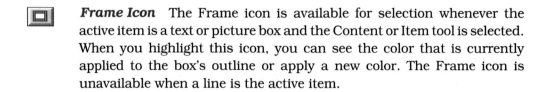

Frame Icon   The Frame icon is available for selection whenever the active item is a text or picture box and the Content or Item tool is selected. When you highlight this icon, you can see the color that is currently applied to the box's outline or apply a new color. The Frame icon is unavailable when a line is the active item.

Box Icon   The Box icon is available whenever the active item is a text or picture box and the Content or Item tool is selected. Highlight this icon to begin applying a color to the background of a box, or to see which color is currently assigned. This icon is also unavailable when a line is active.

Picture Box Icon   The Picture Box icon is available when the Content tool is active and a picture box containing a grayscale or black-and-white bitmapped image is selected. When you highlight this icon, you can assign color to the picture or see which color is currently assigned.

Text Icon   The Text icon, available when the Content tool is active and a text box is selected, lets you assign color at the cursor position to selected characters, or to a selected paragraph. You can also view current color assignments for text.

Line Icon   The Line icon is available when the Item tool is active and a line is the currently selected item. Click on this icon to see the current color assignment for the line or to assign a new color.

Shades List

To apply a tint of the currently selected color to the active design element, click on the desired shade in the Shades drop-down list box. If you prefer to assign a custom shade, enter its percentage value in the Shades field.

Colors List

The colors currently available to the active document appear in the Colors list. To apply a color to a document element, select the element, highlight the appropriate icon at the top of the Colors palette, and click the desired color in the list. If no item in the document is selected, the colors are grayed and you cannot apply them.

If a text or picture box is the active item, you can apply either a solid color fill or a blended fill composed of two different colors or shades. See the section on "Assigning Color to a Background" later in this chapter.

Assigning Color to a Frame

 Quark provides you with two options for applying color to the frame of an active text box or picture box. If the Colors palette is onscreen, you can apply a color by first clicking the Frame icon at the top of the palette and then clicking the desired color name. You can also specify a frame color by choosing the Frame command in the Item menu and setting the Color and Shade fields in the Frame Specifications dialog box.

Assigning Color to a Background

When a text box or picture box is the active item, you can apply color to its background using either the Colors palette or the Modify command in the Item menu. Choosing the Modify command displays the Text Box Specifications or Picture Box Specifications dialog box; set the desired olor using the Color and Shade fields.

To apply color to an active text box or picture box background with the Colors palette, first click the Box icon at the top of the palette. The appearance of the Colors palette changes to include additional fields and buttons as shown here:

You have the option of applying either a solid color or a *linear blend*—a continuous blend of two different colors or two shades of the same color.

Applying a Solid Color Fill

Solid is the default option when you highlight the Box icon in the Colors palette with a text box or picture box active. When Solid is selected, simply click the desired color to apply it to the box background.

Applying a Background Fill of None   A text box or picture box to which you assign a Runaround mode of None (Runaround command, Item menu) automatically takes on a background color of None. This "color" allows the contents of items *behind* the text or picture box to show through transparently. The first text box in Figure 10-3 illustrates an example of this: a picture placed behind a text box that has a background color of None appears as a background graphic. If you reassign some other background color to the item in the foreground, however, your view of any background items will be blocked, as the second example in Figure 10-3 shows. Chapters 11 and 12 provide much more information on how layering and background color affect the appearance of items in a document.

Matching Picture Box Background Color to Picture Color   You may sometimes encounter a situation like the one in Figure 10-4a, in which a perfectly cropped and sized color or grayscale picture created with a solid color background doesn't completely fill its picture box. The following steps give one method of keeping unsightly gaps from occurring in your document:

A foreground item is transparent only when it has both a background color and a Runaround mode of None

Lorem ipsum dolor sit amet, consectetuer adipiscing elit, sed diam nomummy nibh euismod tincidunt ut lacreet dolore magna aliquam erat voluptat.

Ut wisi enim ad minim veniam, quis nostrud exerci tation ullamcorpor suscipit lobortis nisl ut aliquip ex ea commodo consequat. Duis te feugifacilisi. Lorem ipsum dolor sit amet, consectetuer adipiscing elit, sed diam

Text box runaround and background color: None

Lorem ipsum dolor sit amet, consectetuer adipiscing elit, sed diam nomummy nibh euismod tincidunt ut lacreet dolore magna aliquam erat voluptat.

Ut wisi enim ad minim veniam, quis nostrud exerci tation ullamcorpor suscipit lobortis nisl ut aliquip ex ea commodo consequat. Duis te feugifacilisi. Lorem ipsum dolor sit amet, consectetuer adipiscing elit, sed diam

Text box background color: 10% Black

Matching background color to the background color of an imported picture

(a)   (b)

1. View the picture using the image editing or drawing program in which it was created and determine the CMYK color values for the color that forms the picture's background.

2. In Quark, define a color based on these same CMYK values.

3. Apply the newly defined color to the background of the picture box that contains the imported picture. The result should be similar to the example shown in Figure 10-4b.

This solution isn't foolproof, because there is no guarantee that the CMYK values used by a given image editing or drawing program will translate perfectly into the same color in Quark. But in many cases, you may have luck creating the perfect match. Test-print a proof of the page using a color laser printer or a high-resolution color printer at a service bureau.

Applying a Linear Blend

Blended backgrounds are eye-catching design elements in documents. Using the Colors palette, you can fill the background of any text box or picture box with a blend composed of two colors or two shades of the same color. Quark lets you specify not only the colors, but also the angle at which the color transition occurs.

To create a linear blend, follow these steps:

1. With the Content or Item tool active, select the text box or picture box to which you want to apply the blend.

2. Click the Box icon in the Colors palette to display the Solid/Linear Blend list box.

3. Choose Linear Blend from the list box. Fields and buttons for selecting the start and end colors and for specifying the angle of the blend become available, as shown here:

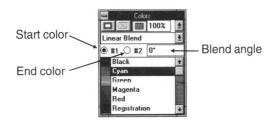

Start color —

End color —

Blend angle

4. To choose a start color, click the #1 button and then choose a color from the list. If you wish, you can also specify a tint of the color in the Shades drop-down list box.

5. To choose an end color for the blend, click the #2 button and then click the desired color in the list. You can specify a shade of this color as well.

Note   You cannot see your blend unless you are using the Item tool to select the text box or picture box. If you use the Content tool, Quark displays only the start color—the color you have specified as #1.

6. Specify an angle for the blend by entering a degree value in the blend angle field. Figure 10-5 shows backgrounds containing color blends at several different angles.

To see the blend, deselect the active text box or picture box, or select the item when the Item tool is active. If your monitor and display adapter lets you see 32,000 or 16 million colors and if the Accurate Blends option in the General Preferences dialog box is checked, you will see a smooth transition from one color or shade to the other. If your monitor can display only 256 or fewer colors, or if the Accurate Blends option in the General Preferences dialog box is unchecked, the onscreen blend will show visible banding. Don't be concerned—the blend will print out correctly as long as your final output device is a high-resolution imagesetter.

Tip   Blended rules can make attractive design elements in the headers of books or other documents. Although you cannot apply a linear blend to a rule, there is a workaround. Create a very narrow rectangular or rounded rectangular picture box and apply the linear blend to its background. The visual effect will be exactly the same as if the picture box were a rule. You can then overlay a text box for the content of the header and assign the same linear blend to it as a background.

Picture box backgrounds featuring linear blends at various angles

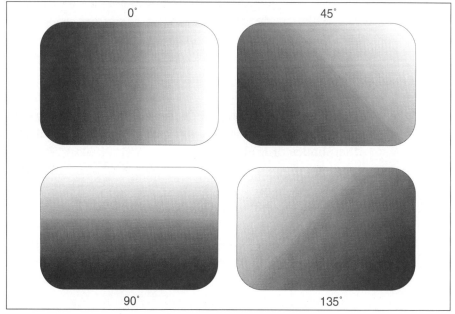

Applying Color to a Line

When the Content or Item tool is active and you have selected a line, you can apply color to the line using either the Colors palette or the Modify command in the Item menu. Choosing the Modify command displays the Line Specifications dialog box shown here:

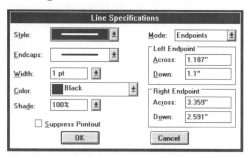

In this dialog box, use the Color and Shade drop-down list boxes to assign a shade of any available color to the line.

To color a line using the Colors palette, select the line. The Line icon in the Colors palette becomes highlighted, and any color or shade you select applies to the line immediately.

Applying Color to Text

QuarkXPress offers several options for assigning color and shading to text. At the character level, you can color selected characters using the Colors palette or the Character or Color commands in the Style menu. At the style sheet level, you can use the Style Sheets dialog box to assign a given color or shading to all instances of the style sheet in a document.

Assigning Color to Selected Characters

 To apply color at the character level using the Colors palette, highlight the desired characters with the Content tool, click the text icon in the Colors palette, and then click the color and/or shade percentage you want to apply. If you click on a color when the text cursor is at the insertion point, without first selecting any characters, the chosen color applies to text you type from that point on.

If the Colors palette is not visible, you can apply color to selected characters (or at the insertion point) by choosing the Color command in the Style menu and selecting a color from the submenu that appears, as shown here:

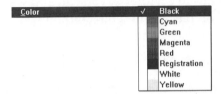

To adjust the tint of a color selected in this way, choose the Shade command in the Style menu. Or, if you prefer to assign both color and shade in a single step, choose the Character command in the Style menu (keyboard shortcut: CTRL-SHIFT-D) and adjust the Color and Shade fields as desired.

Note If you highlight a text string that contains characters of different colors and then choose the Character command, the Color field in the Character Attributes dialog box displays "Mixed Colors" as the current color assignment.

Assigning Color to a Style Sheet

The Colors palette and Style menu commands are fine for applying color to text as local formatting. When you need to apply color consistently and automatically to entire paragraphs, however, you should define a color as part of a style sheet. Follow these steps:

1. Access the Style Sheets dialog box using either the Style Sheets palette or the Style Sheets command in the Edit menu.

2. Click the name of the style sheet you want to edit and then click the Edit button to access the Edit Style Sheet dialog box.

3. Click the Character button to display the Character Attributes dialog box. Use the Color and Shade fields to assign an available color and/or shade that will apply to all instances of the style sheet in the current document.

Applying Color to a Picture

  As you saw in Chapter 9, you can apply a color and/or tint to an active grayscale or black-and-white bitmapped picture using the Color and Shade commands in the Style menu. If the Colors palette is visible, you can achieve the same results by activating the picture box, clicking the Picture Box icon in the upper area of the Colors palette, and then applying the desired color and/or shade from the palette.

 Note The Windows version of QuarkXPress does not allow you to apply color to a color photograph or to a bitmap that is already in color.

Misregistration on the printing press can result in thin white gaps between colors that overlap

Trapping Color in Quark

Any experienced desktop publisher will tell you that the biggest headache involved in using color is getting it to print perfectly. Many color-related slipups can occur at the service bureau or on the printing press, but one of the most problematic is *misregistration*—the slight misalignment of separate color plates. If a document contains overlapping elements of different colors, misregistration can cause unsightly white gaps to appear between the overlapping items, as Figure 10-6 shows. Fortunately, QuarkXPress includes a feature called trapping to help you compensate for potential misregistration problems before they occur.

Basically, *trapping* is a set of techniques for creating overlaps between adjacent colors so that misregistration won't cause a problem during commercial printing. Quark lets you control the trapping process at three different levels:

- ☐ At the application level you control trapping by specifying general trapping parameters in the Application Preferences dialog box.

- ☐ For specific colors in a document, control trapping using the Trap Specifications dialog box that you access through the Edit Trap button in the Colors dialog box. This level of trapping control takes precedence over any trapping parameters you specify in the Application Preferences dialog box.

- ☐ On a case-by-case basis, control trapping using the Trap Information palette to adjust trapping for the currently selected object. This level of trapping control takes precedence over all others.

The more intensively you use color in a Quark document, the more you need trapping. Before we delve any further into the ins and outs of setting trapping specifications, first gain an overview of common trapping terms and techniques in the next section.

Trapping Terms and Techniques

Trapping is all about the relationship between the color of a foreground *object* and the color of an overlapping *background* item behind it. Take the document page shown here, for example:

Imagine that the text in the foreground text box—the object—is 100 percent blue and that the image in the background picture box is tinted a 70 percent shade of red, and that both blue and red are defined as spot colors in the document. The printing industry terms knockout, overprint, spreads, and chokes describe the various techniques that determine how an object color prints on top of the background color.

Knockout and Overprinting

As we mentioned earlier in this chapter, color separations constitute the basis for the color plates that print vendors use on the printing press. One of two things can happen when you print color separations for a page that contains overlapping colored items. A *knockout* occurs when overlapping areas of the background item (here, the red picture) are removed so that the object color can be printed in that area without mixing inks on the press. *Overprinting* occurs when the object color (here, the blue of the text) prints directly on top of the background color, allowing inks to mix. Figure 10-7 shows examples of how knockouts and overprints look on spot color separation plates relative to the original items in a Quark document.

Overprinting colors rarely yields good results because the background color shows through the object color and degrades it. This explains why knockouts are the customary method by which color plates for commercial printing are produced. The only time Quark recommends that you overprint overlapping colors is when the object color is a 95 percent shade or higher.

In an ideal world, knockouts would yield perfect color overlaps every time. This doesn't happen, largely because misregistration can occur either at the service bureau (during film generation) or on press. That's where trapping, quite literally, comes in to "fill the gap."

Spreads and Chokes

The terms spreads and chokes refer to the two techniques used to trap overlapping colored items in a Quark document. If a foreground object is lighter in color than the background item, Quark enlarges or *spreads* it slightly when you print color separations. The object color thus overlaps the background knockout area by a miniscule amount. If a foreground object is darker than the background item, Quark *chokes* the background color, reducing the "knocked out" area slightly so that the object color again overlaps it. Figure 4-3 in Chapter 4 shows an exaggerated example of spreads and chokes at work.

Two common trapping techniques—overprinting and knockouts—determine
how Quark generates color separations for object and background colors

Lorem ipsum dolor sit amet,
consectetuer adipiscing elit,
sed diam nomummy nibh
euismod tincidunt ut lacreet
dolore magna aliquam erat
voluptat. Ut wisi enim ad
minim veniam, quis nostrud
exerci tation ullamcorpor
suscipit lobortis nisl ut aliquip

Quark document
(unseparated)

blue and red color plates, knockout

Lorem ipsum dolor sit amet,
consectetuer adipiscing elit,
sed diam nomummy nibh
euismod tincidunt ut lacreet
dolore magna aliquam erat
voluptat. Ut wisi enim ad
minim veniam, quis nostrud
exerci tation ullamcorpor
suscipit lobortis nisl ut aliquip

blue and red color plates, overprinting

Lorem ipsum dolor sit amet,
consectetuer adipiscing elit,
sed diam nomummy nibh
euismod tincidunt ut lacreet
dolore magna aliquam erat
voluptat. Ut wisi enim ad
minim veniam, quis nostrud
exerci tation ullamcorpor
suscipit lobortis nisl ut aliquip

Remember The lighter of two overlapping items determines which trapping method you should apply. If the foreground color is lighter, spread it. If the background color is lighter, choke it.

Checking with Your Print Vendor

Based on your trapping settings, Quark intelligently determines which trapping *technique* (spread or choke) to apply in a given instance. The *amount* of trapping you should specify for any color or item in a document, however, depends on the type of paper and printing press used for the job. Always discuss color trapping requirements with your print vendor well in advance of press time, and refer to Chapter 14 for more guidelines on printing color documents.

 Caution Trapping parameters that you specify using the Trap Information palette or the Edit Trap dialog box are saved with the current document. However, trapping parameters specified in the Application Preferences dialog box are saved in the XPRESS.PRF file on your computer. If you plan to output your color documents through an imagesetter at a service bureau and you have nonstandard application-wide trapping preferences, either inform the service bureau operator of your settings or generate your own output files. Generating your own output files is the better alternative, since it minimizes the risk of trapping error and ensures that the settings on your computer—not the service bureau's—determine all trapping parameters for a document. See Chapter 14 for information on creating output files.

Application Preferences: Establishing the Rules

The options in the Trap area of the Application Preferences dialog box establish the ground rules by which Quark determines how to create trap and how much trapping to apply. You access the Application Preferences dialog box, shown here, by choosing the Preferences/Application command in the Edit menu:

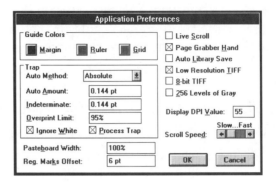

Auto Method

The Auto Method list box determines the basic technique Quark uses to apply trapping.

☐   If you select the Absolute option, Quark spreads lighter object colors and chokes lighter background colors by the exact amount you specify in the Auto Amount field.

☐   If you select the Proportional option, Quark determines the differences in *luminance* (darkness) between object and background colors and then applies a fraction of the trapping amount you specify in the Auto Amount field. The formula Quark uses to determine this amount is:

Auto Amount × (object darkness – background darkness)

Auto Amount

The value you enter in this field determines how much automatic trapping Quark applies to all colors by default. The preset value, 0.144 points, is somewhat low for most color jobs, but you should consult with your print vendor to arrive at the best value for a particular project. You can enter values from 0 pt to 36 pt in increments of .001 points.

Indeterminate

The term *indeterminate* refers to any background composed of multiple colors. Text overlaying an imported EPS or TIFF color picture has an indeterminate color background. So does a rule that lies on top of two overlapping objects of different colors. The value you specify in the Indeterminate field tells Quark how much trapping to apply automatically in such cases.

 Tip   If you want Quark to use overprinting instead of knockouts as the default trapping method for all colors, enter the word **overprint** in the Auto Amount and Indeterminate fields.

Overprint Limit

The Overprint Limit value defines the shade percentage at which an object color overprints its background color instead of creating a knockout. At the default value of 95 percent, for example, an object that is 90 percent yellow would trap a blue background, but an object that is 96 percent yellow would overprint it. The Overprint Limit value also governs trapping for black and for individual colors for which you specify the overprint method in the Trap Specifications dialog box.

Ignore White

Suppose you are producing a document in which a shaded picture overlays a text box containing a linear blend from a solid color (say, magenta) to white. If you don't tell Quark to ignore white when determining trapping relationships, Quark assumes that the picture has an indeterminate color background and bases trapping values on the relationship between the picture color and Indeterminate. However, if you check the Ignore White option, Quark bases trapping values only on the relationship between the picture color and the solid background color (here, magenta).

Process Trap

The Process Trap option applies only to documents for which you create process color (CMYK) separations instead of spot color (single-color) separations. The Process Trap check box determines whether Quark traps CMYK color separation plates individually or applies the same trapping value to all CMYK plates equally. If Process Trap is checked, Quark uses an algorithm to determine the exact amount of trapping for each CMYK plate. The amounts may be different for each plate, which some designers feel gives them more control. If you leave this option unchecked, Quark traps all CMYK plates equally based on the trapping relationship between each pair of object and background colors.

Editing Trapping Specifications for a Specific Color

The Application Preferences dialog box may set up default trapping parameters, but you can override these on a color-by-color basis through the Trap Specifications dialog box shown here:

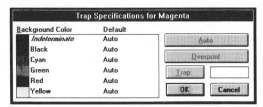

You can access this dialog box in one of two ways:

☐ Choose the Colors command in the Edit menu, select a color in the Colors dialog box, and then click the Edit Trap button.

☐ Press CTRL and click on a color name in the Colors palette, then select a color in the Colors dialog box and click the Edit Trap button.

If you change settings in the Trap Specifications dialog box when no document is open, you are editing the default trapping specifications. If you change Trap Specifications settings when a document is open and active, your edits affect colors in that document only.

You may ask why you would choose to change trapping parameters for a specific set of foreground and background colors. The answer depends on how you are using a specific color in a document. Text at very small point sizes, for example, should feature especially small trapping values to avoid losing definition on individual letters. If you assign a given color only to a style sheet that appears in such small point sizes, you might do well to redefine trapping values for that color.

To define trapping values for specific object and background colors, follow these steps:

1. Access the Colors dialog box using either the Colors palette or the Colors command in the Edit menu.

2. Click the name of the object (foreground) color for which you want to redefine trapping values and then click Edit Trap. The Trap Specifications dialog box appears.

The list box on the left side of the dialog box includes all the currently defined colors that can serve as background colors for the object color you have selected, together with their default trapping relationships to the object color. An *Auto* relationship indicates that the background color is knocked out with trapping applied, while an *Overprint* relationship indicates that the object color completely overprints the background with no knockout.

3. Click the background color whose relationship to the object color you want to redefine. The Auto, Overprint, and Trap buttons become available for selection.

4. To change the default trapping relationship for the specified color pair from Auto to Overprint or vice versa, click the Auto or Overprint button. Quark updates the Default column in the list box immediately.

5. To change the current default trapping value for the specified color pair, enter a new value in the Trap field.

6. If you wish, continue editing trapping parameters for other background colors in the same way.

7. Click OK to return to the Colors dialog box and Save to retain your settings for the chosen object color.

Editing Trapping Information for a Specific Instance

Whereas the Application Preferences dialog box defines default trapping parameters and the Trap Specifications dialog box lets you modify these defaults for specific color pairs, the Trap Information palette shown next lets you customize trapping for specific *instances* of a given color in a document. To display the Trap Information palette, choose Show Trap Information in the View menu. You can move the palette around on the screen by dragging it by its title bar. Double-clicking the palette's control menu box or choosing the Hide Trap Information command in the View menu hides the palette from view.

The content of and options in the Trap Specifications palette vary, depending on which item is currently selected and which tool is active. In every case, the palette provides information about the current trapping relationship between the selected item and its background. You can change the trapping relationship by clicking in the drop-down list box and then highlighting an option in the list. The full range of trapping relationship options include Default, Overprint, Knockout, Auto Amount (+), Auto Amount (–), and Custom, as shown here:

However, not all options are available for every item you select.

☐   *Default* When Default is selected, the name of the default trapping relationship and a gray box containing a question mark appear to the right of the list box. Click the question mark to display a message box that explains the rationale for the default trapping relationship as in this example:

☐ *Overprint* Select Overprint to cause the object color to overprint the background color in this one instance.

☐ *Knockout* Select Knockout if you want the object color to knock out the background color precisely, without adding any trapping.

☐ *Auto Amount (+)* Choose Auto Amount (+) to spread the object color by the amount specified in the Auto Amount field of the Application Preferences dialog box.

☐ *Auto Amount (–)* Choose Auto Amount (–) to choke the background color by the amount specified in the Auto Amount field of the Application Preferences dialog box.

☐ *Custom* Choose Custom to specify a custom trapping value for the currently selected pair of object and background colors. A field appears to the right of the list box for you to enter a value, as shown here:

Any discussion of color and trapping is bound to lead to the subject of printing. After all, color in a document cannot reach the outside world without the printing press as an intermediary. This chapter has looked at several aspects of the relationship between color and printing. When you are ready to print documents that contain color design elements, you may want to refer to Chapter 14.

CHAPTER

Layout Basics

*P*age layout is the process of putting it all together—combining text and graphics into an integrated document with its own special design. So far in this book, you've explored all the essential QuarkXPress features, from document setup techniques, to manipulating text and pictures, to defining and working with color. Now, you're ready to lay out your own documents using some of the skills described in this chapter and Chapters 12 and 13.

On its most basic level, layout in QuarkXPress is the process of modifying, arranging, and grouping the three types of items—text boxes, picture boxes, and lines—that make up the building blocks of any document. This chapter focuses on the skills you need to handle these layout-related tasks:

☐ Setting up your workspace for greater layout efficiency

☐ Setting up preferences and defaults for a new document

☐ Selecting and modifying single and multiple items

☐ Grouping, constraining, and locking items so you can implement and protect your design more automatically

☐ Duplicating items and creating item "patterns"

☐ Arranging items in layers

☐ Setting up automatic page numbering

☐ Creating and using libraries that store any combination of reusable items in your documents

Creating an Efficient Layout Workspace

Layout productivity depends in part on using the right tool for the right job. Quark provides you with a multitude of intuitive tools that enhance precision and productivity; to take full advantage of them, use this checklist to set up the application window for the most efficient layout session possible. Figure 11-1 shows the tools and elements you will usually find most helpful as an aid to page layout.

FIGURE
11-1

Visual aids that help make the layout process more efficient

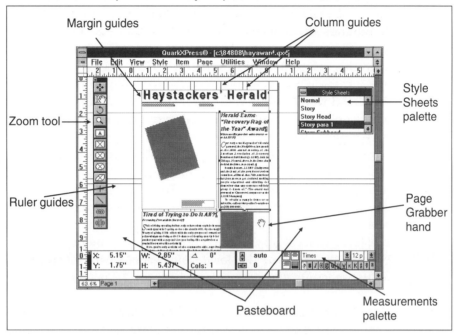

Make the Most of Guides and Rulers   Rulers, ruler guides, column guides, and margin guides are among the best tools for positioning and aligning items on a page. Activate the Snap to Guides and Show Rulers commands in the View menu, and be sure to drag out vertical and horizontal ruler guides as needed. When you first create a document, try setting up multiple column guides based on your page design plan, too. No matter how many "actual" columns a document contains, you can use column guides as a flexible layout grid.

Several controls in the General Preferences dialog box (Preferences/General command, Edit menu) let you adjust settings for rulers and guides. To adjust the distance at which items snap to guides in a particular document, use the Snap Distance field. Use the Horizontal Measure and Vertical Measure fields to change the ruler unit of measure; use the Item Coordinates list box to control where the ruler's zero point is placed in spreads and facing pages documents.

Keep the Measurements Palette Handy   The Measurements palette lets you resize and reposition items precisely, without using menu commands or dialog boxes. You can also edit other item attributes, depending on the active tool (Item or Content) and the type of item currently selected.

Know All the Tricks for Adjusting Document View   If you can't see what you're doing, both your productivity and the accuracy of your work may suffer. Use the Page Grabber hand to view a different area of the page at the current viewing magnification (press ALT and drag with any tool active). Use the Zoom tool to adjust viewing magnification in fixed increments that you set in the Tool Preferences dialog box (Preferences/Tools command, Edit menu). To obtain a more WYSIWYG view of text, adjust the Display DPI value in the Application Preferences dialog box (Preferences/Application command, Edit menu). Use the View Percentage indicator in the lower-left corner of the document window to adjust magnification to any level between 10 percent and 400 percent.

Use the Pasteboard   If you prefer to design "on the fly," create a wide enough pasteboard so you can drag items on and off the page comfortably. You can adjust pasteboard size relative to page width through the Pasteboard Width setting in the Application Preferences dialog box (Preferences/Application command, Edit menu).

Preparing for Layout

Before you begin to lay out a document, you should already have set up a template and/or master pages (see Chapter 3). Other advance preparations will speed your progress, too.

Defining Colors

Using the Colors and Edit Color dialog boxes (Colors command, Edit menu), define the basic palette you will be using in the document. If you prefer, you can access these dialog boxes from the Colors palette by pressing CTRL as you click on an existing color name. Remember to use a hard-copy swatchbook if you specify colors according to a proprietary color system such as PANTONE, TRUMATCH, or Focoltone.

Defining H&Js

As you saw in Chapter 6, hyphenation and justification (H&J) rules can affect copyfitting and layout. Using the H&Js command in the Edit menu, define in advance all the sets of H&Js that you might need to apply to various style sheets and paragraphs in a document. You can then assign these when setting up basic style sheets for the document.

Defining Style Sheets

Style sheets tend to grow and change organically during the layout process, but you should set up commonly used style sheets and their attributes in advance. Access the Style Sheets dialog box either by choosing the Style Sheets command in the Edit menu or by pressing CTRL as you click a style sheet name in the Style Sheets palette. A good strategy is to base related style sheets on one another—for example, to make lower-level heads and subheads dependent on the attributes of a first-level head. That way, if you need to make changes to one style sheet during layout, the attributes of the style sheets that depend on it will change automatically.

Setting Tool Preferences

Quark's ability to predefine tool behavior for a particular document is an oft-overlooked feature that can automate the layout process to a great extent. For example, if you know that the design of a document calls for picture boxes that conform to a standard frame width, background color, and runaround mode, you can predefine these attributes for the Picture Box tool of your choice. Every picture box you draw will then have these attributes automatically. Predefine attributes for all the item creation tools and the Zoom tool using the Tool Preferences dialog box (Preferences/Tools command, Edit menu).

Document "Layers" in Quark

You construct a document in Quark by layering the items—text boxes, picture boxes, and lines—that constitute its basic building blocks. As you add new items to a page, Quark layers them in the order in which you create them. Thus, if you create a text box followed by a picture box, the picture box lies on top of the text box. If you then add a text box for the picture box caption, it becomes the topmost layer of the three. Change the layering or *stacking order* of existing items on a page using commands in the Item menu (see the "Arranging Items" section later in this chapter).

Figure 11-2 shows a brochure as it appears during layout and the order in which its component items are layered. The text boxes that comprise the two left panels are on the bottom, with the castle photograph in a polygon picture box above it. The rightmost panel of the brochure consists of a background picture box on the bottom, with two text boxes overlaid on top of it; both the background picture box and the upper picture box have a runaround mode of None so that the picture can show through. The ruling line that spans the brochure horizontally lies above all the other items. Not every document requires background graphics, however. In your own work, you may find that the "normal" layering order for most documents is a text box on the bottom with other items layered above it.

Three factors—the stacking order of items, the runaround characteristics of each item, and the item that is currently selected—determine what is visible onscreen when items on a document page overlap. This chapter steps you through the processes of selecting, modifying, and arranging items regardless of their stacking order. Chapter 12 deals extensively with runaround and its creative uses in document design.

Selecting and Modifying Items

Positioning, resizing, or otherwise manipulating an item is possible only when the item is selected. You can select and modify a single item or multiple items, regardless of their position in the stacking order of a document.

FIGURE
11-2
Quark documents are constructed in layers from bottom (1) to top (3)

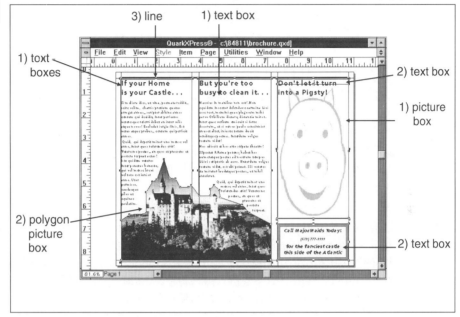

 Remember You can modify a master page item either on its master page or in the document pages on which it appears. Be careful about modifying a master page item on a document page unless you are sure

TABLE
11-1
Selecting, Modifying, and Arranging Items: Keyboard Commands

To Do This	Press
Select a hidden item (Content tool)	CTRL-ALT-SHIFT + click
Modify multiple selected items	CTRL-M
Group multiple selected items	CTRL-G
Ungroup grouped items	CTRL-U
Duplicate item(s)	CTRL-D
Delete item(s)	CTRL-K or DEL
Lock item(s)	CTRL-L

you no longer need to update the design of that page automatically. Refer back to Chapter 3 for further details.

Selecting, Modifying, and Arranging Items: Keyboard Shortcuts

Table 11-1 lists a few handy keyboard commands for selecting, editing, grouping, and otherwise arranging items in a QuarkXPress document. You will encounter these shortcuts one by one in the sections that follow.

Selecting Items

The technique and tool you use to select items depend on the number of items you want to select, the type of modifications you plan to make, and whether the item overlaps other items.

Selecting a Single Item

To select a single item, click it when either the Content tool or the Item tool is active. If the item is a text box or picture box and you plan to move or resize it using the mouse, the Item tool should be active. If you intend to edit the contents of a text box or picture box using the Measurements palette, the Content tool should be active. Either tool is effective if you plan to edit item or content attributes using menu commands.

If an item that you want to select lies wholly underneath another item, first click the item on the top layer, press CTRL-ALT-SHIFT, and then click again. This keyboard shortcut cycles through and selects each item in an overlapping series of items.

Selecting Multiple Items

The Item tool must be active in order for you to select more than one item at a time. Use either of these techniques for selecting multiple items:

☐   Drag a marquee around the items you want to select as shown in Figure 11-3. When you release the mouse button, all of the items that fall at least partially within the marqueed area become selected.

☐   Select the first item by clicking it. Then, press and hold SHIFT and click each additional item you want to select.

If all the items you select are of the same type (text box, picture box, or line), you can modify some of their attributes as a group. See the section "Modifying Multiple Selected Items," coming up shortly in this chapter.

Modifying a Single Selected Item

Quark lets you modify any selected text box, picture box, or line in at least three different ways: through the Measurements palette, through commands in the Item menu, or by using the mouse and the Item or Rotation tool.

FIGURE 11-3   Selecting multiple items with the marquee (Item tool active)

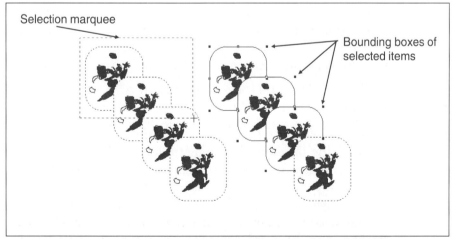

Selection marquee

Bounding boxes of selected items

Modifying a Text Box

Chapter 5 describes how to modify text box attributes that are applicable to Quark's word processing functions. Chapter 10 describes how to apply colors and tints to text or to the background of a text box. For layout purposes, you can also rotate a text box and its text at any angle using the Rotation tool, the Box Angle field in the Text Box Specifications dialog box, or the Rotation field in the Measurements palette.

Modifying a Picture Box

See Chapters 8 and 9 to review techniques for modifying the attributes of selected picture boxes and the pictures they contain.

Modifying a Line

When the Item or Content tool is active, change the length of a selected line by dragging one of its endpoints. To change the position of the line, drag the line itself. When the Rotation tool is active, you can change the angle of the line by dragging, too. The point where you click and begin dragging defines the axis of rotation, as this illustration shows:

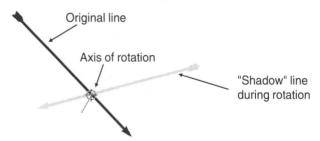

You can also use the Modify and Runaround commands in the Item menu or the Measurements palette to edit the attributes of a line. The Modify command accesses the Line Specifications dialog box shown in Figure 11-4. There are fields for changing the line style; the *endcap* or line endings style; the width, color, and shade of the selected line; the *mode* (the point or points relative to which you define the coordinates of the line); and the coordinates, length, and angle of the line. Figure 11-4a

| FIGURE 11-4 | The Line Specifications dialog box for lines in a) Left Point, Center Point, Right Point and b) Endpoints modes |

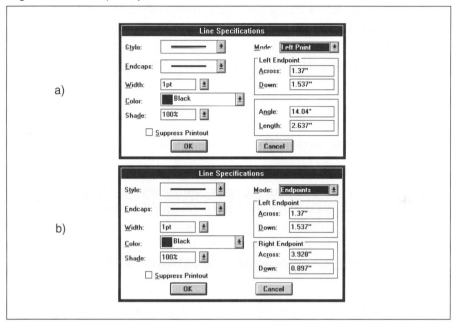

shows the fields available when the line is in Left Point, Center Point, or Right Point mode; Figure 11-4b shows the options you have when defining line attributes in Endpoints mode. You can also use this dialog box to suppress the printout of a selected line.

When you use the Measurements palette to modify a selected line, the mode or measurement start point you choose determines the options that are available. Figure 1-26 in Chapter 1 shows examples of these options.

Modifying Multiple Selected Items

When multiple items are selected, you can still modify some of their attributes. The types of items selected and the tool or command you are using to modify them determine which attributes you can edit.

Moving Multiple Selected Items Interactively

To move multiple selected items of any type when the Item tool is active, simply drag the items to a new location. As you drag, a dotted outline indicating the total area occupied by all the selected items follows the pointer as in Figure 11-5.

Sizing Multiple Selected Items Interactively

Although you cannot resize multiple selected items as a group, Quark lets you resize each one interactively using the mouse and the Item tool. Position the pointer over a selection handle of the item you want to resize and drag to make it larger or smaller. The other items remain selected as you do so—another testament to Quark's flexibility.

FIGURE 11-5   Moving multiple selected items (Item tool active)

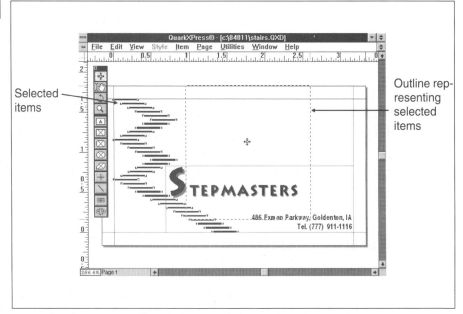

Rotating Multiple Selected Items Interactively

To rotate multiple selected items interactively, activate the Rotation tool and click it where you want to locate the axis of rotation. You can locate the axis of rotation anywhere within the area occupied by the selected items. Then, drag in the desired direction. A dotted outline and the axis handle pointer indicate the direction of rotation. Release the mouse button to reposition the selected items at the desired angle.

Tip   To view the items themselves rather than a dotted outline as you rotate them, click with the Rotation tool and then pause briefly (until the hourglass disappears) before dragging. Be aware, though, that rotation occurs more slowly when you view the items in real time.

Editing Attributes with the Measurements Palette

Whenever multiple items are selected, the Measurements palette displays information in only three fields, as shown here:

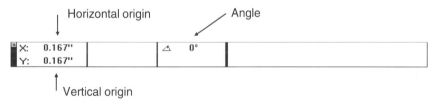

The X and Y fields indicate the ruler coordinates of the leftmost and uppermost points in the area occupied by the selected items. Changing these values moves the group as a whole. Changing the value in the angle field rotates all the selected items by the same angle, though without allowing you to specify a custom axis of rotation.

Editing Attributes with the Modify Command

Another way to edit attributes of multiple selected items is to use the Modify command in the Item menu (keyboard shortcut: CTRL-M). The types of items currently selected determine which dialog box appears when you choose this command.

Modifying Attributes of Multiple Text Boxes

When all the selected items are text boxes, choosing the Modify command displays the Text Box Specifications dialog box shown next. The Width and Height values in the dialog box are grayed out, but you can change all other text box attributes. The Origin Across and Origin Down values show the leftmost and uppermost points in the entire group of selected text boxes, while the Box Angle value shows the angle of the leftmost text box. Blank fields in the left side of the dialog box indicate that the selected text boxes have different values; if you enter a new value in those fields, you reset the values of all the selected text boxes. The appearance of the term "mixed" in a field in the right side of the dialog box indicates that the text boxes have different values. Entering or selecting a new value resets the current values of all the selected text boxes.

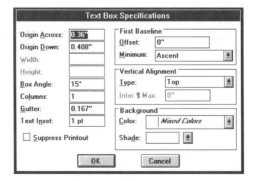

Modifying Attributes of Multiple Picture Boxes

When all the selected items are picture boxes, choosing the Modify command in the Item menu displays the Picture Box Specifications dialog box shown next. This dialog box lets you change all the attributes of the picture boxes except width and height, which must be changed interactively using the Content tool. Blank fields or fields containing the term "mixed" indicate that the selected picture boxes have different settings. If you enter a fixed value in these fields, all the selected picture boxes change in the same way.

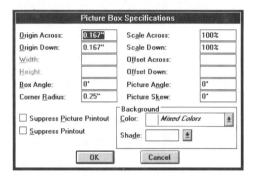

Modifying Multiple Lines

When all the selected items are lines, choosing the Modify command in the Item menu displays the Line Specifications dialog box shown next. The mode defaults to Left Point, regardless of the mode chosen for any individual line among those selected. The Length field is unavailable; to change the length of any selected line, you must use the Item tool as described earlier. Blank fields or fields containing the term "mixed" indicate that the selected lines have different settings. If you enter or select a fixed value in those fields, you change all the selected lines in the same way.

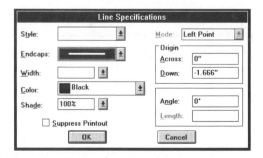

Modifying Multiple Items of Different Types

If multiple selected items are of different types, choosing the Modify command in the Item menu accesses the Group Specifications dialog box shown next. The only attributes you can specify for mixed items are the leftmost point of the item furthest to the left (Origin Across), the highest point of the uppermost item (Origin Down), the collective angle, the background color and shade, and whether to suppress printing of all the selected items. The Angle value corresponds to the current angle of the first item you selected.

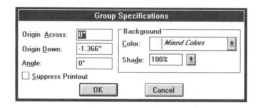

Editing Frame Attributes

If the selected items are either all text boxes or all picture boxes, the Frame command in the Item menu is available (keyboard shortcut: CTRL-B). The same attributes that are available for single selected text or picture boxes—style, width, color, and shade—are available for multiple items, too. The Frame command is unavailable when the selected items are of mixed types.

Grouping and Ungrouping Items

Selecting multiple items is fine if you want to keep the items together only temporarily. If you want two or more selected items to continue acting as one item, though, apply the Group command to them (keyboard shortcut: CTRL-G). Grouping items protects the individual components from being separated, moved, or rotated accidentally. You can also create groups within groups. To break grouped items apart so you again can edit them individually, choose the Ungroup command in the Item menu (shortcut: CTRL-U).

It isn't always easy to tell when selected items are grouped. When the Item tool is active, clicking on any grouped item causes a dotted outline to appear around the entire group, as Figure 11-6 shows. This is the equivalent of a bounding box. If the group is contained within a rectangular text box or picture box, however, you won't be able to see this dotted line. In such cases, the only visual clue that you have selected grouped items is the pointer, which takes on the appearance of the Item tool as you pass it over any of the selected items.

Modifying Grouped Items

You can modify grouped items in much the same way as multiple selected items (see the "Modifying Multiple Selected Items" section earlier in this chapter). If you use the Measurements palette, you can change only the position and angle of the group. If you choose the Modify

FIGURE 11-6　Activating grouped items causes a dotted outline to appear around the group

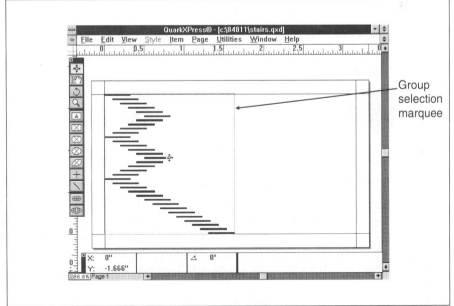

command in the Item menu, the dialog box that appears depends on the types of items selected. Just as with multiple selected items, you can move and rotate grouped items interactively.

Note The Modify command is unavailable for groups within groups.

Quark is especially flexible in the way it lets you edit individual items within a group. Although you can't resize the grouped items together, you can resize individual items within the group by first selecting the Content tool and then dragging a selection handle of one of the items. If the Measurements palette is visible when you select a grouped item with the Content tool active, all the normal attribute fields for the item become available. This means that you can move the item separately from other items in the group, edit its content, color, and angle separately, and so on.

Tip To move a single item within a group when the Content tool is active, press CTRL and drag the item to the desired location.

Constraining and Unconstraining Grouped Items

The Constrain command in the Item menu is useful for forcing grouped items to remain within a fixed area or aligning a group of picture boxes with a background text box. This command is available only when the item on the bottommost layer is the largest in the group and contains all the other items in the group, as in the example in Figure 11-7. Choosing the Unconstrain command removes the constraint from items in the group, allowing you to move individual items freely again while keeping them grouped together.

When the Content tool is active, you can move individual items within a constrained group by pressing CTRL and dragging the item. However, you cannot move any item beyond the confines of the background item.

Tip To constrain items automatically as you create them, activate the Auto Constrain option in the General Preferences dialog box.

FIGURE 11-7 A constrained item cannot be moved beyond the outermost item that constrains it

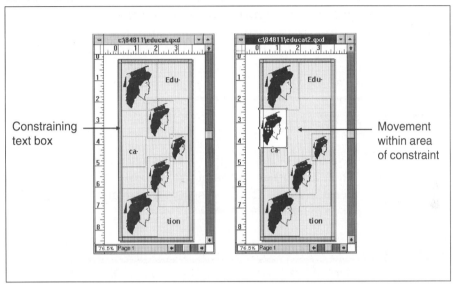

Constraining text box

Movement within area of constraint

Locking and Unlocking Items

The Lock command in the Item menu (keyboard shortcut: CTRL-L) lets you protect selected items or groups from being moved, resized, or rotated accidentally with the mouse. When you select a locked group or item with the Item tool, the pointer turns into a padlock, as shown here:

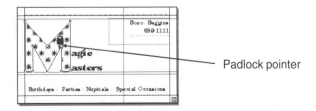

Padlock pointer

You can still edit an item that is locked—you just cannot use the mouse to edit it. Use the Measurements palette or commands in the Item menu whenever the locked item is active. You can also use the Content tool to edit the content of locked text boxes and picture boxes normally.

Choose the Unlock command in the Item menu to unlock the item or group so you can manipulate it with the mouse again. If a group of items is locked, unlock individual items within the group by first activating the Content tool, then selecting one item and choosing the Unlock command. The other items in the group remain locked.

Deleting Items

To delete one or more selected items when the Item tool is active, press DEL. When any other tool is active, choose the Delete command in the Edit menu instead. Quark displays a warning message box when you attempt to delete several items at once.

Duplicating Items

Duplicating items can be a creative part of the design and layout process, as the group of patterned line segments shown in Figure 11-8 suggests. Quark offers you two different options for duplicating any item in a document. The Duplicate command in the Item menu creates one copy of the selected item or group, while the Step and Repeat command lets you create any number of copies at the exact intervals and positions you specify.

The Duplicate Command

Choose the Duplicate command in the Item menu to create one copy of the currently selected item(s) or group(s). Quark offsets the copy at the distance currently specified in the Step and Repeat dialog box. The newly created duplicate becomes the active item; you can begin editing or manipulating it immediately.

FIGURE 11-8 The Step and Repeat command lets you duplicate items at fixed intervals to create interesting designs

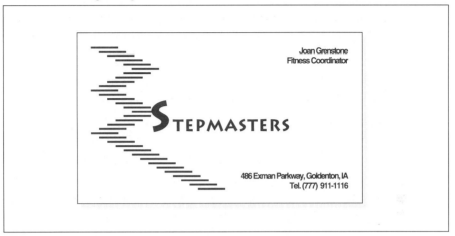

The Step and Repeat Command

The Step and Repeat command offers a wonderful way to create repeating designs in a document layout (see Figure 11-8). You can also use it to create multiple same-size text boxes or other repeating items on master pages. This command gives you complete control over the horizontal and vertical intervals at which copies of the selected item or group appear on the page.

To duplicate one or more items or groups using the Step and Repeat command, follow these steps:

1. Select the item(s) or group(s) with the Item tool active. Keep in mind that you cannot step and repeat a text box that is linked to other text boxes.

2. Choose the Step and Repeat command in the Item menu to display the Step and Repeat dialog box shown here:

3. In the Repeat Count field, enter the number of times you want to duplicate the selected item(s) or group(s).

4. In the Horizontal Offset field, enter the horizontal distance at which you want each copy to appear relative to the original or previous copy. A positive value places each copy to the right of the previous copy, while a negative copy places each copy to the left of the previous one.

5. In the Vertical Offset field, enter the vertical distance at which you want ea·h copy to appear relative to the original or previous copy. A positive value places each copy below the previous copy, while a negative value places each copy above the previous one.

6. Click OK. Quark automatically creates the desired number of copies at the specified inte·vals.

 Tip To create repeating designs that change directions like the example in Figure 11-8, create a specified number of copies, and then change the Horizontal or Vertical Offset values and create additional copies.

Arranging Items

The Send Backward, Send to Back, Bring Forward, and Bring to Front commands in the Item menu let you rearrange the stacking order of items in a document. Most documents contain multiple layers of overlapping items, so you will find this series of commands essential to basic layout work.

☐ *Send Backward* moves the selected item(s) or group(s) one level backward in the stacking order. The Send Backward command is available only when a selected item is not already on the bottommost layer.

☐ *Send to Back* moves the selected item(s) or group behind every other item on the page, whether overlapping or not. The Send to Back command is available only if a selected item is not already on the bottommost layer.

Note The largest item in a constrained group must always remain the bottommost layer in the group. If you apply the Send to Back command to one of the other items in a constrained group, Quark places it immediately in front of the background item within the group, not on the bottommost layer of the page.

❑ Bring Forward moves the selected item(s) or group forward one layer and is available only when a selected item is not already on the top layer of a page.

❑ *Bring to Front* moves the selected item(s) or group(s) to the front of the stack on the current page. It is available only when a selected item is not already on the top layer.

Changing the stacking order of items may have unexpected visual results, hiding previously visible text or graphics from view. If a picture or a text box disappears, don't panic—you can remedy the situation by making transparent the item just in *front* of the one that has vanished. See Chapter 12 for details.

Spacing and Aligning Multiple Items

The Space/Align command in the Item menu offers convenient options for aligning two or more selected items or for adjusting the positions of items relative to one another. You can adjust spacing vertically, horizontally, or in both directions at once. You can specify spacing as a fixed measurement or as a percentage of current spacing, or distribute space evenly between selected items. You can even choose the point relative to which alignment or spacing adjustment occurs. The Space/Align command is the fastest, most precise way to create perfectly spaced page designs automatically.

This section gives briefly the steps involved in aligning or adjusting space among items automatically. The sections following this one give options for aligning and spacing items creatively.

1. Select the items that you want to align or for which you want to adjust relative position. If any of the items is a group or constrained group, its component items will move together as a single unit.

2. Choose the Space/Align command in the Item menu to access the Space/Align Items dialog box shown here:

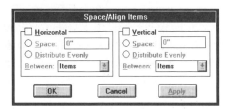

3. Click the check box(es)—Horizontal, Vertical, or both—that indicate the directions in which you want alignment or spacing adjustment to occur.

4. Using the Between drop-down list box, choose the point relative to which spacing or alignment should occur: whole items, item edges, or centers of items. The options available depend on the spacing direction you chose in step 3. If you checked both Horizontal and Vertical, adjust the Between drop-down list box for both directions.

5. Specify the amount of spacing between items, their centers, or edges using the Space field or Distribute Evenly button. Use the Space field if you want to specify a fixed amount or percentage of spacing. If three or more items are currently selected, the Distribute Evenly option is available; clicking this button places an equal amount of space between each selected item.

Note   Quark measures text boxes and rectangular boxes from their sides, nonrectangular picture boxes and groups from their bounding boxes, and lines from their endpoints.

6. To preview the results of your choices, click Apply.

7. If you like the results of your settings, click OK. If your settings didn't yield the desired effects, click Cancel and choose the Space/Align command again.

Note   If one or more of the selected items is a group or a constrained group, its component items move together as a single unit.

Defining the Direction of Alignment or Spacing

The status of the Horizontal and Vertical check boxes in the Space/Align Items dialog box determines the type of alignment or the direction in which spacing is adjusted. When Horizontal is checked, you can align items horizontally or adjust spacing among items from left to right. When Vertical is checked, you can align items vertically or adjust spacing from top to bottom. Check both options to space or align items in any direction as determined by your other settings in the dialog box.

Aligning Items Horizontally

To align items horizontally, activate the Horizontal check box only, click the Space button, set Space to 0 percent or zero in any unit of measurement, and choose Left Edges, Centers, or Right Edges from the Between drop-down list box. Figure 11-9 shows examples of items aligned horizontally relative to their left edges, their centers, and their right edges. The item whose left edge lies furthest to the left does not move.

FIGURE 11-9   Aligning items horizontally

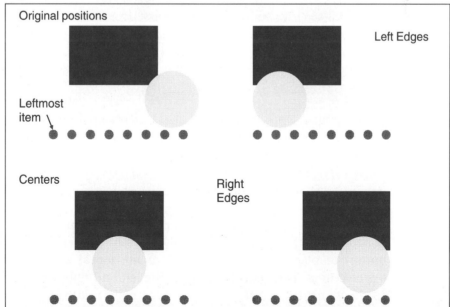

Adjusting Spacing Horizontally

To adjust spacing among items horizontally, activate the Horizontal check box, click the Space button, and set Space to either a fixed value or a percentage. If you set Space to a fixed measurement value, Quark places the specified amount of space between each item, center, or edge in a left-to-right direction. The item whose left edge lies furthest to the left does not move. If the left edge of more than one item is located at the same position, Quark positions the items relative to the item that lies uppermost.

You can also define spacing in relative terms, as a percentage of the *current* spacing between selected items, their centers, or left or right edges. You can specify any percentage from 0 percent to 1000 percent. Percentages above 100 percent increase horizontal spacing among selected items, centers, or edges relative to their current spacing; percentages below 100 percent decrease relative spacing. Again, the item originally furthest to the left does not change its position. Here is an example of three items in their original positions and then with spacing increased by 195 percent relative to their centers:

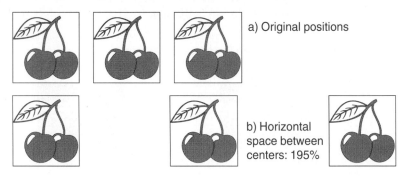

a) Original positions

b) Horizontal space between centers: 195%

Distributing Horizontal Spacing Equally

If three or more items are selected when you are spacing items horizontally, the Distribute Evenly button is available. Activate this button to place an equal amount of horizontal space between each selected item. The items furthest to the left and right remain stationary, as shown next; the other selected items move relative to them.

Aligning Items Vertically

To align items vertically, activate the Vertical check box, click the Space button, set Space to 0 percent or zero in any unit of measurement, and choose Top Edges, Centers, or Bottom Edges from the Between drop-down list box. Figure 11-10 shows examples of items aligned vertically relative to their top edges, their centers, and their bottom edges. The item whose top edge lies highest among the selected items does not move.

FIGURE 11-10   Aligning items vertically

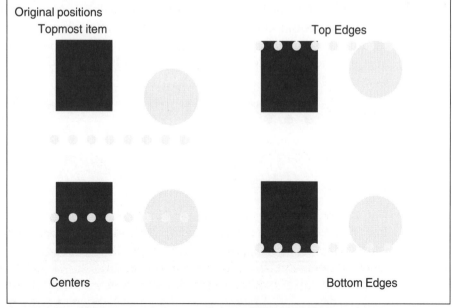

Adjusting Spacing Vertically

To adjust spacing among items vertically, activate the Vertical check box, click the Space button, and set Space to either a fixed value or a percentage. If you set Space to a fixed measurement value, Quark places the specified amount of space between each item, center, or edge in a top-to-bottom direction. The item whose top edge lies highest among the selected items does not move. If the top edge of more than one item is located at the same position, Quark positions the items relative to the item that lies furthest to the left.

You can also define spacing in relative terms, as a percentage of the current spacing between selected items, their centers, or their edges. As the percentage increases, so does the relative top-to-bottom spacing between each pair of items. You can specify any percentage from 0 percent to 1000 percent. At percentages below 100 percent, selected items move closer together; at higher percentages, they move further apart from one another.

Distributing Vertical Spacing Equally

If three or more items are selected when you are spacing items vertically, the Distribute Evenly button is available. Activate this button to place an equal amount of vertical space between each selected item within their current span. The highest and lowest items remain stationary, and the other selected items move relative to them, as shown in this example:

Original positions     Vertical, Distributed Evenly, Items

In most of your day-to-day layout work, you will adjust both vertical and horizontal spacing simultaneously. Figure 11-11, for example, shows a magazine layout in progress, with a set of bleed tabs lying helter-skelter in the pasteboard area of the right-facing master page. After selecting the text boxes that comprise the tabs and applying the Space/Align options shown in the dialog box in Figure 11-11, the tabs are evenly spaced and perfectly aligned, resulting in a document page like the one shown in Figure 11-12. You can generate your own creative designs using picture boxes and lines as well as text boxes.

Numbering Pages and Sections Automatically

Page numbering is an issue that you grapple with twice: once when you initially set up a document, and then on an ongoing basis as you lay

FIGURE 11-11 Using the Space/Align Items dialog box to organize small text boxes...

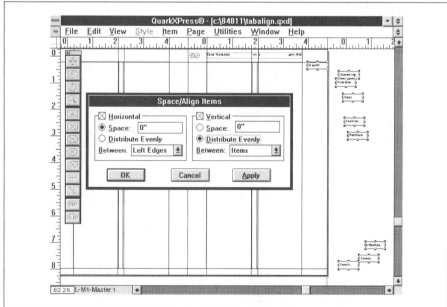

FIGURE
11-12

. . .into perfectly spaced and aligned bleed tabs

Total Woman   *33*   *July 1993*

Lorem ipsum

Once again, folks, we are greeking text in Latin, or even in English, all for the sake of design. Of course, you won't be reading this anyway, ad hoc, ad nauseum, and so forth. Feast your eyes, but don't overtire the brain.

Naevius in manibus

Non est, to be or not to be, that is always the question. Whether 'tis nobler in the slime to put up with the daily grind, or become a hermit and, by forgetting the daily grind, end it.

Non est, to be or not to be, that is always the question. Whether 'tis nobler in the slime to put up with the daily grind, or become a hermit and, by forgetting the daily grind, end it.

Once again, folks, we are greeking text in Latin, or even in English, all for the sake of design. Of course, you won't be reading this anyway, ad hoc, ad nauseum, and so forth. Feast your eyes, but don't overtire the brain.

Once again, folks, we are greeking text in Latin, or even in English, all for the sake of design. Of course, you won't be reading this anyway, ad hoc, ad nauseum, and so forth. Feast your eyes, but don't overtire the brain.

I scream, you scream, we all scream for ice cream, scooby dooby do, exchangus glancus. Gluteus maximus to the minimus and even tighter if at all possible, don't you agree? and other gibberish.

Si meliora dies

I scream, you scream, we all scream for ice cream, scooby dooby do, exchangus glancus. Gluteus maximus to the minimus and even tighter if at all possible, don't you agree?

Once again, folks, we are greeking text in Latin, or even in English, all for the sake of design. Of course, you won't be reading this anyway, ad hoc, ad nauseum, and so forth. Feast your eyes, but don't overtire the brain.

Non est, to be or not to be, that is always the question. Whether 'tis nobler in the slime to put up with the daily grind, or become a hermit and, by forgetting the daily grind, end it.

Factotum

And that's what they called Shakespeare, too. So names really can never hurt you, as his example shows.

Non est, to be or not to be, that is always the question. Whether 'tis nobler in the slime to put up with the daily

Health

Grooming

Exercise

Food

Fashion

Partners

Lifestyle

Career

Family

it out. During the document setup phase (covered in Chapter 3), your page numbering strategies are intimately connected with setting up master page designs, linking master page text boxes, and planning for automatic page insertion.

During the layout phase, the type of document you are working with determines the kinds of automatic page numbering aids you should use. Long documents such as books and manuals, for example, often need to be divided into separate, consecutively numbered sections. Copyfitting in magazines and newsletters often requires using automatic page number references for the continuation of a story. Quark can handle the page numbering needs of these and other types of documents.

Automatic Page Numbering for Continuously Numbered Documents

Entering the automatic page numbering code CTRL-3 in a master page text box causes the current page number to appear on every document page based on that master page. As long as every master page contains a text box with the automatic page numbering code, Quark will number every page in the document consecutively. If you later divide the document into sections, Quark changes the numbering on document pages automatically to reflect any special number formatting or prefixes you have specified.

Section Numbering for Long Documents

Longer publications such as books, manuals, and major reports often comprise multiple chapters, sections, and appendixes. Whether you string together a series of independent documents or include the entire publication in a single document, you can renumber the pages in each section automatically. The Section command in the Page menu and the Document Layout palette offer two different paths for reaching this goal.

Starting a New Section with the Section Command

Imagine you are laying out a manual in which page numbering resets for each section rather than remaining sequential throughout. The first page of a section, for example, would be numbered 2-1 for Chapter 2, 3-1 for Chapter 3, B-1 for Appendix B, and so on. You can incorporate this type of numbering scheme into document pages automatically with the help of the Section command in the Item menu.

To renumber pages by section in a Quark document, follow these steps:

1. Using the Go To command in the Page menu (keyboard shortcut: CTRL-J), display the document page that you want to be the first one in a section.

2. Choose the Section command in the Page menu to access the Section dialog box shown here:

3. Activate the Section Start check box to make the other controls in the dialog box available.

4. To add a prefix to all page numbers in the new section, enter up to four characters in the Prefix field. These can be letters, numbers, or special characters such as dashes or periods.

5. To change the starting page number of the first page of a section to something other than 1, enter the desired number in the Number field.

Tip   The Number field is useful for continuously numbering long publications that you have split into several component documents. Simply create a new section on the first page of each component document and assign a starting page number that is one number higher than the last page of the previous section.

6. Choose a numbering format from the Format drop-down list box. You can use Arabic numerals, uppercase Roman numerals, lowercase Roman numerals, uppercase letters, or lowercase letters as shown here:

7. Click OK to create the new section and implement the numbering you have specified.

The Page Number indicator in the lower-left corner of a document window always reflects any section numbering that applies to the current page. If the current page is the start of a new section, an asterisk (*) appears after the page number, as shown in this example:

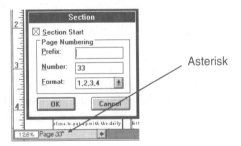

Asterisk

Starting a New Section with the Document Layout Palette

When the Document Layout palette is visible, you can use it instead of the Section command to create and renumber sections. One advantage of using the palette is that you do not need to display a page in order to designate it as the starting page of a new section.

To create and renumber a section using the Document Layout palette, follow these steps:

1. Open the document in which you want to create a new section and display the Document Layout palette (Show Document Layout command, View menu). Make sure that the palette is in document pages mode, not master pages mode (see Chapter 3).

2. In the Document Layout palette, click the icon of the document page that you want to designate as the first page in the section. As the following example shows, this need not be the page that is currently displayed.

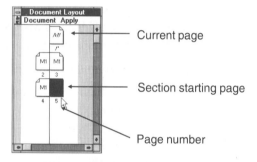

3. Click the page number beneath the icon of the chosen page. The Section dialog box appears.

4. Set the prefix, number, and/or format for the page numbers in the new section, then click OK.

The page numbering of document page icons in the palette does not change when you create a new section. Still, you can distinguish the first page of a section by the asterisk that appears after its page number, as shown here:

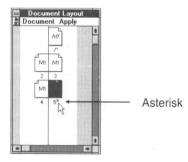

Merging Sections

Section numbering schemes are not written in stone. Quark makes it easy to merge two adjacent sections and renumber their pages if you decide the second section is no longer needed. Again, you can use either the Section command in the Page menu or the Document Layout for this task.

Using the Section Command   To delete a section within a document and merge it with the previous section, follow these steps:

1. Display the page that starts the section you want to delete. The page number indicator at the lower-left corner of the document window displays an asterisk (*) to indicate that this is the first page of the section.

2. Choose the Section command in the Page menu to display the Section dialog box.

3. Deactivate the Section Start check box and then click OK. Quark renumbers the pages in the former section so that they continue automatically from the previous section.

Using the Document Layout Palette   To delete a section within a document when the Document Layout palette is visible, follow these steps:

1. Click the document page icon that represents the start page of the section you want to delete. An asterisk next to the icon's page number indicates that this page is the first in the section.

2. Click the page number of the document page icon to access the Section dialog box.

3. Deactivate the Section Start check box and then click OK. Quark renumbers pages continuously, as though the deleted section had never been independent of the rest of the document.

Creating Jump Lines with Automatic Page References

Stories in magazines, newsletters, and other serial publications usually start on one page but continue on some other, nonconsecutive page. If you have linked the text boxes that contain the separated parts of a story (see Chapter 3), you can use Quark's automatic page number characters to create automatic "Continued on page" and "Continued from page" *jump lines* for such stories. Here is a recommended layout strategy:

1. In document pages, link the text box that contains the first part of the story to the text box in which the story continues. Do this *before* both text boxes become filled with text. Refer back to Chapter 3 if you need to review this process.

2. Import the text file into the first of the linked text boxes; it will flow automatically to the linked text box on the continuation page.

3. Create a small text box for the "Continued on page" jump line and place it within and at the bottom of the text box that contains the first part of the story.

4. Group the first text box with the jump line text box so that they will stay together if you have to move the main text box later.

5. With the Content tool active, click in the jump line text box and enter the text **Continued on page** followed by the keyboard command CTRL-4. The page number of the next linked text box appears automatically at the text cursor location.

 Caution If you see only <None> when you enter the CTRL-4 command, you have not linked text boxes properly for the story.

6. Display the page that contains the continuation text box. Create another small text box for the "Continued from page" jump line, place it at the top of the continuation text box, and group both text boxes so they will remain together.

7. With the Content tool active, click in this jump line text box and enter the phrase **Continued from page** followed by the keyboard command CTRL-2. The page number of the previous linked text box

appears at the text cursor location automatically. Figure 11-13 shows a sample layout that you can follow to create jump lines for your own documents.

Creating separate text boxes for the jump lines is the safest way to ensure that the jump lines will not reflow if you have to edit the text of a story. As long as the jump line text boxes overlap the linked text boxes that contain the story, automatic page number references will appear correctly.

Automatic Page Number References: Keyboard Shortcuts

Table 11-2 lists the three types of automatic page number references you can create in Quark and the keyboard commands for each. XPress Tags codes for each of these page number references are also included in case you want to enter them in a text file in your word processor.

FIGURE 11-13 Creating jump lines with automatic page references and overlapping text boxes

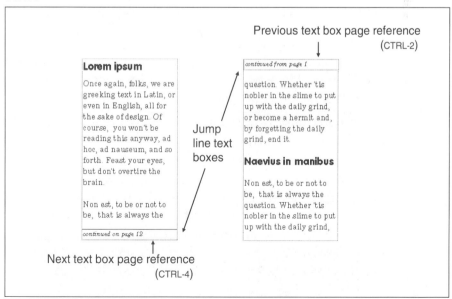

Previous text box page reference
(CTRL-2)

Lorem ipsum

Once again, folks, we are greeking text in Latin, or even in English, all for the sake of design. Of course, you won't be reading this anyway, ad hoc, ad nauseum, and so forth. Feast your eyes, but don't overtire the brain.

Non est, to be or not to be, that is always the

continued on page 12

Next text box page reference
(CTRL-4)

Jump line text boxes

continued from page 1

question. Whether 'tis nobler in the slime to put up with the daily grind, or become a hermit and, by forgetting the daily grind, end it.

Naevius in manibus

Non est, to be or not to be, that is always the question. Whether 'tis nobler in the slime to put up with the daily grind,

| TABLE 11-2 | Creating Automatic Page Number References in Quark and in a Word Processor |

Page Number to Insert	Quark Command	XPressTag Word Processor Code
Previous linked text box	CTRL-2	<\2>
Current page	CTRL-3	<\3>
Next linked text box	CTRL-4	<\4>

Creating and Using Libraries

When you collect large numbers of books, you organize them by categorizing and storing them in a library. Quark's Library palette, available through the Library command in the Utilities menu, lets you organize document components in the same way.

Many types of documents contain large numbers of text and graphic elements that need to be labeled and catalogued for repeated use. Serial publications such as magazines and newsletters are especially strong candidates for libraries—mastheads, columnist photos, table of contents text boxes, and feature story design elements are just a few of the items that you might use frequently, if not in every issue. Long documents, particularly those that need to be updated occasionally, can benefit from library organization as well. Technical manuals, for example, might contain reusable schematics, standardized picture boxes and caption text boxes, headers, and footers.

You don't have to use libraries strictly for single documents, either. Create libraries to hold picture boxes that contain clip art graphics on a single subject, or boilerplate text boxes, or favorite rule combinations.

The Library palette offers you tremendous flexibility in how you manage documents. You can create any number of library files for any purpose, and each library can contain up to 2000 separate items. Storing items in a library is as easy as dragging them into a palette; inserting library entries into a document is simply a matter of dragging them back out again. You can also "label" library entries and display them selectively by name.

Creating or Opening a Library

You must open or create a library in order to insert items into it or extract items from it. A Quark library is actually a file with the extension .qxl. To create a new library or open an existing one, follow these steps:

1. Choose the Library command from the Utilities menu. The Library dialog box shown here appears, with the List Files of Type drop-down list box set to Libraries (.QXL):

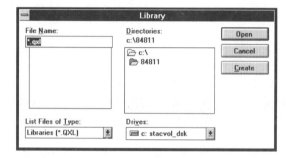

2. To open an existing library, locate the library file using the Drives and Directories list boxes and then double-click the library filename. The Library palette that corresponds to the library file appears to the right of the active document window.

3. To create and open a new library, locate the drive and directory where you want to store the library file—perhaps in the same directory as the document file with which you want to use it. Type the desired filename in the File Name list box and then click the Create button.

The Library Palette

If you are creating a new library, its palette will be empty when you first open it. An existing library may contain up to 2000 separate entries: single items, multiple-selected items, groups, and constrained items. Like Quark's other floating palettes, the Library palette always appears in front of all your open document windows. As the following illustrates, a typical Library palette contains several common components:

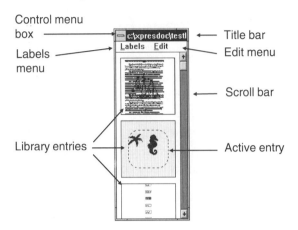

Title Bar   The title bar of a Library palette includes the path and filename of the associated library file. You can move the palette to another location by dragging its title bar.

Control Menu Box   The Control menu box contains commands for moving, sizing, maximizing, and closing the Library palette and its associated file. To close an open Library palette, double-click the control-menu box. If you choose the Maximize command, the palette opens up to fill the Quark application window as shown in Figure 11-14. In maximized view, library entries appear in horizontal rows; dragging the items to different locations rearranges their order relative to one another. Use maximized view whenever you need to reorganize or prune library entries. Clicking the Restore command in the control menu of a maximized Library palette returns the palette to its normal elongated shape.

Labels Menu   The Labels menu of the Library palette contains commands for displaying library entries selectively. It also lists any library entries that you have labeled. See "Displaying and Labeling Library Items" later in this chapter for more information.

Edit Menu   The Edit menu contains commands for copying, cutting, and pasting items between an open document and the Library palette. You can also delete library entries using this menu.

Library Entries   The items contained in a given Library palette appear in the palette's main area. Each entry is represented by a same-size

FIGURE 11-14

A maximized Library palette

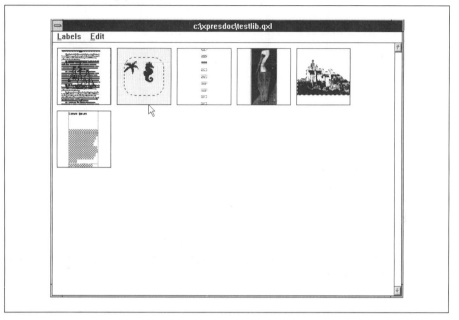

rectangle, and the currently selected entry (if any) is highlighted. While entries may not be completely WYSIWYG, they do give you a general idea of their contents. Use labels to describe the contents more exactly.

Scroll Bar The scroll bar enables you to view library entries beyond those that fit in the normal-sized palette. You can always widen the palette manually by dragging its border to the right. If a library contains a large number of items, you may wish to maximize it.

Adding Items to a Library

What can you store in a Quark library? Just about anything that includes a single item, a grouped item, or multiple selected items. If you want to store text in a library, you must also store the text box that contains it; to store a picture, you must store its picture box as well.

You can add items to an open library either by dragging them or by copying and pasting them. To add items to an open library by dragging, follow these steps:

1. With the Item tool active, select the item or items you want to place in the library.

2. Drag the selected item until it overlaps with the Library palette. When the dotted outline representing the selected item touches the palette, the pointer changes to a pair of glasses and the library placement icons appear, as shown here:

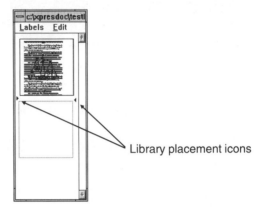

Library placement icons

3. If you don't want to place the selected item where the library placement icons indicate, drag the item's dotted outline into a position that you prefer. The library placement icons appear every time you drag the item after or between existing library entries.

4. Release the mouse button to drop the selected item into position. It becomes highlighted to indicate that it is the active entry, as shown here:

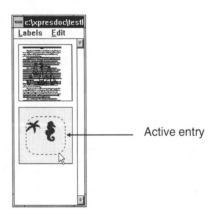

Active entry

An alternate method of placing an item in a library is to copy or cut it from a document and then paste it into the Library palette. Follow these steps:

1. Select the item(s) you want to archive using the Item tool.

2. Copy the selected item(s) into the clipboard using the Copy command in the Edit menu or the keyboard shortcut, CTRL-C. Copying an item is preferable to cutting it unless you truly want to remove it from the active document.

3. Click the point in the Library palette at which you want to insert the item(s). The black library placement icons appear at this point.

4. Choose the Paste command in the Edit menu of the Library palette, as shown here:

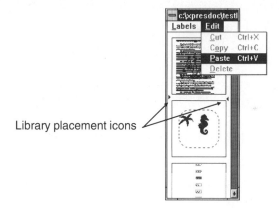

Library placement icons

The pasted item appears in the palette and is immediately highlighted as the active entry.

Tip   You cannot drag a locked item into a Library palette, but you can copy and paste it in.

Text placed in a Library palette automatically includes all the style sheets and attributes you have assigned to the text in the document. The case with high-resolution EPS and TIFF pictures is a little different, however. Just as in a document, Quark retains a pointer to the picture file location rather than retaining the picture file itself. If you delete or move the original picture file, you can still copy the library entry into a document, but the picture will print at low resolution. Always check the Picture Usage dialog box (Picture Usage command, Utilities menu) to verify the status of a picture placed into a document from a library.

Saving a Library's Contents

Quark automatically saves the contents of a library whenever you close its palette. If you activate the Auto Library Save check box in the Application Preferences dialog box (Preferences/Application command, Edit menu), Quark saves a library's contents every time you add a new entry.

Placing a Library Item into a Document

You can place any library entry into an open document, either by dragging or by using the clipboard. To place a library item into a document by dragging, click the library entry once to highlight it and then drag it into position in a document page. To place a library entry using the clipboard, follow these steps:

1. Highlight the library entry in the palette.

2. Choose the Copy command in the palette's Edit menu.

3. Display the document page into which you want to insert the library entry.

4. Choose Paste from the Edit menu of the Quark application window.

Of course, you can also cut the entry from the library before pasting it in the document, but the entry no longer remains in the library if you do so.

Displaying and Labeling Library Items

Using the Labels menu in the Library palette, you can give each library entry a name that corresponds to its function. You can also use this menu to display library items selectively.

Labeling a Library Entry

QuarkXPress lets you name or *label* any entry in an open Library palette. Later, you can use the label to display or hide the entry. To label an entry, follow these steps:

1. Using the scroll bar if necessary, bring into view the library entry you want to name.

2. Double-click the entry to display the Library Entry dialog box shown here:

3. In the Label field, enter a name for the library entry. The label can consist of any sequence of characters. If you prefer, you can assign an existing label name to the entry by selecting a label from the drop-down list box, as shown here:

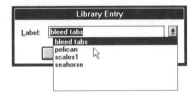

    Multiple library entries can have the same label.

4. Click OK to exit the dialog box and confirm the new label name.

Once you have labeled a library entry, its label appears in the Labels menu of the current Library palette.

Displaying Library Entries Selectively

The options in the Labels menu of the Library palette let you determine which library entries are visible at any one time. You can choose to view all entries in the open library, unlabeled entries only, or a specific labeled entry that you select.

Displaying All Library Entries To view all the entries in the open library, activate the All command. Both labeled and unlabeled library entries become visible. If you have applied labels to any entries, the labels appear in alphabetical order as shown here:

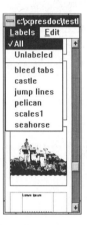

Displaying Unlabeled Entries Only Activate the Unlabeled command in the Labels menu to view only the unlabeled entries in the open library. Any entries to which you have applied specific labels remain hidden from view.

Displaying a Specific Labeled Entry To display a library entry to which you have applied a specific label, activate its name in the Labels menu of the palette. All other entries remain hidden from view.

Managing Library Entries

Like a conventional library, a digital Quark library needs to be pruned occasionally to reorganize or replace some entries and delete unneeded ones.

Replacing Library Entries To replace an existing library entry, copy a document item to the clipboard, click the library entry in the palette that you want to replace, and then choose the Paste command in the Edit menu of the open Library palette. Quark presents a warning message that you will not be able to recover the deleted entry. The previous entry vanishes and is replaced by the item you copied to the clipboard.

Rearranging Library Entries   To change the order of entries in an open Library palette, choose the Maximize command in the palette's control menu so that you can see all available entries. Then, drag items into different positions within the palette. If the number of entries in a library is small, you can leave the palette unmaximized and rearrange entries by copying or cutting them and then pasting them into new positions.

Deleting Library Items

To remove an entry from an open library, highlight the entry and then choose the Cut command from the palette's Edit menu. You can also delete the entry by pressing DEL or choosing the Delete command in the Edit menu, but this is a nonreversible operation.

This chapter has introduced you to the basic layout operations that you encounter in every document. Chapter 12 delves into more advanced techniques for combining graphics with text in a creative way.

CHAPTER

Merging Text with Graphics

*M*anaging how text and graphics interact on a page is like playing hostess or host at a crowded party. At a party, you have to foster connections between people who might have something in common, make sure that incompatible persons stay out of each other's hair, and generally keep all the guests on friendly terms. The role calls upon all your diplomatic and social skills. In much the same way, merging text with graphics in a Quark document is the ultimate test of your "social" page layout skills. Should the pictures and text stay far away from one another? Should they mingle to the point where they are visually inseparable? How can you determine the proper mutual distance in every case?

QuarkXPress for Windows provides two types of features—runaround and anchored boxes—that enhance document design as they help you automate how text and graphics interact.

☐ *Runaround* manages the spatial relationships between any combination of text boxes and picture boxes that overlap. You can manipulate runaround, which is controlled by the Runaround command in the Item menu, to achieve everything from transparent pictures to cutouts, background graphics, and more.

☐ *Anchoring* picture boxes or text boxes within a line of text lets them travel automatically wherever text flows, no matter how many edits you make. This feature is useful for creating run-in heads and automating the placement of figures, captions, tables, and small in-line graphics.

This chapter instructs you in techniques for creating runarounds and anchored boxes and suggests uses for these features that will enhance the design of real-world documents.

Managing Runaround

As mentioned in previous chapters, Quark arranges document items in layers. If a text box overlays a picture box or vice versa, which one "wins"? Runaround is the referee, and the critical factor is the current runaround setting for the item on the *foreground* layer. This setting determines how the overlapping text and graphic elements interact.

The Runaround command in the Item menu, available when the Content or Item tool is active, controls runaround for the currently selected text box, picture box, or line. Refer to Chapters 5, 8, and 11 if you need a refresher course on the basics of setting runaround for text boxes, picture boxes, and lines, respectively.

Note   The Runaround command is unavailable when multiple items or grouped items are selected. However, you can edit runaround for individual items within a group by selecting an item when the Content tool is active.

Table 12-1 offers a quick "cookbook" summary of common design effects that you can achieve by adjusting item layers, runaround settings, and background color. The next few sections describe each runaround setting in detail and offer examples of using runaround creatively in document layout.

No Runaround: Transparent Words and Pictures

Any Text box or Picture box to which you assign a runaround setting of None adopts a background color of None and becomes transparent. If that item is already on the bottommost layer, this setting has no effect. But if some other item lies beneath it, you can view the background item through the transparent foreground item. Figure 12-1 shows several examples of this feature at work.

The types and relative positions of two overlapping items determine what happens when the foreground item is transparent. When a picture box is the foreground item and a text box is the background item, as shown in Figure 12-1a, text flows beneath the picture box, and text directly beneath the picture itself is obscured. When the order of items is reversed and the text box falls above the picture box, the picture becomes a background graphic, as shown in Figure 12-1b, and all text remains legible. The same thing happens when the background item is a ruling line as Figure 12-1c shows.

TABLE 12-1   Adjusting Stacking Order and Runaround Settings for Common Design Effects

Design Effect	Foreground Item/ Runaround	Background Item
Background picture visible under transparent text box	Text box, None (background color None)	Picture box
Text flows under transparent picture box	Picture box, None (background color None)	Text box
Text flows under opaque picture box	Picture box, None (any background color but None)	Text box
Text flows around picture box	Picture Box, Item	Text box
Text flows around picture contours	Picture box, Auto Image	Text box
Custom text flow around picture	Picture box, Manual Image	Text box
Text flows to fit shape of picture	Picture box, Manual Image & Invert (picture deleted)	Text box
Text flows around foreground text box	Text box, Item	Text box
Background text appears behind transparent text box	Text box, None (background color None)	Text box
Background picture visible behind transparent picture box	Picture box, None (background color None)	Picture box

Tip To ensure that text in a transparent foreground text box remains legible, avoid using dark colors or shades for ruling lines or pictures in the background.

One caveat: Both the runaround mode *and* the background color of the uppermost item must be None in order for it to be transparent. If a foreground item has a runaround setting of None and you later change

Foreground items with a runaround setting of None become transparent, allowing background items to show through

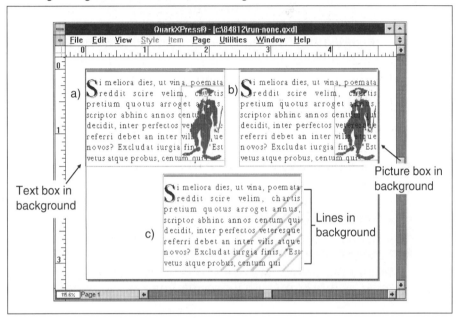

Text box in background

Picture box in background

Lines in background

its background color to something other than None, you will no longer be able to view the text or graphics beneath it, as this example shows:

Background color: None   Background color: 15% gray

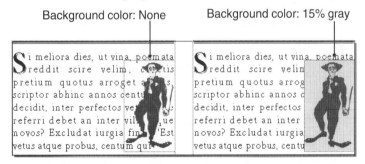

Transparent runaround effects are especially suitable for magazines, newsletters, brochures, posters, and other types of documents that emphasize striking designs.

Item Runarounds

When you assign the Item runaround mode to a text or picture box, text in the background flows around the contours of the box as shown in Figure 12-2. The Runaround Specifications dialog box (Runaround command, Item menu) also lets you control the distance by which background text skirts the foreground text or picture box. If the foreground item is a text box or a rectangular picture box, you can assign a separate runaround distance to each of the four sides: Top, Bottom, Left, and Right. Other fixed-shape and polygon picture boxes can have only a single Text Outset value assigned to them, which means that text flows around these boxes by an equal amount on all sides.

 Note   You cannot assign a custom runaround distance to ruling lines that have an Item runaround.

Books, manuals, business documents, and periodicals that aim at projecting a conservative or professional appearance tend to use rectangular picture boxes with Item runarounds as standard. In a book or other

FIGURE 12-2   Background text flows around the contours of an item that has a runaround setting of Item

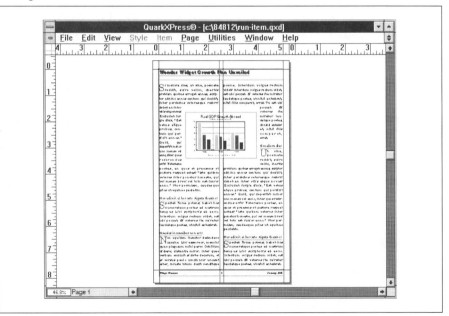

long document, Item runarounds let you separate text and graphics by a uniform distance throughout. Don't write off Item runarounds as a staid design option, though. There are plenty of imaginative ways to use them, as the examples in the following sections show.

Adding Visual Variety to Single-Column Documents

If you place a picture box or text box with an Item runaround in front of a one-column text box, text flows only to one side of the item—the side with the greatest amount of horizontal space. The design issue is simple as long as the foreground text or picture box fills the entire width of the underlying column. If the foreground item is narrower than the column, though, you have some choices to make. Should you standardize and place all pictures at the left edge of the column or at the right edge? Can you place pictures in the white space to the left of text (assuming you have defined style sheets that don't extend all the way to the left margin of the text box)? What about varying the placement of pictures to add visual interest to your design as shown in the example in Figure 12-3?

FIGURE 12-3

Varying the placement of pictures on a page (Item runaround)

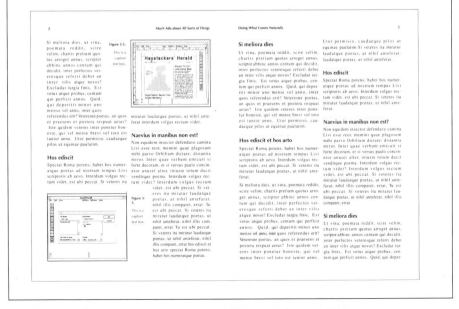

Straddling Pictures Between Two Text Columns

Newsletters, magazines, or other multicolumn documents can also use Item runarounds to enhance design. To achieve results like the example shown in Figure 12-2, a foreground text or picture box that has an Item runaround should *straddle* two text boxes or two columns of text in a single text box. That way, each column moves out of the way of the foreground item in one horizontal direction. This type of treatment is useful not only for graphics, but also for shaded text sidebars within longer articles.

There are many other design-enhancing applications for Item runarounds. For example, you can use a polygon picture box with an Item runaround to create an exceptionally smooth text runaround for a picture cutout. You will see how in the "Auto Image Runarounds" section next.

Auto Image Runarounds

Auto Image runarounds, available only for picture boxes, generally offer more flexible design possibilities than do Item runarounds. When a picture has an Auto Image runaround, text in the background can flow around the contours of the picture rather than around the edges of the picture box itself, as this example shows:

Auto Image runaround

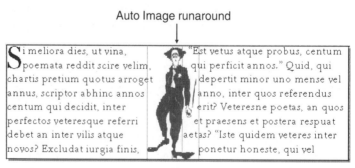

The Text Outset value you assign to a picture box determines how much space separates the picture's contours from surrounding text. Just as with a Runaround setting of None, text moves to one side of an image only, unless the image straddles multiple columns.

Note A picture box to which an Auto Image runaround is assigned takes on a background color of None.

 Note An Auto Image runaround setting has no visible effect unless the picture box to which you apply it is one layer above a text box.

Auto Image runarounds do have their limitations. Most of these stem from the fact that Quark bases an Auto Image runaround on the onscreen representation of a picture, which, in the case of EPS and TIFF pictures, is not completely WYSIWYG. The "Defining Runaround Specifications" section of Chapter 8 suggests a technique for achieving more perfect auto image runarounds for object-oriented EPS graphics. TIFF Auto Image runarounds encounter a slightly different set of problems, but there are solutions for those, too.

Creating "Pseudo" Auto Image Runarounds for Polygon Picture Boxes

Typically, the TIFF photographs or bitmaps you use in documents are at fairly high resolutions (150-300 dpi) to ensure acceptable print quality. The display resolutions of computer monitors, however, are in the much lower range of 72-120 dpi. As a result, imported TIFF images in a Quark document always look more jagged onscreen than they do in print. If the Low Resolution TIFF option in the Application Preferences dialog box is active, Quark represents TIFF images at only *half* the display resolution of your monitor, making them look even more jagged.

It is no wonder, then, that Auto Image runarounds for TIFF images may sometimes be a little more jagged than you might like. In many documents, it may not matter whether text follows a less than neat path when flowing around a TIFF with an Auto Image runaround. But if you require that background text flow along pristinely clean, sharp lines, consider using a polygon picture box with an Item runaround to achieve your goal. Refer to the example in Figure 12-4 and follow these general steps to generate a clean text runaround for a TIFF image:

1. Import the TIFF image into a rectangular picture box as shown in Figure 12-4a. Leave Runaround in its default Item mode.

FIGURE
12-4

Simulating Auto Image runaround by using a polygon picture box with an Item runaround

2. Activate the Polygon Picture Box tool and create a new picture box by tracing around the part of the image behind which you want text to flow, as shown in Figure 12-4b. To close the polygon when you have traced completely around the desired area, click at the starting point. The new picture box hides part of the original picture because it is one layer above it. Refer to Chapter 8 if you need to review how to create and close a polygon picture box.

Tip To simulate smooth curves when tracing around an image area that contains many contours, zoom in on the image and click (create corners) at intervals of every few pixels. This generates very small line segments that are practically indistinguishable from curves.

3. With the Item tool selected, activate the rectangular picture box and press DEL to delete both the image and the picture box that contains it.

4. Activate the newly created polygon picture box and then activate the Content tool. Using the Get Picture command in the File menu, import the same image into the polygon picture box and position it so that the area of the image you want to be visible shows through as in Figure 12-4c.

5. Check the Runaround Specifications dialog box (Runaround command, Item menu) and make sure that the polygon picture box is set to the default Item mode. Adjust the Text Outset value according to the distance from the image at which you want text to flow, and then click OK. Text should now run cleanly around the outline of the polygon.

The printed result looks similar to an Auto Image runaround but may well feature smoother text runaround contours.

Manual Image Runarounds

Think of a Manual Image runaround as an Auto Image runaround that you can tweak. When you apply a Manual Image runaround mode to a picture box, the picture box takes on a background color of None (transparent), and a *runaround polygon* like the one in Figure 12-5 appears around the image inside it. The Text Outset value you assign determines how much space lies between the contours of the runaround polygon and text in the background.

The runaround polygon contains corner points, just like a polygon picture box when the Reshape Polygon command in the Item menu is active (see Chapter 8). The default runaround polygon doesn't always conform exactly to the contours of the image; Quark just creates a good guesstimate. You can edit the runaround polygon, though, in much the same way that you reshape a polygon picture box. To customize the runaround polygon to the exact shape and size you want, use one or more of these techniques when the Content or Item tool is active:

☐ To adjust the position of a line segment within the runaround polygon, click the nearest corner point and drag it. You can even drag the runaround polygon outside the picture box.

☐ To add a corner point (and thus another line segment that you can adjust), move the mouse pointer to the desired point on the run-around polygon and press CTRL. When the corner point symbol appears, click to add the new corner point.

☐ To delete a corner point, move the mouse pointer over the corner point (where it takes on the appearance of a corner point symbol with an "x" through it), press CTRL, and click.

Tip To prevent the screen from redrawing every time you adjust, delete, or add a corner point, press and hold the SPACEBAR until you finish editing the runaround polygon.

FIGURE 12-5 Pictures with a Manual Image runaround feature a runaround polygon

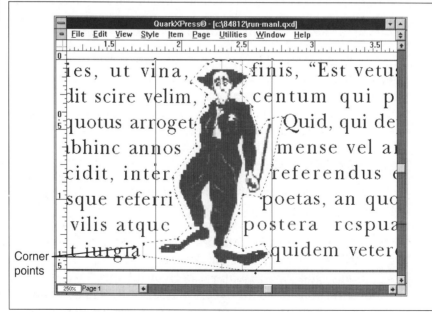

Corner points

Tip Manual runarounds don't work very well with EPS graphics, because the EPS header is usually smaller than the actual picture. If you need to create a manual runaround for an EPS picture, temporarily import a copy of the graphic saved in some other format and edit the runaround polygon for it, as described in Chapter 8. Then, delete the substitute image (with the Content tool active) and reimport the original EPS file in its place. The picture box retains the runaround polygon shape you have created with the substitute image.

The Manual Image runaround offers more varied design possibilities than just the ability to fine-tune the way text surrounds an image. Here, we'll delineate two important examples: wrapping text around a blank shape, and shaping text to the form of an image.

Wrapping Text Around a Blank Shape

One useful application for a Manual Image runaround is to force text to wrap around a picture that isn't there. You can create a blank shape like the one shown in Figure 12-6 in one of two ways: by adjusting the runaround polygon for an image and then deleting the image, or by editing the runaround polygon starting from a picture box that contains no picture.

To create a blank runaround shape starting from an actual image and then delete the image, follow these steps:

1. Import a graphic into a picture box and assign a Manual Image runaround to it.

2. Reshape the runaround polygon until it fits exactly to the contours you want to emphasize. If you have to add or subtract several corner points, remember to press and hold SHIFT as you work to avoid too-frequent screen redraws.

3. Delete the image from the picture box; the runaround polygon remains, and text continues to wrap around it.

To create a runaround polygon based on an imaginary shape rather than on a photo or other bitmap, try this technique instead:

1. Assign a Manual Image runaround to a picture box that contains no picture. The runaround polygon assumes the shape of the picture box and contains exactly eight corner points.

2. Set up horizontal and vertical ruler guides that will help you position corner points precisely according to your imagined design.

FIGURE 12-6

Wrapping text around an empty runaround polygon

Win Back That Hourglass Figure!

Si meliora dies, ut vina, poemata reddit, scire velim, chartis pretium quotus arroget annus, scriptor abhinc annos centum qui decidit, inter perfectos veteresque referri debet an inter vilis atque novos? Excludat iurgia finis, Est vetus atque probus, centum qui perficit annos. Quid, qui deperiit minor uno mense vel anno, inter quos referendus erit? Veteresne poetas, an quos et praesens et postera respuat aetas? Iste quidem veteres inter ponetur honeste, qui vel mense brevi vel toto est iunior anno. Utor permisso, caudaeque pilos ut equinae paulatim. Veteresne poetas, an quos et praesens et postera respuat aetas? Iste quidem veteres inter ponetur honeste, qui vel mense brevi vel toto est iunior anno. Utor permisso, caudaeque pilos ut equinae paulatim.

Fat is Not Funny!

Spectat Roma potens; habet hos numeratque poetas ad nostrum tempus Livi scriptoris ab aevo. Interdum volgus rectum videt, est ubi peccat. Si veteres ita miratur laudatque poetas, ut nihil anteferat.

Naevius in?

Non equidem insector defendave camina Livi esse reor, memini quae plagosum mihi parvo Orbilium dictare; distantia miror. Inter quae verbum emicuit si forte decorum, et si versus paulo concinnior unuset alter, iniuste totum ducit venditque poema. Interdum volgus rectum videt? Interdum volgus rectum videt, est ubi peccat. Si veteres ita miratur

laudatque poetas, ut nihil antefarat, nihil illis comparet, errat. Tu est ubi peccat. Si veteres ita miratur laudatque poetas, ut nihil anteferat, nihil illis comparet, errat. Inter quae verbum emicuit si forte decorum, et si versus paulo concinnior unuset alter, iniuste totum ducit venditque poema. Interdum volgus rectum videt? Interdum volgus rectum videt, est ubi peccat. Si veteres ita miratur laudatque poetas, ut nihil antefarat, nihil illis comparet, errat. Tu est ubi peccat. Si veteres ita miratur laudatque poetas, ut nihil anteferat, nihil illis comparet, errat. Interdum volgus rectum videt, est ubi peccat. Si veteres ita miratur laudatque poetas, ut nihil antefarat, nihil illis comparet, errat.

Si meliora dies

Ut vina, poemata reddit, scire velim, chartis pretium quotus arroget annus, scriptor abhinc annos centum qui decidit, inter perfectos veteresque referri debet an inter vilis atque novos? Excludat iurgia finis, Est vetus atque probus, centum qui perficit annos. Quid, qui deperiit minor uno mense vel anno, inter quos referendus erit? Veteresne poetas, an quos et praesens et postera respuat aetas? Iste quidem veteres inter ponetur honeste, qui vel mense brevi vel toto est iunior anno. Utor permisso, caudaeque pilos ut equinae paulatim.

Hos ediscit atro?

Spectat Roma potens; habet hos numeratque poetas ad nostrum tempus Livi scriptoris ab aevo.

Wonder Weight Loss Centers 3 *January 1993*

3. Add and adjust corner points as necessary to fit the runaround polygon to the desired shape.

When you are finished, text wraps around the shape. Of course, you may need to edit and/or kern the background text in order to force the text wrap to have smooth contours.

Flowing Text into a Runaround Polygon

Imagine text flowing *into* a runaround polygon shape rather than around it. Inverting text flow can be an exciting way to create word pictures in a document, shaping text to the contours of an image or blank shape as shown in Figure 12-7. You can achieve this effect—with a bit of work—by activating the Invert option in the Runaround Specifications dialog box when you assign a Manual Image runaround to a picture box.

Because text doesn't flow automatically into a runaround polygon unless there is more space for the text inside than outside, you must trick Quark into inverting text flow by increasing the size of the picture box until it crowds out the text box in the background, as shown in the sequence in Figure 12-7. The size of the runaround polygon remains unchanged when you resize the associated picture box.

 Note If a picture box contains an image when you invert text flow, you must delete the image in order to make the text visible.

Using Anchored Text and Picture Boxes

Do you find document revisions tedious because you have to reposition graphics and tables manually every time you edit text? Are you looking for a way to make icons, figures, outdented heads, or tables flow automatically with text? Look no further. QuarkXPress includes a feature called *anchoring* that lets you insert either a text box or a picture box within a line of text as though it were a character. As you edit the text, the anchored item flows along with it. Quark gives you advanced control over the position of the anchored item, so the design possibilities for anchored items are almost endless.

FIGURE
12-7

Using the Invert option to force text to flow into a runaround polygon

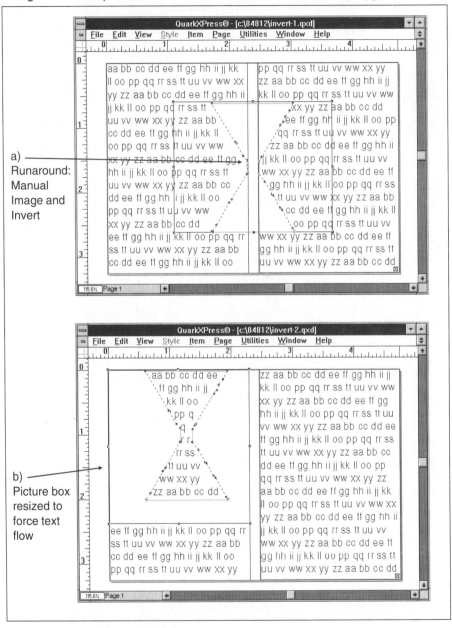

a) —
Runaround:
Manual
Image and
Invert

b) —
Picture box
resized to
force text
flow

Note You cannot anchor grouped or multiple selected items or a line.

Anchoring a Text or Picture Box

Anchoring a text or picture box to text takes only a few steps:

1. With the Item tool (*not* the Content tool) selected, activate the text or picture box that you want to use as an anchored character.

2. Choose the Cut command from the Edit menu (keyboard shortcut: CTRL-C) to cut the selected item to the clipboard. (If you also wanted to leave the original item where it is, you could use the Copy command instead.)

3. Activate the Content tool and position the text cursor at the point where you want to anchor the text or picture box. This must be within a line of text or in front of a paragraph mark (it may help to have the Show Invisibles command in the View menu turned on).

4. Choose Paste from the Edit menu or press CTRL-V to paste the item from the clipboard. The item is now a single anchored text character and will move with the surrounding text.

By default, the bottom of an anchored character aligns flush with the baseline of the paragraph into which you place it. You can easily change its position and many other attributes as well.

Editing an Anchored Text or Picture Box

As far as Quark is concerned, you are editing text when you manipulate an anchored text or picture box. To select an anchored character in order to edit it, click on it with either the Content or the Item tool active. You can then alter its attributes using your choice of the mouse, commands in the Style or Item menu, or the Measurements palette.

Deleting an Anchored Item

To delete an anchored item, activate the Content tool, place the text cursor immediately after the anchored character, and press BACKSPACE. You can also place the cursor immediately before the anchored character and press DEL.

Changing Your Mind about an Anchored Item

Oops! What can you do if, once having anchored a text or picture box, you decide that you'd rather have it back as an independent item again? The simplest method for achieving this is to select the anchored item with the Content or Item tool and then choose the Duplicate command from the Item menu. You can also select the anchored item with the Item tool active, choose Copy from the Edit menu, and then choose the Paste command. Either of these techniques places a duplicate of the anchored item as a freestanding item on the page. You can then safely delete the anchored character that still remains as an in-line graphic.

Editing Attributes Interactively

The only attribute of an anchored text or picture box that you can edit with the mouse is its size. If you select an anchored item when the Content or Item tool is active, resize it by dragging one of its selection handles, just as you would with any freestanding text or picture box.

Editing Attributes with Style Menu Commands

Remember to treat an anchored item like a text character, and you can't go wrong. If you select an anchored character by dragging over it when the Content tool is active, the anchored item becomes highlighted as shown in Figure 12-8, and commands in the Style menu become available.

Only two character attribute commands in the Style menu—Kern/Track and Baseline Shift—are available once you highlight an anchored character using the Content tool. The Kern/Track command lets you adjust horizontal spacing between an anchored item and surrounding text. If you position the text cursor before or after the anchored

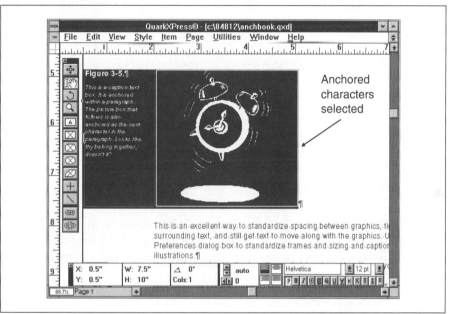

FIGURE 12-8

Dragging over an anchored character with the text cursor causes it to become highlighted

character, the Kern command is available, and you can adjust spacing to one side of the anchored character only. If you highlight the anchored character to select it, the Track command is available, and any values you edit adjust spacing on both sides of the character. Refer to Chapter 6 if you need to review the basics of kerning and tracking.

By editing the baseline shift value, you can move a character up or down relative to the baseline of surrounding text. This technique is especially helpful when you are using anchored characters as in-line icons.

Editing Attributes with Item Menu Commands

One of the first things you will notice when you begin working with anchored text and picture boxes is that the Runaround command in the Item menu is not available for them. This is because the leading and kerning attributes of the "host" paragraph control the spacing between the anchored character and its neighbors above, below, and to each side. The Modify command in the Item menu also gives you an option for determining the relative vertical position of the anchored character.

When the anchored character is a text box, selecting the Modify command in the Item menu (keyboard shortcut: CTRL-M) accesses the Anchored Text Box Specifications dialog box shown here:

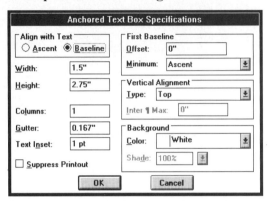

Most of the options in this dialog box are the same as for a freestanding text box. You can change the width, height, number of columns, text inset value, first baseline parameters, vertical alignment, and background color and shade. One option, however, is different. The Align with Text option gives you two choices: you can align the top of the anchored text box with the ascent of the text line in which you have placed it or align the bottom of the anchored box with the text baseline. The result of each option is shown here:

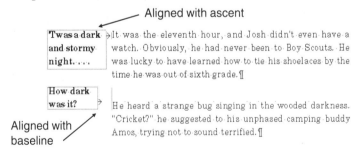

When the anchored character is a picture box, choosing the Modify command from the Item menu accesses the Anchored Picture Box Specifications dialog box shown next. Again, most of the options in this dialog box are identical to those you would find if the selected picture box were freestanding. You can edit the picture box's width and height, background color, and shade, and you have the same flexibility regarding the scaling, offset, rotation angle, and skew angle of the picture it contains. As with anchored text boxes, the Align with Text option lets you choose how to position the anchored picture box relative to the line of text in which it appears.

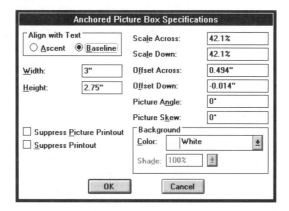

Editing Attributes with the Measurements Palette

If you prefer having attributes always handy rather than hidden in a dialog box, use the Measurements palette to edit an anchored text or picture box. When an anchored text box is the selected item and the Content tool is active, you can edit the box's width and height, number of columns, and all text attributes, as shown here:

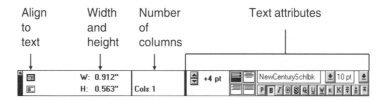

The two icons at the left edge of the Measurements palette let you select a relative alignment for the anchored text box. Highlight the upper icon to align the top of the box with the ascent of text; highlight the lower icon to align the bottom of the box with the text baseline.

Note   If you select an anchored text box when the Item tool is active, only the options on the left side of the Measurements palette are available.

When you select an anchored picture box with the Content tool, the Measurements palette contains the options shown next. You can edit the box's width, height, and alignment, as well as the normal picture attributes: scaling, offset, rotation angle, and skew angle. When you select an anchored picture box with the Item tool, only the alignment, width, and height attributes are editable.

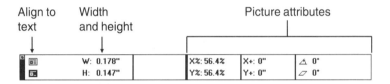

Document Design with Anchored Text and Picture Boxes

There are many ways to use anchored text and picture boxes in a Quark document, and users come up with new applications for them every day. While any type of document can include anchored characters, anchoring is a real lifesaver for users who produce long documents, which tend to have a multitude of graphic components and involve many revisions to text during the layout process. The next few sections give a few suggested applications for anchored characters and ways to implement them.

Outdented Heads

An *outdented head* is a paragraph that appears in the margin to the left of body text, yet is separate from it. Using style sheets alone, Quark offers no way to create independent side-by-side paragraphs like the example shown next. You could, of course, use tabs, a negative first line indent, and local character formatting to achieve this look, but you would lose the local formatting if you applied another style sheet to the paragraph later in the layout process. The safest, most foolproof way to create an outdented head is to use an anchored text box containing text in a style sheet different from body text.

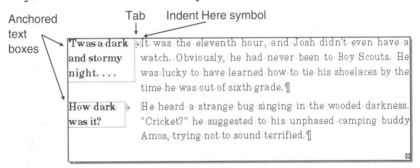

To create an outdented head using an anchored text box, follow these steps:

1. Define a body text style sheet that is indented considerably from the left margin of the text box. This leaves enough room for an outdented head in the margin.

2. Define a special style sheet for the paragraph that is to *contain* the anchored text box. This style sheet should be similar to body text in all respects except one: it should *not* be indented from the left margin of the text box. (This precaution has to do with the way an anchored text box pushes adjacent text out of the way, as you will see shortly.)

3. Create a separate text box for the outdented head. Using the Modify command in the Item menu, set Text Inset to 0 points. Choose the Runaround command and set the Top, Bottom, Left, and Right margins to 0 points as well. These settings ensure that the ascent of text in the anchored text box will align with text in the adjacent paragraph.

4. Enter the text of the outdented head into the text box you just created.

5. Define a separate style sheet for the outdented head text. Set up the font, point size, and so on to contrast with body text. Assign this style sheet to the text you entered in step 4.

6. Select the text box with the Item tool and cut it to the clipboard.

7. Activate the Content tool, position the text cursor in front of the first character of the paragraph with the negative first line indent, and choose Paste from the Edit menu. The anchored text box appears, with a ready-made outdented head in place.

8. With the Content tool still active, click the anchored text box and, using the Modify command or the Measurements palette, align it with the *ascent* (not the baseline) of the accompanying text. The anchored text box may still push text in the adjacent paragraph out of the way, causing the horizontal alignment to look irregular.

9. Define a tab for the style sheet to which the outdented head box is anchored. The tab should be left-indented to the point at which normal body text aligns.

10. Position the text cursor after the anchored box. Press TAB to push the *first* line of the accompanying paragraph into alignment with other body text paragraphs. Some other lines in the paragraph may still look out of alignment, but you will fix that anomaly in the next step.

11. Enter the Indent Here code (CTRL-\) to indent the remaining lines of the paragraph at the same point. You can see the Indent Here character, pointed out in the previous illustration, only if you have Show Invisibles turned on in the View menu.

Tip   If you want text in the outdented head to align with the baselines of text in the adjacent paragraph, define the same font, point size, and amount of leading for both style sheets.

Run-In Heads

A *run-in* head is a paragraph that fits side by side with body text but is typographically different from it, like the examples shown here:

> **'Twas a dark and stormy night.** It was the eleventh hour, and Josh didn't even have a watch. Obviously, he had never been to Boy Scouts. He was lucky to have learned how to tie his shoelaces by the time he was out of sixth grade.¶
>
> **How dark was it?** He heard a strange bug singing in the wooded darkness. "Cricket?" he suggested to his unphased camping buddy Amos, trying not to sound terrified.¶

Like an outdented head, it requires a separate style sheet. A run-in head differs from an outdented head in two respects:

☐ It does not appear in the margin.

☐ Depending on how you define your style sheets, it can align with either the baseline or the ascent of accompanying text.

As already mentioned, Quark does not allow you to create a separate run-in head paragraph using style sheets alone. With the help of an anchored text box, though, the task is easy. Here is how you might proceed:

1. Define a special style sheet for the run-in head paragraph that you will insert into the anchored text box. This style sheet should contrast typographically with body text so that it is visibly set off from it, but it should have the same amount of leading.

2. Create a separate text box for the run-in head and enter text or paste text into it.

3. Assign the run-in head style sheet to this text. If necessary, adjust the size of the text box so that it is exactly as wide as needed to fit the head on a single line, but no wider. Size the text box vertically so no extra space is left.

4. Using the Modify and Runaround commands in the Item menu, set Text Inset and the margins for this text box to 0 points.

5. Select the text box with the Item tool and cut or copy it to the clipboard.

6. Activate the Content tool, position the text cursor in front of the first character of the paragraph into which you want to insert the run-in head, and choose Paste from the Edit menu. The anchored text box appears at the cursor position, already aligned to the baseline of the accompanying paragraph.

7. Add an en space after the anchored text box (CTRL-ALT-SHIFT-6) to leave a little breathing room between the run-in head and the body text that follows.

If for some reason the text in the anchored box does not align perfectly with adjacent text, select the anchored character by dragging over it with the Content tool active. Then, shift the baseline downward until the character does align. If the font in both style sheets is the same height, you might prefer to anchor the text box to the ascent of adjacent text rather than to its baseline.

Custom Drop Caps

As you saw in Chapter 6, Quark already has an automatic drop cap feature that you can access through the Paragraph Formats dialog box when you define a new style sheet. If you want a unique drop-cap, such as a special-effects letter imported from a drawing program or clip art package, import it into a picture box and then anchor the picture box in front of the first character of the target paragraph, as in this example:

Character in anchored picture box

bviously, he had never been to Boy Scouts. He was lucky to have learned how to tie his shoelaces by the time he was out of sixth grade. So when he heard the cacophony of critters (and no flashlight to boot), he was terrified.

Typically, you would anchor such a picture box with the ascent of the accompanying text. If desired, you can always shift the anchored character up or down by drag-selecting it with the Content tool and then choosing the Baseline Shift command in the Style menu. If the custom letter is an EPS or other object-oriented graphic, you can make it fit an exact number of lines by resizing the text box and then pressing CTRL-ALT-SHIFT-F to fit the graphic exactly to the box. You can also kern the space between the anchored character and the next letter in the paragraph.

Icons that Flow with Text

A favorite use for anchored picture boxes—one dear to the hearts of writers and page layout professionals who deal with technical documentation—is to create small in-line graphics that flow within a text paragraph. These may be program icons like the example shown next, representations of computer keys, or any small graphic symbol that you want to use as text.

Anchored picture box

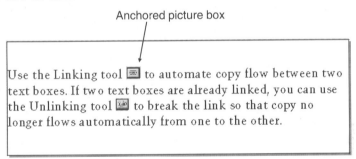

Here are a few guidelines that will help you achieve perfect results for in-line graphics every time:

☐ Avoid using auto leading for any paragraph in which an anchored graphic appears. Although auto leading will automatically adjust interline spacing to accommodate the size of the graphic, too visible a difference in interline spacing is considered a typographic no-no. If you must use auto leading for a paragraph that contains a large anchored graphic, place the graphic in the *first line* of the paragraph.

☐ Whenever possible, size the picture box for the in-line graphic so that its height exactly matches the baseline-to-ascent height of lowercase letters such as "f", "h", "l", and "t". Then, set the anchored graphic to align with the ascent of text; it will also align perfectly with the baseline without needing adjustment.

❑ If the in-line graphic must be slightly larger than the baseline-to-ascent height in order to be legible, try fitting it within a picture box that is exactly as high as the distance between the ascent and the descent of surrounding text. Set the anchored graphic to align with the ascent of text; it will then sit nicely balanced within the paragraph.

❑ If an icon or in-line graphic is much larger than the interline spacing of a target paragraph, anchor it in the margin using a technique similar to the one described in the "Outdented Heads" section earlier in this chapter. Define a separate style sheet for the paragraph in which you place the anchored graphic and set it up for no left or first line indent, but rather for a tab stop that left-aligns with the text in other body text paragraphs. Align the anchored graphic with the ascent of text, then press TAB and enter the Indent Here character (CTRL-\) to align all the other lines in the paragraph neatly. The result will look similar to this example:

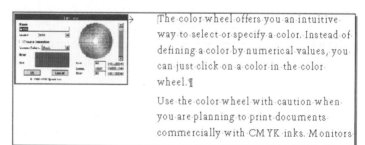

❑ Standardize background color and framing attributes for repeating in-line graphics within the same document.

❑ Add the in-line picture boxes to a library so you can insert them repeatedly into a document with a minimum of effort. Label these elements so you can remember their purposes within the document.

 Tip Use the Baseline Shift command in the Style menu to adjust an anchored graphic up or down a few points relative to the surrounding text.

Figures and Captions that Flow with Text

In Quark, you create figures and their captions using two separate items: a picture box for the figure proper and a text box for the caption. You can group these two items to keep them together, of course, but that solution only works for short newsletters and other documents that contain few pictures. If you are producing a long document that contains many figures, you need a more efficient way to move the figures and their captions automatically with text.

The solution for documents like these is to use anchored text and picture boxes as the *sole characters* within a paragraph. If your document calls for captions that always appear to the left or right of a figure, for example, you can anchor both the picture box and its caption box within the same paragraph. If your document requires that you place captions above or below a figure, you can anchor a picture box in one paragraph and the caption in the next or vice versa.

The paragraph attributes of the style sheet(s) in which you anchor these items determine the horizontal placement of the figure and caption as well as the amount of space Quark leaves above and below the figure. Here is a brief summary of how to generate figures as anchored characters when the caption appears to the left of a picture box:

1. Create a picture box and import the graphic that you want to use as a figure. Size the picture box to fit the picture if necessary. (If you are producing a long document, assign standardized attributes to all picture boxes that contain figures.)

2. Create a text box for the figure's caption. The design of your document should determine the dimensions of this text box. For captions that appear to the left of a figure, for example, all caption boxes should feature a consistent width. Match the height of each caption box to the height of the associated picture box.

3. Define a style sheet for the caption that takes into account its vertical and horizontal alignment within the caption text box.

4. Define a special style sheet for paragraphs that will contain only the anchored items (picture box and caption text box) that make up each figure. In the Paragraph Formats dialog box, pay attention to the following settings:

Alignment Choose Left, for example, if you want the caption to be left-aligned, or Centered if you want the figure and caption to be centered within the column.

Indent Define the indents for this paragraph to accommodate the desired horizontal placement for figures. For instance, create a negative left indent if you want the caption text box to appear out in the margin beyond normal body text for the document.

Leading Assign auto leading to this style sheet so that the space between anchored figure paragraphs and surrounding paragraphs will adjust to the height of each figure automatically.

Space Before, Space After Define the interparagraph spacing for this style sheet according to the amount of space you want to place between figures and surrounding text.

5. With the Item tool active, select the caption text box and cut it to the clipboard.

6. Activate the Content tool. At the point where you want the figure to appear in the text, press ENTER to generate a new blank paragraph. Apply the anchored figure style sheet to this paragraph.

7. With the text cursor still at the beginning of the blank paragraph, choose Paste from the Edit menu to anchor the caption text box. It appears aligned with the baseline as shown in Figure 12-9.

8. Activate the Item tool and select the picture box that contains the figure graphic. Cut this to the clipboard, too.

9. Activate the Content tool and position the text cursor immediately *after* the anchored caption box.

10. Choose Paste from the Edit menu. The picture box drops into position adjacent to the caption text box as shown in Figure 12-10.

There are many variations on this theme. For example, if your document design calls for captions to be placed below figures, you would design two style sheets for the anchored elements. The first style sheet, the one for the anchored figure, would feature a Keep with Next setting, leading equal to the point size of the paragraph, and no spacing after the paragraph. You would anchor the picture box aligned to the baseline of this paragraph. The second style sheet, the one for the caption, would

FIGURE
12-9
Anchoring a caption text box in a left-aligned paragraph with no indents

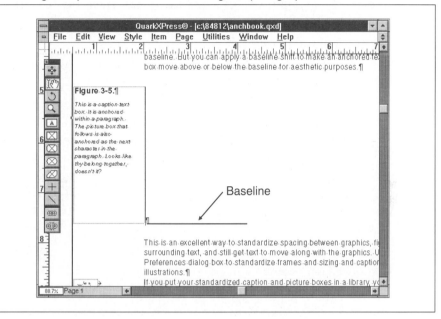

FIGURE
12-10
Anchoring a picture box to complete an anchored figure

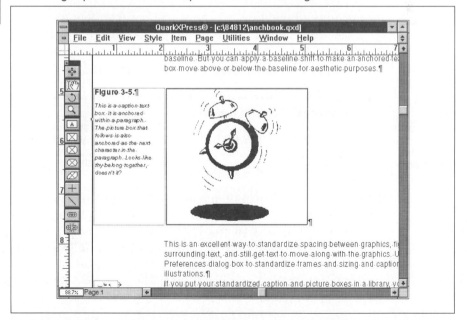

need to have the same indent, leading, and alignment settings as the first, but would feature no spacing before the paragraph. To ensure that an anchored text box abuts the picture box above it, align it with the *ascent* of the paragraph, not with its baseline.

Tables Within Picture Boxes

Chapter 8 covered the basics of using OLE to import graphics into a picture box in their native format. What many users don't realize is that they can also take advantage of OLE to import a table or spreadsheet from Microsoft Excel or from any other database application that can act as an OLE client server. You can make such a table flow along with the text before and after it, using basically the same technique as when you want to anchor figures and captions. Here is a brief summary of how to carry out this task:

1. Link or embed the database cells to a Quark picture box using the Paste Link or Paste Special command in the Edit menu (see Chapter 8).

2. Define a special style sheet for the paragraph in which you will anchor the picture box containing the table. Pay careful attention to the Space Before and Space After options in the Paragraph Formats dialog box, as these will control how much space Quark inserts above and below the table to separate it from other text. You should also define auto leading for this style sheet so that leading will adjust to fit the height of the picture box.

3. Select the picture box containing the table with the Item tool and cut or copy it to the clipboard.

4. At the point in the text where you want to insert the table, press ENTER to create a new blank paragraph. Apply the newly defined style sheet to this paragraph.

5. With the Content tool active, position the text cursor in the blank paragraph and then choose Paste from the Edit menu. The table falls into place, with the requested amount of spacing above and below it.

If tables in your document have separate captions, you can anchor the caption text boxes as described in the "Figures and Captions that Flow with Text" section of this chapter.

We've aimed at providing some tips and tricks for generating attractive designs that merge text seamlessly with graphics. Here's hoping that the examples given in this chapter stimulate your imagination when you design your own documents with Quark.

CHAPTER

Producing Specific
Types of Documents

Quark's rich and powerful features let you produce just about any type of document imaginable. Before you sit down at your computer, though, you should do some preliminary planning and designing. Often, the primary factor that influences design is budget. For example, if you can afford to print only two colors, you should not design a six-color document with full-color photographs! Budget will usually dictate choices regarding document size, binding and trim, colors, artwork and photography, the type and weight of paper used for printing, and the method of distribution (self-mailer, bulk mail, and so forth).

Once you have settled these issues, you can begin to sketch some ideas with pencil and paper. Even the most computer-savvy graphic designers admit that in this preliminary design phase, rough hand-drawn sketches, or *comps*, offer more flexibility than any computer hardware or software can. Think about how your intended audience, the purpose of your document, and the desired response all affect design considerations. When the preliminary sketches have been made, you can start creating the document with QuarkXPress.

In this chapter, types of documents that share common design elements and production techniques are grouped together for discussion. The major categories are periodicals, promotional materials, books and manuals, and business documents.

The discussion of each category should give you direction and spark your own creativity. It is not within the scope of this book to give detailed, how-to instructions for designing different kinds of publications. Many good books on design can be found in your local bookstore; consider purchasing at least one if you are not a trained artist or designer.

Producing Periodicals

Periodicals, publications that are produced on a regular basis, include magazines, newspapers, newsletters, bulletins, and catalogs. Some of the design elements common to these publications are columns, continued text with jump lines, photographs, headers and footers, page numbers, and the use of color.

Setting Preferences for Periodicals

To facilitate working with periodical-type documents, you may want to make some changes to Quark's Preferences settings, which Chapter 4 discusses in detail. If you edit General, Typographic, and Tools preferences while working on your periodical, Quark will save the new settings with the document. Application preferences, on the other hand, apply to all documents until you change them again.

Suggested Application Preferences

A few of Quark's application-wide preferences have special relevance to how you work when producing periodicals. To make changes to these preferences, choose the Preferences/Application command in the Edit menu.

Trap   Magazines, newsletters, catalogs, and bulletins tend to use color more extensively than do books and manuals. Whether you use spot or process color in your periodicals, adjust settings in the Trap section of the Application Preferences dialog box to avoid color-related problems caused by slight misalignment of plates on the printing press. The type of printing press and paper stock used to publish a document are the chief factors in determining the amount of trapping you should use. Publications printed on glossy paper stocks and using slow printing presses designed for color work require smaller amounts of trapping; documents printed on uncoated paper stocks and using high-speed presses call for higher trapping amounts. Refer to Chapter 10 for background information on trapping, and always consult with your print vendor to obtain recommended trapping settings for a specific publication.

Remember   When adjusting Trap settings, keep in mind that only PostScript printers and imagesetters can interpret trapping information.

Caution   If you set Trap Amount to something other than the default 0.144 pt and plan to output your documents through an imagesetter at a service bureau, you should either create your own PostScript output files or inform your service bureau that your settings may differ from theirs. Failing to do so could lead to incorrect trapping values being applied during imagesetting.

Pasteboard Width   Keep the pasteboard wide for layout flexibility, because periodicals typically undergo lots of local formatting changes. The maximum size for the pasteboard is 100 percent of page size.

Remember   The pasteboard in Quark is always attached to the page on which you are currently working.

Suggested General Preferences

Several settings in the General Preferences dialog box (Preferences/General command, Edit menu) apply specifically to how you work when producing periodicals. Edit these settings when your periodical is open so that your changes will affect only the current document.

Auto Page Insertion   Since most periodicals have a fixed number of pages, set Auto Page Insertion to Off. If you are creating a four-page newsletter, for example, you would not want Quark to insert a page when a text box overflows. Instead, reformat text to make more room, or cut portions of the articles so that all the information fits within the fixed number of pages.

Guides   Set Guides to Behind so you do not accidentally relocate guides when you move text boxes, picture boxes, or ruling lines.

Item Coordinates   If you want continuous ruler increments across facing pages or across pages in a spread, choose Spread for the Item Coordinates option. This setting gives you the flexibility so important for the many layout changes to which most periodicals are subject. It also helps you determine measurements when you set up design elements using the Step and Repeat command in the Item menu as described in Chapter 11.

Auto Picture Import   The recommended setting for the Auto Picture Import option is On (verify), because periodicals often contain many pictures that are updated frequently. This setting triggers the Missing/Modified Pictures dialog box, described more fully in Chapter 8, which lets you preview and update the view of modified pictures.

Master Page Items   Set the Master Page Items option to Keep Changes, not Delete Changes. This affords you the flexibility of performing local formatting and copyfitting that will not be overridden on the given page even if you apply a different master page or reapply the existing one.

Greek Pictures   Periodical publications usually contain a large number of pictures. Since it takes more time for the monitor to redraw a page that contains pictures, it is recommended that you check the Greek Pictures option so that pictures will appear as gray silhouettes or solid gray boxes. This will decrease your production time, but it does not limit your ability to work with the individual pictures. If you want to see a greeked picture or manipulate it, simply click its picture box when the Item, Content, or Rotation tool is active.

Suggested Typographic Preferences

To change or review the typographic settings for a periodical document, choose the Preferences/Typographic command in the Edit menu when the document is open. The settings you adjust most often for a periodical are the Maintain Leading option and the options in the Baseline Grid section of the dialog box. These are the ones most likely to affect copyfitting and text alignment in adjacent columns.

Suggested Tool Preferences

You usually want to aim for stylistic consistency when creating text and picture boxes for a periodical publication. Setting the options in the Tool Preferences dialog box (Preferences/Tools command, Edit menu) is a great way to achieve this consistency so that every text or picture box you create has the same characteristics automatically.

The Text Box Tool   Clicking the Text Box tool icon in the Tool Preferences dialog box lets you modify the default characteristics of text boxes in a specific document. Characteristics that you should standardize for stylistic consistency include the number of columns, gutter width, text box margins (Text Inset), first baseline placement, and background color and shade. You may also want to standardize text box frame (outline) characteristics and runaround settings. Chapters 4 and 5 discuss most standardized settings for text boxes; if you are interested in the design potential of text runarounds, also review Chapter 12.

The Picture Box Tools   There are four Picture Box tools, and you may want to set options differently for each one. Like Text Box tool settings, Picture Box settings made in the Tool Preferences dialog box affect all picture boxes you create in the active document. You can standardize the background color of picture boxes as well as their outline (frame) characteristics, if any. As you may recall from Chapter 8, you can also use this dialog box to standardize the scaling and cropping of imported pictures or even to specify a stylized angle of rotation or skew at which all pictures are imported automatically. Don't forget to set default runaround characteristics for picture boxes if your periodical makes use of background graphics or automatic text runarounds (see Chapter 12).

Designing a Usable Template

You saw in Chapter 3 that templates are a wonderful timesaving feature of QuarkXPress; templates can be used to great advantage when creating periodical-type documents. By definition, a periodical is published periodically; you must create variations of the document over and over again. By designing a template that can be used repeatedly, you can be much more productive.

A template is created exactly like a regular document, but it does not have the text and pictures of the final product, although it *can* contain text and pictures that are repeated from one edition of the periodical to the next. A good template for a regularly published periodical should also define the following:

☐   All the basic style sheets commonly used in the document (Chapter 6)

☐   The spot or process colors (Chapter 10) that you use in every issue

☐   Sets of hyphenation and justification rules (Chapter 6) that you apply to various style sheets

Setting Up Column Guides and Grids

In Chapter 2 you practiced setting up margin, column, and ruler guides when you created the *Haystackers' Herald*. (Remember that Quark provides column guides automatically when you specify the number of columns and the gutter space between columns.) Some designers prefer to use Quark's column guides as a flexible grid against which to align the text boxes on which they base a periodical's actual text columns.

Ruler guides are useful for positioning elements precisely on the page. Ruler guides are especially important for periodicals, in which layout and item positioning are more flexible than for longer documents. You may want to create repeating ruler guides by setting them upon master pages.

Designing Multiple Master Pages

Most periodical-type documents require multiple master pages. For example, newsletters and newspapers may need cover pages, inside facing pages, calendar pages, special editorial content pages, classifieds, and display ads. Magazines need master pages for the cover, table of contents, special columns, feature stories, classifieds, and display ads. Catalogs may need master pages for the cover, table of contents, feature product page, and the index.

Chapter 3 discusses master pages in detail. Refer to that chapter if you need to review how to set up and apply master pages.

 Tip Use the techniques described in Chapter 3 for naming master pages so you can identify the purpose of each master page when displaying it in the Document Layout palette.

Master Page Elements Typical master page elements for periodical-type documents include headers and footers, picture boxes, caption text boxes, *sidebars* (specially blocked off stories, usually with a different background color), pull quotes, screens, and bleeds.

 Tip If you cannot afford to use color on every page in a periodical, find out the *imposition* your print vendor is planning to use—the order in which page plates will be arranged on the printing press. Then, assign color only to pages that will be printed in the same signature or set of plates. Taking this step will reduce printing costs significantly.

To create multiple master pages for a newsletter, follow these steps:

1. Create a new document with Facing Pages, the desired number of columns, and no Automatic Text Box.

2. Create a master page with alternating headers and footers. (Left page headers and footers should be flush left, and right page headers and footers should be flush right.) A typical footer might be a text box that contains the automatic numbering code inserted by pressing CTRL-3. The header on the left page might be a text box with the name of the publication, and the header on the right page might be a text box with the date of the publication.

3. Insert another master page based on the first master page so that it retains the headers and footers.

4. On the second master page, add a picture box and a caption box. Define runaround settings for both.

5. Insert another master page based on the first master page.

6. On the third master page, create a text box to be used for sidebars.

7. Continue creating master pages with different elements such as groups of picture boxes, different-sized text boxes, and so on.

To create a master page for a special feature such as a calendar of events, follow these steps:

1. Insert a new master page based on the first master page so that the headers and footers are retained.

2. Create a text box.

3. Type the heading "Calendar of Events" in the text box.

4. Apply a color, font, and size to the headline with the Style options or create a style sheet and apply it to the text.

5. Draw another text box under the first one to list the events.

6. Draw a picture box inside the text box and define the Runaround Mode as None.

7. Import a picture into the box and use a tint or shade of a color, preferably less than 50 percent. You can import any picture on the master page because you will replace it each month on the actual page with a picture appropriate to the month.

Tip   If you do not wish to import a sample picture into the picture box, use the Colors palette or the Picture Specifications dialog box to apply a background shade. The Shade command in the Style menu is available only if the active picture box contains a picture.

Each month you can put a different picture in the box on the document page, and type the events for the month in the text box. Since the text box is transparent, it will overprint the shaded picture in the background as shown in Figure 13-1.

Using the Step and Repeat and Space/Align Commands
Periodicals often feature repeating design elements such as multiple same-size columns on facing pages. The Step and Repeat command in the Item menu, featured in Chapters 3 and 11, is especially handy for setting up items like these on master pages. When using Step and Repeat in a facing-pages document, remember to set Item Coordinates to Spread in the General Preferences dialog box so you can measure and position items continuously from left to right. Another timesaving tool for positioning design elements in periodicals is the Space/Align command featured in Chapter 11.

Copy Flow

There are two ways to control copy flow between text boxes in a Quark document: through the Automatic Text Box option in the New dialog box or by linking text boxes. Linking text boxes is the recommended method for periodicals, which tend to contain multiple stories that start on one page and continue on nonsequential pages. As you may recall from Chapter 3, you can link text boxes on either master pages or document pages.

Tip   Keep layout flexible for periodical-type documents by linking text boxes in document pages rather than in master pages.

Result of a picture box created on a master page

Vol. 8, No. 2

Company Takeover Thwarted by Employee Buyout

As you all know, our parent company, Consolidated Conglomerates, was threatened last year with a takeover by corporate raiders. Low profits, which prompted heavy stock sell-offs, put the company in a weak position and opened the way for the takeover which was spearheaded by A. J. Kronin and Associates.

Negotiations between Consolidated Conglomerates' CEO, John Compton, and the corporate raiders stalled the takeover allowing the employees time to amass enough stock to take voting control of the company.

"Valiant efforts will be richly rewarded."

At the annual stock meeting, the employees voted to retain ownership of the company, thus saving the company from being dismantled by the corporate raiders. Since last November profits have been increasing steadily and worker turnover has decreased dramatically. Compton attributes the current successes to employee involvement and said the valiant efforts to save the company would be richly rewarded.

Employee committees met daily during the takeover negotiations to come up with ways to save the company and increase

profits. Workers agreed to take a small cut in salary and work an additional fifteen minutes a day to help the company get back on its feet. In return, the employees will receive yearly stock options and profit-based bonuses. The committee continues to meet bi-monthly. ♣

Calendar of Events

March 2 ♣ 9:00 AM
Safety Committee Meeting - Board Room

March 5 ♣ 3:00 PM
Retirement Ceremony - Auditorium

March 9 ♣ 10:00 AM
Contest Awards - The Stanley Room

March 10 ♣ 1:00 PM
Executive Board Meeting - Board Room

March 16 ♣ 7:00 PM
Company dinner and dance - Essex House

March 19 ♣ 9:00 AM
User Group Meeting - Conference Room A

March 23 ♣ 12:00 PM
Award Luncheon - Cafetorium

March 30 ♣ 11:00 AM
OJT Training - Conference Room B

25 Year Service Awards Will Be Given in December

Picture box in background

Page 4

When setting up a newsletter or magazine, for example, you might create standard-sized text boxes on master pages, but without linking them. These text boxes would then be available on every document page, and you could resize them there or discard them as your layout requires. If you begin an article on page one and want to continue it on page four, you can make copy flow automatically between the two pages by linking the two text boxes manually.

Jump lines ("Continued on page x" and "Continued from page x") that display the appropriate page numbers automatically can also be created for linked articles. See the "Creating Jump Lines with Automatic Page References" section of Chapter 11 for a detailed example.

 Tip   You do not need to link jump line text boxes to each other, as long as they overlap the linked text boxes that actually contain the article.

Copyfitting

Before desktop publishing, copyfitting was a major headache for a layout artist. Too much copy meant that the layout artist had to redesign the page or have the copy reset in a smaller size type. An alternative was to cut some of the copy. Perhaps the artist could do this manually (a time-consuming chore), but if not, the copy would have to be reset. Copy that did not fill the given space was just as problematic. The remedies were similar (and as tedious) to having too much copy: artists either redesigned the page, reset the type in a larger size, or added more copy.

With the advent of desktop publishing, copyfitting is no longer a major task. Redesigning, resetting type, or cutting or adding copy can all be accomplished quickly.

When designing periodical-type publications, body copy for articles is usually set in the same size type, but justification, hyphenation, and font selection can affect copyfitting. Once the font and size are selected, page design and length of copy become the overriding factors in copyfitting. Figures 13-2 and 13-3 show a newsletter before and after copyfitting. The after version is more readable yet has more copy on the page. The article entitled "Union Vote" is not even in the first version of the newsletter.

 Tip   Typically, catalogs contain many different product entries with a photo and a little text for each. Copyfitting for such catalogs is easier if you use a separate text box for each product entry rather than linking a single text file across multiple text boxes.

The original newsletter

The Tool Time

Tool Workers Union Local 378   Committee for Worker Safety

January 1993 - Volume 5, Number 1

Retooling

The special government task force, funded by Resolution HR123-AC23456, has been gathering and correlating safety information particular to the tool and dye industry for the last five years. The final report from the task force is expected to be presented at the end of this year.

Preliminary findings were released this month, and the principal area of concern for the tool and dye industry is the number of accidents that occur during retooling.

Retooling is a big part of the tool and dye industry. It must be done quickly and efficiently to keep the production flow smooth. As we all know, because of the intricacy and the enormity of some retooling projects, accidents and injuries occur too frequently. The final report will give national statistics which are alarming.

When the report is given, another task force, funded by Resolution HR198-AJ34987, will study the findings and make recommendations. These recommendations could take several forms: federal inspection guidelines, industry standardization, and industry mandates.

Mandated recommendations will, of course, be made into law. At the current time our industry is not inundated with federal laws, but such could be the case when the final recommendations are acted upon. The first legislation is expected by the third quarter of next year.

Safety lobbyists are now organizing to be sure that the recommendations made are not only in the best interest of safety, but also in the best financial interests of our industry. The lobby group will study proposed legislation and report to local unions.

If you are interested in contributing funds to the lobby group, contact your union representative for more details.

Inside this Issue:
From the Editor - p. 2
Tool Maintenance - p. 2
Union Meeting - p.3
Election of Officers - p.3
What's New - p.3
Calendar - p.4
New Labor Laws - p.4

Design Tips

When designing periodical-type documents, use headlines, pull quotes, reversed type, rules, framed text boxes, and screens to enhance

FIGURE 13-3   The makeover

Tool Workers Union
Local 378

Committee
for
Worker
Safety

January 1993
Volume 5, Number 1

Retooling

The special government task force, funded by Resolution HR123-AC23456, has been gathering and correlating safety information particular to the tool and dye industry for the last five years. The final report from the task force is expected to be presented at the end of this year.

Preliminary findings were released this month, and the principal area of concern for the tool and dye industry is the number of accidents that occur during retooling.

Retooling is a big part of the tool and dye industry. It must be done quickly and efficiently to keep the production flow smooth. As we all know, because of the intricacy and the enormity of some retooling projects, accidents and injuries occur too frequently. The final report will give national statistics which are alarming.

When the report is given, another task force, funded by Resolution HR198-AJ34987, will study the findings and make recommendations. These recommendations could take several forms: federal inspection guidelines, industry standardization, and industry mandates.

Mandated recommendations will, of course, be made into law. At the current time our industry is not inundated with federal laws, but such could be the case when the final recommendations are acted upon. The first legislation is expected by the third quarter of next year.

Safety lobbyists are now organizing to be sure that the recommendations made are not only in the best interest of safety, but also in the best financial interests of our industry. The lobby group will study proposed legislation and report to local unions.

If you are interested in contributing funds to the lobby group, contact your union representative for more details.

Union Vote

In the last monthly meeting of Local 378, held December 2, 1992, a vote was taken on the motion to change the monthly meeting to a bimontly meeting. The motion carried by a vote of 123 to 62.

The next meeting will be held on Februray 5, 1993. During this meeting vendors from several large tool manufacturers, names to be announced at a later date, will be present to demonstrate new technology.

Inside the Tool

the text components of page layouts (see Chapter 6). Size headlines, subheads, and bylines to indicate the hierarchy of importance. Use subheads and pull quotes to break up long blocks of text. Use rules, tinted text box backgrounds, shadow boxes, and screens to emphasize important or special features. For examples of some of these design tips, see Figure 13-4.

Use the right number and size of columns for the overall layout, but avoid boring regularity by balancing the columns with visual interest such as white space, pictures, double-column spreads, or an occasional odd-sized column. Background graphics, rotated or otherwise stylized

Examples of design tips

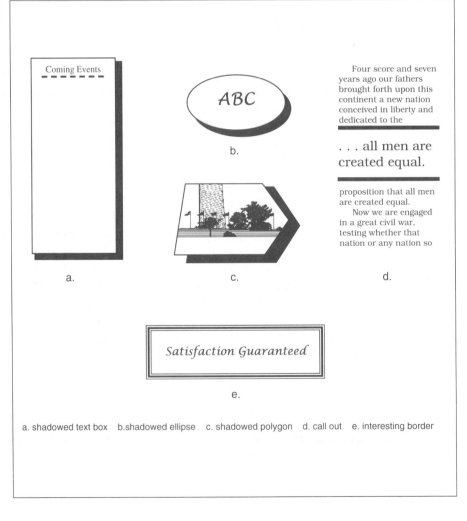

a. shadowed text box   b.shadowed ellipse   c. shadowed polygon   d. call out   e. interesting border

pictures, picture box outlines, and picture or picture box background tints can add liveliness, too.

Producing Promotional Materials

When you produce promotional materials such as advertisements, flyers, brochures, and posters, some of the basic design rules fly out the window. The purpose of promotional material is to get attention, and sometimes it is necessary to *break the rules* to get that attention. A good promotional piece must stand out from all the others so the reader will get the intended message and act on it.

Since promotional pieces are so "free-wheeling," you will probably not be able to use a template for most of the pieces that you create. And because you will not have a template, you will also have to set preferences each time you create a new document.

Setting Preferences for Promotional Pieces

The type of promotional piece that you are creating will dictate the preferences that you set, so it is impossible to make any recommendations beyond a few general ones. Naturally, you will want to keep the pasteboard as wide as possible; with promotional materials as with periodicals, layout changes are likely to be frequent. Since color and pictures often play a more important role than text in such documents, you will also want to pay special attention to all preferences having to do with graphics. For example:

☐ Application Preferences: Guide Colors, Trap, Low Resolution TIFF, 8-Bit TIFF, 256 Levels of Gray

☐ General Preferences: Framing, Guides, Auto Picture Import, Greek Pictures, Accurate Blends

☐ Tool Preferences: Magnification tool, Picture Box tools, Line tools

Note See the "Setting Preferences for Periodicals" section earlier in this chapter for tips on determining trap settings and working with a service bureau when you have changed Quark's default trap preferences.

Grabbing Attention with Design

The purpose of a promotional piece is to grab attention. You can do this with brilliant color, stylized graphics, lots of white space, and minimal text. You may also want to use a sophisticated drawing or image editing package to generate the original graphics that you stylize in Quark.

The basic design principles that govern promotional pieces are simplicity, contrast, organization, and identity. Simplicity makes a piece easier to read so the reader can find your message faster. Contrast emphasizes the most important parts of your message. Organization leads the reader through the logical progression of your message, and a strong identity establishes the reader's positive feeling for your message. Figures 13-5 and 13-6 show examples of these four basic design principles.

Figure 13-5 is an ad that might be placed in a newspaper or magazine. It uses a minimal amount of text and great contrast in font size. The organization is logical and the typeface used in the ad establishes a feeling of trust and professionalism.

Figure 13-6 shows a simple flyer. Notice the logical organization of information. The most important information, the fact that there will be an auction, is displayed prominently at the top of the flyer. Other important details about the auction such as where and when are listed next. The least important information (about the gallery and credit cards) is displayed at the bottom of the flyer. Notice that the typeface used conveys the idea of "fine art."

Using QuarkXPress as a Word Processor

Because text is usually kept to a minimum in promotional pieces, it is easier to enter text directly with QuarkXPress than to import text from

An ad that uses the four basic design principles

a word processor. Since Quark provides a spell checking feature, you won't have to worry about misspelled words in the copy.

Producing Longer Documents

There is a wide range of design and layout possibilities among books and manuals. This category of documents includes, for example, company procedural or policy manuals, instruction booklets for equipment,

FIGURE
13-6

A flyer that uses the four basic design principles

Auction

important works of

Fine Art

Agam❖ Altman ❖ Alvar ❖ Boulanger ❖ Cambier ❖ Cezanne
Chagall ❖ Chemiakin ❖ Cobelle ❖ Dali ❖ Dus ❖ Erte ❖ Fanch
Goya ❖ He Neng ❖ Huchet ❖ Kipniss ❖ Lautrec ❖ Lebadang
Maimon ❖ Manet ❖ Markos ❖ Mouly ❖ Nierman ❖ Picot
Rembrandt ❖ Renoir ❖ Tarkay ❖ Vasarely ❖ Wolfson and more . . .

Oakmont Hotel
1900 West Continental Boulevard
New York, New York

Sunday July 26, 1992
Preview 2:00 p.m.
Auction 3:00 p.m.

The auction will include the following:
- ❖ More than 300 custom framed works
- ❖ Paintings and watercolors
- ❖ Original Old Master prints
- ❖ Signed and numbered original lithographs
- ❖ Etchings, engravings and serigraphs
- ❖ 18th and 19th century Ukiyo-e Japanese prints

Bidding expected in the range of $100 to $4000, some items higher. Collection exceeds $525,00 at gallery list prices. Prices are printed in catalog.

Credit lines available up to $50,000. Credit line approvals may be made by phone, fax, or at the auction. We are please to fill your requests for catalogs and buyers' guides at the auction.

1-800-752-6000
Fax 1-800-752-5000

❖

All Major Credit Cards Accepted

documentation for software, fiction and nonfiction books, cookbooks, and anthologies.

Setting Preferences for Longer Documents

Template documents are useful when a manual will require occasional updating, or when a book is part of a series that features a standard design. If you design a template for a long document that will be part of a series, set preferences when the template document is open. That way, your settings will apply to every spin-off document that you create from the template.

Suggested Application Preferences

Application preferences apply to all documents, not just to the one you are working on. Still, there are several options in the Application Preferences dialog box that can make your work with long documents more efficient.

Trap   Although books and manuals usually make less flamboyant use of color than do other types of publications, color is becoming more economical to use in long documents. Books and manuals are usually printed on high-speed presses, where the likelihood of color registration problems is higher than for full-color documents printed on specialized equipment. So if your long documents use at least one spot or process color in addition to black, you should pay careful attention to the Trap settings in the Application Preferences dialog box. Find out from your print vendor how many fractional points of trapping are advisable for the press and the paper stock that will be used for the printing job.

Auto Library Save   While mass-market books and policy manuals are mostly text, technical books and corporate manuals tend to contain many pictures and/or rules. You may find it useful to use Quark's Library feature (discussed in Chapter 11) to archive reusable design and picture items in a book, in which case you may want to activate the Auto Library Save option in the Application Preferences dialog box. If the Auto Library Save option is checked, Quark saves a library automatically each time you add an item to or delete it from a Library palette.

Low Resolution TIFF   If the long documents you produce contain TIFF images in the form of screen shots or digital photographs, activate the Low Resolution TIFF option. This setting causes Quark to represent TIFF images at only half the display resolution of your monitor (see Chapter 4), which should help speed screen redraw.

Reg. Marks Offset   Some print vendors are particular about the placement of registration and crop marks on the imagesetter output they receive for long documents. Inquire about the ideal settings for the press that will run the job, and adjust the Reg. Marks Offset value accordingly.

Suggested General Preferences

Several preferences in the General Preferences dialog box are relevant to long documents. The type of book or manual you are producing (text-heavy or graphics-intensive) and the complexity of your design determine which settings are appropriate for the job at hand.

Auto Page Insertion   If a book or manual is divided into chapters and you are creating the publication as a single document, use the End of Section setting. If each chapter is a separate document, choose End of Document.

Item Coordinates   Most long documents are facing-pages documents. During the master page design phase, you may want to set Item Coordinates to Spread. During the layout process, you may find it more convenient to reset this option to Page so that the horizontal ruler begins at zero on the page you are working on.

Auto Picture Import   If a long document contains pictures, set Auto Picture Import to On (verify) so that Quark will warn you if any picture files have been modified. This is especially important if you are part of a documentation team working on a network, where many team members have access to and can edit the files that make up the document.

Master Page Items   With books and manuals, it is often more important to be stylistically consistent throughout than to try adventurous local modifications on individual document pages. Therefore, in most cases you may want to set this option to Delete Changes so that local modifications to a document page will be removed when you apply a master page to it.

Greek Pictures   The longer the document, the more you need to greek any pictures that it contains. If a book or manual contains more than a few pictures, activate the Greek Pictures option to speed screen redraw as much as possible.

Suggested Typographic Preferences

Since books and manuals are often text-heavy, be sure the settings in the Typographic Preferences dialog box meet your needs. The default settings in this dialog box are fairly standard and are probably suitable for your document. Refer to Chapters 4 and 6 for more information on optimizing these settings.

Tip   If you plan to lock body copy to the baseline grid (Paragraph Formats dialog box), set the Increment option in the Typographic Preferences dialog box to the same value as (or a multiple of) the leading used in the body copy.

Suggested Tool Preferences

In the Tool Preferences dialog box, standardize settings for at least the Text Box tool and the most commonly used Picture Box tool. Many books and manuals require *vertical justification*, or facing pages in which text aligns evenly at both the top and bottom of the pages. For such documents, you may want to set Vertical Alignment to Justify for the Text Box tool. Avoid setting the Inter Paragraph Max value to higher than a few points, however, unless you want to risk irregular-looking spacing between style sheets for the sake of copyfitting.

Tip   There are alternatives to setting up automatic vertical justification through the Vertical Alignment and Inter Paragraph Max options. For example, you could achieve vertical justification by adjusting text run-around specifications for picture boxes or by locally formatting paragraphs on specific document pages. If copy flow then changes due to editing of the manuscript, you can remove local formatting to modified paragraphs by applying first No Style and then the original style sheet to them (refer to Chapter 6).

Be sure to specify the desired Frame settings and Runaround settings for both the Text Box tool and the Picture Box tool(s). Designs for serious books and manuals tend to be less graphically adventuresome than designs for periodicals and promotional material; in most cases, you should set Runaround to the Item mode for both text boxes and picture boxes.

Designing a Usable Template

Once again, it makes sense to design a template for books in a series or for manuals that have to be updated occasionally. For example, if you have to edit an existing instruction booklet every time the product is revised or create a new instruction booklet every time a new product comes out, it would be wise to design a template that can be used for all instruction booklets.

Designing Multiple Master Pages

Whether or not you design a template, you should set up separate master pages for body copy pages, chapter opener pages, part openers, body text pages, front matter, the table of contents, the index, appendixes, bibliographies, and so on.

Tip Remember to link text boxes at the master or document page level so that text will flow automatically between pages that use different masters—between the opening page in a chapter and the body copy page that follows it, for example.

Setting Up Page Numbers for Different Sections

Books and manuals frequently use different types of numbers for different sections. For example, the pages in a book that precede the first chapter page may use lowercase Roman numerals (i, ii, iii, and so on), while the chapter pages use Arabic numbers.

To designate a special section for numbering, display the Document Layout palette in document pages mode. Click the icon for the page where the section should begin and then click the page number under the icon to display the Section dialog box described in Chapter 11 and shown here:

(You can also access the Section dialog box by displaying the document page you want to use as the first in a section and then choosing the Section command in the Page menu.) You can specify a prefix, the starting number, and the format. For preliminary pages in a document, you could specify a starting number of 1 and a lowercase Roman numeral format. For the first page of chapter one, you could specify a prefix of "1-", a starting number of 1, and an Arabic format. For the first page of chapter two (page 15, for example), you could specify a prefix of "2-", a starting number of 15, and an Arabic format. See Chapter 11 for more information about setting up section numbering in a document.

 Remember Quark displays page numbers in a document automatically only if you have created a text box on the master pages that contains the page number code (inserted by pressing CTRL-3). If you set up multiple master pages for the document, be sure to create such a text box on every master page.

 Caution Sections started on right-facing pages should have odd starting numbers and sections starting on left-facing pages should have even starting numbers. You may have to insert blank pages to accomplish this.

Designing and Archiving Repeating Items

Some items such as standard-sized picture boxes, text boxes for captions, and icons are used repeatedly throughout a book or manual. These repeating items can be created once and added to a library (see Chapter 11). When ready to use them, you can drag them from the Library palette and position them in the document at the desired location. This is a great timesaving technique when compared to copying a standardized item from a template document every time you need it and then pasting it into the current document page.

 Tip Store all your library items for a given document in a single directory to prevent deleting or moving them accidentally. Library items are valid only if the corresponding files (in the case of external picture files, that is) remain in their original locations on the hard drive or network server.

Designing Style Sheets

Various style sheets should be designed in advance for books and manuals. You will need style sheets for chapter titles, subheads, captions, and tables that use intricate tab stops. (See Chapter 6 to review style sheet design.)

 Tip Using style sheets to format a document that is text-heavy is always preferable to local formatting. Reserve the use of local formatting for special purposes such as copyfitting.

Word Processing and Production Tips

Due to the large amount of text that books and manuals contain, it is likely that you will produce the text with a word processing program and import it rather than input the text within Quark. If you do use a word processing program, you have the added capability of inserting XPress Tags codes as you type. You may wish to set up macros in your word processor for inserting some of the more complex XPress Tags code strings. (Refer to Chapter 7 to review the exact codes for XPress Tags.)

Because books and manuals are subject to multiple revisions that cause text to *walk* from one page to another, it is advisable to insert picture boxes near the end of the production process if possible. If the layout depends on the placement of pictures, then it is best to anchor them with the text that they refer to as explained in Chapter 12. Then, even if revised text walks to another page, the picture will follow it.

Many books and manuals spread the text of each page so that the first and last lines of text align on facing pages. This is called vertical justification, and it can be set in the Tools Preferences dialog box if you click Modify for the Text tool and then select Justify for the Vertical Alignment.

If you are creating a book that contains a list of items, such as a directory or a catalog, your data probably originates in a database program, not in a word processor. If you import the data directly into Quark, you will have to do a tremendous amount of formatting—or will you? There are at least two solutions that can greatly speed layout time in such situations.

If the database is Microsoft Excel or another Windows application that can act as an OLE server (see Chapter 8), you can link or embed it directly into a Quark document, retaining the native formatting of the source program. You may also be able to purchase a third-party utility for formatting database information according to XPress Tags codes. As Appendix A explains, the Macintosh version of QuarkXPress has an established tradition of third-party developers who provide utilities for every conceivable Quark documentation need, including database publishing. A number of these independent developers have announced intentions to provide similar utilities for the Windows version of QuarkXPress. Some of these utilities may be available by the time you read this—call Quark XChange at 1-800-788-7557 for details.

Producing Business Documents

Like books and manuals, business documents are mostly text-based, but they tend to be shorter and more highly structured. Typical business documents include forms, invoices, purchase orders, price lists, business cards, stationery, business plans, proposals, resumes, quarterly reports, annual reports, and so on.

Setting Preferences for Business Documents

Of all the document categories discussed in this chapter, the business documents category probably contains the most divergent group of documents. Therefore, it is not easy to recommend preference settings. If you create documents such as reports, proposals, resumes, and price lists, you can refer to the preference settings discussed in this chapter for books and manuals. Preferences for business cards and stationery most closely resemble those for the promotional category. That leaves forms, invoices, and purchase orders. These documents, which can be referred to collectively as *preprinted forms*, do have some recommended preferences that you will want to note.

Suggested Application Preferences for Preprinted Forms

Pay close attention to settings for the following options in the Application Preferences dialog box: Guide Colors, Pasteboard Width, and Auto Library Save. When designing preprinted forms, you will rely heavily on column and ruler guides, so set colors for these that will be easily distinguishable on your monitor. Make the pasteboard as wide as you can, too. Activate the Auto Library Save option so Quark updates any open library files automatically each time you add or delete an item.

Suggested General Preferences for Preprinted Forms

Base the Horizontal and Vertical Measures settings on how the form will be filled out. Will the form be rolled into a typewriter, or will it be used with a word processing program? If users fill out the form using a typewriter, it is easy enough for the typist to adjust the platen (for each line on the form if necessary) so the cells in the form line up with the print element.

If users fill out the form using a word processing program and a printer, take care to position the lines so that they fall at standard increments. Most word processing programs still use a vertical scale of six or eight lines per inch. Word processor operators who must use preprinted forms are usually very frustrated because forms designed using non-standard spacing increments are almost impossible to align. When creating forms with Quark, pay as much attention to mechanics as you do to aesthetics.

Other settings to be carefully considered are Auto Page Insertion, Framing, Guides, Item Coordinates, and Master Page Items. How you set these depends on the particular document you are creating.

Suggested Typographic and Tool Preferences for Preprinted Forms

The most important option in the Typographic Preferences dialog box is the Baseline Grid. If the form will be filled out on a typewriter or printer that prints at six lines per inch, begin by defining a Baseline Grid increment of 12 points (one line is equal to 12 points). Then, when you define style sheets for the form, activate the Lock to Baseline Grid option in the Paragraph Formats dialog box so that all lines in the form are spaced automatically in increments of 12 points. See Chapters 5 and 6 for more details on Baseline Grid settings.

In the Tool Preferences dialog box, the Text Box tool is probably the most important tool to standardize for creating preprinted forms. Depending on the form you are designing, you will probably want to specify one column for the text box, no frame, and an Item runaround.

Designing a Usable Template

Some business documents should have templates; other documents that are one-time designs do not need them. Reports, resumes, proposals, and price lists are candidates for templates because they are repeatable.

Setting Up Column Guides and Grids

If you are designing preprinted forms, column guides and grids are extremely important when it comes to placing items on the form. Displaying the baseline grid can also be helpful, especially if you define the increment between grid lines to match the spacing that will be used by the typewriter or printer on which users will fill out or print out the forms.

Designing Multiple Master Pages

If you are working with reports or other documents that contain several pages with varying designs, design multiple master pages as discussed in this chapter and in Chapter 3.

Creating Style Sheets

Style sheets for reports, proposals, price lists, and so on are no different from style sheets designed for books and manuals. If you are defining style sheets for a preprinted form, however, you should include style sheets that use the underline character as a leader for tab stops. (See Chapter 6 for a detailed explanation of tabs and an example of a form that is created with a right-aligned tab and an underline fill character.) You can use tab stops to simulate the look of multiple columns, even if the form contains only a single one-column text box.

To standardize the spacing between lines on the form, use the Space Before and the Space After options in the Paragraph Formats dialog box. If you have text locked to the baseline grid, be sure that the Space Before and the Space After measurements work well with the Baseline Grid increment specified in the Typographic Preferences dialog box. (See Chapters 5 and 6 for a full discussion of the baseline grid.)

Using Single or Multiple Text Boxes

When designing some business documents, you will be able to use one or two text boxes per page. For example, a one-column report could use a single text box, while a two-column report might use two text boxes. When you are designing forms, however, it is better to work with multiple text boxes. If you have to redesign the form it is much easier to move the text boxes around than to cut and paste individual segments of text.

PART

V

Output

CHAPTER

Printing Your Documents

After you lay out a Quark document, what happens next? How do you get that masterpiece out into the world where your message can finally reach the intended audience? By printing it, that's how. The ability to print or *output* a document without errors is the foundation upon which all desktop publishing rests.

There are four steps involved in printing any document from Quark:

☐ Educating yourself about the *output requirements* for the document—matching the content of the document to the way it should be printed for best results

☐ Managing fonts, picture files, and *auxiliary files*—any custom kerning tables, tracking tables, and hyphenation exceptions that go with your document

☐ Choosing a printer or other *output device* and setting it up correctly

☐ Using the Print dialog box in Quark

The bulk of this chapter is devoted to the *mechanics* of printing from Quark—managing files, setting up an output device, and actually printing the document. But your ability to make the final printed product look as you intended often depends on your understanding of the document's output requirements. See the "Quark and Prepress Basics" section near the end of this chapter for more background information.

Printing from Quark: An Overview

We make some basic assumptions in this chapter about what kinds of documents you produce in QuarkXPress for Windows and how you output them. Most likely, you create some documents for informal distribution within an organization and others that are printed commercially for higher-quality results. When you produce "informal" documents, a 300-dpi laser printer may be the only printing device you need. When producing more commercial documents, however, you will probably use a laser printer only to print draft versions. To output the final version of the document in a format that a print vendor can use (photographic paper or film), you will use an imagesetter or other high-resolution output device (600-3600 dpi) at your company or at a service bureau. Working with a service bureau and creating PostScript output files are discussed in more detail in the "Quark and Prepress Basics" section at the end of the chapter, but you will see references to these subjects wherever they apply throughout the chapter.

This chapter discusses three common types of output devices: low-resolution non-PostScript printers, low-resolution PostScript printers, and high-resolution PostScript imagesetters. The options available to you in Quark's Printer Setup and Print dialog boxes depend not only on the general type of output device you are using, but also on the features provided with a specific printer model. In explaining dialog box options, this chapter uses the Hewlett-Packard LaserJet III and the QMS PS-810 to represent low-resolution non-PostScript and PostScript printers, respectively. Two popular imagesetter lines—the Agfa 9000 Series PS and the Linotronic 530—represent high-resolution PostScript imagesetters.

 Note   Many low-resolution non-PostScript printers can perform like PostScript printers if you use PostScript cartridges or software-based PostScript emulators. If you have adapted your non-PostScript printer in this way, use a PostScript printer driver, not the driver for your specific printer model.

Managing Font, Picture, and Auxiliary Files for Printing

Most Quark documents use pictures, special fonts, and/or auxiliary files such as custom kerning or tracking tables. If you have used your own system to lay out the document you want to print, you already control the fonts, picture files, and auxiliary files that compose the document. If, however, you are printing a document that was created by someone else who used a different system and a different type of printer, you may have to make some adjustments. For example, you might have to change a font because your system does not have the font used on the original system.

Most settings in Quark are saved automatically with the document to which they apply. Font files and picture files, though, are exceptions. So are any custom kerning and tracking tables or custom hyphenation exceptions that you may have created for a specific document. Before you choose the Print command from Quark's File menu, make sure you have these files where Quark expects to find them.

Managing Fonts

When you open a document, if the document contains any fonts not currently installed on your system, Quark displays a warning like this:

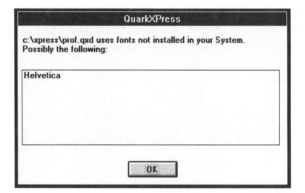

At this point, you have two choices. If you want to use the font originally specified for the document, you must install it on your system using the Windows Control Panel (for TrueType fonts) or Adobe Type Manager (for Adobe Type 1 fonts). If you cannot obtain the required font, use the Font Usage dialog box to replace the missing font or fonts with others that *are* available on your system. To display the Font Usage dialog box shown next, choose the Font Usage command from the Utilities menu. This dialog box recognizes both Adobe Type 1 and TrueType fonts.

Caution If you substitute a new font for one that was originally in the document, text may reflow. Check the document thoroughly before printing to ensure that line endings are correct.

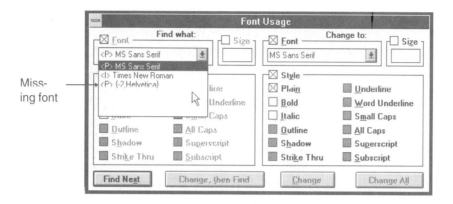

The left side of the dialog box displays information about the fonts that are currently used in the document. If a specific font is not installed on your system, it appears enclosed in brackets with a –2 in front of it, like the Helvetica font in the example just shown.

To substitute another font, use the fields on the right side of the dialog box. Use the Font drop-down list box to substitute a specific font available to your system, the Size field to change the point size, and the Style options to make any changes to the occurrences of specific type styles. The Font Usage dialog box works just like the Find/Change dialog box; refer to the "Using Quark's Search and Replace Features" section of Chapter 5 for more information on how to use this dialog box.

Managing Picture Files for Printing

As you may recall from Chapter 8, you can incorporate pictures into a Quark document in one of several ways: by importing them, by linking or embedding them, or by pasting them from the clipboard. Embedded and pasted pictures are actually part of the Quark document, so you do not have to take any special steps to keep track of them for printing purposes. Imported and linked pictures are another matter, however. Before beginning any print operation, always check the Picture Usage dialog box to monitor the status of imported pictures and the Links dialog box to update OLE-linked pictures that have been changed. Unless Quark knows where these pictures are, you will obtain only a low-resolution version of them when you print.

Managing Imported Pictures

When you import a picture into a document using the Get Picture command in the File menu, Quark takes note of where the file is stored and expects to find that file in the same place every time you open the document. If you move or delete the original picture file and then print the document into which you imported it, Quark will print only the low-resolution representation of the picture that you normally see on your monitor. This can lead to unpleasant surprises, especially if you are using an imagesetter to output the document at high resolution!

To help Quark keep track of picture files associated with a document, set Auto Picture Import to On (verify) in the General Preferences dialog box. With this setting, Quark notifies you upon opening a document if one or more pictures have been modified or are missing from their expected locations. Then, you can use the Picture Usage dialog box (described in Chapter 8) to update Quark's pointers to the picture file. Routinely check the Picture Usage dialog box before printing in any case, to monitor the name of each imported picture file, the page on which it appears, and the format and current status of the file.

Managing Linked Pictures

The Picture Usage dialog box works well for imported pictures, but it does not check the status of pictures that you have linked to a document using OLE (see Chapter 8). To monitor the status of linked pictures, use the Links dialog box, accessed through the Links command in the Edit menu. Chapter 8 includes an illustration of the Links dialog box.

The Update option in the Links dialog box determines whether Quark updates a modified linked picture automatically or only when prompted. When you set Update to Automatic, Quark updates any modified linked pictures automatically as soon as you open the document that contains them. Set Update to Manual if you prefer to be prompted for an update. If a linked picture file has been moved from its original location, the Links dialog box lists the picture as Unavailable; you can click the Change Links button to find the missing file and reestablish the link.

Managing Auxiliary Files and Custom Typographical Settings

Many Quark users may never create custom kerning tables, tracking tables, or hyphenation exception dictionaries for their documents (see Chapter 7). If you are one of the typographical experts who does, be aware that these auxiliary files and custom settings can spell trouble if a document is printed from a computer system other than the one in which it was laid out (at a service bureau that outputs a document for you, for example). That's because the kerning, tracking, and hyphenation settings in Quark's main preferences file, xpress.prf, *must* be the same in both the system in which the document was laid out and the system that outputs it. Otherwise, the text may reflow incorrectly in the printed document.

There is an important step you can take to avoid havoc caused by custom typographical settings that don't match. The next time you open a document whose kerning, tracking, or hyphenation settings you edited during a previous session, Quark displays the "Non-Matching Preferences" dialog box described in the "Editing Kerning and Tracking Tables" section of Chapter 7. Choose the Keep Document Settings option in this dialog box to save these altered settings with the *document file only*, leaving the xpress.prf file unaltered.

Caution   Do not choose XPress Preferences, or you will alter your xpress.prf file permanently.

Tip   If you send a .qxd document file to a service bureau to be output from their copy of QuarkXPress, instruct them to choose the Keep Document Settings option if they encounter a non-matching preferences message when they open your document. This step will protect the typographical integrity of your document.

Tip   The most trouble-free way to output a document to an imagesetter at a remote service bureau is to create your own PostScript output file rather than let the service bureau output the document from the original .qxd file. When you create your own output files, there is no risk of encountering non-matching preferences in someone else's copy of QuarkXPress. It won't matter if you have altered your xpress.prf file settings.

Choosing and Setting Up a Printer

After ensuring that your fonts, picture files, and any custom typographical settings for a document are in order, the next step is to select an output device and set it up. You can select and set up a printer either by choosing the Printer Setup command in the File menu or by choosing the Print command and then clicking the Setup button in the Print dialog box. Either way, the Printer Setup dialog box appears. Figure 14-1 shows settings available for a typical low-resolution PostScript printer (the QMS PS-810) and for the Agfa 9000 Series PS of high-resolution imagesetters.

The Printer Setup dialog box includes options for selecting a printer and adjusting orientation, paper size, image settings, halftone frequency, resolution, material, and settings related to the output medium. Several of the options in this dialog box apply to high-resolution imagesetters only. Only options that are available for the current printer are selectable.

Printer, Orientation, and Paper Settings

To select a printer, click the Default Printer button or select a printer from the list under the Specific Printer button. If you select the Default Printer, the printer installed as the default printer in Windows will be used. (The name of the printer appears below the Default Printer button.)

If you select a different printer from the drop-down list, Quark automatically activates the Specific Printer button. Only printers that have been installed in Windows appear in this list. If you need to install an additional printer driver, do so from the Windows Control Panel.

 Tip If you are creating a PostScript output file to be printed by an imagesetter at a remote service bureau, use the Windows driver that is specifically tailored to the type of imagesetter that will be used. Get a

FIGURE
14-1

The Printer Setup dialog box with Agfa 9000 PS and QMS PS-810 printers chosen

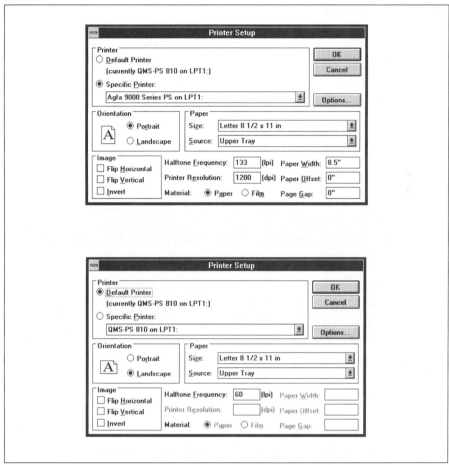

driver from the service bureau if the correct driver is not available in your version of Windows.

Orientation

Page orientation gives you two choices—Portrait and Landscape. Click Portrait to output the document in a format that is taller than it is wide. Click Landscape to choose a format that is wider than it is tall.

Tip When printing a long document to a roll-fed imagesetter, you can save on the amount of RC paper or film used by choosing Landscape orientation.

Paper

The Paper settings include Size and Source. Each option has a drop-down list that displays the choices available for the particular printer or imagesetter that you have selected. The paper sizes available will vary, depending on the specific printer or imagesetter model selected.

The paper Source determines how paper is fed into the printer. Choices may include Upper Tray, Lower Tray, Envelope, Manual, Envelope Manual Feed, and so on. For most popular imagesetters, Upper Tray is the only option, because paper or film is fed into the imagesetter from a roll that is housed in a cassette.

Caution Always specify a paper size that is at least as large as the document Page Size, or only part of a page will print on a single sheet of paper. If you print crop marks and registration marks with a document, the paper size must be larger than the Page Size. You control the Page Size through the Document Setup command in the File menu.

Image Settings

Use the Flip Horizontal, Flip Vertical, and Invert options to output a document to an imagesetter in film negative format. To reverse the pages from left to right, select Flip Horizontal. To reverse the pages from top to bottom, select Flip Vertical. To print a negative image, select Invert.

When sending a document to a service bureau as a PostScript output file, ask your service bureau for recommended Image settings *before* you make adjustments in the Printer Setup dialog box. For example, if the imagesetter is set for negative, emulsion side down, and you want a positive, activate the Invert and Flip Horizontal options.

Halftone Frequency

Halftone Frequency, available for PostScript printers and imagesetters only, determines the number of lines per inch (lpi) that Quark uses to print halftone pictures, shaded text, picture and text box backgrounds and frames, process color separations, and images with Normal Screen applied. The settings range from 15 to 400, with 60 lpi as the default. Laser printers give their best results with halftone frequencies between 53 and 75 lpi. For imageset documents, line frequencies typically range from 85 to 200 lpi depending on the nature of the document, the type of printing press that will be used, and the paper stock on which the document will ultimately be printed. Ask your service bureau and print vendor for recommendations. The "Quark and Prepress Basics" section later in this chapter contains additional guidelines for selecting a halftone frequency based on the content of a document.

 Tip Although imported photographic pictures normally output at the number of lines per inch specified by the Halftone Frequency option, you can override this value by accessing the Picture Screening Specifications dialog box (Other Screen command, Style menu). Any adjustments you make in the Picture Screening Specifications dialog box apply only to the currently active image. Other images in the document print at the default Halftone Frequency.

 Tip See Chapter 9 for a discussion of the relationship between halftone frequency, printer resolution, and the number of gray shades that can be reproduced.

Printer Resolution

The Printer Resolution option is available only for printers and imagesetters that support multiple resolutions. Imagesetters typically print at one of several available fixed resolutions. If you are creating a PostScript output file for output by an imagesetter, make sure that the imagesetter actually supports the resolution you define. Ask your service bureau about your options.

Material

The Material options let you specify the *output medium*—the paper or film on which your document will be printed. Click Paper for photographic paper (also known as *RC paper*) or Film for clear film. Only imagesetters support both RC paper and film.

Paper Width, Paper Offset, Page Gap

The last three options in the Printer Setup dialog box apply only if the currently selected printer is a roll-fed imagesetter. These options are grayed if you are setting up a non-PostScript printer or a PostScript printer that is not an imagesetter. Ask your service bureau for the recommended settings for their imagesetter model.

The Paper Width field specifies the width of the paper or film in the imagesetter. Quark centers the printed image on the width specified in the Paper Width Field.

The Paper Offset value specifies the distance from the left edge of the paper or film at which the pages will be printed. The default value is 0", but you may wish to increase this distance so that you or your service bureau can cut the pages apart more easily. If you adjust this option, keep the page size in mind and be careful not to shift the normal position of the page beyond the size of the paper or film.

The Page Gap option establishes a vertical distance between pages as they are printed on the roll. Use this option to separate the images (pages).

 Tip   For documents that contain multiple-page spreads, the Page Gap setting specifies the amount of space placed between spreads, not between individual pages in the spread.

Options

The Options button in the Printer Setup dialog box provides access to another dialog box containing options that are available for the currently selected printer. These options originate in Microsoft Windows, not

Quark, and vary according to which version of Windows you are using and the type of printer you have selected. The next two sections discuss options for PostScript output devices (represented by the Agfa 9000 series of imagesetters) and non-PostScript printers (represented by the Hewlett-Packard LaserJet III). Keep in mind that the available options may look slightly different for other printers.

PostScript Device Options

When you select options for a PostScript printer or imagesetter, a dialog box similar to this appears:

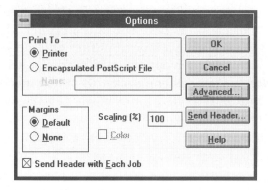

Print to Printer   Select this option to send the output directly to the printer. The currently selected printer must be physically connected to your system in order for this to work.

Print to Encapsulated PostScript File   Select this option and enter a filename to send the output to an .eps or .prn file. Typically, you choose this option when preparing a PostScript output file that an imagesetter at a remote service bureau will print. Such files consist of PostScript code that tells the imagesetter how to reproduce the document.

 Note   Under Windows 3.1, Print to Encapsulated PostScript File is activated automatically if the currently selected printer is not physically connected to your computer.

Margins   For this option, select Default (as defined in Windows) or None.

Scaling   Enter a percentage in the Scaling field if you want to reduce or enlarge the document when it prints. To enlarge each page, enter a number greater than 100. To reduce the size of each page, enter a number less than 100.

Color   The Color option is available (and activated) only for printers, such as the QMS ColorScript 100, that can actually print multiple colors. Although imagesetters can prepare color separations by printing shades of gray on separate sheets of paper or film, they are actually black-and-white printing devices.

Send Header with Each Job   To print using a PostScript device, Windows must send header information to the printer or imagesetter. If the header information is not sent to the printer, the file will not print. If printing to a file or to a shared printer on a network, activate the Send Header with Each Job option. If the currently selected printer is directly connected to your system, leave this option inactive and click the Send Header button to access the Send Header dialog box shown next. This dialog box lets you send a header manually to the printer or to a file the very first time you print during a work session.

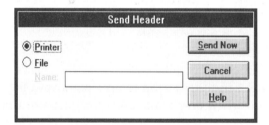

Non-PostScript Printer Options

If you are using Windows 3.1 with a Hewlett-Packard LaserJet III printer driver selected, the Options dialog box will look like this:

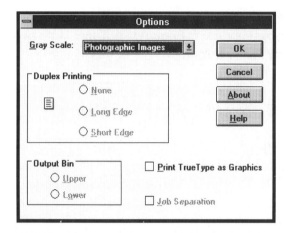

Notice that Duplex Printing options, Output Bin options, and Job Separation are not selectable for this printer. Remember that the Options menu can look different for various non-PostScript printers. For example, if you are setting up the Hewlett-Packard LaserJet IIID printer, which is a duplex printer, the Duplex Printing and Output Bin options will both be selectable.

Gray Scale   The Gray Scale settings determine the type of pattern that is applied to images when printed. The pattern choices are Photographic Images, Line Art Images, and HP ScanJet Images.

The Photographic Images setting uses a clustered dot pattern to provide soft contrasts between various shades of gray. This setting works well for images that are originally designed with color. It produces 60 different levels of gray—good enough for draft printing, but not sufficient to reproduce photographic images at high quality.

The Line Art Images setting uses the dispersed dot pattern to provide sharp contrasts between shaded areas. This setting is best for clip art or other artwork within a document that contains intricate lines and fine detail.

The HP ScanJet Images setting is specifically for images that have been scanned by the HP ScanJet. It uses a variation of the clustered dot method to provide exceptional clarity with 60 levels of gray.

Print TrueType as Graphics   Use this option if your document has many graphics but few TrueType fonts. When you print, TrueType fonts are printed as graphics, which means the printer requires less memory but printing time may increase. There is no perceptible difference in the quality of the output.

Advanced PostScript Options

In the previous sections you learned about the Options menu for both the PostScript and non-PostScript printers. Look again at the PostScript Options dialog box. Notice the Advanced button on the right side of the menu. Clicking this button displays the Advanced Options dialog box shown here:

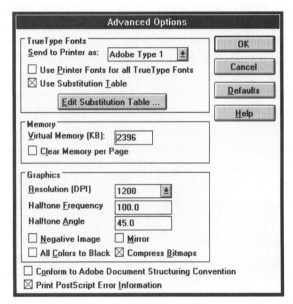

Whether you are using an inexpensive PostScript printer or an expensive imagesetter as your output device, the options on this menu are the same, but the defaults will vary with the printer type and model.

TrueType Fonts

This section of the menu allows you to control how TrueType fonts are printed. TrueType fonts, the latest advance in scalable font technology, are downloadable fonts that produce the same font for the screen as for the printer. A *downloadable* font is a font that is not built into the printer but instead is sent to the printer via software. Any kind of printer that is supported by Windows 3.1 can output TrueType fonts. This includes dot-matrix printers, laser printers, and imagesetters.

Most PostScript printers and imagesetters support downloadable fonts. If yours cannot, it can only use the fonts that are *resident* in the printer. Resident fonts are programmed internally in the printer or reside on cartridges that are inserted in the printer.

 Tip   Many experienced desktop publishers feel that Adobe Type 1 fonts are superior typographically to the easy-to-use TrueType fonts. If you are producing documents for a sophisticated or mass audience, consider using Adobe Type 1 fonts. Reserve TrueType fonts for business documents that will be circulated either in-house or to smaller, more informal audiences.

Send to Printer As   This option specifies how TrueType fonts will be printed. Most TrueType fonts are converted to bitmaps by the computer before they are sent to the printer, but large fonts (above 14 points) are converted in the printer. (Bitmaps, rows of black and white dots in a checkerboard pattern, form each character in the font.) If you select Bitmap (Type 3), all point sizes of TrueType fonts will be sent as bitmaps. If you select Adobe Type 1, all the fonts below 14 points will still be sent as bitmaps, but the larger fonts will be sent as outline fonts. The Adobe Type 1 outline fonts are particularly good for large point sizes because they are not jagged like bitmap fonts.

Use Printer Fonts For All TrueType Fonts   If your printer does not support downloadable fonts, you must use resident printer fonts. If you check this option, the printer driver will determine which printer fonts most closely match the TrueType fonts and substitute them automatically. If you do not want the print driver to make the font decisions for you, use the substitution table, explained next.

Use Substitution Table   If you check this option, you can specify the fonts that you want to use by making the appropriate selections in the Substitution dialog box that is displayed when you select Edit Substitution Table. The Substitution dialog box is shown here:

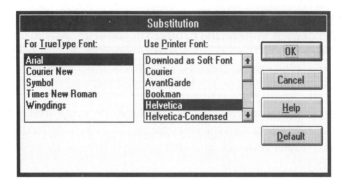

Tip   Since downloadable fonts must be sent to the printer each time you print, using them can slow print operations noticeably. If you are only interested in proofing text on a low-resolution PostScript laser printer, use the Edit Substitution Table to speed up printing even if your printer supports downloadable fonts.

Memory

The amount of memory that your printer has available (called *virtual memory*) is set by the manufacturer, but you can change this amount using the Virtual Memory option. To see how much virtual memory the manufacturer recommends, print the Windows file called testps.txt found in the Windows subdirectory called SYSTEM. This is the DOS command to send the file to a printer connected to the LPT1 port:

copy c:\windows\system\testps.txt lpt1:

If you specify virtual memory correctly, the printer driver will automatically clear the fonts from memory when memory space is low and resend the needed fonts. The Memory option becomes an important one if you have a document that uses a large number of fonts that must be downloaded to the printer.

Even if you have a large number of downloadable fonts in a document, you can reduce the amount of virtual memory if you check Clear Memory per Page. Instead of downloading all the fonts that are used in the entire document, only the fonts used on the next page to print are downloaded.

These fonts are cleared from memory after the page is printed. This option saves memory but slows printing.

Graphics

The Graphics options for PostScript printers include Resolution, Halftone Frequency, Halftone Angle, Negative Image, All Colors in Black, Mirror, and Compress Bitmaps. These options control how graphic images are printed.

Resolution   This option duplicates the Printer Resolution option found in Quark's Printer Setup dialog box. Most of the time, you will specify output resolution under Printer Setup. Together, the resolution, halftone frequency, and halftone angle determine the quality of the printed graphic images. Higher resolution reproduces graphics more perfectly but takes longer to print.

Halftone Frequency   This option duplicates the Halftone Frequency setting in Quark's Printer Setup dialog box; you don't need to set it in both places.

Halftone Angle   The Halftone Angle option applies to any images in a Quark document to which a Normal Screen applies (see Chapter 9). The default value for this option is usually sufficient. (Windows will supply you with the default values for value fields if you click the Defaults button.)

Negative Image   If you select Negative Image, the black and white (light and dark) areas of a page will be reversed. Activating this option has the same effect as the Invert option in Quark's Printer Setup dialog box.

All Colors in Black   All Colors in Black prints color images in black and white only. Use this option for draft printing if you are losing detail in light-colored areas.

Mirror   The Mirror setting prints a mirror image of a graphic, much like the Flip Horizontal option in the Printer Setup dialog box.

Compress Bitmaps The Compress Bitmaps option compresses graphics before they are sent to the printer. Windows sends documents to the Print Spooler faster when you activate this option, but the actual time required for printing will usually increase.

Conform to Adobe Document Structuring Convention

This option is useful if you are creating a PostScript output file that will be printed from within another page layout application such as Aldus PageMaker or Ventura Publisher. You can also use it when generating an output file if you want the service bureau to control the document's halftone frequency and angle for printing. When you activate Conform to Adobe Document Structuring Convention, Windows strips from the output file any PostScript instructions specific to a particular printing device. This allows the imagesetter operator at the service bureau to control PostScript settings directly. Inform your service bureau if you have activated this option, as it may slow printing.

Print PostScript Error Information

The PostScript printer driver has the ability to detect certain errors that the Windows Print Manager cannot detect. If you select this option, information about the detected errors and how to correct them will print after the document has printed. Having this information would help you or a support technician troubleshoot problems in your document.

Using the Print Command

When all the information in the Printer Setup dialog box is correct, you are almost ready to print. With a document open, Print from the File menu or press CTRL-P to access the Print dialog box shown here:

```
┌─────────────────────────────────────────────────────────┐
│ ▬                          Print                          │
├─────────────────────────────────────────────────────────┤
│  Printer:    Agfa 9000 Series PS  (LPT1:)      ┌─────────┐│
│                                                │   OK    ││
│  Copies: [1]    Pages: ● All ○ From: [    ] To: [    ]    └─────────┘│
│                                                ┌─────────┐│
│  Cover Page: ● No  ○ First Page  ○ Last Page   │ Cancel  ││
│                                                └─────────┘│
│  Output:     ● Normal  ○ Rough    □ Thumbnails ┌─────────┐│
│              ● All Pages ○ Odd Pages ○ Even Pages│ Setup...││
│              □ Back to Front □ Collate □ Spreads ⊠ Blank Pages└────┘│
│              □ Registration Marks ○ Centered ○ Off Center │
│              OPI: [Include Images        ▼]              │
│                                                          │
│  Tiling:     ● Off  ○ Manual  ○ Auto, overlap: [3"]      │
│  Color:      □ Make Separations    Plate: [All Plates ▼] │
│              □ Print Colors as Grays                     │
└─────────────────────────────────────────────────────────┘
```

Print Dialog Box Options

The Print dialog box allows you to specify exactly what part of a document will be printed and how it will be printed. Notice that the currently selected printer is listed at the top of the dialog box. If you need to choose a different printer, click the Setup button to access the Printer Setup dialog box.

Copies

This option lets you specify the number of copies to be printed for all of the pages specified in the Pages option.

Pages

The Pages option allows you to print all of the pages in a document or a range of pages. The default is All, but to print a range you can enter a beginning page number for From and an ending page number for To.

When specifying a range of pages for a document that has more than one section (see Chapter 11), enter the page numbers exactly as they appear in the lower-left corner of the document window. If your document has more than one section and you are unsure of the user-defined section number, use the absolute page number. Precede an absolute page number with a plus sign (+) so that Quark will recognize the number as valid.

Imagine, for example, a document that has ten pages and two sections. Section one is numbered 1-1, 1-2, 1-3, 1-4, 1-5, and section two is numbered 2-1, 2-2, 2-3, 2-4, 2-5. These are the numbers that will appear in the lower-left corner of the screen. If you want to print page 2-1, which is the sixth page of the document, specify the page as either 2-1 or +6 (the absolute page number).

Hint   If the To and From fields are dimmed, you have a master page displayed instead of a document page. Master pages can be printed, but you can print only a single master page or facing master pages.

Cover Page

As a reference, you can print a cover page as either the first or last page of the document. The cover page contains the name of the document and the date and time it was printed; it is not actually part of the document. This option is useful if you are using a shared printer or imagesetter on a company network and want to identify your print jobs to distinguish them from others.

Output Options

Several Output options are listed in the Print dialog box, but not all options are available for every printing device.

Normal, Rough   If you select Normal, the document will be printed as it is displayed on the screen. If you select Rough, pictures will be replaced with boxed x's and complex box frames will be replaced with simpler frames. Text will not be affected. See Figure 14-2.

Thumbnails   The Thumbnails option is available for PostScript devices only. Thumbnail pages are one-eighth the size of the normal pages. If you

FIGURE 14-2 Normal printing versus rough printing

Professionals Prefer. . .

service

quality

value

Normal

Professionals Prefer. . .

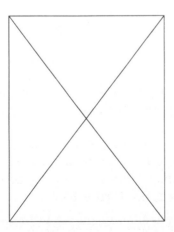

service

quality

value

Rough

select this output option, Quark will print as many thumbnail pages as it can on a single sheet of paper. Thumbnails are ideal for reviewing the overall layout of a document or producing rough comps for company approval. The following shows the thumbnail printing of a four-page document that is normally printed on 8.5-by-11-inch paper. The actual print size of each thumbnail page in this case is approximately 6 picas by 8 picas.

 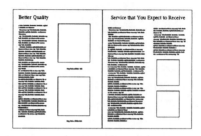 

All Pages, Odd Pages, Even Pages   This option allows you to print all of the pages specified through the Pages option or just the odd or even pages specified through the Pages option. You might want to print the odd and even pages separately, for example, if you plan to make double-sided copies with a copier that copies on one side of the page only. You could copy the odd pages on a copier and then turn the odd pages over and send them through the copier again, copying the even pages on the back.

Back to Front   Use this option to print the pages of a document in reverse order.

Collate Copies   Use this option if you are printing multiple copies of a document and you want each copy to be printed in its entirety (that is, in numerical order) before the next copy is printed. If you print multiple copies without collating, you will have to collate the pages manually.

 Tip   Multiple copies print faster if you do not activate the Collate Copies option.

Spreads   The Spreads option allows you to print facing pages or multipage spreads together as contiguous output. Of course, the paper size that your printer or imagesetter is using must accommodate the entire spread. This option is most useful for output by a roll-fed imagesetter.

Tip Before you select this option, check with your print vendor about page *imposition*—the order in which page plates will be arranged for your printing job. If page imposition differs from normal page order (and it usually does), it may not make sense to print spreads contiguously.

Blank Pages If you have blank pages in the document, select this option when you want to include them in the printing. Many times, blank pages are included in a document to force text to begin on a right-hand page. For example, if the first page of a chapter in a book falls on an even-numbered page number, you might routinely insert a blank page before it to force the page to an odd numbered, right-hand page. Commercial print vendors often prefer to have blank pages included in the camera-ready copy you supply to them. Check with your print vendor.

Registration Marks (Centered, Off Center) Registration marks help commercial print vendors align plates on the printing press and are especially important to include when printing color separations. When you activate the Registration Marks option, choose between Centered or Off Center. Click Centered to print registration marks and crop marks outside the document margins, but centered relative to all four sides of the page or plate. Many print vendors prefer off-center crop and registration marks, which decrease the likelihood that a press operator will accidentally rotate a square plate 180 degrees. Figure 14-3 shows off-centered registration marks and crop marks on a business card.

Caution If you select Registration Marks and the paper size is the same as the page size, only part of each page will fit on the paper or film used to output the document.

OPI Options

OPI, or Open Prepress Interface, is a PostScript file convention designed by Aldus Corporation. It provides a standard format for sending files from color desktop publishing programs to high-end prepress systems. These prepress programs minimize the stripping and other work that print vendors must do to prepare plates for the printing press.

Crop marks and off-centered registration marks

If you are using a PostScript printer, three options are available in the OPI drop-down menu: Include Images, Omit TIFF, and Omit TIFF & EPS. Your selection depends on how you will output the document and whether or not you have high-resolution picture files for the graphics included in the document.

Include Images   If you select this option, all TIFF and EPS pictures will be printed. OPI comments for TIFF pictures are included in the output data, but OPI comments for EPS pictures are not. Use this option when outputting to draft printers or PostScript imagesetters.

Omit TIFF   This option suppresses the printout of TIFF pictures, but EPS pictures are printed normally. OPI comments are included for the TIFF pictures, but not for EPS pictures. Use this option when outputting to a high-end Scitex or similar dedicated prepress system rather than to an imagesetter. Most of these systems replace TIFF pictures only.

Omit TIFF & EPS   This option suppresses the printout of both TIFF and EPS pictures, but OPI comments are included in the output. Use this option for dedicated, high-end color prepress systems that replace both TIFF and EPS images.

Tiling

Activate the Tiling option to print a document that is too large to print on the paper size that you have specified. The document will be printed in sections or "tiles." After printing the tiles, you can cut off the marginal white space plus any overlapping output and assemble the tiles to form the complete page. The tiles can be defined manually by you or automatically by Quark.

Figure 14-4 shows a page divided into four tiles.

 Note   This option can be used with both PostScript and non-PostScript printers.

Manual   To specify the size of the tiles yourself, first define the tile and then select the Manual Tiling option in the Print menu. To define the tile, drag the ruler origin so that the lower-right quadrant of the intersection is positioned for the desired tile. See Figure 14-4.

Auto, Overlap   If you want Quark to control tile sizing automatically, enter a value in the overlap field. This value should reflect the amount of space by which each tile is separated so you (or a service bureau operator) can cut tiles to size more easily.

Color

If you have defined and applied spot colors, process colors, or both in your document, Quark can print separations that commercial print vendors can use to make plates for the printing press. Refer to Chapter 10 for more details on the relationship between color and printing.

Make Separations   If you activate the Make Separations option, Quark can print a separate page for each color or component of a color on a

FIGURE
14-4

A page divided into tiles

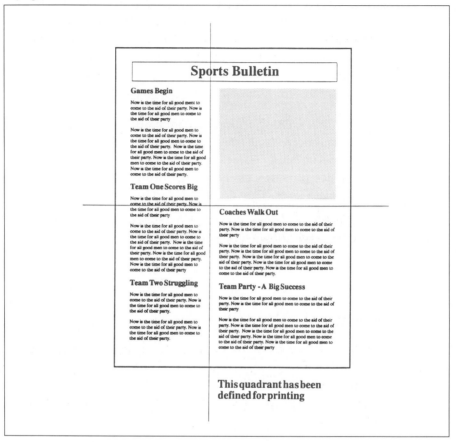

page. You probably remember from Chapter 10 that each page containing a specific color is called a plate.

Note   If you have activated both Registration Marks and Make Separations, Quark prints a color test strip indicator on each separation plate.

Plate   To print a separate plate on each page for every color you have defined *and used* in a document, activate the Make Separations check box and choose All Plates from the drop-down list box. If you have defined all colors as process colors (activating the Process Separation check box in the Edit Color dialog box for every defined color), exactly four plates will be printed—Cyan, Magenta, Yellow, and Black. Additional plates will be printed for each color that you have defined as a spot color (Process Separation check box deactivated in the Edit Color dialog box). If you have used only spot colors in the document, a separate plate will be printed for each spot color on each page. Chapter 10 gives more information about defining colors as spot colors or as process colors.

To print a single plate for a specific color only, select the desired color from the drop-down list in the Plate option. All the colors you have defined in the current document will be included in the list.

Print Colors as Grays   This option is available if you are using a PostScript printer. Instead of printing each color on a separate sheet, this option prints a composite of all the colors on one page using shades of gray to represent each color.

Making a Trial Run

Now that you have learned about the intricacies of printing, open the haystack.qxd document you created in Chapter 2. Choose the Printer Setup command in Quark's File menu and define settings for your printer. Next, define options in the Print dialog box and click OK to print the document.

Quark and Prepress Basics

Before you concern yourself with the mechanics of printing from Quark, find out as much as you can about the output requirements of your document. There are many issues to consider. Will you be using spot color, process color, or just shades of gray? What fonts are you using? Does your document contain pictures? What about color photographs? How should you define halftone screen settings? Should you work with a service bureau? Should the service bureau output the document to paper or to film? If a document will be printed commercially, what kind of printing press and paper stock will be used? And how can you prepare a foolproof PostScript output file, anyway?

While Quark doesn't answer these questions for you, it provides all the options you need to secure high-quality printing results once you have researched the answers for yourself. What follows is a checklist of important prepress issues and basic information on how they can determine the best way to print a particular document from Quark.

Creating a PostScript Output File

As you know from previous references, a service bureau can provide you with high-quality output from an expensive imagesetter, but first you must provide the service bureau with either the document file (extension .qxd) or a PostScript output file (extension .eps or .prn).

 Tip Creating your own PostScript output files and then presenting these to the service bureau is both safer and less expensive than expecting the service bureau to print directly from your .qxd document file.

Delivering a Quark document file can be successful *only* if you provide the service bureau with all the font and picture files used in the document. You should also provide your xpress.prf file to the service bureau, just in case you have any custom trap amount, kerning, tracking, or hyphenation dictionary settings that do not match the settings in the copy of Quark that the service bureau uses. Of course, a service bureau that uses QuarkXPress can revise your .qxd file—substituting fonts, changing preference settings, default trapping amounts, and so forth—but they will usually charge extra for this kind of time-consuming troubleshooting.

The best kind of file to give to a service bureau is a PostScript output file. When you generate your own output files, you have complete control over (and responsibility for) the fonts, pictures, typographic preferences, trapping, and other variables that can wreak havoc when they are not managed properly. An output file is complete in itself and already contains the fonts and pictures used by your document. Of course, it contains them in a coded form that cannot be edited or revised. If you have not made the correct settings when generating the output file, the document will not print correctly, and the service bureau will not be able to fire up Quark Xpress and correct your mistakes like it can if you submit a .qxd document file. On the other hand, any service bureau can print your PostScript output files, no matter what kind of desktop publishing program they normally use.

To generate a PostScript output file for a document, follow these steps:

1. From the Windows Main menu, select Control Panel, and then select Printers. Select the desired imagesetter from the list of installed printers and click Connect. (The output device that you select should be the same model used by the service bureau. You might actually have to get the printer driver file on disk from the service bureau in order to install it in Windows.)

2. Select File from the Ports drop-down list and then click OK. Exit the Control Panel.

3. Next, use the Printer Setup command in Quark's File menu to select all the options that correspond to the settings required by the service bureau. Many of these settings have already been discussed in this chapter, but if you are uncertain about any option, ask your service bureau for recommendations.

4. Choose the Print command in the File menu and adjust options as necessary, then click OK. A small dialog box will pop up, prompting you to name the output file. Quark generates the file; the amount of time required depends on the length of the document, the number of pictures used, and the use of color in the document.

5. Transfer this file to a floppy disk or other medium that the service bureau can accept, and deliver it to the service bureau. If you are using floppy disks and the output file is larger than 1.44MB, you will need to compress the file in order to make it fit on a single disk.

So much for the mechanics of creating an output file. What settings should you define for specific types of documents? The following sections provide some basic guidelines.

Choosing a Halftone Screen Frequency

As discussed earlier in this chapter and in Chapter 9, the halftone screen frequency used in printing determines the sharpness and print quality of the final document. Generally, the higher the screen frequency in lines per inch, the higher the quality of your output. However, you should match screen frequency to the type of document you are producing, the type of printing press that will run the job, and the paper stock that will be used. Table 14-1 lists common ranges of halftone screen settings by document type; check with your print vendor and service bureau for specific recommendations.

 Tip Documents that include tinted or full-color photographs should usually be output at halftone frequencies of 120 lpi or higher.

TABLE **14-1**	Matching Halftone Screen Frequency to Document Type and Printing Parameters		
Screen Frequency Range	**Document Types**	**Press Equipment**	**Paper stock**
45-65 lpi	T-shirts, mugs, imprint products	Silkscreen	Non-paper materials
65-85 lpi	Newspapers	Open web	Newsprint
85-120 lpi	B/W catalogs, informal magazines	Open web	Various stocks
90-133 lpi	Newsletters, trade books	Open web	Uncoated book stocks
120-150 lpi	Commercial magazines, catalogs, 4-color pubs	Heat-set web	Various glossy stocks
150-200 lpi	High-end advertising, color art books	Sheet-fed	Various glossy stocks

What Type of Imagesetter?

Imagesetters from different manufacturers vary widely in their feature sets and output resolutions. If you are producing a document that is text-only or that includes only grayscale object-oriented artwork without linear blends, the type of imagesetter your service bureau uses is not likely to impact the quality of the final output. If, however, a document includes photographs, bitmapped pictures, or any artwork that uses color or linear blends, ask your service bureau about three imagesetter features:

☐ The type of mechanism used to transport paper or film through the imagesetter

☐ The range of output resolutions available

☐ The number of gray shades the imagesetter can reproduce at 1200 or 1270 dpi

Transport Mechanism and Registration Issues

The transport mechanism of an imagesetter is a concern if you are outputting a document that contains color. The way an imagesetter feeds paper or film during imaging can impact the registration of color separation plates on the printing press. Many imagesetters built before 1991 used a flatbed or sheet-fed mechanism to pass paper or film through the imagesetter. This type of mechanism left more room for shifting, which in turn meant that separate color plates from the same page might be misaligned slightly. If your service bureau uses only sheet-fed imagesetters and you are producing color separations for a document, ask about the degree of misalignment that is expected. Once you have this information, consult with your print vendor about how much trapping you should apply. Then, set Auto Amount in the Application Preferences dialog box to the recommended trapping amount *before* you create a PostScript output file. Refer to Chapter 10 if you need to review how to create trap in Quark.

 Caution If you set trapping to an amount other than the Quark default of 0.144 pt, you should definitely create your own PostScript output files. The service bureau may well have different trapping settings in their copy

of QuarkXPress—and since Trap Amount is an application preference, it is saved in the xpress.prf file, not with the document.

Many imagesetters built during the last couple of years are based on a rotary drum mechanism, which is similar in principle to the design of high-end proprietary systems (such as Scitex) long known for their accuracy in color production work. Rotary drum mechanisms, based on a rotating cylinder, greatly reduce the amount of shifting that can occur while RC paper or film is being exposed, thus minimizing the risk of color plate misalignment.

Some newer imagesetters, while not based on the rotary drum concept, tend to have improved transport mechanisms that also reduce shifting and misalignment. Both types of imagesetters are well-suited for color work. If your service bureau or company imagesetter features either a rotary drum or improved sheet-fed transport design, you will not need to set trapping as high as with older imagesetter models.

Output Resolution, Balanced Screen Angles, and Image Quality

The range of output resolutions and the number of gray shades that an imagesetter can reproduce at each resolution are important if your document contains photographs, bitmapped artwork, or any artwork that includes blended colors. At resolutions below 1200 or 1270 dpi, many imagesetters cannot reproduce the full 256 shades of gray per plate needed for realistic-looking photographic or bitmapped images, and blended colors show visible banding. Even at these resolutions, many imagesetters can reproduce 256 shades of gray only at the low halftone frequencies that are suitable for newspapers and informal documents only (see Table 14-1). If you are outputting a book, corporate newsletter, or magazine that contains photographs, bitmaps, or color blends, you should probably request an output resolution of 2400 dpi or higher. Running an imagesetter at these higher resolutions is more time-consuming and expensive but may be necessary for high-quality output.

There is an important exception to this rule, however. Many service bureaus have upgraded their imagesetters recently to include a feature known as *balanced screen angles*. Basically, imagesetters featuring balanced screen angles can reproduce a full 256 shades of gray at output resolutions of 1200 or 1270, as long as the halftone frequency does not exceed 133 lpi. Being able to output documents with photographs at these lower resolutions can save you or your company money.

What Type of Output Medium?

If your document uses only shades of gray or spot colors and contains no photographs or bitmaps, you can save money by outputting to photographic RC paper. If the document uses process colors and/or photographs, however, you should probably output to film for best results. The reason for this is that print vendors cannot make printing plates directly from paper output; they must first create a film negative as an intermediate step. Some risk of degrading image quality always accompanies this intermediate step.

Another reason why film is preferable to RC paper for documents that contain images or process color has to do with the interaction between toner and paper. As the halftone screen frequency increases, so does the risk that toner will spread, causing bigger halftone dots and some degree of blurring. This phenomenon (covered in Chapter 10) is known as *dot gain*, and can happen either at the service bureau during imaging or on the printing press when ink is applied. Minimize the risk of dot gain whenever possible so you have the greatest degree of control during the PostScript output phase of the printing process.

Basically, you can safely specify RC paper output for documents that contain no photographs, or which, like newspapers, are to be output at low halftone screen frequencies. For documents that contain process colors and/or multiple photographs, output directly to film.

Printing Documents That Contain Full-color Artwork

If your document contains full-color photographs or object-oriented artwork, Quark will create automatic color separations for only two types of file formats: TIFF bitmaps that have been saved in CMYK format, and EPS files. The responsibility for saving artwork in these formats lies with the person who created the artwork and the program in which it was created. Here are some tips for ensuring that the artwork is saved in a way that enables Quark to create color separations.

Object-Oriented Artwork

Many drawing programs on both the PC and Macintosh can save artwork to Encapsulated PostScript (EPS) format. When creating a drawing destined for process color separation in Quark, define all colors in CMYK terms. To output the drawing in Quark using spot color separation, your drawing program should support the PANTONE color model and you should define spot colors in PANTONE terms. Drawing programs that support neither PANTONE nor process color specification cannot create artwork that Quark will color separate.

Photographs and Bitmapped Artwork

Quark will color separate a color TIFF image only if it has been saved as a CMYK TIFF image, in which all colors are defined in CMYK terms. On the Macintosh, Adobe PhotoShop is well known for its ability to save color images in this format. Image editing packages on the PC are only just beginning to support the CMYK TIFF format, but by the time you read this, several packages may be able to do so.

 Tip To color separate a color photograph or bitmap that has been saved in a standard TIFF format, first import the TIFF image into CorelDRAW! 3.0 or later. From CorelDRAW!, export this image as an Encapsulated PostScript (.EPS) file. Finally, import the .EPS file into a Quark picture box. At output time, request separations for the Cyan, Magenta, Yellow, and Black component plates, and Quark will separate the image. This technique may also work with other object-oriented programs that run under Windows, as long as they support CMYK color in the .EPS file format.

 Tip PrePress Technologies provides a color separation package for the Windows version of QuarkXPress that is similar to its acclaimed SpectreSeps QX utility for the Macintosh version of QuarkXPress. This utility provides advanced color separation options for many types of picture files. For more information, contact PrePress Technologies directly at (619) 931-2695 or call QuarkXChange (see Appendix A).

QuarkXPress packs a heftier punch in printing capabilities than any other page layout package available on the PC. The issues just discussed should help steer you through the often murky waters associated with printing a color or image-laden document accurately. QuarkXTensions from third-party developers (see Appendix A) may also provide useful utilities for high-powered printing jobs. Above all, keep the lines of communication open to your print vendor and service bureau and discuss Quark print-related settings with them at every step. Good luck, and happy Quarking!

PART

VI

Additional Resources

APPENDIX

Quark's XTended Family

*Q*uarkXPress does it all. And if there is something Quark doesn't do, you can be sure that an add-on utility from Quark or from a third-party vendor does it.

QuarkXPress for the Macintosh has spawned a lively aftermarket of software add-ons—excuse us, *XTensions*—that enrich Quark's powerful publishing capabilities with convenient or advanced features. There are XTensions that create ad agency comps, search and replace colors throughout a document, create fully formatted tables from database files, generate sophisticated color separations, translate foreign-language mainframe documents into XPress Tags formatting, relink text boxes after drastic layout changes, generate an index or table of contents automatically, and arrange pages in the order required by a printing press—just to name a few. There is also a proliferation of smaller-scale utilities that enhance the interface with floating palettes or other tools for accomplishing repetitive everyday tasks. In addition, Quark Inc. develops its own utilities, many of which it makes available to users for free or for a nominal charge.

 Note   Quark Inc. is planning to release a multiple-language international version of QuarkXPress for Windows that is similar to the Passport edition already available for the Macintosh.

The good news is that many of these utilities, along with others that don't even exist yet, will soon be available for the Windows version of QuarkXPress. A number of independent developers are already hard at work translating Macintosh XTensions into their Windows equivalents; some may be available by the time you read this.

QuarkXChange, an independent company not affiliated with Quark Inc., acts as a marketing agency and clearinghouse for Quark's own and third-party XTensions. To find out if there is an XTension that suits your very special publishing needs, contact QuarkXChange through one of the following channels:

Mail:	QuarkXChange
	P.O. Box 8899
	Fort Collins, CO 80525
Voice:	(800) 788-7557
Fax:	(303) 229-3773
CompuServe:	76414,363

Developer Inquiries: (415) 864-7591, 864-7592 (voice)

                                                      (415) 864-7594 (fax)

Index

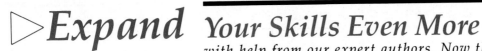
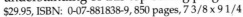

Microsoft Word for Windows 2 Made Easy
by Paul Hoffman
Best-selling author Paul Hoffman will quickly teach you the newest version of Microsoft Word for Windows. Plenty of hands-on examples and helpful illustrations are included to build your skills fast. You'll also explore all of the powerful features including menus, linking documents, macros, and graphics.
$19.95, ISBN: 0-07-881770-6, 303 pp., 7 3/8 X 9 1/4

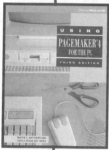

Using PageMaker 4 for the PC, Third Edition
by Martin S. Matthews and Carole Boggs Matthews
The Matthews lead the way as you learn PageMaker Release 4.0, the latest version of Aldus Corporation's full-featured desktop publishing software for your IBM PC or compatible. You'll discover this guide is the easiest route to creating your own newsletters, ads, catalogs, and more.
$26.95, ISBN: 0-07-881629-7, 650 pages, 7 3/8 x 9 1/4

PageMaker for Windows Inside & Out
(Includes One 3.5-Inch Disk)
by Martin S. Matthews and Carole Boggs Matthews
With the Matthews clear instructions, you'll quickly learn how to create flyers, brochures, newsletters, and more. Follow hands-on directions as you work with the accompanying disk containing all the examples from the book.
$39.95, ISBN: 0-07-881852-4, 752 pages, 7 3/8 x 9 1/4
Available Winter 1993

Harvard Graphics 3.0 Made Easy
by Mary Campbell
Campbell covers the basics of the latest version of Harvard Graphics before showing you how to create a variety of charts and demonstrates new drawing features. You'll also learn the latest presentation techniques for producing professional slide shows.
$24.95, ISBN: 0-07-881746-3, 358 pages, 7 3/8 x 9 1/4